The Making of International Criminal Justice

THE MAKING OF INTERNATIONAL CRIMINAL JUSTICE

A View from the Bench

SELECTED SPEECHES

Theodor Meron

OXFORD
UNIVERSITY PRESS

Great Clarendon Street, Oxford, OX2 6DP,
United Kingdom

Oxford University Press is a department of the University of Oxford.
It furthers the University's objective of excellence in research, scholarship,
and education by publishing worldwide. Oxford is a registered trade mark of
Oxford University Press in the UK and in certain other countries

© Theodor Meron 2011

The moral rights of the author have been asserted

First Edition published 2011
First published in paperback 2012

Impression: 1

All rights reserved. No part of this publication may be reproduced, stored in
a retrieval system, or transmitted, in any form or by any means, without the
prior permission in writing of Oxford University Press, or as expressly permitted
by law, by licence or under terms agreed with the appropriate reprographics
rights organization. Enquiries concerning reproduction outside the scope of the
above should be sent to the Rights Department, Oxford University Press, at the
address above

You must not circulate this work in any other form
and you must impose this same condition on any acquirer

British Library Cataloguing in Publication Data

Data available

Library of Congress Cataloging in Publication Data

Data available

ISBN 978–0–19–960893–5
ISBN 978–0–19–966984–4 (pbk.)

Printed in Great Britain
on acid-free paper by
CPI Group (UK) Ltd, Croydon CR0 4YY

Links to third party websites are provided by Oxford in good faith and
for information only. Oxford disclaims any responsibility for the materials
contained in any third party website referenced in this work.

*To my wonderful law clerks,
who have immensely enriched my life at The Hague
and these speeches.*

PREFACE

Since my election to the bench by the UN General Assembly in 2001, I have refrained, for the most part, from publishing. The one notable exception involved my general course on public international law at The Hague Academy, delivered in 2003 but prepared largely when I was still a full-time professor at New York University School of Law.

While I have generally abstained from academic writing in light of my role and duties as a judge, during the past decade I have given a number of speeches to a variety of outside audiences, ranging from diplomats, jurists, and scholars, to legal practitioners, government officials, and the survivors of horrific crimes. I did so in the belief that it is important, in promoting the new universe of international criminal justice, to speak about our achievements, our challenges, and, yes, even our frustrations. It is this same belief that has animated my decision to share a selection of my speeches in the present volume.

In identifying speeches for inclusion here and in preparing them for publication, I have endeavored to abide by three—admittedly somewhat contradictory—principles. First, I have made every effort to be comprehensive, by choosing speeches that address a wide range of topics and that chart the evolution of and prospects for international criminal justice from both substantive and practical perspectives. Although I believe these efforts at breadth have been largely successful, it is, perhaps, inevitable that many of the pieces focus on the jurisprudence and practices of the International Criminal Tribunal for the former Yugoslavia, the court on which I sit as an appeals judge and for which I served as President from 2003 to 2005.

Second, I have attempted, wherever possible, to be selective—that is, to omit those speeches or those portions of speeches that echo too loudly the content or coverage of another speech in the volume. If I have not always succeeded in my efforts to adhere to this second goal, it is because there are certain foundational ideas and events—lodestars—around which the universe of international criminal justice revolves, and without reference to which it would be difficult to find one's way.

Finally, although the perspective I have gained over the past ten years has served as a helpful guide in choosing speeches for inclusion, I have tried to ignore the seductive influence of hindsight during the editing process and, instead, kept the speeches largely in the form in which they were delivered. What small changes I have made were primarily in the interest of enhancing clarity and reducing repetition. These being speeches and not law review articles, I have also added relatively few footnotes so as to retain and reflect the uniquely oral quality of the remarks collected here.

It is my hope and belief that each of these speeches stands on its own. Nevertheless, I have tried to organize these remarks in such a way that, when read together, they also tell a larger story about the making of international criminal justice, starting—after a few brief biographical notes—with Part I's examinations of the evolving bodies of law from which international criminal law is, in great part, derived. Part II proceeds to explore the rise of international criminal tribunals and the difficulties posed, and possibilities presented, by and for such institutions. Part III then invites the reader to reflect upon certain substantive aspects of international criminal law and upon a selection of the jurisprudence of international courts. Finally, Part IV and the Epilogue conclude with thoughts on the themes of responsibility and the role of a judge. With the exception of two formal statements made in my capacity as then-President of the International Criminal Tribunal for the former Yugoslavia and my separate and partially dissenting opinion in the *Galić* appeal judgment, the views expressed in this volume have been offered strictly in my personal capacity and not in my capacity as a judge.

Throughout the process of readying this volume for publication, I have been assisted by several individuals whose contributions and guidance have proven invaluable. I am deeply grateful for the astute advice of Merel Alstein, my excellent editor, and her attentive colleagues at Oxford University Press; the prowess and perseverance of Mohini Ramsoekh, my irreplaceable right-hand, whose task it was to type and re-type many of these speeches; and the exceptional editing of Willow Crystal, one of the outstanding law clerks with whom I have had the great pleasure of working during my first decade on the bench.

Theodor Meron

The Hague
February 2011

CONTENTS

List of Abbreviations   xii

INTRODUCTION

1. The Seven Ages of Man (Charles Homer Haskins Prize Lecture)   3

I. HUMANITARIAN LAW AND HUMAN RIGHTS LAW: EVOLVING BODIES OF LAW

2. The Geneva Conventions and Public International Law   19

3. Customary Humanitarian Law: From the Academy to the Courtroom   28

4. The Humanization of the Law of War (Marek Nowicki Memorial Lecture)   42

5. The Universal Declaration of Human Rights at Sixty   62

6. Improving Compliance by Non-State Actors with Obligations in International Humanitarian Law: A Global Responsibility   66

II. THE RISE OF INTERNATIONAL CRIMINAL TRIBUNALS

7. The Greatest Change in International Law   75

8. Reflections on the Prosecution of War Crimes by International Tribunals: A Historical Perspective   77

9. Anatomy of an International Criminal Tribunal (Manley O Hudson Medal Lecture)   98

10. The Principle of Legality in International Criminal Law   110

11. The Challenges Facing the International Criminal
    Tribunal for the Former Yugoslavia ... 115

12. Statement to the UN Security Council ... 128

13. Does International Criminal Justice Work?
    (Alec Roche Annual Lecture in Public
    International Law) ... 138

14. The Role of the ICC: Accountability, Peace,
    and Justice ... 156

15. The ICC's Relationship with National Jurisdictions:
    What Future? ... 167

16. Making the International Criminal Court a Global
    Reality through Cooperation ... 171

III. INTERNATIONAL CRIMES AND JURISPRUDENCE OF INTERNATIONAL COURTS

17. Human Rights Law Marches into New Territory:
    The Enforcement of International Human Rights
    in International Criminal Tribunals (Marek
    Nowicki Memorial Lecture) ... 181

18. The Protection of Civilians in the Jurisprudence
    of the ICTY and ICTR ... 199

19. Deliver Us Not to Evil: Keeping POWs Safe ... 211

20. International and Non-International Conflicts
    in the Jurisprudence of the ICTY and ICTR ... 217

21. The ICJ's Opinion in *Bosnia and Herzegovina
    v Serbia and Montenegro* ... 231

IV. RESPONSIBILITY AND THE ROLE OF THE JUDGE

22. Judge Thomas Buergenthal and the Development
    of International Law by International Courts ... 239

23.	Fairness in Sentencing (Separate and Partially Dissenting Opinion, *Prosecutor v Stanislav Galić*)	246
24.	Judicial Independence and Judicial Impartiality	255
25.	The Role of Judges in Public Life	267
26.	Decision-Making in International Criminal Tribunals	278
27.	Justice and Leadership Dilemmas in Shakespeare	286

EPILOGUE

28.	Address at Memorial Cemetery at Potočari, Srebrenica	297

Table of Cases	300
Table of Instruments	307
Index	313

LIST OF ABBREVIATIONS

ABiH	Bosnian Muslim Army
ACLS	American Council of Learned Societies
AJIL	American Journal of International Law
CSCE	Conference for Security and Co-operation in Europe
DC	District of Columbia
DRC	Democratic Republic of the Congo
ECOWAS	Economic Community of West African States
FRY	Federal Republic of Yugoslavia
HVO	Croatian Defense Council
ICC	International Criminal Court
ICJ	International Court of Justice
ICRC	International Committee of the Red Cross
ICSID	International Centre for Settlement of Investment Disputes
ICTR	International Criminal Tribunal for Rwanda
ICTY	International Criminal Tribunal for the former Yugoslavia
IHL	international humanitarian law
ILC	International Law Commission
IMT	International Military Tribunal
JNA	Yugoslav Peoples' Army
LRA	Lord's Resistance Army (of Uganda)
MONUC	United Nations Mission in the Democratic Republic of the Congo
NATO	North Atlantic Treaty Organization
NGO	non-governmental organization
NKVD	People's Commissariat for Internal Affairs (Soviet secret police)
NYU	New York University
P-5	Five Permanent Members of the United Nations Security Council
POW	Prisoner of War
RPF	Rwandan Patriotic Front
SS	Schutzstaffel (an organ of the Nazi party)
TO	Territorial Defense
TRC	Truth and Reconciliation Commission
UDHR	Universal Declaration of Human Rights
UN	United Nations

UNAMID	African Union United Nations Mission in Darfur
UNGA	United Nations General Assembly
UNMIL	United Nations Mission in Liberia
UNOSOM II	United Nations Operation in Somalia II
UNSC	United Nations Security Council
UNTS	United Nations Treaty Series
USA	United States of America
USSR	Union of Soviet Socialist Republics
WTO	World Trade Organization

Introduction

1
THE SEVEN AGES OF MAN (CHARLES HOMER HASKINS PRIZE LECTURE)*

The uniform topic assigned to the Haskins Lectures, 'A Life of Learning', is particularly challenging because it compels an inquiry into the private domain, the piercing of the veil on essentially private experiences: motivation, achievement, and failure. Striking the right balance between self-satisfaction and saying something that may be of interest to this distinguished audience is quite a challenge. But there is no question that what we write and when we write can only be explained by our own life experiences. Avoiding autobiography would depart from the tradition of the Haskins Lectures and would provide an artificial and disingenuous reading of one's work.

ᴄ₃ʙᴏ

This leads me to the inevitability of some personal comments. I was born in 1930 in a small town in Poland to a middle-class Jewish family and had a happy but, alas, short childhood. By the age of nine I was out of school for the duration of the war. Ghettos and work camps followed, with most of my family falling victim to the Holocaust. When the war ended, I emerged, lucky to be alive, with a hunger for school, for learning, for normality. In 1945, I left Poland for Palestine and faced the daunting task, never quite accomplished, of catching up with six lost years. High school and military service followed, then studies at the law schools of the

---

* Delivered at the Annual Meeting of the American Council of Learned Societies in Pittsburgh, Pennsylvania, USA, on 9 May 2008. The text of this speech first appeared as *A Life of Learning: Charles Homer Haskins Prize Lecture for 2008* (ACLS Occasional Paper No 65, New York: ACLS, 2008), © Theodor Meron. Used by permission and modified from the original publication.

University of Jerusalem, Harvard University, and the University of Cambridge. At Jerusalem I started focusing on international law. At the two Cambridges I worked on hardly anything else. Jerusalem gave me a solid legal foundation, but I found the old-fashioned educational system, largely based on memorization, to be uninspiring. It was at Harvard, with its analytical method, that I became comfortable with the law, especially international law, and knew it was to be my vocation.

The imprint of the war made me particularly interested in working in areas which could contribute to making atrocities impossible and avoiding the horrible chaos, the helplessness, and the loss of autonomy which I remembered so well. At Harvard, I was fortunate to become a student of and a research assistant to two masters of international law—one specializing in humanitarian law and the law of war, the other in human rights—who became my mentors and models, and with whom I worked on an attempted codification of the law of state responsibility. They were Richard Baxter, later a judge of the International Court of Justice, and Louis Sohn. As it happened, much of my later scholarship and practice found expression in these two areas. My World War II experience was never far away.

When in Cambridge, England, as a Humanitarian Law Scholar, I was approached by another person to whom I owe a great deal of my legal education: Shabtai Rosenne, the legal adviser of the Israeli Foreign Ministry. He offered me a job, which I accepted. I would have preferred an academic job, but none was in sight. I stayed in the Israeli Foreign Service for about twenty years, resigning in 1977 and moving permanently to the United States, where I joined NYU School of Law as a professor of international law.

I have, of course, been very, very lucky. My life has provided me with unusual experiences and my writings have grown of these windows of opportunity. Yet, looking back, I can see something imperfectly resembling an integral whole emerging from the discrete segments. That does not mean that the goal of complete coherence was achievable or even desirable. A combination of chance and seized opportunity has been critically important in shaping my career. Situations, circumstances, needs, and institutional compulsions have often been controlling factors. But when the opportunity arose, I chose activities that fit my chosen purposes.

☙❧

The Israeli Foreign Ministry provided me with an invaluable experience writing legal opinions, participating in international conferences, and litigating cases. It helped me gain a practical perspective. Soon after my arrival in Jerusalem, I joined the team suing Bulgaria before the International Court of Justice in the case of the *Aerial Incident of 27 July 1955* during the height of the Cold War.[1] It was a tragic case, in which an El Al passenger plane strayed over Bulgaria and was shot down, causing the death of all the passengers and crew. Bulgaria contested jurisdiction and admissibility, and the claim was dismissed. But one of the more interesting legal issues was whether in such a case, where the contacts with the territorial state were not deliberate and voluntary, there was an obligation for the claimant to exhaust local remedies in Bulgaria before suing before the International Court. In an article published in the *British Year Book of International Law* in 1959, I argued that there was no such obligation and suggested parameters for the applicability of the doctrine of local remedies.[2] I had already published law review articles based on my studies at Harvard and my doctoral dissertation, but the local remedies article was the first in which my practice resulted in a discrete contribution to the theory of international law.

In 1961 I joined the Permanent Mission of Israel to the United Nations in New York. As a representative on the Fifth Committee (Administrative and Budgetary), most of my work involved the administrative problems of the United Nations and its Secretariat. I became concerned about the growing politicization of the Secretariat, its slide from an international to a multinational institution, the discrimination against women, and the absence of adequate due process provisions. My first articles on the Secretariat quickly followed.

My UN period ended with the Six-Day War in June 1967, a traumatic period in which, from the perspective of a diplomat in New York, the future and the survival of Israel were very much at stake. In June, shortly after the fighting was concluded with a victory for Israel, I was offered the job of the Legal Adviser of the Foreign Ministry in Jerusalem to succeed Shabtai Rosenne, who was being moved to New York. It was, in many ways, a baptism of fire. Within weeks of my arrival in Jerusalem, I was requested to advise the Prime Minister as to whether the establishment of civilian settlements in the occupied West Bank, the Golan Heights, and Gaza was allowed by international law. In a secret legal opinion recently brought to light by the historian Gershom Gorenberg in

---

[1] *Case Concerning the Aerial Incident of July 27th, 1955 (Israel v Bulgaria)* (Preliminary Objections: Judgment of May 26, 1959) [1959] ICJ Rep 127.
[2] Theodor Meron, 'The Incidence of the Rule of Exhaustion of Local Remedies' (1959) 35 *British Year Book of International Law* 83.

The New York Times[3] and subsequently reported by Donald Macintyre in *The Independent*[4] and Christiane Amanpour on CNN, I wrote that the establishment of civilian settlements violated the Fourth Geneva Convention as well as private property rights of the Arab inhabitants. The Israeli government chose to go another way and a wave of settlements followed, making the prospects for a political solution so much more difficult. Although I knew that this was not the kind of opinion that the Prime Minister wanted to receive, I had no doubt that legal advisers must be faithful to the law. To the credit of the Israeli government, I must note that there were no repercussions, of which I was aware, from my unpopular opinion. Of course, the opinion fit naturally into my interest in human rights and humanitarian law. It dealt not only with rights and obligations of states, but with rights of inhabitants.

In 1971, I became Israel's ambassador to Canada, a position I held until 1975. This was a period in which I had time to write, and to teach part-time at the University of Ottawa. During this period I wrote my first articles for the *American Journal of International Law*, of which Richard Baxter was editor-in-chief. Over the years, the *American Journal* became the principal vehicle for publishing my writings; indeed, articles in the *Journal* at times preceded publication of books on the same subjects. I was honored to serve as the co-editor-in-chief of the *Journal* in the 1990s. During those years in Ottawa, I also wrote my first book, *Investment Insurance in International Law* (1976), partly because of my interest in the law of state responsibility and partly to prove to myself that I was capable of writing a technical book on the law.

During that period, the call of academia was becoming irresistible. I obtained a year's leave from the Foreign Ministry to go to New York on a grant from the Rockefeller Foundation to write a book about the UN Secretariat, *The United Nations Secretariat: The Rules and the Practice* (1977). The merit principle, the need to depoliticize, due process, and women's rights were among the principal topics covered. Of course, I was building on the experience I gained as a representative on the General Assembly's Fifth Committee. During that period I also taught at NYU School of Law, and was soon invited to join the full-time faculty.

This was a difficult and critical period in my life. I was looking for ways to leave the foreign service and to enter the academy. NYU was beckon-

---

[3] Gershom Gorenberg, 'Israel's Tragedy Foretold' *The New York Times* (New York, 10 March 2006) Opinion A21.
[4] Donald Macintyre, 'Israelis were warned on illegality of settlements in 1967 memo' *The Independent* (London, 11 March 2006) News 27.

ing, but I was 48 and still a bit uncertain what I should be doing in my future life. I found the shift exciting but also a bit terrifying.

☙❧

Upon my appointment to the faculty, the question arose about my principal teaching subjects. At that time, human rights was not regularly taught, though the law school benefited from some teaching of human rights by visiting professors. There was clearly student interest in the subject, and the law school recognized a need for a regular human rights course offering. I was asked to focus on human rights, and somewhat nervously prepared to teach in what for me was still rather uncharted territory. My background in international law was in state responsibility, treaties, and humanitarian law (to which I was exposed in Israel). My knowledge and experience in human rights were, however, thin. I should perhaps explain briefly that humanitarian law deals with protection by a foreign government of civilians and combatants belonging to the adversary and applicable in time of armed conflict or war. Human rights concern protection of individuals against their own authorities or governments primarily in times of peace, though the law has been expanding to require respect for human rights in time of armed conflict as well.

Teaching human rights proved a blessing, offering a major writing field and a natural partner to international humanitarian law. My books *Human Rights Law-Making in the United Nations* (1986), *Human Rights in Internal Strife* (1987), *Human Rights and Humanitarian Norms as Customary Law* (1989), and eventually *Humanization of International Law* (2006)—the book that is closest to reflecting the quintessence of my work—were made possible by such an integrated approach to human rights and humanitarian law and by grounding both in the general theory of international law. It seemed to me obvious that repression of human dignity occurs in a continuum of situations of strife ranging from normality to full-blown international war, and that all these norms must be treated as a whole to provide for a maximum of protection to human beings. I also dissented from the tendency in academic quarters and among NGOs to treat human rights and humanitarian law as *sui generis* disciplines, and have always insisted on treating them as parts and parcels of general international law. Only thus would they find a place in the general theory of international law. I admit I am a generalist at heart, resenting overspecialization in segments of international law.

NYU provided me with a friendly, nurturing environment for teaching, research, and my more activist or practice-related activities. I continued to write in the fields of international administrative law, human rights and humanitarian law, and, increasingly, international criminal law, as well as on Shakespeare and chivalry, on which I will say a few words later. Apart from Shakespeare, most of my other academic interests were closely related to my extracurricular activities. I tried to make them from one cloth, as seamless as possible.

☙❧

My work with the International Committee of the Red Cross (ICRC), an organization for which I have always had a great admiration, could now begin in earnest. It became a major vehicle for deeper involvement in humanitarian law. Although I was active in a number of human rights organizations, especially Human Rights Watch, my work with the ICRC was continuous and more intensive. I developed and led an annual ICRC/NYU seminar for UN diplomats on international humanitarian law which eventually became an established tradition that recently celebrated its silver anniversary. I have always thought that teaching should not be limited to the academy in the narrow sense, but should be directed to governmental officials and decision-makers.

My additional appointment as Professor at the Graduate Institute of International Law in Geneva for the years 1991–1995 facilitated further work with the ICRC. I began to conduct periodic seminars on humanitarian law in Geneva for young university teachers from all over the world. My involvement in ICRC groups of experts—including the groups on internal strife, on the environment and armed conflicts, on direct participation in hostilities, and on customary rules of international humanitarian law, of which I was a member of the steering committee and one of the rapporteurs—was both demanding and rewarding. The customary law project, which required a significant multi-year commitment, was a perfect fit for my academic interests, especially as it followed *Human Rights and Humanitarian Norms as Customary Law.*

The creation of the expert group on internal strife was, in part, triggered by my earlier advocacy of a declaration of minimum humanitarian standards. When I was first settling in at NYU, an invitation arrived to present a paper at an ICRC conference in Hawaii on the relationship between human rights and humanitarian law. My work on the paper led me to believe that the separate treatment of humanitarian and human rights law left a gaping hole in available protections. In my paper in Hawaii and in follow-up papers for the *American Journal of International Law,* I argued that the conventions on international humanitarian law protect victims of international wars, but offer only limited protections to victims of internal armed conflicts and even less for civil strife. Moreover, disputes on characterization of conflicts create opportunities for states to evade the law altogether. Human rights treaties protect individuals from abuses in times of peace, but many of these protections may be derogated from on grounds of national emergency. In some situations, non-governmental actors exercise control over people while denying that, in doing so, they are bound by international standards. There was thus a significant gap between humanitarian and human rights instruments, to the detriment of victims. As a partial remedy, I proposed the adoption of a declaration of minimum humanitarian standards which would state norms capable of filling the gap for all situations of strife. I was grateful to Oscar Schachter and Lou Henkin, the editors of the *Journal* at the time, for publishing an article that challenged so many sacred cows. I pursued these ideas in my Lauterpacht Memorial Lecture on 'Human Rights in Internal Strife' at the University of Cambridge.

One of the joys of law as a discipline is that it allows a give and take within the profession—the chance to use the profession, which is naturally fluid, to overcome the stark barriers put up by the academic and organizational division of subjects. Fortunately, Alexandre Hay, the president of the ICRC, expressed interest and the first consultations of experts started, eventually resulting in the text of the so-called Turku Declaration (1990). But the proposal encountered opposition. Some opponents feared that a non-binding declaration would dilute existing legal commitments under the treaties in force; others felt that the declaration went too far in trying to impose additional obligations, albeit of non-binding character. Eventually the project went into a deep coma, but the basic idea that drove it is still very much alive. Since then, the world seems to have moved in the direction envisaged by the project, not through the force of a central idea or principle, but through the ICRC project on customary law, the statutes and the jurisprudence of international criminal tribunals, and the work of people everywhere to promote accountability and fight impunity. All of these contributed to expanding the applicability of protective norms to national conflicts and strife. What happened was a kind of bottom-up transition from the field and practice to theory.

Throughout my life, I litigated and advised on only a small number of cases, including two before the International Court of Justice. One case I argued arose from my continuing interest in international administrative law and women's rights. In 1990, Jacqueline Dauchy, a French national working for the United Nations, asked that I represent her before the UN

Administrative Tribunal in a case against the UN Secretary-General. She had expressed interest in being considered for the post of Director of the Codification Division, for which she was fully qualified. That post, however, had been traditionally held by a national of the Soviet Union, and the Secretary-General, in effect, restricted eligibility to nationals of that country. This was an offer I could not refuse. The judgment that Dauchy won limited the sway of the practice of national preserves and helped both men and women in the Secretariat to be considered on the basis of individual merit.[5]

⋙⋘

When I moved to the United States in 1978 and joined the faculty of NYU School of Law, I had to start my life almost from scratch. I found the opportunities given by NYU, the academic community, and the country to be wonderful. In 1984 I became a citizen. I was grateful for the welcome I was given by my adopted country and began looking for an opportunity to make a contribution. I was therefore particularly pleased when, in 1990, the US government invited me to be a public member of the US delegation to the Conference on the Human Dimension of the CSCE (Conference for Security and Co-operation in Europe) held in Copenhagen under the distinguished leadership of Ambassador Max Kampelman.

Additional assignments eventually followed. In 1998, I was invited to join the US delegation to the Rome Conference on the Establishment of an International Criminal Court, where I was involved in negotiating the provisions on war crimes and crimes against humanity. I could not believe my luck. Suddenly, I could deal with major countries on issues of fundamental importance and, as a representative of the United States, have some impact on the emerging provisions.

A few years later, while visiting at the University of California, Berkeley, I was invited to work with the US State Department on the *Oil Platforms* case before the International Court of Justice.[6] Soon thereafter I was appointed Counselor on International Law in the State Department, a post I held in 2000–2001. As Counselor, I was involved in negotiations, litigation, and advising. During my counselorship I was nominated by the

---

[5] *Dauchy v Secretary-General of the United Nations* (Judgement No 492) Administrative Tribunal of the United Nations Case No 548 (2 November 1990).

[6] *Case Concerning Oil Platforms (Islamic Republic of Iran v United States of America)* (Merits: Judgment) [2003] ICJ Rep 161.

US government and elected by the United Nations to be a judge at the UN war crimes tribunal at The Hague.

My judgeship became the most exciting and rewarding assignment in my life. It required a change of instincts, of intuitions, and of habits of work. It allowed me to put into practice my personal commitment to accountability, rule of law, and due process. I know how terribly fortunate I have been in becoming an international criminal judge so late in life, when most people would be retired or planning to retire.

The departure from the academy was more than rewarded by judicial activity. Scholarly activity was not entirely abandoned; it metamorphosed into something else. My position required me to address a myriad of new problems in a focused and precise way. I am grateful to my colleagues and particularly my wonderful law clerks, who had clerked in the US Supreme Court and the DC Circuit Court before coming to The Hague, for making this immense task of learning so much easier. And this transition allowed me to take part in the most exciting literature of all: writing the jurisprudence of international criminal law, such as the seminal Srebrenica case of General Krstić,[7] which established that genocide can be committed even in a circumscribed geographical area, and the *Kunarac* case, which clarified the law on rape and sexual slavery as crimes against humanity.[8]

In 2003, my colleagues, the judges, elected me President of the Tribunal, a post I held for about three years. Being President required me to preside over most appeal cases, to manage the institution, to provide leadership for the judges, to represent the Tribunal, to appear before the Security Council and the General Assembly, and to meet with the Secretary-General of the United Nations and with the leaders of the countries of the former Yugoslavia and of other states. It was a demanding job from which I could never disengage, but I found it truly exciting. My main disappointment was with the failure of the leadership of Serbia to deliver General Mladić for trial at The Hague for crimes he allegedly committed. I was hoping, perhaps naively, that my several meetings with Prime Minister Kostunica would produce results. They did not.

∽·∾

Let me turn to the last part of my lecture: Shakespeare. If my work on general international law, human rights, and humanitarian law repre-

---

[7] *Prosecutor v Radislav Krstić* (Judgement) IT-98-33-A (19 April 2004).
[8] *Prosecutor v Dragoljub Kunarac et al.* (Judgement) IT-96-23&23/1-A (12 June 2002).

sented a commitment or a mission, my work on Shakespeare was pure love and excitement. Like most things in my life, it resulted from chance.

In 1989, I was at All Souls College, University of Oxford, as a visiting fellow. My wife was also at Oxford and used her time to follow courses on Shakespeare, who had always been her great literary hero. She discovered the law of war in Fluellen's comment to Gower in *Henry V*: 'Kill the poys and the luggage! 'Tis expressly against the law of arms' (*Henry V*, IV. vii.1–2).[9] She suggested I write on the origins of the law of war in Shakespeare. After initial resistance, reasonable for a person whose relevant knowledge was limited to *Macbeth*, I went to see Laurence Olivier's and Kenneth Branagh's films of *Henry V* and soon became a born-again amateur Shakespearean.

A second period as a visiting fellow at All Souls in 1991 allowed me to read medieval history and the chroniclers intensively, which is essential for understanding the context for Shakespeare's historical plays on which I concentrated. Oxford medieval historians, and especially Maurice Kean, generously offered advice and guidance. In 1992, I published my first article on this topic, 'Shakespeare's Henry the Fifth and the Law of War', in the *American Journal of International Law*; it was followed in 1993 by my book *Henry's Wars and Shakespeare's Laws* and, in 1998, by my book *Bloody Constraint: War and Chivalry in Shakespeare*. My work on Shakespeare was facilitated by the support of NYU, which encouraged the involvement of faculty members in the humanities. I also started teaching law and literature and was pleased by my students' enthusiasm. There followed articles on Gentili and Grotius and on the authority to make treaties in the Middle Ages, and, later, on leaders, courtiers, and command responsibility in Shakespeare. I felt I would have been a happy medieval historian, had I followed a different path.

In *Henry's Wars* I tried to provide a humanitarian lawyer's commentary on the law-of-war issues arising in Henry V's French campaigns. My goal was to illustrate the law's evolution and to show how Shakespeare used the law of nations for his dramatic purposes. In *Bloody Constraint*, I moved on from the laws of war to broader issues of chivalry. My task required an exploration of the values of chivalry that sustained and reshaped the customs of war in the Middle Ages and the Renaissance, values that continue to surface in the legal, moral, and utilitarian arguments configuring the Geneva and The Hague Conventions and the laws and practices

---

[9] All citations to Shakespeare in this lecture are drawn from Stanley Wells and Gary Taylor (eds), *William Shakespeare: The Complete Works* (Compact edn, Oxford: Oxford University Press, 1988).

of war today. More than anything else, chivalry meant the duty to act honorably, in peace as in war. Indeed, chivalry's role was not limited to war. It implies an all-important code of behavior for a civil society. Its legacy continues to shape our contemporary law and values.

One of my more gratifying (and serendipitous) experiences as a scholar came when the director of Shakespeare in the Park[10] took note of my book *Henry's Laws and Shakespeare's Wars*. Although many productions have tread lightly around the horrific slaughter of the English POWs in Agincourt (*Henry V*), he was persuaded that the atrocity was a central part of the narrative, one that speaks to us even more powerfully today. *The New Yorker* featured an article, 'Take No Prisoners' by Lawrence Weschler, about this paradigm shift,[11] and I was happy to make a contribution towards this new reading of Shakespeare.

Not a literary critic, I did not purport to write as one. Rather, I wrote as a scholar of humanitarian law with an interest in history and literature. I focused not on Shakespeare the poet and dramatist, but mostly on Shakespeare the student of the chroniclers and of Plutarch and Homer, a humanist who had an acute understanding of the affairs of state and war. Above all, I wrote about a dramatist whose characters articulate a moving call for civilized behavior, for mercy and quarter, and for moral responsibility, and whose plays are a powerful instrument for illuminating the humanitarian principle as an ideal for all times.

I tried to show how Shakespeare's characters attempt to discourage war through legal, moral, and utilitarian arguments, and through irony and sarcasm, as in the famous soliloquy by Canterbury in *Henry V*, where Shakespeare lays bare self-serving and hypocritical assertions of just war. In *Hamlet*, he highlights the futility and emphasizes the inevitable cruelty and cost of war. Consider this moving exchange on war in *Hamlet*:

> *Captain*
> ...
> We go to gain a little patch of ground
> That hath in it no profit but the name.
> To pay five ducats, five, I would not farm it,
> ....
> *Hamlet*
> ...
> [T]o my shame, I see
> The imminent death of twenty thousand men

---

[10] Editor's note: Shakespeare in the Park is The Public Theater's annual season of free plays performed in New York City's Central Park.

[11] Lawrence Weschler, 'Take No Prisoners' *The New Yorker* (17 June 1996), 50.

> That, for a fantasy and trick of fame,
> Go to their graves like beds, fight for a plot
> Whereon the numbers cannot try the cause,
> Which is not tomb enough and continent
> To hide the slain.
>
> (*Hamlet*, IV. iv. 9–11, 50–56)

I have already disclaimed any competence in literary criticism. I have therefore avoided literary methodologies and their consequences for literary interpretation. But I have recognized the historicist's concerns and have tried to situate Shakespeare's text in its cultural and political environment, relating it to Tudor and Renaissance societies. I understood that Shakespeare's characters speak with a hundred voices and that there is hardly a text that could not be understood in different, sometimes contradictory, ways. While risking accusations of simplification, I found it worthwhile, nevertheless, to derive from those voices certain themes of chivalry which I dared think were Shakespeare's own.

෪ෂ෫

As I said at the outset, I am reluctant to view my academic journey as one that has taken me along a single path to a single goal. I should be profoundly disappointed if that had been the case—so many of the most rewarding experiences are the result of serendipitous diversions. But, in many ways, the title of my book *Humanization of International Law* could describe the overarching theme of my life's work. My interest in international law evolved from a relatively narrow focus on notions of state responsibility to encompass humanitarian law and human rights law, and my fervent desire to integrate these disciplines.

I have been blessed to be able to pursue my intellectual passions both in the world of the academy, where we enjoy the luxury of exploring Shakespeare and crafting pristine theories, as well as in the nitty-gritty world of handling cases and negotiating instruments of international law. My time as a judge on the International Criminal Tribunal for the former Yugoslavia has been the best of both worlds—shaping doctrines that often have an academic flair, but always doing so with an eye towards their impact on real people's lives. My hope is that, in some small way, these endeavors have contributed to our thinking critically about how to create a more humane world.

The time has come to end this discussion. Given my own age, it is natural that I would think of Jacques' seven ages of man in *As You Like It*.

Whatever my present frailties, my judgeship legitimizes situating me in the fifth age:

> the justice,
> In fair round belly with good capon lined,
> ...
> Full of wise saws and modern instances,
> And so he plays his part.
>
> *(As You Like It,* II.vii.153–157)

It is the future, represented by the sixth and the seventh ages, which is more frightening. For the time being, my intense work, new interests and projects, and helpful genes may delay somewhat the inevitable coming of the seventh age:

> Last scene of all,
> That ends this strange, eventful history,
> Is second childishness and mere oblivion,
> Sans teeth, sans eyes, sans taste, sans everything.
>
> *(As You Like It,* II.vii.163–166)

I thank you for your patience and for the honor you have bestowed upon me.

I
Humanitarian Law and Human Rights Law: Evolving Bodies of Law

2

THE GENEVA CONVENTIONS AND PUBLIC INTERNATIONAL LAW*

With sixty years of hindsight, it seems particularly appropriate to reflect on the trajectory of international humanitarian law (IHL) as shaped by the 1949 Geneva Conventions. Today, the rights and values embodied in the Conventions implicitly underlie rights and duties of states in both war and peace, as well as shaping the ethos of our shared sense of humanity. But the near universal acceptance of the Conventions and their secure integration into the international system can sometimes lead us to underestimate the significance of their impact. It is this transformative impact that I would like to speak about today.

I will focus on three concurrent trends set in motion by the Conventions. The first strand was a movement away from reactively protecting civilians to proactively safeguarding their welfare. Second, IHL shifted its focus from a paradigm of reciprocity to a framework of individual responsibility and rights. Lastly, the near universal acceptance of the Geneva Conventions has led to a non-derogable standard of humane conduct.

To start, I will briefly review the historical context from which the 1949 Conventions materialized. Calamitous events and atrocities have always driven the development of IHL. In 1863, the American Civil War gave rise to the Lieber Code. This ultimately gave birth to the branch of IHL commonly known as Hague Law, which governs the conduct of hostilities. The battle of Solferino—immortalized in Henry Dunant's moving memoir of suffering and bloodshed in battle—inspired the Red Cross movement. Thence began the other branch of IHL, Geneva Law,

---

* Delivered at the British Foreign and Commonwealth Office Conference commemorating the 60th Anniversary of the 1949 Geneva Conventions, London, United Kingdom, on 9 July 2009. The text of this speech first appeared as 'The Geneva Conventions and Public International Law', in *International Review of the Red Cross*, Vol 91, No 875 (30 September 2009), 619–625, © International Committee of the Red Cross. Reprinted with permission and modified from the original publication.

which, starting with the first Geneva Convention in 1864, has provided for the protection of the victims of war, the sick, the wounded, prisoners, and civilians.

In the twentieth century, Nazi atrocities led to Nuremberg, the Genocide Convention, and the adoption of the Universal Declaration of Human Rights and the human rights clauses in the UN Charter. At around the same time, the 1949 Geneva Conventions were adopted. While the First, Second, and Third Geneva Conventions followed earlier, more rudimentary models of IHL, the common clauses of the Conventions and the Fourth Geneva Convention were entirely new conceptions. Not surprisingly, the committee that drafted the common clauses was chaired by one of the eminent international lawyers of the time, Maurice Bourquin. The most famous of these common clauses is, of course, common Article 3, which for the first time in the history of international law introduced regulation of non-international armed conflicts into multilateral treaties. Through international criminal courts, this Article has evolved into a mini-code of criminal proscriptions.

The 1949 Geneva Conventions were the flagship of the post-World War II legal changes that shifted the paradigm of many aspects of IHL from an inter-state archetype to a homocentric system which included rules on individual criminal responsibility. The Geneva Conventions also introduced the system of grave breaches and the obligation of all states parties to prosecute or to extradite for violations listed as such, *aut dedere aut judicare*. The Conventions thus made an important contribution to the principle of universal jurisdiction over crimes *jure gentium*. The rights of states to prosecute crimes *jure gentium* can be seen as an analogue, *mutatis mutandis*, of the prerogative of all states to invoke obligations *erga omnes* against states that violate fundamental human rights. State practice has demonstrated, however, a clear reluctance to prosecute or even extradite alleged offenders of grave breaches where the direct interests of the state are not involved. Notably, although the Conventions contemplated the exercise of jurisdiction by the detaining powers, it is now accepted that international criminal courts may also exercise jurisdiction over grave breaches.

I. FROM THE FOURTH HAGUE CONVENTION TO THE FOURTH GENEVA CONVENTION

To understand how significant the 1949 Geneva Conventions were, it is useful to consider the legal protections that preceded them. The most significant of the latter were found in the Fourth Hague Convention, which contains important but inadequate rules governing the protection of civilians in occupied territory, including the duty to maintain law and order and the prohibition of collective punishment. Of the fifteen Articles of the Hague Regulations on 'Military Authority over the Territory of the Hostile State', only three relate to the physical integrity of civilians. The other provisions deal essentially with the protection of property. The sufferings of populations in Nazi-occupied Europe demonstrated very well the limitations in the Fourth Hague Convention, and the need for a more protective regime.

The International Committee of the Red Cross (ICRC) had prepared a draft civilians' convention (the Tokyo draft) that would have supplemented the Hague Conventions, but the onset of World War II suspended any progress. Of course, it would take a true optimist to believe that the existence of a civilians' convention during World War II would have prevented the worst Nazi atrocities (such as the Holocaust) as well as those committed by Japan and others, but it would at least have given the ICRC more standing to intervene.

Informed by the carnage of World War II, the Fourth Geneva Convention created a new balance between the rights of occupiers and the rights of occupied populations. The Fourth Hague Convention established important limitations on the occupier's permissible activities; by contrast, the Fourth Geneva Convention obligated the occupier, as Sir Hersch Lauterpacht memorably wrote, to assume active responsibility for the 'welfare' of the civilian population under his control.[1] These obligations included ensuring the population's basic needs in terms of food, health, and administration of justice—and, more broadly, protection of individuals' human dignity. By contrast to the Fourth Hague Convention, the Fourth Geneva Convention contains detailed provisions on the protections afforded to civilians—aliens, the general population, vulnerable groups such as children and women, and internees—not only in occupied territories, but also in all territories of the parties to the conflict.

Speaking to a British audience, it may be worthwhile recalling the ancient pedigree of the rules on humane treatment of the civilian population of occupied countries. In the context of theft of a church object during the Hundred Years War, and the hanging ordered for the offender, for example, Shakespeare's Henry V declared: 'We would have all such offenders so cut off, and we here give express charge that in our marches

---

[1] Hersch Lauterpacht, 'The Problem of the Revision of the Law of War', in Sir Elihu Lauterpacht (ed), *International Law: Being the Collected Papers of Hersch Lauterpacht: 5. Disputes, War and Neutrality, Parts IX–XIV* (Cambridge: Cambridge University Press, 2004), 604.

through the country there be nothing compelled from the villages, nothing taken but paid for, none of the French upbraided or abused in disdainful language' (*Henry V*, III.vi.108–112).[2] The Fourth Geneva Convention constitutes a great leap in what has been a very long march toward a more proactive approach to safeguarding civilian welfare.

II. FROM RECIPROCITY TO INDIVIDUAL RESPONSIBILITY AND RIGHTS

How much humanitarian law has already departed from its previous foci can be seen by revisiting the now largely obsolete *si omnes* clause of the Fourth Hague Convention and the question of belligerent reprisals.

The *si omnes* clause found in early law-of-war treaties provided that if one party to a conflict was not a party to the instrument, no parties were bound by the instrument. The Fourth Hague Convention's *si omnes* clause was invoked as a defense during, and threatened the integrity of, the Nuremberg prosecutions. It was only by considering the Hague Regulations—made inapplicable because of the *si omnes* clause—as a mirror of customary law that the argument of the Nuremberg defendants could be answered.[3] While the Fourth Hague Convention is still in force, the fact that most of its provisions are now regarded as customary law means that the Convention's general participation clause can now be regarded as having fallen into desuetude.

And what about the Geneva Conventions? The general participation clause was explicitly reversed in the 1929 Prisoner of War (POW) Convention and in the 1929 Convention for the Amelioration of the Condition of the Wounded and Sick in Armies in the Field. Article 82 of the POW Convention provided, for instance, that: 'In time of war if one of the belligerents is not a party to the Convention, its provisions shall, nevertheless, remain binding as between the belligerents who are parties thereto.'

Common Article 2(3) of the 1949 Geneva Conventions goes even further. It provides that even if one belligerent is not a party to the convention but accepts it for the specific conflict only, the parties shall be bound by the Convention in relation to that state. This idea of broadening the potential contractual reach of a convention had been broached in 1929 but was rejected at that time.

---

[2] Stanley Wells and Gary Taylor (eds), *William Shakespeare: The Complete Works* (Compact edn, Oxford: Oxford University Press, 1988).

[3] International Military Tribunal (Nuremberg), 'Judgment and Sentences' (1947) 41 *AJIL* 172.

The Geneva Conventions also broadened their applicability by excluding the principle of reciprocity. Common Article 1 of the 1949 Geneva Conventions, which provides that '[t]he High Contracting Parties undertake to respect and to ensure respect for the present Convention *in all circumstances*',[4] epitomizes this denial of reciprocity. The ICRC Commentary to the First Geneva Convention further emphasizes the unconditional and non-reciprocal character of the obligations: 'A State does not proclaim the principle of the protection due to wounded and sick combatants in the hope of saving a certain number of its own nationals. It does so out of respect for the human person as such.'[5]

Another aspect of common Article 1, the charge that parties 'ensure respect', also derives from the rejection of reciprocity and goes to the heart of accountability for violations of international humanitarian law. The International Court of Justice held this Article to be declaratory of customary law in its 1986 judgment in *Nicaragua v United States*, concluding that the Geneva Conventions were merely specific expressions of general principles of IHL, which obligated the United States to respect their provisions.[6]

Although the initial purpose of common Article 1 may have been to specify the obligation of a party to ensure that its entire civilian and military apparatus respect the Conventions, it has subsequently been interpreted as providing standing for states parties to the Conventions vis-à-vis violating states. Parties can therefore endeavor to bring a violating party back into compliance, thus promoting universal application. To a large extent, this later interpretation was triggered by the ICRC's Commentaries to the Geneva Conventions and the supportive literature generated by them. The exact scope of the rights of third parties under common Article 1, however, is still unclear. For example, whether the parties must act jointly or may only take individual measures with respect to a violating state is uncertain, as is the precise nature of the actions that may be taken. Nevertheless, common Article 1 can already be seen as the humanitarian law analogue to the human rights principle of *erga omnes*.

We can further observe the departure from the principle of reciprocity in the treatment of reprisals. From the 1929 POW Convention to the 1977 Additional Protocol I to the Geneva Conventions, the domain of

---

[4] Emphasis added.

[5] Jean S Pictet (ed), *Commentary I: Geneva Convention for the Amelioration of the Condition of the Wounded and Sick in Armed Forces in the Field* (Geneva: ICRC, 1952) (*Commentary I*), 28–9.

[6] *Military and Paramilitary Activities in and against Nicaragua (Nicaragua v United States of America)* (Merits: Judgment) [1986] ICJ Rep 14 (*Nicaragua*).

legitimate reprisals has shrunk dramatically. The 1929 POW Convention prohibited reprisals against prisoners of war. The 1949 Geneva Conventions dramatically expanded the prohibition on reprisals to include persons, installations, or property protected by their provisions (including the wounded, the sick and the shipwrecked, medical personnel and objects, prisoners of war, and the civilian population or individuals in the power of a party), as well as prohibiting collective punishment and terrorization of the civilian population and the taking of hostages. Additional Protocol I prohibits reprisals against the entire civilian population, civilian objects, and cultural objects (reprisals against the latter are also prohibited by the 1954 Convention for the Protection of Cultural Property in the Event of Armed Conflict). The Protocol also prohibits reprisals against objects indispensable to the survival of the civilian population, the natural environment, and works or installations containing so-called dangerous forces, such as nuclear or toxic materials. Finally, I note that Protocol II to the Convention on Conventional Weapons prohibits reprisals through the use of mines, booby-traps, and other devices.

In short, modern treaties have reduced legitimate reprisals to those launched against the armed forces. But since attacks against the military are, in any event, lawful under *jus in bello*, these treaties, in effect, have nearly eliminated reprisals against non-military targets. State practice lags, however, behind such enlightened normative texts.

The principle of reciprocity, still prominent in the law of war, has thus undergone important changes. Although reciprocity still applies to the creation of obligations under the Geneva Conventions, its reach is limited. It does not enable the termination of obligations on grounds of breach. For example, the denunciation clause of the Geneva Conventions provides that a denunciation cannot take effect until peace has been concluded and the release and repatriation of the persons protected by the Conventions have been completed.

Article 60(5) of the Vienna Convention on the Law of Treaties resonates with these provisions of the Geneva Conventions. Under this Article, the party victim to a breach of treaty cannot invoke the breach as a ground for terminating or suspending treaty provisions of a humanitarian character relating to the protection of the human person. A breach, and consequently the principle of reciprocity, may therefore not be invoked to justify derogations from humanitarian law with regard to protected persons, especially civilians. As the ICRC Commentary notes, 'the Conventions are coming to be regarded less and less as contracts on a basis of reciprocity concluded in the national interest of each of the parties, and more and more as solemn affirmations of principles [and] unconditional engagements'.⁷

III. INALIENABILITY OF INDIVIDUAL RIGHTS

The transition from contractual principles governing inter-state relations to universal ones is also evidenced in the proposals for a preamble to the 1949 Geneva Conventions. While no preamble was included in the four Conventions because of disagreements on its content, concern for human rights was nonetheless very present among the delegates to the drafting conference. A French proposal for a preamble to the draft Conventions amply demonstrates this concern, stating that: 'The High Contracting Parties, conscious of their obligation to come to an agreement in order to protect civilian populations from the horrors of war, undertake to respect the principles of human rights which constitute the safeguard of civilization[.]'⁸

Although the French proposal was not accepted, much of its language can be found in common Article 3. The International Court of Justice has already paid common Article 3 the highest tribute in the *Nicaragua* decision by describing it as a reflection of 'elementary considerations of humanity'.⁹ The establishment of mechanisms for the repression of grave breaches and the development of universal criminal jurisdiction also demonstrate the intent to reach individuals as the ultimate beneficiaries of humanitarian protection.

While even the early Geneva Conventions conferred protections on individuals, as well as on states, whether those protections belonged to the contracting states or to the individuals themselves was unclear. The 1929 POW Convention first paved the way for recognition of individual rights by using the term 'right' in several provisions. It was not until the 1949 Geneva Conventions, however, that 'the existence of "rights" conferred on protected persons was affirmed' through several key provisions.¹⁰ These provisions clarified that rights are granted to the protected persons themselves, using the language of 'rights', 'privileges', 'entitlements', or 'claims'. States may not waive such rights, nor may individuals renounce them. Indeed, common Article 7/7/7/8 provides that: '[Protected persons] may in no circumstances renounce in part or in

---

⁷ *Commentary I*, n 5 above, 28.
⁸ Jean S Pictet (ed), *Commentary IV: Geneva Convention relative to the Protection of Civilian Persons in Time of War* (Geneva: ICRC, 1958), 12.
⁹ *Nicaragua*, n 6 above, para 218.
¹⁰ Jean S Pictet (ed), *Commentary II: Geneva Convention for the Amelioration of the Condition of Wounded, Sick and Shipwrecked Members of Armed Forces at Sea* (Geneva: ICRC, 1960), 58.

entirety the rights secured to them by the present Convention, and by the special agreements referred to in the foregoing Article, if such there be.' The ICRC Commentary specifies that the prohibition upon renunciation of rights is absolute. This prohibition was adopted in light of experience showing that persons may be pressured into making waivers, but that proving duress or pressure is difficult.

Other provisions introduced into IHL an analogue to *jus cogens*, which is so central to human rights law. In IHL, this analogue—found in common Article 6/6/6/7—preceded by two decades the recognition of *jus cogens* in the Vienna Convention on the Law of Treaties. According to common Article 6/6/6/7, agreements by which either states or individuals themselves purport to restrict the rights of protected persons under the Conventions will have no effect. Admittedly, these invalidating provisions are conceptually different from the concept of *jus cogens* of Article 53 of the Vienna Convention on the Law of Treaties, and the resolution of conflicts between them and later agreements may be difficult. But given the widespread recognition of the Geneva Conventions as customary law—and, in some cases, as peremptory law—the invalidating provisions will probably prevail.

The significance of the rights conferred by the Geneva Conventions is reinforced by the recognition of the broad applicability and customary nature of the Conventions. The International Court of Justice and international criminal tribunals have repeatedly affirmed the universal applicability of the Geneva Conventions. In the case concerning *Armed Activities on the Territory of the Congo (New Application: 2002) (Democratic Republic of the Congo v Rwanda)*, in which the Court acknowledged for the first time the existence of peremptory norms in international law, it confirmed that in the *Nicaragua* decision, it had upheld the four Geneva Conventions as 'concrete expression[s]' of general principles of humanitarian law.[11] The Court also affirmed the expansive applicability of the Geneva Conventions in its 1996 advisory opinion regarding the *Legality of the Threat or Use of Nuclear Weapons*, in which it determined that the fundamental rules embodied in the Geneva Conventions 'constitute intransgressible principles of international customary law'.[12] Moreover, in its advisory opinion on the *Legal Consequences of the Construction of a Wall in the Occupied Palestinian Territory* in 2004, where it recognized Israel had

---

[11] *Armed Activities on the Territory of the Congo (New Application: 2002) (Democratic Republic of the Congo v Rwanda)* (Jurisdiction and Admissibility: Judgment) [2006] ICJ Rep 6, para 122 (internal quotation marks omitted).

[12] *Legality of the Threat or Use of Nuclear Weapons* (Advisory Opinion) [1996] ICJ Rep 226, para 79.

violated certain obligations *erga omnes*, the Court reaffirmed that Article 1 of the Fourth Geneva Convention requires every state party to the Convention to ensure compliance with its provisions, regardless of whether the state is a party to a specific conflict.[13]

IV. CONCLUSION

In conclusion, it should be underscored that the Geneva Conventions of 1949—important as they were even at the time of their adoption—have gained even greater authority with the passage of time, and their impact on public international law is difficult to overestimate.

First, they have achieved universality as the most highly ratified treaties in the world, apart perhaps from the Charter of the United Nations and the Convention on the Rights of the Child. Second, most of their provisions are recognized as customary law, and often as *jus cogens* or peremptory norms. Third, they have shown unusual adaptability to changed circumstances. For example, the strict inter-state obligations pertaining to repatriation of POWs to the country of origin have been attenuated by the principle of individual autonomy of the POW. Another sign of the Conventions' versatility is the change in the requirement of different captor/detainee nationalities for the status of protected persons. This requirement, so difficult to apply to wars involving fragmentation of states, has been superseded in the jurisprudence of international criminal tribunals by the more flexible concept of belonging to adversary groups. This vitality of the Conventions is in a great degree due to another unique aspect: the role of the ICRC and its outstanding reputation as the institutional guardian of the Conventions.

Confronted by crises and atrocities which sadly continue unabated, it is easy to forget how much worse the fate of all humans would be absent the Geneva Conventions. And in the midst of the atrocities that persist today, they hold us to a higher standard of human dignity that cannot be contracted away.

---

[13] *Legal Consequences of the Construction of a Wall in the Occupied Palestinian Territory* (Advisory Opinion) [2004] ICJ Rep 136.

3

CUSTOMARY HUMANITARIAN LAW: FROM THE ACADEMY TO THE COURTROOM*

I. THE ROOTS OF THE REVIVAL OF CUSTOMARY INTERNATIONAL LAW

The roots of the revival of customary humanitarian law can be traced back to the Nuremberg trials. Customary law was essential to the Nuremberg tribunals' ability to convict Nazi war criminals. The tribunals, including the International Military Tribunal (IMT), could not rely heavily on treaties because the Soviet Union had not ratified the Geneva POW Convention of 1929 and because the application of the Hague Convention (No IV) was challenged on the ground that the situation of the belligerents did not conform with its *si omnes* clause, as not all the belligerents were parties. The IMT reasoned, however, that the law of war was to be found not only in treaties but also in the customs and practices of states and in the general principles of justice.[1]

For many years after Nuremberg, there were no other international criminal tribunals. Thus, customary humanitarian law lay dormant for some time, except for its invocation in inter-state disputes. In other areas of international law too, customary international law began to appear less relevant. Where international tribunals *did* rely on customary international law, as in the International Court of Justice's (ICJ's) *Nicaragua* case

---

* Delivered at the Geneva Academy of International Humanitarian Law and Human Rights, Geneva, Switzerland, on 25 September 2008 as the 2008/2009 Master's Programme Inaugural Lecture. Portions of the text of this speech first appeared in 'Revival of Customary Humanitarian Law' (2005) 99 *AJIL* 817, © The American Society of International Law; Theodor Meron. Used by permission and modified from the original publication.

[1] International Military Tribunal (Nuremberg), 'Judgment and Sentences' (1947) 41 *AJIL* 172.

in 1986,[2] they did so in a somewhat relaxed fashion. This approach relied principally on loosely defined *opinio juris* and the existence of widely ratified treaties, resolutions, and 'soft law' instruments as proof of state practice.

Only a few years ago, I would have described customary international law primarily as a theoretical matter, except for the Nuremberg case law, the ICJ's *Nicaragua* decision, and a few other exceptions. Today, however, customary international law has effectively moved from the domain of academia to the courtroom. Customary international law now comes up in almost every international court and tribunal, in almost every case, and frequently has an impact on the outcome. International courts ranging from the ICJ, the Iran-United States Claims Tribunal, and the International Centre for Settlement of Investment Disputes (ICSID) arbitral tribunals to the regional human rights courts have pronounced on important issues of customary international law in recent years. But I believe it is in the international criminal tribunals—particularly in the International Criminal Tribunal for the former Yugoslavia—that the jurisprudence on customary international law has been most rich.

II. CUSTOMARY INTERNATIONAL LAW IN THE NON-CRIMINAL INTERNATIONAL COURTS

Let us begin by looking at the application of customary international law by non-criminal international bodies, such as the ICJ.

Although several classically customary branches of international law have been codified in widely ratified conventions, other branches have so far resisted such codification. Thus, today, customary law is very much alive in institutions treating those latter branches, although it is no longer the dominant source of international law in general.

Likewise, where one or more parties to a dispute have not ratified the relevant international instruments, customary law governs. This is the case with the Eritrea–Ethiopia Claims Commission which, before Eritrea's ratification of the Geneva Conventions, focused on customary humanitarian law.

Even the regional human rights courts, which principally apply their own constituent instruments, occasionally invoke customary law. The Inter-American Court of Human Rights, for example, has relied on the law of state responsibility as a matter of customary international law[3]

---

[2] *Military and Paramilitary Activities in and against Nicaragua (Nicaragua v United States of America)* (Merits: Judgment) [1986] ICJ Rep 14.
[3] *Case of Velásquez Rodríguez v Honduras* (Judgment (Merits)) Inter-American Court of Human Rights Series C No 4 (29 July 1988).

and, more recently, has ruled that amnesties for crimes against humanity violate customary international law and *jus cogens*.[4] The European Court of Human Rights has invoked the customary rules on imputability,[5] has found that the prohibition on torture is both customary and *jus cogens*,[6] and just this month confirmed the customary law character of the prohibition of attacks against persons *hors de combat* and of the principle of *nullum crimen sine lege*.[7]

Notably absent from many of these cases, however, is a detailed discussion of the evidence that has traditionally supported the establishment of the relevant rules as customary law—the practices and legal opinions of a large number of states. The ICJ articulated the textbook methodology for identifying customary law more than thirty-five years ago in its seminal *Continental Shelf* cases.[8] Yet other bodies can hardly be blamed for failing to apply this approach, as the ICJ's modern cases also do not tend to follow it rigorously. Rather, where a treaty exists in a particular area of law, even where it does not bind the parties to the dispute in question, the ICJ has tended to treat the text of the treaty as a distillation of the customary rule, thus eschewing examination of primary materials establishing state practice and *opinio juris*.

For example, in the *Nicaragua* case, the Court held that common Articles 1 and 3 of the Geneva Conventions constitute binding general principles of humanitarian law—in other words, customary law. In doing so, the Court made a major contribution to the vitality of humanitarian law. What is remarkable about the *Nicaragua* case, though, is the complete failure to inquire whether *opinio juris* and practice support the crystallization of common Articles 1 and 3 into customary law, as pointed out in Judge Sir Robert Jennings' dissent.

Another example of the ICJ's reliance on customary international law is the recent *Genocide* case (*Bosnia and Herzegovina v Serbia and Montenegro*, 2007).[9] While the Court was careful to confine much of its ruling to the Genocide Convention itself, it also found that the 'effective control'

---

[4] *Case of Almonacid-Arellano et al. v Chile* (Judgment (Preliminary Objections, Merits, Reparations and Costs)) Inter-American Court of Human Rights Series C No 154 (26 September 2006).
[5] *Assanidze v Georgia* (App no 71503/01) (2004) 39 EHRR 32; *Ilaşcu and others v Moldova and Russia* (App no 48787/99) (2004) 40 EHRR 46.
[6] *Al-Adsani v United Kingdom* (App no 35763/97) (2001) 34 EHRR 11.
[7] *Korbely v Hungary* (App no 9174/02) (2008) 50 EHRR 48.
[8] *North Sea Continental Shelf Cases (Federal Republic of Germany v Denmark; Federal Republic of Germany v Netherlands)* (Merits: Judgment) [1969] ICJ Rep 3 (*Continental Shelf*).
[9] *Application of the Convention on the Prevention and Punishment of the Crime of Genocide (Bosnia and Herzegovina v Serbia and Montenegro)* (Merits: Judgment) [2007] ICJ Rep 43.

standard of attribution contained in the non-binding International Law Commission (ILC) Articles on State Responsibility was reflective of customary international law.[10]

In addition to a generally more relaxed approach to customary international law, the ICJ and other international courts are increasingly relying on precedent rather than repeatedly engaging in detailed analysis of the customary status of the same principles in every case. We might perhaps discern in this practice something similar to a *stare decisis* principle among the international tribunals. For instance, the impact of *Nicaragua* on the subsequent development of the law was such that the customary law character of common Articles 1 and 3, and practically of the entire corpus of the Geneva Conventions, is now virtually never questioned. The same is true, under the influence of the Nuremberg tribunals, of the Hague Convention (No IV) of 1907. It is certainly true that, in practice, courts are giving greater weight to judicial decisions than what is suggested by the text of Article 38 of the ICJ Statute.

In calling attention to this more relaxed approach to customary international law, I do not mean to argue that these courts' holdings have been unfounded or are any less important than they would be had they followed a more traditional approach. To the contrary, at least one aspect of this more relaxed approach has been a very good development. In *Nicaragua*, the ICJ substantially strengthened customary law by downplaying the normative significance of contrary practice. State conduct inconsistent with a norm was to be treated as a breach of the rule rather than as evidence disproving the rule. And if a state defended its inconsistent conduct by appealing to exceptions and justifications contained in the rule, the significance of such a statement was to confirm the rule.

This development was essential to the effectiveness of customary law. A balance must, of course, be struck, as there is a point at which contrary practice reaches such a critical mass that the norm in question cannot be said to be customary. But without an approach acknowledging the reality of contrary practice and articulating a method of dealing with it, it might be virtually impossible to identify any norms of customary international law, for there is almost no norm that every nation consistently obeys.

It is also important to recognize that many of these judicial bodies, perhaps particularly the ICJ, would struggle to apply a more traditional approach to customary law. They lack strong fact-finding powers and their formal rules of procedure and evidence make the presentation of the

---

[10] Ibid., para 401.

large bodies of evidence required to demonstrate 'extensive and virtually uniform'[11] state practice difficult. In addition, we must remember that it is difficult to find positive, concrete state practice with respect to rules that are largely prohibitive—as the rules of humanitarian law generally are—because such rules are largely respected through abstention from violations, rather than affirmative practice.

III. THE CUSTOMARY LAW JURISPRUDENCE OF THE ICTY

International criminal tribunals, particularly the International Criminal Tribunal for the former Yugoslavia (ICTY), have taken a conservative approach to the identification and application of customary international law principles. Both the centrality of customary law in ICTY doctrine and the ICTY's rigorous approach to analyzing and applying it are the result of the Tribunal's obligation, as a criminal court, to respect the fundamental principle of *nullum crimen sine lege*, or the legality principle: a defendant may only be convicted on the basis of legal rules clearly established at the time of the offense.

Given that the Nuremberg tribunals rooted their convictions not only in custom but also in treaties and general principles of criminal law, one might ask why the ICTY has relied principally on customary law. One reason is a desire to honor the statement in the Secretary-General's 1993 authoritative report to the Security Council that the Tribunal should refer to custom—although, it bears noting, the Appeals Chamber has held that this statement does not exclude reliance on treaties where there is no doubt that all the relevant states were party to them.[12] In addition, because of the generality of custom, reliance on it avoids doubts as to succession to treaties, their continuing binding character, the application of reservations, and the validity of ad hoc agreements between belligerents. And, although the Tribunal's jurisdiction is defined by its Statute, reliance on customary law ensures that the principle of legality is respected even where the alleged crimes occurred before the Statute entered into force.

The Tribunal's authority to punish is therefore circumscribed by customary law. If a criminal conviction for violating uncodified customary law is to be reconciled with the legality principle, however, it must be through clear and well-established methods for identifying customary law. The legality principle is thus a restraint on tribunals' ability to be

---

[11] *Continental Shelf*, n 8 above, para 74.
[12] *Prosecutor v Duško Tadić* (Decision on the Defence Motion for Interlocutory Appeal on Jurisdiction) IT-94-1-AR72 (2 October 1995).

'progressive' in developing customary humanitarian law. Rather, tribunals must be 'conservative' in the sense of resisting fast change to the law—in particular, fast expansion of the definition of culpable conduct. This approach respects an accused's procedural right to fair notice of the law.

It might fairly be asked whether a conviction for violating uncodified customary law can ever meet this standard. After all, codification of criminal prohibitions is the modern norm in domestic systems, even in common law countries; in the United States, for example, there are no common law crimes, and in the United Kingdom there are few. Nonetheless, in my view the legality principle does not bar such a conviction.

Thus, customary law can provide a safe basis for a conviction, but only if genuine care is taken in establishing that the relevant legal principle was sufficiently firmly established as custom at the time of the offense so that the offender could have identified the rule he was expected to obey.

This, in a nutshell, has been the approach of the ICTY. In effect, the Tribunal's Chambers have superimposed on the Statute a test of whether each of the crimes within the Tribunal's jurisdiction reflects customary law. The *Galić* case, for instance, concerned a conviction for terrorization of the civilian population. The Trial Chamber based the conviction on Additional Protocol I,[13] while the Appeals Chamber grounded it in customary humanitarian law.[14] The Appeals Chamber concluded that the conduct at issue was clearly prohibited under customary law at the relevant time by examining the drafting history of the Additional Protocols, previous conventions, and soft law norms such as the Turku Declaration of Minimum Humanitarian Standards, as well as the official pronouncements and military manuals of states. As the Appeals Chamber's judgment in *Galić* makes clear,

> the Judges have consistently endeavoured to satisfy themselves that the crimes charged in the indictments before them were crimes under customary international law at the time of their commission.... This is because in most cases, treaty provisions will only provide for the prohibition of a certain conduct, not for its criminalisation, or the treaty provision itself will not sufficiently define the elements of the prohibition they criminalise and customary international law must be looked at for the definition of those elements.[15]

So, does the legality principle require a tribunal to conduct a laborious inquiry into the question of whether a particular legal principle enjoyed

---

[13] *Prosecutor v Stanislav Galić* (Judgement and Opinion) IT-98-29-T (5 December 2003).
[14] *Prosecutor v Stanislav Galić* (Judgement) IT-98-29-A (30 November 2006).
[15] Ibid., para 83.

the status of customary international law for *every* offense with which *every* accused is charged? No—such an inquiry is only required where the unlawfulness of the conduct in question at the time would not otherwise have been clear. As the ICTY Appeals Chamber stated in the *Čelebići* case, acts such as murder, torture, and rape are obviously unlawful and there is nothing unfair about using the international system to punish them.[16]

Many of the Tribunal's cases, however, involve conduct of less obvious criminality. In such cases, the relevant customary law must be ascertained, and it must likewise be determined whether fair notice to the accused—sufficient to satisfy the *nullum crimen* principle—was provided. This may be accomplished through either of two related approaches. The first approach might be characterized as 'methodological conservatism'—that is, the use of only firmly established traditional methods for identifying the applicable customary norms. A second approach might be referred to as 'outcome conservatism'. Under this approach, doubts regarding the customary status of any particular legal principle are resolved in favor of the defendant, *in dubio pro reo*. This is simply another way of stating the requirement that criminal prohibitions be clear. The ICTY has blended these two approaches, and has done so in a way that, I believe, respects the fundamental principle of *nullum crimen*.

An example illustrating the Tribunal's approach is the 2003 decision in an interlocutory appeal in the *Hadžihasanović* case, which presented two issues.[17] The first was whether customary law applied the doctrine of command responsibility to internal conflicts. The five-member panel unanimously agreed that it did. The Appeals Chamber's methodology in reaching this conclusion provides an illustration of its generally meticulous approach. The Appeals Chamber specifically noted that 'to hold that a principle was part of customary international law, it has to be satisfied that State practice recognized the principle on the basis of supporting *opinio juris*'.[18]

The second issue in *Hadžihasanović* proved more contentious. At issue was whether a superior could be held responsible for punishing acts that were committed before he became the superior of the persons who committed the offenses—that is, crimes that took place on his predecessor's watch. By a majority, the Appeals Chamber rejected such culpability, finding no state practice and no *opinio juris* to support the theory of

---

[16] *Prosecutor v Zejnil Delalić et al.* (Judgement) IT-96-21-A (20 February 2001) (*Čelebići*).
[17] *Prosecutor v Enver Hadžihasanović et al.* (Decision on Interlocutory Appeal Challenging Jurisdiction in Relation to Command Responsibility) IT-01-47-AR72 (16 July 2003).
[18] Ibid., para 12.

liability. It also found that an expansive reading of criminal law texts, including the ICTY Statute, adequate to support such liability would violate the principle of legality.

The majority and minority decisions highlight a challenging issue raised by grounding criminal convictions in customary international law. Where a customary law principle can be shown to exist, 'it is not an objection to the application of the principle to a particular situation to say that the situation is new if it reasonably falls within the application of the principle'.[19] The difficulty lies in deciding where to draw the line and how to determine when a new situation is so new that it cannot be said to *reasonably* fall within the principle. On this issue, reasonable judges can differ, as we did in *Hadžihasanović*. Customary international law is not a precise science.

I believe that international criminal tribunals are necessarily constrained by the principle of legality, which is widely recognized as a peremptory norm of international law. While international tribunals can clearly apply a principle of customary international law to new factual circumstances, they cannot cross the line and create new criminal prohibitions that would be applied retroactively. This is the essence of the principle of legality and it serves as a fundamental check on the ability of international *criminal* tribunals to push the progressive development of customary international law.

Still, we must distinguish between the creation of new law and the interpretation of the scope of existing law. In *Prosecutor v Aleksovski*, for example, the accused argued that a previous decision could not be used as a statement of the governing customary law, since that decision was reached after the alleged commission of the crimes. The ICTY Appeals Chamber distinguished the interpretation and clarification of customary law, which is permissible, from the creation of new law, which would violate the *ex post facto* prohibition.[20] As the Appeals Chamber explained in its judgment, the *nullum crimen* principle

> does not prevent a court, either at the national or international level, from determining an issue through a process of interpretation and clarification as to the elements of a particular crime; nor does it prevent a court from relying on previous decisions which reflect an interpretation as to the meaning to be ascribed to particular ingredients of a crime.[21]

---

[19] Ibid.
[20] *Prosecutor v Zlatko Aleksovski* (Judgement) IT-95-14/1-A (24 March 2000) (*Aleksovski* Appeal Judgement).
[21] Ibid., para 127.

The ICTY has also made important contributions to the clarification of the substantive scope of customary international law. Among others, the ICTY has held that torture, slavery, forcible displacement, deportation, and terrorizing the civilian population are prohibited under customary humanitarian law. Here too, I believe, the Tribunal's methodological approach to determining the substance of customary humanitarian law has been sound.

In the *Stakić* case, for instance, the Appeals Chamber had to assess the cross-border requirement of the crime of deportation.[22] In its 2006 judgment the Chamber surveyed existing international law, including the IMT judgment, the Geneva Conventions and their Additional Protocols, the ILC Draft Code of Crimes against the Peace and Security of Mankind, the ICRC study on customary humanitarian law, and its own case law. It concluded that the crime of deportation requires, as a matter of customary law, a transfer across a *de jure* or a *de facto* state border and that the issue of whether a particular *de facto* border was sufficient must be assessed on a case-by-case basis in light of customary international law. On the facts of that particular case, the Appeals Chamber concluded that 'constantly changing frontlines' did not constitute a sufficient *de facto* border.[23]

In the *Kunarac* case—my first case—the Appeals Chamber upheld the Trial Chamber's definition of rape as reflecting customary international law, noting in particular that that there is no victim 'resistance' requirement under the customary international law definition of rape.[24] The Appeals Chamber also emphasized that the definition of rape under customary international law did not require that the victim's lack of consent result from force or threat of force; lack of consent could be inferred from coercive circumstances. Finally, the Appeals Chamber concluded that rape constituted 'a recognised war crime under customary international law, which is punishable under Article 3 of the Statute'.[25] It based this conclusion on

The universal criminalisation of rape in domestic jurisdictions, the explicit prohibitions contained in the fourth Geneva Convention and in the Additional Protocols I and II, and the recognition of the seriousness of the offence in the jurisprudence of international bodies, including the European Commission on Human Rights and the Inter-American Commission on Human Rights....[26]

---

[22] *Prosecutor v Milomir Stakić* (Judgement) IT-97-24-A (22 March 2006).
[23] *Prosecutor v Milomir Stakić* (Judgement), para 303.
[24] *Prosecutor v Dragoljub Kunarac et al.* (Judgement) IT-96-23&23 / 1-A (12 June 2002), para 128 (internal quotation marks omitted).
[25] Ibid., para 195.   [26] Ibid.

The ICTY has relied on customary international law not only for the basis of the underlying, substantive crimes, but also for the modes of liability. Early in its jurisprudence, the Tribunal clarified the customary doctrines of command responsibility and of joint criminal enterprise by reference to customary international law.

In addition, the ICTY has also relied on customary international law in construing procedural protections. In *Aleksovski*, the Appeals Chamber concluded that '[t]he right to a fair trial is, of course, a requirement of customary international law'.[27] In a decision in the *Perišić* case, the Trial Chamber relied on customary international law to define the right to fair trial.[28] It reasoned that

> although the right to a fair trial encompasses an equality of arms between the parties, there is no support in either customary international law, the case law of the [Human Rights Committee] or that of the [European Court of Human Rights] which supports the proposition that the principle of equality of arms affords a party a right to receive resources that are similar to his opponent.[29]

In the *Krajišnik* case, the Appeals Chamber concluded that the case law of domestic jurisdictions did not support a distinction between the right to self-representation during trial and on appeal.[30] Most recently, in the *Strugar* judgment, the Appeals Chamber relied on 'general principles of law recognized by all nations',[31] as exemplified in state practice and the jurisprudence of a range of international tribunals, to conclude that the applicable standard for fitness to stand trial was 'meaningful participation which allows the accused to exercise his fair trial right to such a degree that he is able to participate effectively in his trial, and has an understanding of the essentials of the proceedings'.[32]

In some cases, of course, whether the issue is substantive or procedural, the Tribunal's assessments of the evidence supporting the relevant customary international law principles have been comparatively brief. In most of these cases, the Tribunal has relied on its own precedents instead of revisiting the same issues repetitively, an approach that can hardly be faulted. It has also relied to some extent on proxies—such as the

---

[27] *Aleksovski* Appeal Judgement, n 20 above, para 104.
[28] *Prosecutor v Momčilo Perišić* (Decision on Motion to Appoint *Amicus Curiae* to Investigate Equality of Arms) IT-04-81-PT (18 June 2007).
[29] Ibid., para 9.
[30] *Prosecutor v Momčilo Krajišnik* (Decision on Momčilo Krajišnik's Request to Self-Represent, on Counsel's Motions in Relation to Appointment of *Amicus Curiae*, and on the Prosecution Motion of 16 February 2007) IT-00-39-A (11 May 2007).
[31] *Prosecutor v Pavle Strugar* (Judgement) IT-01-42-A (17 July 2008), para 44 (internal quotation marks omitted).
[32] Ibid., para 55.

long-standing recognition of a principle's customary status by the ICJ—in place of the comprehensive detailing of state practice.

The ICTY is not the only international institution to have approached the analysis of customary international law in such a painstaking manner. The ICRC study on customary international humanitarian law adopted a similarly traditional approach.[33] This important study represents an unprecedented collection of state practice and opinion gathered over the course of ten years, from over fifty countries and forty armed conflicts, and the volume of rules that the study produced represents essentially a restatement of the law. The need for this study, which was requested by states themselves, reflects the increasing importance of customary international law today. The study's two volumes on state practice that accompany the rules are perhaps even more important than the volume on rules, as they demonstrate the methodology applied and the wealth of practice considered.

In general, therefore, both the ICTY and the ICRC study have eschewed the more relaxed approach that has typically characterized modern discussions of customary international law. The two institutions share a synergy in their approach to re-establishing the centrality of customary humanitarian law which, I believe, is mutually reinforcing. Already, the ICRC study has been invoked in the ICTY's jurisprudence. For example, in the *Stakić* appeal judgment, the Appeals Chamber relied on the study as evidence of the customary international legal definition of the crime of deportation. In another interlocutory decision in the *Hadžihasanović* case, the Appeals Chamber cited the study to support the Trial Chamber's conclusions that the prohibitions of wanton destruction of cities, plunder of public or private property, and destruction of institutions dedicated to religion, and, more broadly, of attacks on civilian objects, were customary norms whose violation entails individual criminal responsibility.[34] In both cases, the Appeals Chamber was cautious not to rely on the study's rules alone; in the *Hadžihasanović* decision, the Chamber cited practice, rather than a black-letter rule, and in *Stakić*, the Chamber relied on Nuremberg case law, the Geneva Conventions and their Additional Protocols, the 1991 ILC Draft Code of Crimes against the Peace and Security of Mankind, and its own jurisprudence.

---

[33] Jean-Marie Henckaerts and Louise Doswald-Beck (eds), *Customary International Humanitarian Law*, Vols I–III (Cambridge: Cambridge University Press, 2005).

[34] *Prosecutor v Enver Hadžihasanović and Amir Kubura* (Decision on Joint Defence Interlocutory Appeal of Trial Chamber Decision on Rule 98*bis* Motions for Acquittal) IT-01-47-AR73.3 (11 March 2005).

IV. THE CUSTOMARY LAW JURISPRUDENCE OF THE OTHER INTERNATIONAL CRIMINAL COURTS

Now let me turn briefly to look at the use of customary humanitarian law by the other international criminal tribunals, particularly the International Criminal Tribunal for Rwanda (ICTR), the Special Court for Sierra Leone, and the International Criminal Court (ICC).

Despite the general similarities between the law governing the ICTY and the ICTR, there is a significant difference with respect to custom and the legality principle. Since the conflict in Rwanda was non-international in character, and since Rwanda was a party to the relevant international humanitarian law treaties, it is not generally necessary to consider whether a violation of the ICTR Statute was also a violation of customary law. It is enough that the treaties with domestic force in Rwanda were violated. There has therefore been no obvious need for the ICTR, in its treatment of provisions of these treaties or its own Statute, to examine their customary law underpinnings.

Nevertheless, the ICTR has still made some contributions to the elucidation of customary humanitarian law. In the so-called *Media* case, the Trial Chamber found that hate speech violates the customary international law prohibiting discrimination and, as a result, can constitute the crime against humanity of persecution.[35] In addition, the Chamber confirmed the distinction among hate speech in general, which is not criminalized in and of itself, speech that incites to discrimination or violence, and the crime of direct and public incitement to commit genocide. The Tribunal has also frequently invoked customary law on its decisions on preliminary motions.

I turn now to the Special Court for Sierra Leone. Its Appeals Chamber has held that the *nullum crimen* principle must be applied by reference to customary law.[36] As a matter of substance, the Special Court's greatest contribution to the clarification of customary law so far is the Appeals Chamber's finding that the prohibition on child recruitment in internal and international armed conflicts had crystallized into customary international law prior to November 1996, which is the starting point of the Court's temporal jurisdiction. Based on that reasoning, the Trial Chambers convicted four accused, in two separate cases, of recruiting, enlisting, and using children to

---

[35] *Prosecutor v Ferdinand Nahimana et al.* (Judgement and Sentence) ICTR-99-52-T (3 December 2003).
[36] *Prosecutor v Sam Hinga Norman* (Decision on Preliminary Motion Based on Lack of Jurisdiction (Child Recruitment)) SCSL-2004-14-AR72(E) (31 May 2004).

participate in hostilities. All but one of these convictions were upheld on appeal.

The Special Court's recognition that the recruitment of child soldiers violated a customary international law prohibition has been cited with approval by the ICC in the Pre-Trial Chamber's decision on the confirmation of charges in the *Lubanga* case.[37] There, the Pre-Trial Chamber rejected the accused's argument that the indictment violated the principle of legality because the charge of child recruitment was not prohibited under customary international law at the time of the offense. The Pre-Trial Chamber agreed with the Special Court's conclusion that, as far back as 1996, child recruitment was an offense under customary law.

Primarily, however, the Pre-Trial Chamber based its decision on the fact that the offense of child recruitment is clearly proscribed in the Rome Statute, which was in force in the Democratic Republic of Congo at the time the alleged offense was committed. This approach illustrates a fundamental difference between the ICC and the ad hoc Tribunals. The ICC Statute more closely resembles a civil law code. Unlike pleadings in the ICTY, therefore, the gravamen of future pleadings in the ICC will be the interpretation of the Statute, not its customary law underpinnings.

Nevertheless, Article 21 of the Rome Statute, which concerns applicable law, opens the door wide to additional sources of international law, including custom as well as 'general principles'. If the ICC chooses to take advantage of this Article in defining the scope of criminal liability, it should be guided by the legality principle and should, in my view, adopt a cautious approach to the interpretation of custom. The principle of legality is recognized in Article 11 of the Statute, which provides that the ICC's jurisdiction does not extend to crimes committed before the Statute's entry into force for the ICC or for the state concerned, if it became a party to the Statute at a later date.

Moreover, in the case of a referral of a situation to the ICC by the Security Council acting under Chapter VII of the UN Charter and in accordance with Article 13(b) of the Statute—as, for instance, with the Darfur atrocities—or when the ICC's jurisdiction is based on a special acceptance by the state concerned, a defendant might argue that he or she is subjected to *ex post facto* legislation. The success of such an argument would turn on whether the act constituted an offense at the time of its commission. In such a case, the ICC would have a rare opportunity to clarify the customary law status of the Statute's provisions.

---

[37] *Prosecutor v Thomas Lubanga Dyilo* (Decision on the Confirmation of Charges (Public Redacted Version)) ICC-01/04-01/06 (29 January 2007).

V. CONCLUSION

In conclusion, let me offer you some final reflections on the future of customary humanitarian law. As I have made clear, I believe that—perhaps contrary to what some might assume—customary international law is undergoing a remarkable revival. It has effectively moved from the academy to the courtroom. Nowhere is this more apparent than in the jurisprudence of the international criminal tribunals.

I do not foresee any end to the importance of customary humanitarian law. Sadly, there continues to be a shortage of treaty law regulating non-international armed conflicts—yet almost every conflict in the world today is non-international. It is in these internal conflicts, frequently so brutal, that the great majority of violations of humanitarian law and fundamental human rights occur. International courts will therefore necessarily have to rely on custom to fill the gaps and provide the necessary detail so as to be able to punish those who have committed these offenses.

Clearly, those who predicted the demise of customary law in the era of codification and treaty regimes have been proven wrong, at least with respect to international humanitarian law. As for those who believe that codification is always the best solution, I put to them the danger that diplomatic conferences would drift to the minimum common denominator.

Finally, as the ICJ made clear in the *Nicaragua* case, violations of customary law cannot be allowed to undermine or modify the law. In an age where many states are keen to rely on fears of terrorism and other threats to question fundamental principles of international law such as the absolute prohibition on torture, international courts must stand firm: violations of the law cannot be allowed to 'dictate the law'.[38]

---

[38] International Committee of the Red Cross: Response of Jean-Marie Henckaerts to the Bellinger/Haynes Comments on Customary International Law Study (2007) 46 ILM 959, 961.

4

THE HUMANIZATION OF THE LAW OF WAR (MAREK NOWICKI MEMORIAL LECTURE)*

Since ancient times, rules protecting individuals and rules governing the conduct of war have been contradictory. The Bible says: 'Thou shalt not kill.'[1] But in the Book of Samuel, God tells the Israelites to kill every man, woman, and child of Amalek. We are torn between our conscientious desire to uphold the sanctity of human life and acknowledging the stark reality that warfare has existed since the dawn of humankind. How do we reconcile the two?

The object of this lecture is to show that such a reconciliation is already taking place, thanks to the development and authority of human rights law. Human rights have humanized the law of war, so that even in armed conflict our focus is on protecting individuals to the greatest extent possible.

While there has been a constant tension between the world of human rights and the world of war, over the past century the pendulum has swung firmly towards human rights. This process has resulted in an overlap between these two previously distinct disciplines of law, with human rights law informing interpretations of what is now known as international humanitarian law and vice versa. Neither regime will entirely subsume the other, however; to some extent different rules will always apply to war and to peace. Nevertheless, strengthening the reach of international humanitarian law and the international community's commitment to safeguarding human rights is an inexorable process—and one that should be applauded and fostered.

---

* Delivered in Budapest, Hungary, on 25 November 2008 as one of two Marek Nowicki Memorial Lectures.

[1] Exodus 20:13.

I. THE LAW OF WAR AND THE HUMAN RIGHTS REVOLUTION

To begin the discussion, I would like to briefly review the traditional domains of international humanitarian law and human rights law before moving on to discuss their increasing symbiosis. So let me first ask: what exactly is international humanitarian law?

Most of you here in the audience are able to answer that international humanitarian law refers to the set of rules applicable in armed conflict governing the use of force and the protection of civilians, prisoners of war (POWs), soldiers, and property. The term international humanitarian law is, however, probably a bit more opaque than the previous term—the law of war—which has roots that are centuries old, though the first major multilateral treaties were not negotiated until the latter half of the nineteenth century. The change in terminology is an important one, because it represents not only the unification of Hague Law and Geneva Law, but also—and most importantly—the profound influence of human rights.

The classic law of war, like a number of other areas of international law, was limited in several important respects. First, in the very early days when the term *jus in bello* was in vogue, the law of war chiefly regulated nations' behavior towards one another. If one nation offended the rules, the other nation was justified in taking action against it, including reprisals against civilians that would otherwise be unlawful. The law of war was inter-state law, and, as Georges Abi-Saab put it, driven by 'collective responsibility, with the attendant collective sanctions of classical international law: belligerent reprisals *durante bello* and war reparations *post bellum*'.[2] The legality of such tactics was cold comfort to those caught in the middle: soldiers, POWs, and civilians—civilians who, as individuals, were not subjects of international law, let alone of the law of war.

This state-centric character of classical humanitarian law was reflected in both liabilities and remedies. When a soldier violated the rules, the state for which he—and at that time it was always a man—fought was typically liable for the violation not to the victim, but to the victim's state. The remedies available to the injured state were largely methods of self-help: reprisals, demands for compensation through diplomatic channels, and, after the war, a demand for war reparations. Individuals seldom

---

[2] Georges Abi-Saab, 'International Criminal Tribunals and the Development of International Humanitarian and Human Rights Law', in Emile Yakpo and Tahar Boumedra (eds), *Liber Amicorum Judge Mohammed Bedjaoui* (The Hague: Kluwer Law International, 1999), 650.

benefited from such arrangements. The very notion of an individual seeking and receiving reparations from another state for injuries caused during conflict was improbable; the idea that he or she could seek reparations from his or her own state was inconceivable.

Second, the law of war rested on the principle of reciprocity—the notion that states are legally bound only vis-à-vis those other states that have themselves agreed to abide by the same rules or conventions. While the principle of reciprocity created an important incentive for compliance, it also dramatically limited the reach of the protections afforded by the law of war. If even one of the belligerents was not a party to a law-of-war convention, the convention would not apply to any of the belligerents.

Third, in the tension between military necessity and restraint in the interest of reducing human suffering that has always been the hallmark of the law of war, the traditional law gave wide latitude to the achievement of military goals.

In this period, states were the only players; they were autonomous, sovereign, and, theoretically, equal. Moreover, until the mid-twentieth century, democracies were the exception. Consequently, the concept of states' obligations to their citizens was narrow: states owed their citizens protection from the depredations of outsiders, but little more. Until recently, individuals' rights against states were limited and difficult to invoke. We have progressed quite a bit since then, and the way in which relations between states and individuals have changed constitutes the most profound modern shift in international law.

This shift is the consequence of the human rights revolution. The atrocities of World War II—concentration camps, gas chambers, the Holocaust—gave birth to the human rights movement, and with it a number of important developments: the recognition of human rights as a fundamental principle in the UN Charter; the recognition of individual criminal responsibility for violations of humanitarian law; the judgments of the Nuremberg tribunals; the 1949 Geneva Conventions; the Genocide Convention; and the promulgation of the Universal Declaration of Human Rights. Other core human rights instruments were enacted in the wake of the Universal Declaration, including the International Covenant on Civil and Political Rights (Political Covenant), the International Covenant on Economic, Social and Cultural Rights, and other important declarations and resolutions. During the Cold War, human rights instruments proliferated further. The Helsinki system proved critical in countries under Soviet domination.

These international human rights instruments have been interpreted as conferring rights on individuals against states—and not just an individual's own state, but all states. Under human rights law, states are not autonomous entities with rights and duties only vis-à-vis one another. Rather, they have a responsibility to refrain from certain actions against individuals and, affirmatively, to provide for individuals' basic needs. Under human rights law, rights vest not in the state, but in the individual.

The human rights revolution has, more than anything else, taught us that what states do to their own citizens is the concern of the entire world, a teaching reflected in the development of international law. This does not mean that the old attitude has disappeared entirely—far from it. Nations still frequently invoke sovereignty to prevent others from peering behind their borders. But it does indicate a shift in how we think about human beings and their relationship to the world.

In short, human rights norms—including guarantees of due process of law and the prohibitions of torture and cruel, inhuman, or degrading treatment and punishment, arbitrary arrest and detention, and discrimination on grounds of race, sex, language, or religion—have infiltrated the law of war to a significant degree. More and more, obligations are defined in relation to the rights of individuals, and individuals are increasingly held responsible for their own derelictions. New institutions to enforce this individual responsibility, such as the international criminal tribunal on which I serve, have been established.

Meanwhile, notions of state-to-state reciprocity have given way to the establishment of norms considered to be universally binding. At the same time, many of the larger social changes that have fed the burgeoning of human rights consciousness—notably the globalization of television and the increasing reach of its networks—have helped move public opinion towards greater intolerance for human suffering in times of war as well as in times of peace. And in the tug-of-war between military effectiveness and reduction of suffering, the balance has shifted towards greater protection of individual dignity and freedom.

It is this process that has given the law of war a more humane face and, indeed, a correspondingly new name: international *humanitarian* law.

II. OTHER FACTORS LEADING TO THE HUMANIZATION OF THE LAW OF WAR

By describing recent developments as the humanization of the law of war, I do not mean to suggest that the classic law of war was inhumane or even that the human rights revolution has been the only cause of this humanization trend. On the contrary, efforts to impose legal restraints on the conduct of the murderous violence that is war have always been motivated to some degree by a desire to reduce human suffering. The law of war has long contained rules based on chivalry, religion, and humanity designed for the protection of non-combatants—and especially of women, children, and old men, presumed incapable of bearing arms and committing acts of hostility. It has also long contained rules protecting combatants in matters such as giving quarter, not inflicting unnecessary suffering, and not using perfidious means of killing.

Indeed, calamitous events and atrocities have propelled the development of the law of war throughout history; the more offensive or painful the suffering, the greater the pressure for adjustment of the law. The American Civil War, with its millions of dead and maimed, generated the Lieber Code of 1863 (a manual for the Union Army commissioned by President Lincoln) and ultimately spawned the branch of international humanitarian law known as Hague Law, which governs the conduct of hostilities. The suffering of the thousands of wounded soldiers at the Battle of Solferino inspired the Red Cross movement and what has come to be known as Geneva Law, which, starting with the first Geneva convention in 1864 and developed further in conventions of 1906, 1929, and 1949, emphasizes the protection of victims of war: the sick, the wounded, prisoners, and civilians.

War has never been kind to civilians, but the twentieth century stands out in the horrors and outrages visited upon them—and in the attention paid to those horrific acts. Nazi atrocities helped shift the state-centric focus of the law of war to individuals and, most notably, helped to introduce the idea of individual criminal responsibility. What we think of today as *the* Geneva Conventions (the four conventions promulgated in 1949 that built on the earlier Geneva Conventions) came directly in the wake of World War II's devastation. The atrocities in the former Yugoslavia, Rwanda, and elsewhere have also had a pronounced impact not because of their unprecedented nature—there is, unfortunately, nothing new in atrocities—but because of their breadth and visibility: what is now termed the CNN factor.

The media attention paid to twentieth-century conflicts contributed to humanizing the law of war. Increased media attention has resulted in the rapid sensitization of public opinion, reducing the time between atrocities and international responses. One result was the establishment of the ad hoc criminal tribunals for the former Yugoslavia and Rwanda, which have had a tremendous impact on both the development of international humanitarian law and its humanization. Another was the establishment of the ICC and the indictment of Sudanese President Omar Hassan al-Bashir by Prosecutor Luis Moreno Ocampo for genocide, crimes against humanity, and war crimes in Darfur. As these developments demonstrate, the old *post bellum* paradigm no longer applies: the international community is no longer satisfied to wait for the cessation of hostilities before enforcing international humanitarian law.

Further, before the twentieth century, civilians were generally not seen as worthwhile targets in war. States were less responsive to their citizens' voices, and low morale and the suffering of non-combatants would not necessarily have affected a state's policies. Today, by contrast, a strike on civilians is seen as a strike on the state itself. In addition, conflicts involving non-state actors, such as al-Qaeda and other terrorist groups, have proliferated, increasing the harm to civilians.

Technology and new means of warfare have also made the need to protect civilians from the ravages of war more urgent. The first half of the twentieth century saw the first uses of gas attacks, air power, automatic weapons, tanks, and nuclear weapons. Each one of these implements of destruction has resulted in increased civilian suffering and death.

In short, since the end of World War I, a combination of a greater focus on the individual and a heightened need to protect individuals has forced the international community to look at the law of war from a new perspective. This reflects an effort to protect human dignity in the face of overwhelmingly destructive wars. Though we still accept the idea that civilians can be lawfully harmed and killed during conflict (collateral damage), the ways in which that harm and killing can be done have become much more regulated and limited.

III. EXAMPLES

To illustrate this process of the humanization of the law of war, I am now going to turn to a few specific examples. First, treaty development over the last 150 or so years demonstrates how the law of war has changed to incorporate human rights values. I will then highlight particular aspects of the law of war that have changed as a result of the pressure of human rights, namely: views regarding POWs, protected persons, reciprocity, and reprisals. Finally, we will take a look at interpretations of both human rights and humanitarian law to see how judicial and other bodies have influenced the humanization process.

A. Treaties

I turn first to treaty development. The first treaties that significantly adjusted the traditional view of the law of war came in the mid-nineteenth century and grew with the Hague Conventions on the Laws and Customs of War on Land of 1899 and 1907. These Conventions prohibited weapons of a nature to cause superfluous injury or calculated to cause unnecessary suffering. In this regard, the Conventions are protective of individuals, though more so of combatants than civilians.

Conceptually, the most important part of the 1899 and 1907 Conventions was the so-called Marten's Clause, which states that all people, regardless of any specific provisions in treaties or laws, must be protected by the principles of humanity and the dictates of public conscience at all times. Thus, matters not regulated are not simply left to the discretion of the military commander. The strong language of the Marten's Clause explains its resonance and influence in the formation and interpretation of international humanitarian law; the rhetoric and ethics of the Clause have compensated for its somewhat vague and indeterminate legal content. The notion that there are certain things so abhorrent to our collective humanity that we absolutely forbid them, and that the sphere of forbidden actions can expand in line with public conscience, has been hugely influential in the more than 100 years since it was promulgated.

But it took time for the ideas enunciated by the Marten's Clause to become reality. While the early international humanitarian law treaties concerned individuals, it was unclear whether they gave individuals enforceable rights. It took until 1949 and the Geneva Conventions for individuals to be given inalienable rights. Common Article 7/7/7/8 states that protected persons may in no circumstance renounce in part or in entirety 'the rights secured to them' by the Conventions. The Commentary by the International Committee of the Red Cross further states that the prohibition of the renunciation of rights is absolute. This prohibition was adopted in light of experience showing that persons may be pressured into waiving rights, but that proving such pressure is difficult. Several provisions of the Conventions—Articles 5 and 27 of the Fourth Convention, for example—similarly use the language of 'rights', 'privileges', 'entitle[ments]', and 'claim[s]'. The international community learned lessons from agreements between the Third Reich and the Vichy Regime renouncing rights of French POWs and citizens. Now, states may not waive such rights, and agreements by which states or the individuals themselves purport to restrict the rights of protected persons under the Conventions have no effect. These developments resonate with the concept of *jus cogens*, or peremptory norms of international law.

The Geneva Conventions were followed by the Additional Protocols and conventions on weapons with excessive or indiscriminate effects, mines, booby traps, biological and chemical weapons, and blinding lasers. Each ensuing treaty has placed further restrictions on acceptable methods of warfare and has provided greater protection to individuals, particularly civilians. Thus, for instance, the principal object of Additional Protocol I (on international armed conflicts) was to bring up to date in a single treaty both the 1949 Geneva Conventions for the protection of war victims and the 1907 Hague Convention (No IV) respecting the Laws and Customs of War on Land, and to provide greater protection for victims of war. The Protocol created a new regime for the protection of medical aircraft; developed rules protecting medical personnel and governing relief efforts for the civilian population; and, in reaction to the Vietnam War, codified norms for recovering the missing and the dead and disposing of the remains of the dead. It strengthened civil defense and the protection of women and children. It elaborated a list of fundamental guarantees and human rights for persons affected by an international armed conflict who are in the power of a party to the conflict and are not otherwise entitled to more favorable treatment. And by its definitions of 'attacks', 'civilian[s]', 'military objectives', and proportionality,[3] the Protocol narrowed the parameters of permissible collateral damage to civilians resulting from attacks on military objectives and totally prohibited reprisals against any civilian population, even in cases of persistent violations by one belligerent of the laws of war protecting civilians.

The post-World War II instruments also disallowed many wartime actions once accepted as lawful. For instance, in both human rights and international humanitarian law instruments we now find provisions relating to the right to life, prohibitions on torture, cruel treatment, and arbitrary arrest, detention, guarantees of due process, and rules prohibiting discrimination.

Another important development is that the distinction between internal and international conflicts is being greatly reduced. The Geneva Conventions distinguish between international conflicts as defined in common Article 2, and conflicts not of an international character under common Article 3. The Additional Protocols distinguish among international

---

[3] Protocol Additional to the Geneva Conventions of 12 August 1949, and relating to the Protection of Victims of International Armed Conflicts (Protocol I) (1977) 1125 UNTS 3, arts 49, 50, 51(5), 52(2).

armed conflicts as defined in Article 1 of Additional Protocol I, non-international armed conflicts as defined in Article 1 of Additional Protocol II, and 'situations of internal disturbances and tensions', which are below the thresholds of applicability of Additional Protocol II.[4] Yet distinguishing between international and non-international conflicts is particularly difficult in contemporary conflict situations, which present aspects of both. These 'mixed' or 'internationalized' conflicts create special problems and there is no agreed-upon mechanism available for characterizing situations of violence.

Fortunately, thresholds of applicability have recently been blurred. The ICRC study on rules of customary international humanitarian law, for instance, seeks a broader recognition that many rules are applicable both to international and to non-international conflicts. Some armed forces now recognize that the same rules of international humanitarian law should be applicable in all situations involving armed conflict. The regulations promulgated by the Secretary-General of the United Nations on the observance of international humanitarian law restate a broad set of protective norms distilled from humanitarian law treaties without making any distinction between international and non-international conflicts in which UN forces are involved.[5] And the establishment of the two ad hoc tribunals and their subsequent jurisprudence as well as the drafting and the adoption of the Statute of the International Criminal Court contributed further to this progress. The codification in the ICC Statute of the principle that crimes against humanity can be committed in all situations, without regard to thresholds of armed conflicts, and that they can be committed not only by states, but also in furtherance of the policy of non-state entities, is a signal achievement.

The changing nature of the bulk of modern conflicts from international to internal or even mixed has thus drawn humanitarian law in the direction of human rights law. Common Article 3, the sole Article of the Geneva Conventions expressly applicable to internal conflicts, is now accepted as a minimum standard that is applicable regardless of the territorial nature of the conflict. Protective norms and regulations, including those governing the use of weapons and means of warfare—previously applicable to international conflicts only—are increasingly being applied to internal armed conflicts governed by common Article 3.

---

[4] Protocol Additional to the Geneva Conventions of 12 August 1949, and relating to the Protection of Victims of Non-International Armed Conflicts (Protocol II) (1977) 1125 UNTS 609, art 1(2).

[5] UN Secretariat, Secretary-General's Bulletin, 'Observance by United Nations forces of international humanitarian law' (1999) UN Doc ST/SGB/1999/13.

Such is the case with the revised Protocol II (to the 1980 Convention on Certain Conventional Weapons) on Prohibitions or Restrictions on the Use of Mines, Booby-traps and Other Devices (1996). Even more recently, in December 2001, on the proposal of the United States, the scope of the Convention on Prohibitions or Restrictions on the Use of Certain Conventional Weapons which May be Deemed to be Excessively Injurious or to Have Indiscriminate Effects was amended to provide for application in common Article 3 situations. The Convention will thus apply in any international or non-international armed conflict to which the Geneva Conventions apply. Other instruments already explicitly impose rules for all circumstances, including the Ottawa Convention on the Prohibition of the Use, Stockpiling, Production and Transfer of Anti-Personnel Mines and on their Destruction (1997), the Convention on the Prohibition of the Development, Production and Stockpiling of Bacteriological (Biological) and Toxin Weapons, and on their Destruction (a 1972 arms control treaty), and the Convention on the Prohibition of the Development, Production, Stockpiling and Use of Chemical Weapons and on their Destruction (1993, which concerns both arms control and use).

In short, according to the Appeals Chamber of the ICTY,

A State-sovereignty-oriented approach has been gradually supplanted by a human-being-oriented approach. Gradually the maxim of Roman law *hominum causa omne jus constitutum est* (all law is created for the benefit of human beings) has gained a firm foothold in the international community as well. It follows that in the area of armed conflict the distinction between interstate wars and civil wars is losing its value as far as human beings are concerned. Why protect civilians from belligerent violence, or ban rape, torture or the wanton destruction of hospitals, churches, museums or private property, as well as proscribe weapons causing unnecessary suffering when two sovereign States are engaged in war, and yet refrain from enacting the same bans or providing the same protection when armed violence has erupted 'only' within the territory of a sovereign State?[6]

B. *Particular elements of humanitarian law*

In addition to humanitarian law treaties that increasingly incorporate or are a result of human rights norms, human rights law has had a notable influence on the way we interpret, or even re-interpret, international humanitarian law, particularly the Geneva Conventions.

---

[6] *Prosecutor v Duško Tadić* (Decision on the Defence Motion for Interlocutory Appeal on Jurisdiction) IT-94-1-AR72 (2 October 1995) (*Tadić* Jurisdiction Decision), para 97.

1. POWs' right to repatriation

The notion of rights, and the idea that those rights belong to the individual, has increasingly affected the law governing the repatriation of POWs at the end of hostilities. The Hague Conventions provided only that the repatriation of POWs should be carried out after the conclusion of peace, and the 1929 Geneva POW Convention required that this happen as soon as an armistice was concluded. But there was no formal peace treaty or armistice ending World War II—a problem which the 1949 Geneva Conventions answered. The Third Geneva Convention's Article 118 mandates that repatriation should happen after the cessation of active hostilities. This suggests that POWs are not to be used as a bargaining chip by belligerent states prior to the conclusion of a peace treaty.

But what if certain POWs do not want to be repatriated? This was the situation after the Korean War with respect to North Korean and Chinese prisoners, and the question constituted one of the first direct clashes between human rights law and humanitarian law. The question boiled down to this: whose rights did the Geneva Conventions really espouse? If the right to repatriation belongs to the state, then the POWs must be repatriated when the state of origin demands their return. If the right belongs to the individuals, they should be able to refuse repatriation if they so desire.

The USSR and China felt that the right belonged to the state. But the UN Unified Command, backed by the General Assembly, declared that forcible repatriation was inconsistent with the Geneva Conventions. Rather, the right belonged to the individual.

In the years since the conclusion of the Korean War, the principle of individual autonomy has been further affirmed. As demonstrated by the Gulf Wars and the conflict in the former Yugoslavia, POWs themselves, and not states, can decide whether to be repatriated. Thus, from a right not to be repatriated by force in the Korean War, the practice has evolved to recognize the right of free choice. Of course, POWs who do not wish to be repatriated still need a state to grant them asylum, which might defeat the newly acquired autonomy.

What I find fascinating about the Korean situation is the basis the UN Command gave for its conclusion that forcible repatriation was inconsistent with the Geneva Conventions: forcible repatriation clashed with the Conventions' 'humanitarian basis'.[7] In other words, even in the 1950s, the

---

[7] UNGA, 'Special Report by the Unified Command under the United States: Letter dated 18 October 1952 from the Chairman of the United States delegation to the General Assembly of the United Nations, addressed to the Secretary-General' (18 October 1952) UN Doc A/2228, 18.

laws that regulated the conduct of war were seen as humanitarian. This marks a profound shift from the old state-centric days.

2. Protected persons

Because of its inter-state, reciprocity-based origins, the law of war has traditionally protected enemy persons, but not nationals of a state from their own government. Although this paradigm still prevails in some respects, it is changing by means of a process in which the application of the law of war is being influenced by human rights, a system which addresses the responsibility of governments vis-à-vis populations over which they exercise power, authority, or jurisdiction, regardless of nationality.

The Fourth Geneva Convention defines protected persons as only those persons who 'find themselves, in case of a conflict or occupation, in the hands of a Party to the conflict or Occupying Power of which they are not nationals'.[8] Moreover, this concept of 'protected persons' applies only to international armed conflicts. Since belonging to the category of protected persons was the traditional condition for the applicability of the grave breaches provisions of the Geneva Conventions, where a conflict did not constitute an international armed conflict, the grave breaches provisions of the Geneva Conventions would not apply—a position supported by the ICTY in the *Tadić* interlocutory appeal decision of 1995.[9]

More recent ICTY jurisprudence, however, has departed from that traditional construction, introducing more flexible criteria to replace the formal concept of nationality. Following the ICTY's appeal judgments in *Tadić, Aleksovski,* and *Čelebići*, individuals are now protected persons vis-à-vis all adversaries, regardless of their formal nationality.[10] As the ICRC has said, 'nobody in enemy hands can be outside the law'.[11] Respect for human rights and for a humanitarian interpretation of the Geneva Conventions thus replaced the literal and legalistic approach requiring different nationalities for the definition of protected persons. This is a

---

[8] Geneva Convention relative to the Protection of Civilian Persons in Time of War (Fourth Geneva Convention) (1949) 75 UNTS 287, art 4.

[9] See *Tadić* Jurisdiction Decision, n 6 above.

[10] *Prosecutor v Zejnil Delalić et al.* (Judgement) IT-96-21-A (20 February 2001) (*Čelebići*); *Prosecutor v Zlatko Aleksovski* (Judgement) IT-95-14/1-A (24 March 2000); *Prosecutor v Duško Tadić* (Judgement) IT-94-1-A (15 July 1999).

[11] Jean S Pictet (ed), *Commentary IV: Geneva Convention relative to the Protection of Civilian Persons in Time of War* (Geneva: ICRC, 1958), 51.

critical protection in the case of state fragmentation before the creation of a new system of nationality.

The influence of human rights law has also eradicated in theory, and sharply limited in practice, two key features of the old system: reciprocity and reprisals.

3. Reciprocity

Reciprocity, a natural consequence of a system of states equal to one another, was one of the main justifications for the existence and the development of the law of war and was important for its enforcement. In a world of armies, each agrees to follow the law for one overriding reason: the expectation that your enemies will follow the same law and give you the same protection that you afford them. Derived from the medieval tradition of chivalry, this version of legality guaranteed a modicum of fair play even during war. As long as the rules of the game were observed by both parties, it was permissible to cause suffering, deprivation of freedom, and death.

This rationale tends to leave individuals, especially civilians, without adequate protection. But as humanitarian law has departed more and more from its purely inter-state focus, reciprocity has lost much of its force as a driver of the law. Thus, the *si omnes* clause of the Hague Convention (No IV) was explicitly reversed in common Article 2 of the 1949 Geneva Conventions. This Article provides for the application of the Conventions between all belligerents involved in a conflict, even if one of the belligerents is not a party to the Convention.

Moreover, common Article 1 of the Geneva Conventions epitomizes the international community's rejection of reciprocity by providing that all parties, not only those involved in a particular conflict, undertake to respect and ensure respect for the Conventions in all circumstances. Common Article 1 is thus international humanitarian law's analogue to the human rights principle of *erga omnes*.

Nevertheless, reciprocity is an old and important basis for the law of war, which drove both its development and enforcement. It has never quite lost its impact and importance. The rule against refusing quarter is illustrative. Professional soldiers appreciate this rule because an enemy who knows that he or she will not be given quarter has no incentive to surrender, and will fight all the harder. The enemy soldier may well suffer a greater defeat, but will kill more opponents in the process. Conversely, granting quarter creates the expectation that it will be reciprocated by the enemy.

Normativity also prevailed over reciprocity in the denunciation clauses of the Geneva Conventions, and in Article 76, paragraph 5, of the Vienna Convention of the Law of Treaties. The latter excludes humanitarian provisions from termination or suspension for breach. Thus, a breach by one party does not allow the aggrieved party to suspend operation of the agreement.

4. Reprisals

The limitation of legitimate reprisals is an even clearer illustration of the influence of human rights. The classical definition of reprisal in international armed conflict is an act by one belligerent, otherwise in violation of the law of war, in response to an unlawful act of war by another belligerent, and carried out to compel that other belligerent to cease the unlawful act and to comply henceforth with its obligations.

Of course, even lawful reprisals cause suffering to innocent persons. We all know of mass executions of civilians during World War II under the guise of reprisals. Fortunately, the domain of legitimate reprisals has shrunk dramatically. Treaty law, particularly Additional Protocol I, has essentially outlawed any reprisals against civilians and civilian objects. On this matter, however, there may be a gap between norms promulgated by treaty and the maturation of customary international law. The United States, for one, does not accept as customary law a total ban on reprisals against civilians and civilian objects.

C. *Interpretation by judicial and other organs*

Judicial and other bodies have also encouraged the process of convergence by interpreting both human rights and humanitarian law as legal regimes that have more commonalities than distinctions.

Institutionally, human rights law and international humanitarian law are often applied in tandem; however, this was not always the case. In the early years following World War II, the separation between human rights law and what is now known as international humanitarian law was enhanced by institutional duality. The ICRC and the 'protecting powers' under the 1949 Geneva Conventions were in charge of the enforcement of international humanitarian law, while human rights bodies were in charge of implementing and enforcing human rights law. As conflicts became more internal in nature, the institutions charged with enforcing international humanitarian law and human rights law began to branch out—neither could avoid application of the other law. The institutional duality of the system was largely eroded. Now, human rights organs often review acts committed in wartime, and humanitarian law tribunals frequently rely on human rights norms.

For instance, the UN Commission on Human Rights has condemned violations of both human rights law and international humanitarian law in the conflicts in Kuwait, the former Yugoslavia, Rwanda, the Sudan, and elsewhere. Indeed, when looking at Kuwait, the Commission's special rapporteur said that his mandate included 'violations of all guarantees of international law', including those enshrined in both international humanitarian and human rights law instruments.[12] The Commission's rapporteur similarly noted that many actions in Colombia had violated both international humanitarian and human rights law, and he applied both bodies of law in his analysis. UN missions, such as the observer mission in El Salvador, have looked at both human rights law and international humanitarian law, as has the Inter-American Commission on Human Rights.

Another example that many here in Budapest may be familiar with is the case of *Korbely v Hungary*, which was recently decided by the European Court of Human Rights.[13] In that case the applicant, a former military officer, had been convicted of murder as a crime against humanity for shooting and killing an insurgent during the 1956 Hungarian revolution. The applicant argued that he had been convicted in violation of Article 7 of the European Convention on Human Rights, which provides that no one shall be held guilty for an act that did not constitute a criminal offense under national or international law at the time it was committed.

Let me remind you briefly of the provisions of common Article 3 of the Geneva Conventions. Common Article 3 is a virtual mini-convention which provides for the humane treatment of non-combatants and prohibits torture, murder, mistreatment, and unlawful executions. In *Korbely*, the European Court concluded that, although murder within the meaning of common Article 3 could have provided a basis for a conviction for crimes against humanity in 1956, other elements were also required in order for a conviction to be entered. For example, the Court reasoned that while a link with an armed conflict was probably not required in 1956, the crime in question should not be an isolated act, but should form part of a widespread or systematic attack on the civilian population. The Court further found that the victim was not a non-combatant for the

---

[12] UN Commission on Human Rights, 'Report on the situation of human rights in Kuwait under Iraqi occupation, prepared by Mr Walter Kälin, Special Rapporteur of the Commission on Human Rights, in accordance with Commission resolution 1991/67' (1992) UN Doc E/CN.4/1992/26, para 12.

[13] *Korbely v Hungary* (App no 9174/02) (2008) 50 EHRR 48.

purposes of common Article 3. Consequently, a violation of Article 7 had occurred.

In the examples just mentioned, what is interesting is not simply the penetration of human rights law into international humanitarian law, but, in fact, the converse—that is to say, the application of international humanitarian law by human rights bodies. If these and other bodies were established to deal with violations of human rights, should they really be deciding on violations of international humanitarian law?

Various states have thought not. The United States argued that the Inter-American Commission on Human Rights, when deciding a case arising from the invasion of Panama, could not even assert its jurisdiction over the invasion because the Organization of American States had not given it competence to adjudicate humanitarian law. Not surprisingly, the Inter-American Commission disagreed.[14] In a later case, it explained why a human rights body was competent to apply international humanitarian law.[15] First, the charge before it—an alleged arbitrary deprivation of the right to life—was clearly within its competence. But, more importantly, human rights law, it found, did not supply all the answers when the alleged violation occurred during an armed conflict; the Commission had to look to international humanitarian law to fill in the gaps. This gap-filling has much to commend itself, but it bears noting that such a move will probably result in less protection for individuals, who face a greater risk of lawful killing under international humanitarian law than under human rights law.

Important milestones in the convergence of human rights and humanitarian law have been achieved by international judicial bodies. For instance, the Inter-American Commission of Human Rights found that common Article 3 of the Geneva Conventions is 'pure human rights law',[16] and in *Nicaragua*, the ICJ held that common Article 3 provides rules which 'constitute a minimum yardstick' and reflect 'elementary considerations of humanity' from which no derogation is permitted.[17] Based on these findings, it is now accepted that common Article 3 is customary law that requires minimum standards of humane treatment during all forms of armed conflict.

---

[14] *Salas et al. v United States* (Admissibility: Report no 31/93) Inter-American Commission on Human Rights Case 10.573 (14 October 1993).
[15] *Juan Carlos Abella et al. v Argentina* (Merits: Report no 55/97) Inter-American Commission on Human Rights Case 11.137 (18 November 1997) (*La Tablada*).
[16] Ibid.
[17] *Military and Paramilitary Activities in and against Nicaragua (Nicaragua v United States of America)* (Merits: Judgment) [1986] ICJ Rep 14, para 218 (internal quotation marks omitted).

The contributions made by the ad hoc criminal tribunals such as the ICTY and the ICTR should also be noted. Due to lack of humanitarian law precedent, these tribunals have frequently turned to human rights jurisprudence to interpret and elaborate both the procedural and substantive provisions of their respective statutes. In so doing, the tribunals have ensured that the full range of due process rights provided by human rights law have been accorded to the accused and, as a result, have met the international community's expectation of fair trials. Moreover, by drawing on human rights precedents, the tribunals have ensured that serious violations of humanitarian law have not gone unpunished for lack of specificity.

One of the most important recent achievements is the widespread acceptance of the notion that human rights continue to apply in wartime. In the *Nuclear Weapons* opinion, the ICJ first determined that human rights provisions continue to apply during armed conflict, unless a party has lawfully derogated from them.[18] In particular, the provision of the Political Covenant that '[n]o one shall be arbitrarily deprived of... life'[19] did not cease in times of armed conflict.

Of course, humanitarian law permits a number of acts, including killing, that may constitute violations of human rights. How can this conflict be resolved? The ICJ provided an answer in the *Nuclear Weapons* opinion by turning to the notion of *lex specialis*. Human rights law can be understood as an umbrella law generally applicable to everybody. International humanitarian law, on the other hand, is applicable only in times of war. Therefore, where there is a conflict between the two bodies of law, we need to resort to a *renvoi* to the system which is most particular to the situation. Through a *renvoi* to the applicable *lex specialis*, the legality of a deprivation of life would turn on humanitarian, not human rights, law. The Court thus interpreted the right to life provision of the Political Covenant in light of principles of international law applicable in armed conflict, and found that a deprivation of life is arbitrary if it does not conform to that law.

The holding of the ICJ in the *Nuclear Weapons* opinion raises another question: if human rights law is applicable during times of armed conflict, where is it applicable and to whom? I have spoken today about how human rights law has infiltrated the law of war in general. It is equally clear that a consensus has developed that human rights law, like international

---

[18] *Legality of the Threat or Use of Nuclear Weapons* (Advisory Opinion) [1996] ICJ Rep 226.
[19] International Covenant on Civil and Political Rights (1966) 999 UNTS 171, art 6(1).

humanitarian law, is applicable extraterritorially. Like international humanitarian law, human rights law applies to all actions taken by a state or its agents that involve the exercise of the state's power over individuals. This is so whether the individuals are in the state's sovereign territory or not, such as in areas under temporary occupation.

The extraterritorial application of human rights law was central to the 2004 ICJ advisory opinion on the *Legal Consequences of the Construction of a Wall in the Occupied Palestinian Territory*.[20] The *Construction of a Wall* opinion set squarely before the Court the question of whether human rights law applies to territories beyond a state's borders, yet under its control. The answer was an unequivocal yes. The Court, citing the *lex specialis* holding in *Nuclear Weapons*, concluded that—except for derogations which relate to issues of security in times of emergency, such as in Article 4 of the Political Covenant—the protections offered by human rights instruments do not cease in case of armed conflict. As such, both humanitarian and human rights law were applicable in the Occupied Territories. Israel had argued that international humanitarian law is the sole law governing a conflict situation, while human rights law is intended only for the protection of citizens from their own government in times of peace. This argument reflected antiquated notions of mutual exclusivity of international humanitarian and human rights law. In rejecting the arguments of Israel, the Court decided that human rights law and treaties applied wherever the state exercised jurisdiction, alongside humanitarian law and subject to lawful derogations.

The Court turned to numerous sources to support its conclusion, including the jurisprudence of the Human Rights Committee. The ICJ also relied on the texts of the core human rights instruments. The Political Covenant, for instance, is interpreted to mean that states must protect the rights of not only individuals within their territory but also those subject to their jurisdiction. The reasons for this are clear. As the Human Rights Committee has said in regard to Uruguay, it would be 'unconscionable' to interpret the Covenant so as to permit a state to perpetrate 'violations of the Covenant on the territory of another State, which violations it could not perpetrate on its own territory'.[21]

So, what does this all mean? The primary message is that there is always space for human rights law—it never disappears, whether at home

---

[20] *Legal Consequences of the Construction of a Wall in the Occupied Palestinian Territory* (Advisory Opinion) [2004] ICJ Rep 136.
[21] *Lilian Celiberti de Casariego v Uruguay*, UNHRC Communication No 56/1979 (29 July 1981) UN Doc CCPR/C/13/D/56/1979, para 10.3.

or abroad, in times of peace, war, or in one of the gray areas in between. The actions of states must be looked at through the prisms of both international humanitarian law and human rights law. The ruling in the *Construction of a Wall* opinion, and the development it exemplifies, will result in increased protection for individuals.

IV. DIFFERENCES

Although I have spent quite a bit of time arguing that the classic law of war has been humanized by human rights, and that as a result there are increasing similarities between these two regimes, I must acknowledge that human rights law and today's humanitarian law have not become one and the same.

The law of armed conflict regulates aspects of a struggle for life and death between contestants who operate on the basis of formal equality. As long as the rules of the game are observed, suffering, deprivation of freedom, and death are allowed. By contrast, human rights protect human dignity and physical integrity in all circumstances. Human rights concern relationships between unequal parties, protecting the governed from governments. Under human rights law, no person may be deprived of his or her life except for serious crimes pursuant to a judgment by a competent court—except in countries that have ratified Protocol No 6 to the European Convention or the Second Optional Protocol to the Political Covenant.

The differences do not stop there. The Geneva Conventions permit certain deprivations of freedom without judicial process; they allow warring powers to intern people in camps, to limit their appeal rights, and to put broad restrictions on the right to freedom of speech and assembly. Yet human rights law strictly forbids all of these actions, except where there are lawful derogations.

V. THE FUTURE

In sum, while the humanization of the law of war has been immensely beneficial for both combatants and civilians affected by armed conflict, this process must take into account the reality of armed conflict. We will never be able to make war completely safe. Yet, under the influence of human rights law, international humanitarian law has come to offer far greater protections for both civilians and combatants. We can, I believe, expect these protections to continue to grow. There is no doubt that the state-centric old regime of the law of war has been replaced in large part by a new homocentric regime. And this is due, largely, to the influence of human rights law.

In practice, of course, respect for international humanitarian law and human rights law has not always developed as rapidly as relevant legal doctrines. Indeed, the tremendous progress we have made in humanizing the law of war brings into sharp relief the stark contrast between promises made in treaties and declarations, on the one hand, and the harsh, often barbaric practices continually employed in times of war, on the other. Fortunately, however, our arsenal of newly humanized norms is accompanied by an emerging system of international criminal courts and various sanctions against the violators. These courts will help encourage combatants and non-combatants alike to take the norms of international humanitarian law and human rights law more seriously.

5

THE UNIVERSAL DECLARATION OF HUMAN RIGHTS AT SIXTY*

Because of its simplicity, its wide reach into political, economic, and social rights, and its rhetorical force, the Universal Declaration of Human Rights has moved human rights from the domestic world of citizen and civil rights to the universe of international entitlement, providing them additional legitimacy and making them a basis of expectations for peoples everywhere. The rights the Universal Declaration promises are increasingly accepted as international customary law. The Universal Declaration, in conjunction with the Helsinki Accords, has also provided inspiration for and played a major role in the overthrow of the Communist regimes in Eastern Europe. Through its recognition of people's rights the Universal Declaration was instrumental in the struggle against colonialism and in advancing self-determination. More recently, through international criminal courts and tribunals, some of its norms have even been transformed into binding rules of international criminal law.

But while the normative and theoretical impacts of the Universal Declaration have been extraordinary, the gap between expectations on the one hand, and implementation and enforcement on the other, was and continues to be significant. There is thus no question that much remains to be done in advancing the cause of human freedom and dignity.

In assessing the achievements and future potential of the Universal Declaration at sixty, it is appropriate to ponder first whether its fundamental values are still those that should frame the debate over human rights. Conceptions of equality and rights for human beings derived from the ashes of World War II sometimes appear removed from the broader

---

* Delivered at the Ditchley Foundation, Enstone, Chipping Norton, United Kingdom, in December 2009.

concerns we face today; for example, the Universal Declaration is virtually silent on the subject of non-state entities which so often control the lives of large populations. It is also obvious today, and has been for some time, that the General Assembly of 1948 which adopted the Universal Declaration was much less diverse, and much more Eurocentric, than the global community that emerged from the struggles for decolonization and the end of the Cold War. Even during the early and middle stages of the Cold War, divergent philosophical views on society produced debates on cultural relativism, with vigorous discussion of the role of human rights in value systems derived from, for example, socialism. This involved the question of whether the authoritarian regimes of the Eastern Bloc claimed to prioritize social and economic rights as a fig-leaf for efforts to preserve their own power.

However, the full extent to which the Universal Declaration opened the way for relativist debates became apparent to the broader world community only towards the end of the Cold War, as decolonization was completed. To be sure, the Universal Declaration includes references to people's rights and the concept of duties which depart from purely European cultural conceptions, and it helped to promote sovereignty for nations and groups that were once officially subservient. Yet this sovereignty, once achieved, opened the door wider to debates about human rights and claims of cultural relativism as justifying derogation or modification of rights stated in the Universal Declaration.

It bears noting that the Geneva Conventions of 1949 did not give rise to a similar controversy concerning the tensions between universality and cultural relativism. This was, perhaps, because humanitarian law contains fewer basic norms and is based on a smaller number of elementary principles, such as the prohibitions of attacks against civilians or the taking of hostages, which have always commanded at least rhetorical support from all nations.

One of the reasons for increased clashes about the meaning of the Universal Declaration is globalization—which, in this context, I would define as increased communication between different societies, including their ideas about different conceptions of human rights. In the long term, I would expect this increased communication to result in similar ideas about the rights of human beings and perhaps entities as well. In the short term, however, exposure to alternative conceptions of rights tends to raise the profile and the sharpness of debate, rather than decrease it. Globalization has made it easier for western countries to voice claims for universal application of rights, and for Asian and African states to lodge counterclaims or advocate different conceptions of universal rights.

On the whole, I would posit that the vigorous debate still taking place about the meaning and appropriate parameters of the Universal Declaration is encouraging, and demonstrates its relevance as a living document. Sadly, despite this healthy dialogue, human rights as understood by the Universal Declaration and the legally binding covenants to which it gave rise are violated all too often in many, if not most, countries. The promises of the Universal Declaration have clearly not been fulfilled, quite apart from the question of whether the Universal Declaration is over-expansive or too narrow.

But is every divergence from the human rights recognized in the Universal Declaration and other human rights instruments necessarily a violation? It must be admitted that human rights law has always contained some space for deviation from the general norms through reservation clauses. Where such reservations are not disallowed under human rights treaties, states parties can modify their obligations through reservations that take account of their national conditions. Although not referred to in the context of the debate on universality versus cultural relativism, in substance, reservations often reflect a concept of pluralism, in contrast to the traditional concept of the uniformity of human rights. Western countries that are at the forefront of the opposition to cultural relativism elsewhere have not themselves hesitated to take ample advantage of reservations clauses.

The most heated of these emerging debates relate to potential clashes between the bold statements of the Universal Declaration and cultural and religious traditions that may question the types of freedoms the Universal Declaration promises. For example, even if you believe, as I do, that equality between human beings of both sexes is a non-negotiable human right, it is indisputable that certain explicitly patriarchal traditions have survived for centuries and continue to enjoy much support in certain societies, raising the question of whether some accommodation of these groups' values is necessary or appropriate.

In the middle of this dichotomy between sharp rhetorical claims on the one hand, and limited results in terms of human rights protections in many nation states on the other, is the United Nations, and especially its Human Rights Council. By their nature, these are political and politicized institutions; yet, despite these limitations, both have significantly assisted in the promotion of human rights. It would appear, however, that the Council is not less politicized than the Commission that preceded it.

The record of the United Nations and the Human Rights Council means that even as the world community continues to debate the appropriate parameters and application of the Universal Declaration and its accompanying human rights treaties, I believe that we must urgently focus on ways for these institutions to improve their work. However, if even the limited promises of the Universal Declaration are to have any bite, I believe the United Nations, and the global community more generally, will need to focus on the increased enforcement of human rights norms. Achieving this aim, while at the same time considering legitimate objections to the current structure of the Universal Declaration and other human rights treaties, is a major challenge of our time.

Assuming that philosophical differences between approaches to human rights will continue, can something be done to improve the cross-cultural common denominators? If universalism across the board should continue to escape our reach, should we aim at establishing a list of fundamental rights which can and should be universally followed, and which would not be subject to any doubts on the basis of cultural relativism? Such a vision of a more limited list of 'hard' or non-derogable rights has been advanced in recent scholarship by Professor Wiktor Osiatyński, who has identified a difference between the universal acceptance of specific human rights as binding rules and the western philosophy of human rights, which may not be universal.[1]

But even if the international community agrees to commit itself to a narrow list of particularly sacrosanct rights, the task of creating such a list will not be easy. Freedom and equality rights will have to be balanced by economic and social rights and by the goal of eliminating abject poverty as a critical impediment to the attainment of rule of law. The question overshadowing such an approach is, of course, whether a shorter list, even if it could be agreed upon, would result in a greater respect for human rights. Moreover, the very attempt to 'trim' the Universal Declaration may erode its iconic character. It would shift the basis of discussion to a lower common denominator and probably reduce the prospects of compliance with the totality of the norms stated in the Declaration.

Alternatively, one might stay with a broad approach, maintaining an equal focus on all the rights stated in the Universal Declaration and even considering their expansion. In adopting this latter approach, the international community could attempt—through outreach, education, and, if necessary, pressure—to increase global compliance with the Universal Declaration. Additional institutions that could be created to channel this focus include regional commissions and courts or perhaps a World Court of Human Rights.

---

[1] Wiktor Osiatyński, *Human Rights and Their Limits* (Cambridge: Cambridge University Press, 2009), 175–8.

6

IMPROVING COMPLIANCE BY NON-STATE ACTORS WITH OBLIGATIONS IN INTERNATIONAL HUMANITARIAN LAW: A GLOBAL RESPONSIBILITY*

In terms of conflict, non-state actors—and the problems they pose for the workings of the international system—were catapulted into the limelight by the World Trade Center attacks. It is not that non-state actors did not exist before that time, but rather that a new type of non-state actor seized the agenda and forced the international community as a whole to focus on the issue.

Non-state actors, of one kind or another, have been around for centuries, but the post-World War II age of self-determination brought countless rebel and liberation groups to the fore. In the last two decades, the weakening of state power associated with the end of the Cold War, coupled with the forces of globalization, has further fueled the emergence of non-state groups. As some control mechanisms were dismantled or reduced due to the perceived imperative of economic efficiency, power became rapidly decentralized and dispersed in a large part of the world and ethnic divisions became accentuated.

The most potent problems we face are associated with these newer types of non-state actors. Seemingly committed to the destabilization of many states, they have no discernible territorial aims and no wish to join the international system of states as it currently stands. They oftentimes publicly denounce the values expressed in international humanitarian law and one of their key tactics—that of deliberately targeting civilians—runs

---

* Delivered at the College of Europe, Bruges, Belgium, on 12 September 2003.

contrary to the fundamental rationale for having a body of international humanitarian law in the first place.

This is not to suggest we forget the more 'traditional' non-state actors—such as rebel and liberation movements—as they too pose real challenges for international humanitarian law. Although these groups generally aspire to statehood within the parameters of the traditional Westphalian system, and have usually enunciated—if not immediately implemented—a commitment to international humanitarian law, they still present a clear challenge. This is particularly true in the early stages of their existence, when they are struggling for recognition and will use any means to seize attention and control of the political agenda.

What hope, then, is there that these increasingly radical non-state actors can be brought into the international system? How can non-state actors—of all types—be persuaded to accept obligations under international humanitarian law and how can the international community ensure that humanitarian standards are enforced? These are the key issues for discussion today.

※

There is no doubt, of course, that non-state actors *should* recognize and abide by basic humanitarian obligations under international law, and international lawyers are beginning to actively define these obligations. For example, the Berlin Resolution of the Institute of International Law declared that all participants in armed conflicts were bound to respect international humanitarian law, and specifically cited non-state entities alongside states. Other initiatives, such as the Turku Declaration, aimed to establish minimum humanitarian standards in international law, applicable in all circumstances and to all actors.

The incentives for rebel and liberation movements, at least, to comply with international humanitarian law are also clear. First, they are unlikely to be admitted to the international community if their ascent to power was tainted by grave violations of fundamental principles of international law. Humane behavior helps to establish the legitimacy of a group and its struggle. Second, rebel and liberation movements are usually concentrated within a particular geographic area, making it difficult for the groups' leaders to escape criminal responsibility for violations of international humanitarian law if prosecutions are commenced. Finally, rebel and liberation movements aspiring to control and govern a territory will often find it in their long-term interest to preserve the civilian population and infrastructure.

There is, however, one key reason why non-state actors tend to deliberately flout international humanitarian law. Operating in small groups, with limited military hardware and resources in comparison to the state entities with which they are in contention, their only hope of real influence is to employ guerrilla tactics and attack the opposition at its weakest points—and in terms of security, the weakest points invariably involve civilian targets and, inevitably, civilian casualties. The principle of reciprocity, which helped to shape international law as a system of mutual, inter-state obligations and works well among equal opponents who share common values, is not an effective enforcement mechanism when it comes to non-state actors engaged in asymmetric warfare.

The need for enforcement mechanisms to compel compliance by non-state actors with international humanitarian law is thus evident. However, there is no consensus among members of the international community as to the form such control structures should take. The danger is that this will remain the case for years to come. Yet, even if states can agree on enforcement mechanisms, most non-state actors operate outside of what is considered international consensus—they are not consulted about, nor do they contribute to, humanitarian law standards, and they may perceive there to be little reason for voluntary compliance. For example, although the Rome Statute provides that non-governmental bodies can be responsible for crimes against humanity, it is still uncertain whether the threat of individual prosecution has been an effective deterrent of terrorist acts or violations of international humanitarian law in internal armed conflicts.

Nevertheless, while there is no perfect solution, enforcement mechanisms of various types can have an impact, and the imposition of new compliance regimes could ensure more civilian lives are saved in the future.

০৪৮০

It must be remembered that non-state actors—be they the more traditional rebel or liberation groups, or the newer, global terrorist organizations—do not operate in a vacuum. They are supplied arms, allowed access to financing, and given sanctuary by states within the international system, and we should explore how we can use the leverage associated with supplying financing and arms to enforce compliance with international humanitarian law.

This can be—and already has been—done. Under the weight of just such pressure, post-World War II rebel and liberation movements have, in general, been willing to accept the principles, even if not immediately the practice, of international humanitarian law. Examples of liberation movements that have been persuaded to abide by obligations under international humanitarian law include groups in Algeria in 1956, Cuba in 1958, Congo in 1960, Yemen in 1962, and Nigeria in 1967. Political and economic pressure was also effective when placed on the Palestinian Liberation Organization during the 'Black September' of 1970 by Saudi Arabia, which threatened to cut off funding, and by the Soviet Union, which threatened to stem the flow of arms to the group. It is, however, still uncertain whether the shutting down of tranches of al-Qaeda funds has had some impact on that group's operations.

On top of these measures, enforcement mechanisms that compel compliance at collective, regional, and individual state levels can all play their part in getting non-state actors to abide by international humanitarian law. The institutional structures of the United Nations can be used to respond to actual or potential humanitarian crises and put the actions of non-state actors under the microscope of the international community. An even better mechanism, although more costly, would be to have permanent UN monitoring agencies in areas undergoing civil strife or those likely to become unstable. Establishing an expansive network of observers would facilitate the transfer of information from the front lines and could help alleviate the harm to civilian populations through deterrence or outright intervention. In both cases, one of the main benefits of collective security operations authorized by the UN Security Council is the universal legitimacy associated with them. On the other hand, collective security operations can also be somewhat inefficient and difficult to mobilize, and the slow pace of generating consensus for a collective security operation can have dire consequences.

Regional coalitions, such as NATO or ECOWAS (Economic Community of West African States), are sometimes more efficient and effective at reacting to humanitarian crises than collective security mechanisms at the global level. Additionally, they offer a degree of legitimacy to the intervention, although actions taken in the absence of Security Council approval may give rise to problems under the UN Charter.

Finally, unilateral state action has sometimes been utilized to compel compliance by non-state actors with international humanitarian law. Such measures can draw a great deal of criticism, however, if viewed as lacking legitimacy or violating the law.

In addition to mechanisms designed to compel compliance, there are ways in which the international community can create incentives for non-state actors to comply with international humanitarian law. While there are long-term strategic reasons for rebel and liberation movements to accept obligations under international humanitarian law, often there is a time-lag between the commencement of armed conflict and observance of international humanitarian law. History has shown that during this period of time, horrific atrocities often take place, and this will continue to occur unless more expedient mechanisms are developed. Such mechanisms include establishing opportunities for rebel and liberation movements to unilaterally declare their commitment to international humanitarian law or to enter into bilateral special agreements with the adversary state, possibly through a third-party facilitator such as the United Nations or the ICRC. The less time there is for non-state actors to operate in an uncontrolled and unobserved environment, the lower the likelihood that atrocities will be committed.

Another possibility would be to grant immunity from criminal prosecution to armed groups that observe international humanitarian law. There are, of course, obvious drawbacks to this—states will be understandably reluctant to confer any kind of recognition on, or legitimacy to, insurgent movements within their borders. Also, the paramount danger is that immunity would promote impunity and defeat accountability. Still, a more diluted version of the same policy—such as guaranteed reductions in punishment for non-state actors if they observe international humanitarian law—may satisfy the same goal and be more palatable to states. Conversely, the threat of effective prosecution by international criminal courts, in addition to national jurisdictions, may be, I hope, a powerful deterrent.

෬෩

Both types of measures—external monitoring or enforcement and internal incentives—would help regulate an armed conflict in order to achieve policy goals under international humanitarian law. Nevertheless, although such measures may lead non-state actors to reduce, or even stop, operations which violate international humanitarian law, they do not get to the heart of the matter. While taking resources away from non-state actors and policing their actions may reduce their ability to perpetrate atrocities and terrorist acts against civilians, the key task is to get all parties to agree that the way forward necessarily involves the protection of non-combatants.

This problem goes far beyond technical questions of international humanitarian law. There is no doubt that the powerful states of the international community need to take a more strategic and long-term view in their foreign policy—both to stem the alienation of the growing number of disaffected individuals and groups, and to avoid the specific 'growing' of radical non-state groups such as the Afghan Mujahideen, which enjoyed considerable clandestine support from the United States in the 1980s. More fundamentally, we must strive to create a common set of values shared not only by states but by non-state actors as well.

The stress on the system caused by terrorism might bring about a retrogression in the recent trend to humanize international humanitarian law and might encourage resort to reprisals—even indiscriminate reprisals. Al-Qaeda's type of terrorism is also causing major stresses on the *jus ad bellum*, affecting the traditional understanding of concepts of self-defense in the UN Charter, of the legitimate parties to war, and of war itself.

Yet, humanitarianism in the application of the law of war must continue and become a part of public consciousness if the protection of civilians and respect for the rule of law are to be ensured. The core of the difficulty is not the inadequacy of the law, but a lack of shared values between state and non-state actors. Education, training, persuasion, and emphasis on values that lie outside the law, such as ethics, honor, mercy, and chivalry, must be vigorously pursued. Organizations and individuals deliberately flouting the most basic humanitarian rules should be universally condemned, delegitimized, and shamed. The creation of a culture of values is thus indispensable. This job cannot be left to lawyers alone, we must do our bit.

II
The Rise of International Criminal Tribunals

7

THE GREATEST CHANGE IN INTERNATIONAL LAW*

The greatest change in international law over my lifetime has been the creation of a new universe of international criminal and hybrid tribunals and courts in various manifestations. The creation of these courts constituted a sea change in the enforcement of international law.

These courts carry forward the spirit of their famous forerunner in Nuremberg. But after the International Military Tribunal and the Allied occupation courts in Germany closed their doors, no further international tribunals were established for half a century. International law continued to develop, along with its principle of universality, but states were reluctant to prosecute those who breached international law in the absence of a nexus with their territories or citizens. Impunity thus blossomed.

Not even the most fervent advocates of international tribunals could have predicted their current prominence. Originally born from the shock waves triggered by atrocities in the former Yugoslavia and the genocide in Rwanda, international tribunals now signify a revolutionary approach to assessing individual responsibility for serious violations of international humanitarian law.

The UN ad hoc tribunals, in particular, have established that fair international prosecutions of war crimes, genocide, and crimes against humanity are feasible, striking a blow to the practice of impunity, leading to the establishment of the International Criminal Court and additional tribunals, and paving the way to more effective deterrence. The tribunals' most significant contributions include:

---

* Delivered at the 104th Annual Meeting of the American Society of International Law, Washington, DC, USA, on 26 March 2010. These remarks will be published in *American Society of International Law Proceedings* (forthcoming), © The American Society of International Law; Theodor Meron. Used by permission.

(A) spawning a revival of customary international law driven by the jurisprudence of the ad hoc tribunals, which needed to ensure that they avoided violating the principle of legality;

(B) creating a set of evidentiary and procedural rules that even the Nuremberg tribunals did not bequeath, as well as a corpus of substantive law expressed in detailed jurisprudence and hundreds of judicial decisions;

(C) criminalizing for individuals an increasing number of norms previously only applied to states as a matter of civil responsibility; and, finally,

(D) laying to rest the age-old question of whether international law really is law. The direct enforcement of international law through international courts and tribunals leaves no doubt that it is.

8
REFLECTIONS ON THE PROSECUTION OF WAR CRIMES BY INTERNATIONAL TRIBUNALS: A HISTORICAL PERSPECTIVE*

Sixty-three years ago, the international community, seeking to heal the wounds of a brutal war, embarked on a bold legal experiment. For the first time in history, legal mechanisms were invoked to bring to justice the perpetrators of war crimes and crimes against humanity in international tribunals specifically erected for that purpose. The resulting trials at Nuremberg and Tokyo were endeavors both extraordinary and risky. Above all, they were unique in their time.

In his famous opening statement for the Prosecution at the outset of the Nuremberg trial, Justice Robert Jackson eloquently remarked on the trial's novelty: 'That four great nations, flushed with victory and stung with injury, stay the hands of vengeance and voluntarily submit their captive enemies to the judgment of the law, is one of the most significant tributes that Power ever has paid to Reason.'[1] Indeed, the idea of bringing perpetrators of war crimes before a tribunal was so novel that it almost never happened. At a conference at Yalta, Stalin suggested that 50,000 people should simply be killed after the war, and Churchill 'thought a list of the major criminals... should be drawn up here... [and] they should

---

* Delivered as part of the Lecture Series of the UN Audiovisual Library of International Law in February 2008. Portions of the text of this speech first appeared in 'Reflections on the Prosecution of War Crimes by International Tribunals' (2006) 100 *AJIL* 551, © The American Society of International Law; Theodor Meron. Used by permission and modified from the original publication.

[1] Opening speech by Justice Robert H Jackson, Chief Prosecutor for the United States of America, in *The Trial of German Major War Criminals by the International Military Tribunal Sitting at Nuremberg Germany: Opening Speeches of the Chief Prosecutors* (Buffalo: William S Hein & Co, 2001) (Opening Statement), 3.

be shot once their identity is established'.[2] Yet the American government forcefully advocated trials—and, in particular, trials conducted not by national courts of the vanquished state or any victorious power, but by an international court. In the end, the Allies agreed, and they set up trials in which judges rigorously examined whether the actions of individual accused amounted to offenses under international law. Many of the accused were convicted but some were acquitted, much to the shock of people who expected the trials to be mere formalities. The fact that the trials were honest and objective may be one of the reasons why Germans and Japanese overwhelmingly accepted the conclusion that the officials eventually punished were, in fact, guilty and deserving of sanction. Moreover, as Professor Herbert Wechsler, a participant at Nuremberg, observed, the trials may have helped to stave off unauthorized acts of retribution against those believed to have been Nazis.

The trials at Nuremberg and Tokyo were, then, by many measures a success, and this is part of the reason that the concept of international criminal tribunals is less radical to us today. To be sure, Nuremberg and Tokyo had their shortcomings, and some of those shortcomings were endemic to the nature of the courts themselves. On the whole, however, the Nuremberg experiment in particular proved to be, as Justice Jackson had hoped, a triumph of reason. And, in time, that triumph allowed the international community to establish the international criminal courts that now sit at The Hague and elsewhere.

There are obvious similarities between the modern international courts and the experiences of the post-World War II tribunals. There are also, however, a number of differences between the exercise of justice in the wake of World War II and the exercise of justice today. One of the principal criticisms leveled against the post-World War II tribunals, for instance, was (and still is) that they were an exercise in victors' justice—a trial of the losers by and for the winners. In this lecture, I will highlight some of the similarities and differences between the post-World War II tribunals and the modern tribunals to show how humanitarian law has evolved. To demonstrate how the mechanisms for enforcement of humanitarian law have changed over the past hundred years, I will begin by examining the status of war crimes law as it existed before Nuremberg and Tokyo. I will then turn to Nuremberg and Tokyo themselves and compare them to the modern international tribunals.

---

[2] *Foreign Relations of the United States: Diplomatic Papers: The Conferences at Malta and Yalta 1945* (Washington, DC: US Government Printing Office, 1955), 849.

I. WAR CRIMES LAW BEFORE NUREMBERG AND TOKYO

A. *The landscape before the First World War*

Until the mid-nineteenth century, the laws of war were largely uncodified and existed solely as custom, evidenced in national laws, military manuals, and religious teachings. The second half of the nineteenth century witnessed the beginning of a trend towards codification focused on the law governing certain narrow issues. This period was marked by the 1856 Paris Declaration on Maritime Law, the 1864 Geneva Convention on wounded soldiers, and the 1868 St Petersburg Declaration barring the use of certain small explosive projectiles. Yet it was not until the turn of the twentieth century, at the 1899 and 1907 Hague Peace Conferences, that the modern law of war and war crimes began to take shape in a more comprehensive manner.

Spurred by fears that modern weapons technology would permit wars to get out of hand, delegates first met at The Hague in 1899 in response to a call from the Russian Czar. The conference produced a convention on maritime war and the Convention with respect to the Laws and Customs of War on Land—the first general, multilateral codification of the laws of land war. Far more productive than the 1899 Conference, the 1907 Conference produced ten agreements on the laws of war, including the Fourth Hague Convention—a revamped version of the 1899 Convention with respect to the Laws and Customs of War on Land.

While the law of war developed significantly over the course of the two Hague Conferences, mechanisms to enforce that law did not. The Fourth Hague Convention of 1907 provided no mechanism for the imposition of individual criminal responsibility. Instead, payment of compensation by states was the chief form of punishment set out in the Convention. Moreover, states had to negotiate over the amount of compensation, and these negotiations proved long and complex. Not surprisingly, the Fourth Hague Convention's provision on compensation was criticized as having little deterrent effect.

Other means of enforcing the laws and customs of war at the turn of the century also lacked teeth. States could try their own nationals for war crimes, but they rarely did so. And although an aggrieved state could take military action against the offending state, such reprisals were often criticized for simply escalating the hostilities. Even if a belligerent state wished to prosecute foreign war criminals, it was not clear that it would have jurisdiction over captured enemy combatants, and, in any event, the act-of-state defense traditionally immunized heads of state from prosecution in foreign courts.

B. *World War I and its aftermath*

War crimes law came very much to the fore at the end of World War I. Even as the war raged, commentators began calling for justice to be done in the wake of the atrocities committed by the armed forces of German and Austrian states.

The process of establishing a legal framework to address the atrocities began shortly after the war ended. At its first plenary meeting in January of 1919, the Paris Peace Conference appointed a multinational commission to inquire into the war's causes and consequences.

After two months of secret meetings, the Commission issued its final report. The Commission determined that Germany and Austria-Hungary bore primary responsibility for the war, criticized Bulgaria and Turkey for supporting the German and Austrian aggression, and found that all of these states practiced 'barbarous or illegitimate methods' of warfare.[3] Seeking to precisely classify the criminal acts committed by officials from these states, the Commission prepared a catalogue of thirty-two offenses that, according to its report, fell within the meaning of war crimes. These included, among other things, murders and massacres, torture of civilians, rape, and internment of civilians under inhuman conditions. In an annex listing instances in which the Central Empires and their Allies committed such offenses, however, the Commission said that the listed acts constituted violations of 'the laws and customs of war *and* of the laws of humanity'.[4] Among the atrocities listed were some committed by Turkish and German forces against Turkish subjects (Armenians), and by Austrian forces against Austrian subjects. These were likely the acts that, in the Commission's view, violated the 'laws of humanity' and not the 'laws of war'.

Having concluded that officials and soldiers from Germany, Austria-Hungary, Bulgaria, and Turkey had committed illegal acts, the Commission recommended the creation of an international tribunal to try officials responsible for some of the worst. The Commission also concluded that

---

[3] Commission on the Responsibility of the Authors of the War and on Enforcement of Penalties, 'Report Presented to the Preliminary Peace Conference: March 29, 1919' (1920) 14 *AJIL* 95 (Commission Report), 115 (emphasis omitted).

[4] Violations of the Laws and Customs of War: Reports of Majority and Dissenting Reports of American and Japanese Members of the Commission of Responsibilities, Conference of Paris (Carnegie Endowment for International Peace, Division of International Law Pamphlet No 32, Oxford: Clarendon, 1919), Annex I, 16 (emphasis added).

criminal liability should extend to all persons responsible for war crimes, including heads of state. According to the Commission, a prohibition on the prosecution of heads of state who were guilty of war crimes 'would shock the conscience' of the world.[5]

On 28 June 1919, several months after the Commission filed its report, the Treaty of Versailles was signed. The Treaty contained several critical provisions relating to wartime conduct.

Despite American and Japanese objections, Article 227 of the Treaty provided that: 'The Allied and Associated Powers publicly arraign William II of Hohenzollern, formerly German Emperor, for a supreme offence against international morality and the sanctity of treaties', and specified that '[a] special tribunal will be constituted to try the accused'. This marked the first time that a treaty addressed the individual responsibility of a head of state for initiating and conducting what we now call a crime of aggression or crime against peace. As a practical matter, however, Article 227 was a dead letter. Rather than adopting the strident language of the Commission's recommendation, the Treaty spoke in more abstract terms of the Kaiser's 'supreme offence against international morality'. That phrase had as little meaning then as it does now. 'Article 227 articulated a "moral", rather than a "legal", offense.'[6] But that was part of its intent. In any event, it was clear that The Netherlands, where the Kaiser was in exile, would not permit his extradition.

In other respects, the Treaty fell short of the Commission's recommendations. Although the Treaty contained two other provisions related to the prosecution of individuals for war crimes, Articles 228 and 229, these clauses did not call for an international criminal court; instead, they merely contemplated the use of military tribunals. Article 228 stated in part: 'The German Government recognises the right of the Allied and Associated Powers to bring before military tribunals persons accused of having committed acts in violation of the laws and customs of war.' Moreover, through Article 228, the German government recognized only the victorious powers' right to prosecute 'violation[s] of the laws and customs of war', and not violations of the 'laws of humanity'.

After the Treaty of Versailles had been signed, German opposition to Allied-conducted trials proved considerable, prompting the Allies to worry that such trials would weaken the German government and enable

---

[5] Commission Report, n 3 above, 116.
[6] M Cherif Bassiouni, 'World War I: "The War to End All Wars" and the Birth of a Handicapped International Criminal Justice System' (2002) 30 *Denver Journal of International Law and Policy* 244, 271.

militarists or Bolsheviks to take over. With fears about unrest in Germany mounting, the Allies agreed to allow Germany to conduct the trials of alleged war criminals in the Supreme Court in Leipzig. The Allies also agreed to reduce the list of people to be prosecuted to only forty-five individuals. But even that number was too high for the Germans, and, since the Procurator General of the Supreme Court retained prosecutorial discretion, ultimately only twelve military officers were brought to trial.

Two and a half years after the signing of the Armistice, the trials finally commenced before the Penal Senate of the Reichsgericht in Leipzig. Of the twelve defendants, six were convicted. But even in those cases, the German court imposed lenient punishments.

Other attempts to achieve justice for atrocities committed during the war period similarly fell short. The Treaty of Lausanne that was eventually signed by the Allies and Turkey in 1923 contained no war crimes clauses; instead, it was accompanied by a 'Declaration of Amnesty' that covered all offenses committed during the wartime period. Rather than insist on war crimes clauses, the Allies agreed that Turkey itself would prosecute offenders. Those trials, known as the Istanbul trials, were no more successful than the Leipzig trials: many defendants were absent, the sentences were light, and there was no popular support for the proceedings.

In sum, while international humanitarian law saw considerable doctrinal development in the half century preceding Nuremberg, enforcement lagged far behind. Nobody faced an international tribunal after World War I, few faced domestic prosecution in Germany and Turkey, and in those cases that were actually brought, the few-and-far-between convictions resulted in light penalties. Thus, while war crimes law had increasingly well-established contours going into World War II, persons violating that law faced only a hypothetical possibility of criminal sanction. In a sense, war crimes law had not yet truly become a form of criminal law.

II. FROM NUREMBERG TO THE HAGUE

The Treaty of Versailles and the disappointing results of enforcement efforts in the wake of World War I sowed the seeds for the development of international criminal law that followed World War II. The Allies realized that entrusting trials of alleged war criminals entirely to the courts of the criminals' own countries would not produce real justice. Instead, an international tribunal was required, and it had to be as impartial as possible.

During the course of the war the Allies began to set up mechanisms for addressing the atrocities that were occurring. In two early documents—the St James Declaration of 1942 and the Moscow Declaration of 1943—the Allies resolved to prosecute war crimes. By 1945, their intention to establish international military tribunals became manifest.

Nuremberg—and also Tokyo—represented a substantial step forward in the development of the law of war crimes. My aim in this part of the lecture is to highlight the similarities and differences between Nuremberg and Tokyo and the modern tribunals. Importantly, while the Nuremberg and Tokyo tribunals were established by the victorious powers, the International Criminal Tribunal for the former Yugoslavia (ICTY) and the International Criminal Tribunal for Rwanda (ICTR) are the first ever truly international criminal courts, established and funded by the United Nations. The ICC, by contrast, is a treaty body established by states parties to the Treaty of Rome of 1998.

A. From battlefield violations to prosecutions of abuses against civilians

Most of the post-World War I prosecutions concerned classical violations of the law governing the conduct of hostilities. World War II prosecutions, however, were focused mostly on abuses committed against civilians and civilian populations, whether as crimes against humanity or as violations of the provisions on occupations in the Fourth Hague Convention. This focus was a result of the sheer immensity of abuses against civilian populations. The focus can also partially be explained by the desire to avoid *tu quoque* arguments, which could have arisen during the prosecution of conventional war crimes.

While the ICTY has dealt with some Hague Law matters, such consideration has been rare in the ICTR. In both Tribunals, as in the World War II prosecutions, abuses against civilians have taken pride of place.

B. Paper trails and the availability of evidence

Seemingly mundane facts about evidence and the profile of defendants also reveal much about how the prospects for enforcement of humanitarian law are evolving.

The case that a prosecutor is able to make in any given criminal trial is dictated largely by the available evidence. This truism is often overlooked in international law, but it actually explains critical differences between the trials at Nuremberg and at The Hague and Arusha—differences which demonstrate the pervasive difficulties facing the modern tribunals.

Gathering evidence after World War II was comparatively easy. One thing can be said of the Nazi regime: they kept good records. Rather than basing its case primarily on witness testimony, the Prosecution at Nuremberg was able to rely heavily on the defendants' own words and documents to prove its accusations. Add to that the extensive police powers that the Allies exercised in occupied Germany, and you have an evidence-gathering apparatus that any prosecutor would envy.

Things are different in the modern tribunals. We do not have the benefit of a police power to search for evidence or a paper trail. The ICTY instead must rely on the cooperation of supportive governments and of individuals who often may realistically fear reprisals if they cooperate openly. The Security Council resolution adopting the ICTY Statute requires all member states of the United Nations to comply with the ICTY's requests and orders. Yet governments do not always cooperate, and, when they do, they are often willing to share information only if its sources are kept confidential, a demand clearly in tension with the defendant's right to challenge the evidence against him or her.

The ICTR has enjoyed the solid support of the government of Rwanda, except when the ICTR Prosecutor tried to investigate crimes allegedly committed by the Tutsis. This further reveals how national-political considerations continue to affect the work of the Tribunals. The ICC, as a treaty organization not created by the Security Council, may have equal or even greater difficulties in marshalling evidence.

The problem of an incomplete evidentiary base is also much more common at the ICTY than in domestic criminal cases. There have been cases in which defendants have claimed that governments have deliberately withheld information to shield some defendants and implicate others. These are challenges facing any tribunal that tries accused from states that have not been completely vanquished.

These difficulties in gathering evidence thus make it apparent that the bodies enforcing international criminal law still lack muscle within the international community.

C. *The profile of defendants*

More optimistic signs can be seen in the profile of the defendants being tried. Just as the strengths of Nuremberg paved the way and, indeed, made possible the modern project of international criminal law, so the legitimacy earned by the ICTY has both encouraged national governments to turn over more senior figures and, more importantly, spurred the international community to exert pressure on those governments.

Again, Nuremberg and Tokyo, with the might of the victorious Allies behind them, could prosecute *almost* anyone involved. Hitler escaped judgment only because he committed suicide. A political decision was taken by the powers constituting the Tokyo tribunal not to prosecute Emperor Hirohito, but there was never a suggestion that the tribunal could not have prosecuted him had it wanted. Both tribunals, like their modern counterparts, dealt with defendants of varying status and level of responsibility.

The first trial at Nuremberg is the best known, because it involved the most senior defendants. This first (and only) trial by the International Military Tribunal (IMT)—with twenty-two leading Nazi war criminals in the dock—began in Nuremberg on 20 November 1945, and lasted nine months. The tribunal rendered its judgment on 1 October 1946.[7] Three of the defendants were acquitted, seven received prison terms, and twelve were sentenced to hang.

Following the IMT trial, American occupation authorities conducted twelve proceedings at Nuremberg pursuant to Allied Control Council Law No 10. In all, 177 defendants were tried in these later proceedings. While less prominent than the chief Nazi leaders tried by the IMT, the defendants were leaders of Nazi Germany's government, military, and economy, and they were charged with playing central roles in the crimes perpetrated by the Nazi regime.

The Allied authorities in Japan also held separate sets of trials for senior officials and lower-ranking officials. In the first set of trials, held at Tokyo, twenty-five senior officials, known as Class A criminals, were tried for war crimes. The group included premiers, foreign ministers, ambassadors, generals, and others. After more than two years, all were found guilty on at least one charge.[8] Seven were sentenced to death. In the second set of trials, held at Yokohama, another 980 less senior officers and officials—Class B and C criminals—were tried for war crimes and crimes against humanity. Some of them were of quite low rank.

Early on, the trials at The Hague looked less like the IMT trial of the top Nazi leaders and the first trial in Tokyo, and more like the later proceedings against significant, but less prominent, officials. But as time went on, the impression of the tribunal's worthiness grew, and international and local pressure led to fuller cooperation by national governments,

---

[7] International Military Tribunal (Nuremberg), 'Judgment and Sentences' (1947) 41 *AJIL* 172 (IMT Judgment).

[8] Judgment of the International Military Tribunal for the Far East, reprinted in BVA Röling and CF Rüter (eds), *The Tokyo Judgment: The International Military Tribunal for the Far East, 29 April 1946– 12 November 1948*, Vol 1 (Amsterdam: University Press Amsterdam BV, 1977).

resulting in a greater number of senior government officials and military commanders being held responsible. Slobodan Milošević is the most obvious example. And among those being tried are President Milan Milutinović, senior generals, and chiefs of staff of the armed forces and security service.[9] The ICTY has also increased its focus on top-level officials as a part of its completion strategy—a recognition of the ICTY's status as a temporary tribunal. Nevertheless, the ICTY remains largely at the mercy of the national governments in the Balkans to apprehend such important leaders as Radovan Karadžić and Ratko Mladić.[10]

Unlike the ICTY, the ICTR has always been able to focus on senior-level accused. From the beginning, the Arusha-based Tribunal received substantial cooperation not only from the government of Rwanda, but also from the governments of other African nations to which many of the suspected war criminals had fled. As a result of this cooperation, the ICTR was able to begin trying former cabinet ministers and high-level military commanders quickly.

It makes sense for international tribunals to focus on top officials who helped to orchestrate atrocities. International tribunals have resources far more limited than those of national legal systems. Of necessity, this dictates some selectivity in who will be tried by such a tribunal. Just as important, trials of those who orchestrate atrocities help to demonstrate international condemnation of the crimes involved and provide vindication for substantial numbers of victims.

By contrast, if nations where atrocities took place are capable of conducting adequate trials, even if only for lower-level accused, and such trials are marked by a vigorous, good-faith prosecution, due process rights for the defendant, impartial judging, and the protection of witnesses from intimidation and reprisals, there would be significant benefits to letting those nations conduct the trials. Trials close to home may be better followed than those occurring in a distant forum, serving to better educate people about atrocities that occurred in their country. Moreover, condemnation of atrocities by a country's own legal system may serve to better inspire the people of that country to condemn the atrocities themselves. The ICTY has begun referring cases involving intermediate- and lower-level accused to local courts in the former Yugoslav republics,

---

[9] Editor's note: Milan Milutinović was acquitted in *Prosecutor v Milan Milutinović et al.* (Judgement) IT-05-87-T (26 February 2009).

[10] Editor's note: Radovan Karadžić was arrested and transferred to the ICTY in July 2008. His trial commenced in October 2009.

and these courts will have an opportunity to prove that local trials, in fact, produce such benefits.

D. *Recognized offenses*

Prior to Nuremberg, customary international law, of course, existed, but it had never been applied in an international court. The challenge for Nuremberg, then, was to find a way to bring the existing law to bear in a multinational court.

The London Charter that created the IMT dealt with this issue by identifying the crimes within the IMT's jurisdiction. These crimes fell into three categories, which the London Charter termed 'crimes against peace', 'war crimes', and 'crimes against humanity'.[11] It then defined each of these classes of crimes. The Charter also allowed prosecutors to charge major war criminals with conspiracy, and it stated that defenses of state immunity and superior orders would not be relevant to guilt.

Each of the legal grounds set forth in the London Charter was controversial. Never before had crimes against peace, or aggression, been treated as a legal—rather than merely political—wrong, and never had senior officials been held criminally liable as individuals. The concept of conspiracy liability was not only novel in international law, but it was especially foreign to lawyers from civil law traditions. And although the notion of 'crimes against humanity'—with its criminal liability including citizen-to-citizen acts—seems second nature to us now, it had never formed the basis for international criminal liability before World War II.

In Japan, the trials were conducted by the International Military Tribunal for the Far East. That tribunal was not created by an international diplomatic conference but by a charter issued as a military order by General Douglas MacArthur, the Supreme Commander for the Allied Powers in Japan. Nevertheless, the Charter tracked Nuremberg's closely.

Despite the initial controversy, Nuremberg's legal legacy was rapidly and broadly established. The Genocide Convention soon followed (1948), as did the Geneva Conventions for the protection of victims of war (1949), and pressure to establish a permanent international criminal court began to build. Nuremberg's major premise—that individuals who lead their nations into aggressive wars should be held criminally liable as individuals—was widely accepted for crimes against peace, but

---

[11] Charter of the International Military Tribunal—Annex to the Agreement for the prosecution and punishment of the major war criminals of the European Axis (1945) 82 UNTS 284, art 6.

remained controversial enough not to have been adopted in the ICC Statute.[12]

These developments stimulated a number of doctrinal developments. Then came Vietnam. The acts of war by both the United States and North Vietnam sparked a new debate over the applicability of international legal norms and, more broadly, about inadequate compliance with the law. The disagreement was not over the definition of the offenses, but rather over the inadequacy of the law in dealing with the conduct of hostilities, the protection of medical evacuation aircraft, and the treatment of prisoners of war. These difficulties were heightened by questions concerning the applicability of international humanitarian conventions to internal and mixed internal–international conflicts. These concerns created pressure to renew the law through the elaboration of the two Additional Protocols to the Geneva Conventions, which were adopted in 1977.

This brings us to the modern tribunals at The Hague and Arusha. Using the London Charter as a model, the UN Security Council, exercising its authority under Chapter VII of the UN Charter, enacted the Statutes that created the ICTY and ICTR. Those Statutes set forth in detail the crimes over which the ad hoc Tribunals have jurisdiction. As at Nuremberg, those crimes include war crimes and crimes against humanity. Unlike the London Charter, however, the ICTY and ICTR Statutes do not include crimes against peace. They are also more detailed in their definitions and broader in scope, encompassing war crimes in internal conflicts.

Although the definitions in the Statutes of the ad hoc Tribunals are more detailed, they still require extensive judicial interpretation. In adding that judicial gloss, the Tribunals, like the court at Nuremberg, refer to the customary underpinnings of the crimes. Our resort to customary law, however, is more methodical than Nuremberg's, and this is partly because of the criticisms leveled against the Nuremberg convictions. Critics of Nuremberg charged that the law applied at Nuremberg originated in the London Charter and that it was unlawfully applied *ex post facto* to the German defendants. This is not correct: the law applied at Nuremberg was grounded in existing conventional and customary international law. But to forestall similar criticisms of the ad hoc Tribunals, we take pains to explain the customary and conventional underpinnings of our decisions. Consequently, ICTY and ICTR judgments are helping to

---

[12] Editor's note: The Review Conference of the Rome Statute adopted a definition of the crime of aggression in 2010.

revitalize customary law and to give international law a solid foundation in both codified law and judicial decisions. The ICC is different in this respect. Its Statute resembles more of a civil law code and is to be applied as such.

E. Gender crimes

Rape and violence against women had long been accepted as natural consequences of war. The Nuremberg and Tokyo tribunals recorded a substantial amount of evidence of sex crimes committed during World War II, but they gave little attention to these crimes in their judgments.[13] The ICTY and ICTR, in contrast, have been groundbreaking in this area. Both Tribunals' Statutes explicitly include rape as a crime against humanity, and the Tribunals have successfully prosecuted various forms of sexual violence as instruments of genocide, crimes against humanity, and crimes of war, thus developing a crucial area of international humanitarian law.[14] The Tribunals also made a major contribution in grounding the prohibition of rape in customary international law.[15] And the ICC's Statute specifically defines sexual crimes such as rape and sexual slavery.

F. Jurisdiction

The respective jurisdictions of the post-World War II and modern tribunals differ in another respect. There is no question that the elaboration of crimes against humanity constituted the most revolutionary contribution Nuremberg made to international criminal law. In particular, the London Charter extended international criminal responsibility to atrocities committed within a single country, even between its own citizens. But the scope of that liability was limited, because the offenses were required to be *wartime* atrocities. Thus, the Nuremberg tribunal had no jurisdiction over atrocities committed within and by Germany in the years leading up to the outbreak of World War II.

Over time, however, the definition of crimes against humanity lost the required nexus with an armed conflict. For instance, the UN Convention on the Non-Applicability of Statutory Limitations to War Crimes and Crimes Against Humanity (1968) applies to '[c]rimes against humanity

---

[13] See generally Theodor Meron, Editorial Comment, 'Rape as a Crime under International Humanitarian Law' (1993) 87 *AJIL* 424.
[14] See, eg, *Prosecutor v Anto Furundžija* (Judgement) IT-95-17/1-T (10 December 1998).
[15] *Prosecutor v Dragoljub Kunarac et al.* (Judgement) IT-96-23&23/1-A (12 June 2002); *Sylvestre Gacumbitsi v Prosecutor* (Judgement) ICTR-2001-64-A (7 July 2006).

whether committed in time of war or in time of peace'.[16] At the ICTY, Article 5 of the Statute defines crimes against humanity subject to the jurisdiction of the Tribunal as certain crimes 'committed in armed conflict, whether international or internal in character'. Although this provision appears to require a nexus with an armed conflict, the Appeals Chamber has interpreted the requirement as related only to the Tribunal's subject matter jurisdiction.[17] Under the case law of the ICTY, a war nexus is not required under customary law. The ICTR Statute does not mention an armed conflict requirement for crimes against humanity. And the ICC Statute also confirms that no nexus with an armed conflict is required. Under Article 7, crimes against humanity can be committed in all situations—international wars, internal wars of whatever intensity, and peacetime.

These changes relate to another significant legal development: the international criminalization of internal atrocities. The Statutes for the ad hoc Tribunals have contributed significantly to the extension of international humanitarian law to non-international armed conflicts. And the ICC Statute also sets forth serious violations of the laws and customs applicable in armed conflicts not of an international character—within the established framework of international law. These developments are a welcome extension of Nuremberg's principles.

G. *Due process*

The next substantive area of comparison I wish to discuss is due process. The provisions on criminal procedure in the London and Tokyo Charters were rudimentary at best. For instance, the convicted persons could ask for clemency from senior military officers, but there was no mechanism for appeal to a higher court. As mentioned earlier, one of the principal criticisms of Nuremberg and Tokyo was, and is, that they were victors' courts trying the vanquished. And that criticism resonates most strongly in the context of due process protections.

Two examples illustrate this point. The London Charter expressly provided in Article 12 that trials could be conducted *in absentia*. The IMT tried, convicted, and sentenced to death one defendant—Martin Bormann, Head of the Party Chancellery—even though the Allies were unable to locate and arrest him. The Charter also contained no protection

---

[16] Convention on the Non-Applicability of Statutory Limitations to War Crimes and Crimes Against Humanity (1968), 754 UNTS 73, art 1(b).
[17] *Prosecutor v Duško Tadić* (Decision on the Defence Motion for Interlocutory Appeal on Jurisdiction) IT-94-1-AR72 (2 October 1995).

against double jeopardy; on the contrary, Article 11 stated that persons convicted by the tribunal could be separately charged and punished by a national, military, or occupation court. At least three Nuremberg defendants were prosecuted in German courts following prosecution by the tribunal.

But Nuremberg's track record on due process protections was not all bad. Fairness norms inevitably crept into the proceedings. Although the Soviets were of the view that the burden should rest on the Defense rather than the Prosecution, the tribunal imposed a rigorous Anglo-American burden on the Prosecution—so rigorous that some of the accused were acquitted.

Due process protections also triumphed over the American plan to focus at Nuremberg on trials of Nazi organizations such as the Gestapo. The intention had been to convict these organizations at trial and then use the convictions in follow-on proceedings to bring to justice thousands of individual members. But the tribunal thwarted this plan by interpreting conspiracy narrowly and by reading additional elements of specific intent into the conspiracy and aggressive war charges.

The Japanese trials had much greater problems with due process and bias. The Defense lacked time and resources, and was denied access to some relevant material. Justice Pal of India published a long dissent, in which he argued that the rules of evidence had been slanted against the Defense.[18]

One of the enduring lessons of Nuremberg and Tokyo, then, is that due process protections are not an impediment to the administration of international justice; rather, they are indispensable. Tokyo's more cavalier attitude to the law and the defendants is the major factor in its relative marginality in the past sixty years, and its near-total lack of influence on international law.

Today, the ad hoc Tribunals at The Hague and Arusha and the permanent ICC are supported by detailed Statutes and extensive Rules of Procedure and Evidence that are a far cry from the brief London Charter. At the ICTY and ICTR, the accused has a right to be present at his or her trial, and the Tribunals have primacy over national courts, thus preventing concurrent or consecutive convictions by multiple jurisdictions for the same charges. The Tribunals' Statutes also expressly created an Appeals Chamber to which defendants may appeal not only their convictions, but also certain interlocutory issues. Moreover, in general, the

---

[18] Judgment of Mr Justice Pal, reprinted in Röling and Rüter (eds), *The Tokyo Judgment*, Vol II, n 8 above.

modern tribunals adhere to the catalogue of human rights protections embodied in the International Covenant on Civil and Political Rights, and, increasingly, those in the European Convention on Human Rights. So, while Nuremberg was hardly a failure from the perspective of due process rights, its shortcomings and those of the Tokyo tribunal have inspired its heirs to do better.

H. *The criminalization of norms*

The post-World War II tribunals built on a body of law that had clearly prohibited certain actions during wartime. However, before Nuremberg and Tokyo, it was far from clear whether these actions could be *criminalized* or whether, instead, they could only form the basis for state responsibility. Indeed, as a practical matter, Nuremberg was the first international court to try defendants on the basis of this body of law.

The Nuremberg and Tokyo tribunals appear to have taken it for granted that violations of the substantive provisions of the Hague and Geneva Conventions were criminal. Thus, although neither the Geneva Conventions that preceded those of 1949 nor the Fourth Hague Convention contained explicit penal provisions, they were accepted as a basis for prosecutions and convictions in the post-World War II tribunals.

Following Nuremberg and Tokyo, the Geneva Conventions of 12 August 1949 introduced the grave breaches system, which explicitly criminalized certain acts. The grave breaches system requires the states parties to the Conventions to criminalize specific acts domestically, and to prosecute or extradite the perpetrators.

Until recently, however, the accepted wisdom was that neither common Article 3 (which is not among the grave breaches provisions of the Geneva Conventions) nor Additional Protocol II (which contains no provisions on grave breaches) provided a basis for an obligation by third states to prosecute or extradite, and that they constituted, at least on the international plane, an uncertain basis for individual criminal responsibility. It has been asserted that the normative customary law rules applicable in non-international armed conflicts do not encompass the criminal element of war crimes.

As early as the discussions of the ICTY Statute, however, voices urging the international criminalization of violations of common Article 3 and Additional Protocol II had been heard. With amazing speed, international conceptions of common Article 3 have changed and a perception that its violation triggers individual criminal responsibility in non-international armed conflicts has emerged. Indeed, when the ICTR Statute was debated in the Security Council, there was no opposition in the Security Council to treating violations of common Article 3 and Additional Protocol II as bases for the individual criminal responsibility of perpetrators.

That an obligation is addressed to governments is not dispositive of the penal responsibility of individuals if individuals clearly must carry out that obligation. The Nuremberg tribunals, however, considered as binding not only on Germany but also on individual defendants those provisions of the 1929 Geneva POW Convention and the Fourth Hague Convention of 1907 that were addressed to 'belligerents', the 'occupant', or 'an army of occupation'.[19] As the IMT so eloquently stated: 'Crimes against international law are committed by men, not by abstract entities, and only by punishing individuals who commit such crimes can the provisions of international law be enforced.'[20] This principle should, however, not obscure the fact that in some crimes states play a critical role, and that the criminal responsibility of individuals is cumulative with state responsibility. States must remain answerable for such collective crimes as those committed by the Nazis during World War II.

Typically, norms of international law have been addressed to states. With increasing frequency, however, international law, and especially the law of war, has directed its proscriptions both to states and to individuals and groups. Indeed, a principal purpose of the punishment of war criminals is to improve compliance with the law. The trend towards imposing individual criminal responsibility for violations of an increasing number of norms of international law is clearly ascendant. International conventions that proscribe certain activities of international concern without creating international tribunals to try the violators characteristically obligate states to prohibit those activities and to punish people under their jurisdiction.

I. *Sources of law*

Like the ICTY, other international criminal tribunals are bound by the principle of *nullum crimen sine lege*. Indeed, this principle has been much discussed with respect to the Nuremberg tribunals. Customary law was essential to the Nuremberg tribunals' ability to convict Nazi war criminals. The Nuremberg tribunals were faced with the problem that the applicable provisions of the 1929 Geneva POW Convention and the

---

[19] *United States v Wilhelm von Leeb et al.* (*The High Command Case*), reprinted in *Trials of War Criminals Before the Nuernberg Military Tribunals Under Control Council Law No 10*, Vols X–XI (Buffalo: William S Hein & Co, 1997).

[20] IMT Judgment, n 7 above, 221.

Fourth Hague Convention defining the relevant substantive proscriptions and considered declaratory of customary law did not expressly *criminalize* their violation. Thus, there was some question as to whether offenders had been sufficiently on notice that their conduct entailed criminal liability. The IMT described the London Charter as both the exercise of the sovereign power of the victorious countries and 'the expression of international law existing at the time of its creation'.[21] In dismissing a challenge based on the principle of legality, the IMT noted that the law of war was to be found not only in treaties, but also in the customs and practices of states and the general principles of justice.

Some criticized the Nuremberg tribunals for this relatively loose approach to the legality principle, which looked not just to treaties or customary law defined in the traditional sense, but also to the notion of 'general principles' of law 'common to civilized nations'.[22] And to be sure, the Nuremberg tribunals did not provide a very satisfactory explanation as to how aspects of the 1929 Geneva POW Convention and the Fourth Hague Convention of 1907 so quickly metamorphosed into customary norms. Nonetheless, I believe that the tribunals' general approach was, under the circumstances, appropriate. The crimes with which the Nuremberg defendants were charged—including murder, torture, and enslavement carried out on an enormous scale—were so clearly criminal under every domestic legal system in the world that it could hardly be said that the prospect of criminal liability for them was unpredictable. In my view, it cannot be said that the Nuremberg war crimes proceedings compromised basic fairness. Moreover, it is clear that the Nuremberg tribunals rooted the legality of the crimes charged not only in custom, but also in treaties and general principles of criminal law. And it bears noting that the criticism of Nuremberg for violating the legality principle was directed primarily to crimes against peace, and secondarily to crimes against humanity. Its war crimes jurisdiction triggered few dissents.

The ICTY has likewise declined to engage in an overly formalistic assessment of custom in instances where the criminality of conduct is obvious. In its seminal interlocutory decision on jurisdiction in the *Tadić* case, the ICTY Appeals Chamber stated that to be subject to prosecution by the Tribunal as a violation of laws and customs of war, an offense must violate either customary law or a treaty that was unquestionably binding on the parties at the time of the alleged offense. Nuremberg, of course,

---

[21] Ibid., 216.
[22] *United States v Wilhelm List et al.* (*The Hostage Case*), reprinted in *Trials of War Criminals*, Vol XI, n 19 above, 1239.

provides a precedent for the principle of legality to be satisfied by reference to treaties that were in force at the time of the offense. However, in the case of the ICTY, such reliance on treaties must be reconciled with the statement in the UN Secretary-General's 1993 report that the Tribunal 'should apply rules of international humanitarian law which are beyond any doubt part of customary law'.[23]

Why has the ICTY preferred to rely on customary principles rather than treaty law? One reason obviously was to follow as closely as possible the language of the Secretary-General's report. Another may have been to avoid doubts as to succession to treaties, their continuing binding character and reservations, and the scope and validity of ad hoc agreements between the belligerents. Reliance on customary law provides additional comfort because of the generality of that law.

The legality principle likewise governs the other international and mixed criminal tribunals operating today, including the ICTR, the Special Court for Sierra Leone, and the ICC. As much as possible, the Rome Conference sought to reflect customary international law in the language of the ICC Statute. Where the Statute goes beyond customary law, the ICC may encounter particular difficulties if nationals of non-state parties are prosecuted.

III. WAR CRIMES LAW GOING FORWARD: THE INFLUENCE OF NUREMBERG AND THE MODERN TRIBUNALS ON THE FUTURE OF INTERNATIONAL LAW AND THE AVOIDANCE OF ATROCITIES

Nuremberg had an almost incalculable effect on normative international law. But sadly, the second half of the twentieth century—and, now, the beginning of the twenty-first—have been so marked by atrocities that one commentator has termed the period 'the age of genocide'.[24] These atrocities have continued, not only in spite of Nuremberg and its legacy, but also in spite of the increasing interest in international humanitarian law. So, if such atrocities still occur, what is the legacy of Nuremberg and its latter-day heirs?

It would be wrong to conclude that international tribunals do not work simply because atrocities have continued to occur. After all, we would hardly say that domestic criminal law has no deterrent force simply

---

[23] UNSC, 'Report of the Secretary-General Pursuant to Paragraph 2 of Security Council Resolution 808' (1993) UN Doc S/25704, para 34.
[24] Samantha Power, *'A Problem from Hell': America and the Age of Genocide* (New York: Basic Books, 2002).

because some citizens continue to commit murder or assault. Furthermore, international criminal tribunals serve a variety of noble goals beyond deterrence. By throwing into stark relief the consequences of ethnic and religious hatred, the modern tribunals have demonstrated the viciousness of war criminals and have contributed to the rule of law in affected regions. The ICTY, for one, has made a fundamental and lasting contribution to bringing justice to the peoples of the former Yugoslavia. Due in no small part to that Tribunal, international humanitarian and human rights law today holds greater currency and is better understood than it was just a decade ago. And the very existence of the ICC may cause more prosecution of war criminals in the courts of countries within its jurisdiction.

Moreover, after some ten years, the ICTY and ICTR have established an impressive body of jurisprudence on both substantive international humanitarian and criminal law and, equally important, on criminal procedure and evidence. Their judgments have filled the gaps in international procedural and evidentiary law left by Nuremberg, and their success serves as a model for future prosecutions. Over the past decade, in dozens of trials and appeals, the Tribunals have shown that it is possible to apply international criminal and humanitarian law in actual cases. They have helped to instill the idea that justice, not retribution or impunity, should be the response to horrific crimes.

Still, it is important to remember that international criminal law does not provide all of the answers. It is only one component of the international community's highly complicated response to humanitarian emergencies. Just as we do not expect domestic criminal law to address all the effects of serious crimes, we should not expect international criminal trials to address all the effects of large-scale atrocities. I hope that a multifaceted approach that includes not only legal judgments, but also other tools—asset freezes, travel restrictions, and political stigmatization, among others—will have a meaningful effect in deterring future crimes.

Of course, in the shifting landscape of international relations, progress on crimes committed by sovereign entities is only part of the picture. More and more, atrocities are being perpetrated by non-governmental actors who purport to operate entirely outside of international norms. Casting themselves as interstitial players, exempt from legal rules and bound only by their own moral code, these groups—primarily terrorists and religious fanatics—are challenging all accepted rules of humanitarian and criminal law. The challenge for international humanitarian and criminal law, in return, is to reassert itself in the face of this impunity—to maintain the foothold it gained at Nuremberg and to continue to extend the principle of universality to all peoples, groups, and nations. As the ad hoc Tribunals move towards the completion of their mandates, the future of ensuring effective compliance with international criminal law will depend on the ICC, and on national and mixed tribunals.

The mission of Nuremberg, in Justice Jackson's words, was to 'summon such detachment and intellectual integrity' to the task that the trial would 'commend itself to posterity as fulfilling humanity's aspirations to do justice'.[25] Work always remains to be done, but with these noble goals as our lodestar, we are making progress, and the expanding universe of international humanitarian law is stronger as a result.

---

[25] Opening Statement, n 1 above, 5.

9
ANATOMY OF AN INTERNATIONAL CRIMINAL TRIBUNAL (MANLEY O HUDSON MEDAL LECTURE)*

I am going to focus on the ad hoc Tribunals on whose Appeals Chambers I serve—the International Criminal Tribunal for the former Yugoslavia (ICTY) and the International Criminal Tribunal for Rwanda (ICTR). Established by the UN Security Council in 1993 and 1994, respectively, these Tribunals were a real experiment. Since the Nuremberg and Tokyo trials almost a half century before, theories of international criminal justice had not been tested in courts. Hence, at the time the ICTY and ICTR were created, one could hardly have taken for granted that an international court applying international criminal law would be a success. Yet both the UN Security Council and the UN General Assembly have recently praised the Tribunals for their efficiency, their contribution to ending impunity, and their development of a whole new corpus of substantive, evidentiary, and procedural jurisprudence.

A few weeks ago, after the death of Slobodan Milošević, a handful of pundits called the ICTY's success into question. Their skepticism is unwarranted. The fact that one defendant died as his trial was concluding does not detract from the fact that, in dozens of other cases, the ICTY and ICTR have shown that international criminal law can be fairly and impartially applied, and that persons who violate that law cannot expect impunity. The ad hoc Tribunals have also helped to create an impartial record of atrocities, and to offer victims a sense of vindication.

---

* Delivered upon receipt of the Manley O Hudson Medal at the Centennial Annual Meeting of the American Society of International Law in Washington, DC, USA, on 31 March 2006. The text of this speech first appeared as 'Anatomy of an International Criminal Tribunal: Hudson Lecture' (2006) 100 *American Society of International Law Proceedings* 279 © The American Society of International Law; Theodor Meron. Used by permission and modified from the original publication.

Moreover, Mr Milošević's trial itself contributed to all of these goals. The mere fact that he was brought to The Hague to answer the very serious allegations against him signified that even the most powerful are subject to the rule of law. Scores of witnesses for both sides travelled from afar to tell their stories. The body of evidence thereby created remains relevant, not for the ICTY's judgment, but for that of history. And the ICTY also amply demonstrated its serious commitment to ensuring a fair trial for defendants, including by accommodating Mr Milošević's medical needs and his desire to conduct his own defense. This, more than anything else, was the reason his trial was so long.

Now let me turn to my main focus. I am not going to spend much time on the ad hoc Tribunals' broader social and political goals. Rather, I want to talk nuts and bolts. How do the Tribunals actually work?

The ad hoc Tribunals' anatomy is not just the sum of many disjointed solutions to disconnected practical problems. Rather, this anatomy has developed, in significant part, as a result of two broad considerations. The first is the need to ensure substantive and procedural fairness and to ensure that the Tribunals are perceived as acting legitimately. The second is the fact that the Tribunals exist outside the framework of any state, and that they therefore must function in the absence of any corresponding legislative or executive body. Despite these challenges, the Tribunals have done a good job of ensuring both fairness and efficacy outside the framework of a state.

○₈₰

To begin, I want to highlight a few points of contrast between the ad hoc Tribunals and the Nuremberg tribunals, which were, along with the Tokyo tribunals, the modern international criminal tribunals' sole antecedents, and thus serve as an important point of reference.

Although Nuremberg was the principal ancestor of the modern ad hoc Tribunals, when they were established it was neither possible nor desirable to simply clone the Nuremberg model. The Nuremberg tribunals were established by occupying powers, and they tried members of a regime that had been completely defeated. Because the Allies had total control over German territory, they had little difficulty arresting indictees, seizing evidence, or compelling the production of documents in government archives. Moreover, for the most part, defendants could not intimidate witnesses or pose an immediate continuing danger to society.

The modern ad hoc Tribunals, by contrast, were established by the United Nations, which lacks direct control over most places where suspects or evidence are to be found. Gathering evidence, making arrests, and protecting witnesses thus pose serious challenges. The cooperation of national governments in these tasks is essential—but these same governments often have interests at stake in the cases, and sometimes have strong links to the suspects themselves. The ad hoc Tribunals derive their authority from Chapter VII of the UN Charter—which gives the Security Council the power to respond to threats to international peace and security—and the Tribunals' Statutes require UN member states to cooperate with requests for assistance. Yet compliance by some Balkan governments was, at least in the ICTY's early years, the exception rather than the rule. Furthermore, the ICTY was initially established while the conflict in the Balkans was still ongoing, which presented obvious practical complications. And in Rwanda, cooperation was suspended when the Prosecutor tried to investigate crimes alleged to have been committed by the Tutsis.

Recently, however, enhanced cooperation by governments in the Balkans has made it easier to meet the challenges arising from the ICTY's lack of police powers, as the arrest in Spain of former Croatian General Ante Gotovina, one of the ICTY's most wanted fugitives, illustrates. Moreover, last year saw a 50 percent increase in the ICTY's docket, and by now 96 percent of the ICTY's indictees have surrendered or been captured. This compares favorably with national law enforcement results.

Of course, the ICTY still does not receive complete cooperation from all governments in the Balkans. Radovan Karadžić and Ratko Mladić—who served, respectively, as the political and military leaders of the Bosnian Serbs—are still at large.[1] The fact that they remain at large illustrates that challenges stemming from the ICTY's lack of police powers remain quite real. Nonetheless, the gradual improvement in cooperation from states in the Balkans has itself been a remarkable achievement. It speaks, not just to the value of a little prodding by the United States and European Union, but also to the fact that the ICTY's handling of cases has led people to view it as legitimate, and as an institution worth assisting.

೮೦

Another reason why Nuremberg could not be cloned stems from the need for procedural rules—the production of which formed one of the ad hoc Tribunals' first institutional challenges. Although the Nuremberg tribu-

---

[1] Editor's note: Radovan Karadžić was arrested and transferred to the ICTY in July 2008. His trial commenced in October 2009.

nals were supported by the Allies' legislative power—at least at first—
the Allies provided these tribunals with shockingly little guidance in the
way of procedure. Few rules were promulgated in advance of the Nuremberg trials, and the tribunals were instructed to apply 'expeditious and
nontechnical procedure'.[2] Although this did not render the Nuremberg
proceedings defective, it probably was not ideal, and when the Security
Council established the ad hoc Tribunals, it decided that there should be
written rules of procedure and evidence.

The ad hoc Tribunals' approach, with rules spelled out *ex ante* clearly
and in detail, lends certainty to the process, enabling litigants to plan
their cases with the rules in mind. This approach also ensures consistency
in the procedures adopted from case to case, minimizing allegations of
bias. Hence, the Tribunals' detailed procedural rules represent an important fairness-related advance over Nuremberg.

Although it clearly seems desirable to have rules of procedure and
evidence, it is less clear, in the case of the ad hoc Tribunals, how these
rules should be created and amended, and, in particular, who should do
the creating and amending. After all, unlike the International Criminal
Court, the ICTY, for example, was not the product of a treaty resulting
from extended negotiations. And without a treaty process, there was no
assembly of state parties to serve as a legislature, as it were, that would
assume functions such as drafting rules of procedure and evidence. In a
sense, the Security Council was the legislature. It adopted the Statute,
and it could be called upon and is still called upon to amend the Statute
when major policy questions arise, such as the appointment of *ad litem*
judges. But when it came to the rules of procedure and evidence which
were needed to put meat on the bones of the Statute, the Security Council
was not a particularly good body to turn to. It has no experience in the
area of criminal procedure, and its time is taken up dealing with urgent
international security-related matters. It cannot be bothered every time
some procedural rule at an ad hoc Tribunal needs tweaking. And the
political morass that might have resulted from hashing out every detail of
those rules in the Security Council might have adversely affected the
Tribunal's work.

With regard to the rules, it was therefore left to the judges of the ICTY
to act as the legislators. And, as I mentioned, this secondary legislative
flesh has been substantial. This role of the judges as quasi-legislators may

---

[2] Charter of the International Military Tribunal—Annex to the Agreement for the prosecution
and punishment of the major war criminals of the European Axis (1945) 82 UNTS 284, art 19.

seem strange. In most civil law countries, it is the legislature that revises the code of criminal procedure. For the International Criminal Court, a preparatory commission drafted the rules of procedure and evidence, and it is the Assembly of States Parties that has adopted them. In the United States, the system, at least on the federal level, is a little closer to that of the ICTY. For although it is Congress that must approve changes in the rules, it is the judges who propose them—and, much of the time, the judges get their way.

Despite the novelty of the ICTY's approach, I think entrusting the judges with the authority to write their own Rules of Procedure and Evidence has largely proven a success. Admittedly, there have been many, perhaps too many, revisions: some thirty-five versions of the Rules in less than eleven years.[3] But the high frequency of changes reflects in significant part two attributes of the ICTY that have nothing to do with the Rules' judicial authorship: (i) the challenge of bringing together concepts from different legal traditions in a workable amalgam; and (ii) the problems I mentioned above resulting from our dependence on cooperation by sovereign governments for arrests and evidence. The large number of revisions also reflects one of the main advantages of having the judges do the rule-writing: the ability to quickly take into account lessons learned from concrete experiences in the courtroom. The absence of a legislature capable of revising or adjusting the substantive law has meant that the law had to be developed through the case law of the Tribunals, a function which requires tremendous care to avoid clashing with the prohibition of *ex post facto* criminal legislation.

∞

In the source of authority that appears to stand behind convictions, there is another fairness and legitimacy-related difference between Nuremberg and the modern Tribunals. The Nuremberg tribunals have often been attacked as exercises in victors' justice. This criticism is largely unfair. At the time the Nuremberg tribunals were created, many advocated summary execution of Nazi war criminals, as was the historical norm. Instead, the defendants were provided with adversarial trials with due process protections. Some defendants were, in fact, acquitted.[4] Still, the charge of victors' justice has persisted, and the modern Tribunals were specifically

---

[3] Editor's note: As of February 2011, there have been forty-five revisions to the ICTY's Rules of Procedure and Evidence.

[4] See, eg, International Military Tribunal (Nuremberg), 'Judgment and Sentences' (1947) 41 *AJIL* 172.

designed to foreclose any similar objection. As noted, they were established by the UN Security Council. Judges are nominated by UN member states, short-listed by the Security Council, and then elected by the General Assembly, representing every nation in the world. Likewise, the Prosecutors of the ICTY and ICTR are nominated by the UN Secretary-General and approved by the Security Council. Together, these procedures ensure that the ad hoc Tribunals are not composed of individuals from any one nation or group of nations. Rather, they are the world's first truly international criminal courts.

This does not eliminate all criticism, of course. There will always be those, particularly in the regions we directly affect, who will insist that the Tribunals are biased against one side. This is inevitable—we are handling politically charged cases arising from wars and crimes against humanity in the very recent past. Nationalist sentiments and ethnic tensions do not disappear overnight, but we cannot pander to them. We cannot shape our judgments to try to please everybody. We have to call it as we see it based on the evidence and the law. We provide a fair and impartial process. That is the best that can be done.

The Statutes of both Tribunals state that judges must be persons of high moral character, impartiality, and integrity who possess the qualifications required in their respective countries for appointment to the highest judicial offices. The ICTY and the ICTR Statutes add that due account shall be taken of the experience of the judges in criminal law and international law, including humanitarian law and human rights law. Typically, most experts on humanitarian law and human rights law are found in academia rather than the criminal bar and bench. But today, for example, only about a quarter of the ICTY's sixteen permanent judges come from academia or foreign ministries; the vast majority of judges originate in their national judiciaries, including supreme courts. In contrast, out of the five presidents of the ICTY who have been elected by the permanent judges, three have come from academia. The composition of the judges has struck a good balance. I know the ICTY has benefited from the expertise that several of my colleagues developed through years of scholarship. Still, I think that the decision to select mostly experienced judges has been wise. We have much to learn from them. New judges must rapidly adopt the values, duties, and instincts of a person holding judicial office.

ଓଃଡ

The substantive law and procedural rules applied at the ad hoc Tribunals further enhance their legitimacy. Notably, the ad hoc Tribunals apply substantive law in a way that assiduously respects the principle of *nullum crimen sine lege*—also known as the principle of legality.

The ad hoc Tribunals frequently judge crimes committed before their Statutes were enacted. The potential for *ex post facto* problems was particularly acute when the ICTY's Statute was approved. The break-up of Yugoslavia had created uncertainty about which treaties applied in different parts of the territory that had belonged to that nation. So, for instance, how can the ICTY apply its Statute to a crime committed in 1992, before the Statute was passed but within the temporal jurisdiction of the Tribunal? The ICTY would not, unless the act in question was already a crime under customary international law in 1992.

Of course, there are some gray areas in which customary law might be less well defined or in which international law exceeds the scope of applicable domestic law. In such cases, the ICTY has erred on the side of caution. And it has employed a relatively conservative methodology in defining custom. This caution has no doubt limited the ICTY's ability to contribute to the progressive development of the law, and some might bemoan that fact. But in my view, such limitations are inherent in our role as a criminal court obliged to respect defendants' rights.

This point, however, illustrates that there is no one-size-fits-all model for an international tribunal. Although the ICTY and ICTR share an Appeals Chamber, most of the Articles of their Statutes and procedural rules, and most of their doctrines, there are some differences, and these are tailored to the differences in the situations to which the Tribunals were designed to respond. Thus, for instance, violence in Rwanda and surrounding areas did not lead to the break-up of states. Hence, at the ICTR, no treaty-succession problems arise, and acts criminalized by treaties forming part of the law of the land may be judged without creating *ex post facto* problems. So, unlike in the ICTY, where custom at the time of the crime is the litmus test for the permissibility of prosecution, in the ICTR it is possible to refer either to custom or to treaties to satisfy the legality principle.

෬෩

I want to return to the procedural rules for a bit. Consider the ICTY's rules governing evidence in the possession of states and its rules governing provisional release, both of which show how the Tribunals account for their lack of police power. With regard to the former, as the ICTY must obtain information from states, its rules protect national security-related information in a manner consistent with the rights of the accused.

In particular, the purpose of Rule 70 of the ICTY's Rules of Procedure and Evidence is to encourage states to share sensitive information on a confidential basis by offering them a guarantee that the confidentiality of both the information they provide and the information's sources will be protected. The Prosecution must obtain the consent of the state that provided the information before the information can be presented in evidence and certain limitations are placed on what Trial Chambers may do with respect to the information. Rule 70 also makes explicit that, subject to these limitations, '[t]he right of the accused to challenge the evidence presented by the Prosecution shall remain unaffected'.[5]

Because the Tribunals have no police force to catch those who abscond while on provisional release, the Rules create a presumption in favor of pre-trial detention. Provisional release may be granted only when the defendant can satisfy the relevant Chamber that he or she will surrender to the Tribunal and will pose no danger to others. This is a substantial difference from many domestic systems that have a presumption in favor of provisional release. At first, provisional release was available only in extraordinary circumstances in the ICTY, but the Rules have been liberalized as a result of changing circumstances. Provisional release has been granted increasingly often as better government cooperation has made it possible to trust states' guarantees to re-arrest the accused. In Rwanda, the situation is different. The rules governing provisional release have somewhat different language, but the real distinction is that, in practice, the risk of flight is often serious. As a result, provisional release is almost never granted.

గ8౦

As I mentioned earlier, the ad hoc Tribunals represent a blend of the civil and common law traditions, although weighted in favor of the common law, adversarial system. The majority of the judges come, however, from civil law systems. Sometimes, one might say, this blend makes for a strange brew.

Consider, for example, the rules governing hearsay. In contrast to the rules of procedure, the rules of evidence applicable at the Tribunals are, for the most part, not spelled out in extensive detail. Rather, the judges have broad discretion to admit probative evidence. This is in keeping with civil law traditions, and it also reflects the fact that facts are found by judges, not juries. In particular, there is no blanket prohibition on hearsay

---

[5] ICTY, Rules of Procedure and Evidence, Rule 70(E).

statements. After all, hearsay can be highly probative, and judges may be better equipped than lay jurors are to account for a statement's hearsay nature when assessing its value. Yet as trials are largely adversarial, and as the judges lack civil law judges' power to independently investigate and check facts, there is still a risk that, in some circumstances, hearsay evidence could threaten the fairness of trials. To account for this problem, the Rules of the ICTY, for example, authorize exclusion of evidence 'if its probative value is substantially outweighed by the need to ensure a fair trial'.[6] In my view, this nuanced treatment of hearsay demonstrates how judges should and do account for the ad hoc Tribunals' hybrid nature when determining the optimal solution to procedural or evidentiary questions.

On one very important subject, plea bargaining, the ad hoc Tribunals have largely adopted common law rules. The ICTY and ICTR have made the controversial decision that, like the courts of common law countries, they will accept plea bargains. In civil law countries, acceptance of plea bargains is still rare. Hence, some lawyers and judges coming out of civil law systems approach plea bargains with apprehension. Additional apprehension about plea bargaining at the ad hoc Tribunals arises due to the extraordinary nature of the crimes prosecuted and the need for sentences to reflect the crimes' gravity.

I believe, however, that the ad hoc Tribunals have again struck the right balance. To be sure, these Tribunals strive to create an accurate record of atrocities and provide vindication for victims. Yet in accepting plea bargains, the ICTY and ICTR have taken care not to abdicate these important responsibilities. Not bound by sentence recommendations made pursuant to plea agreements, judges of the ad hoc Tribunals have frequently imposed sentences beyond the recommended range if the recommendation appeared not to adequately reflect the gravity of the crime—although such sentences have been appealed. When accompanied by genuine expressions of remorse and properly detailed acknowledgment of the defendant's participation in crimes, a plea can be highly constructive. For instance, in a recent sentencing proceeding, one defendant demonstrated that his admission of responsibility for participating in the Srebrenica genocide had a major impact on the region, making revisionism and denial of that genocide much more difficult.[7] A forthright and specific acknowledgment of guilt may also offer victims as much consolation as a conviction following repeated protestations of innocence.

---

[6] Ibid., Rule 89(D).
[7] *Prosecutor v Momir Nikolić* (Judgement on Sentencing Appeal) IT-02-60/1-A (8 March 2006).

One rule that, in my personal opinion, reflects a rather unwise resolution of the tension between common and civil law approaches is the provision in the Tribunals' Statutes permitting appeals by the Prosecution. Such appeals—routine in the civil law system—are anathema to those of us from common law systems. Perhaps it was felt that such a rule was required by the immensity of certain crimes. This rule renders less meaningful the right to a speedy trial.

〇〇〇

Conscious of the fact that the ad hoc Tribunals were meant to be temporary, we judges take seriously the need for the Tribunals to rapidly complete their missions while still applying a full panoply of due process protections. To help achieve this goal, the Tribunals have, in response to requests from the Security Council, prepared completion strategies. These strategies entail some basic, practical steps, such as maximizing our usage of our limited courtroom space. Some aspects, however, involve complex legal challenges, such as the referral of cases involving lower-ranking accused to national war crimes courts in the Balkans, as allowed, subject to due process considerations under our rules.

The Security Council's desire for the ad hoc Tribunals to close at the end of this decade challenges judges to ensure that, while proceedings move quickly, the push for efficiency does not unfairly prejudice the accused. For instance, the Prosecutor of the ICTY has recently requested joinder of numerous cases involving related acts. Although consolidated trials will frequently be shorter than a series of separate trials, judges must take care not to approve joinder when doing so would unfairly prejudice the Defense. Some joinder motions have therefore been rejected. Joinder also poses a practical problem: what happens if, over the course of a long trial involving multiple defendants, judges need to be replaced? Although this could potentially be a problem with any case, it is more likely with the new trials of multiple defendants because of their length, and the costs of starting over would be much greater. This is an example of a problem that working closely with the Security Council enabled us to solve. The Council amended our Statute recently to create the new position of reserve judges, who will serve in addition to the three-judge bench and will step in if necessary.

Similarly, the length of proceedings, combined with the Tribunals' need to complete their work, makes it more difficult for their Appeals Chambers to use remand as a means of curing errors. Consequently, the Appeals Chambers must reverse a conviction if an error caused prejudice to an accused. This approach tends to benefit defendants, since they will simply be acquitted of the charges in question instead of being tried again by the Trial Chamber. In an appeal by the Prosecutor, the Appeals Chamber may, however, enter a conviction *de novo*. This is obviously not a perfect solution.[8]

It bears noting that even the existence of the Appeals Chamber is an improvement over Nuremberg, where the only recourse for a convicted defendant was a request for clemency from superior military officers. Moreover, like appellate courts in some civil law countries, the ad hoc Tribunals' Appeals Chambers even have the power to consider new evidence. This power has helped to ensure fairness in situations where states do not furnish evidence at first but later disclose relevant materials.

Persons convicted by the ad hoc Tribunals, moreover, still have the ability to seek a pardon or commutation of their sentence. Although they serve sentences in countries that have signed cooperation agreements with the Tribunals—another function of the Tribunals' lack of police power—these persons may seek pardon or commutation from the President of the Tribunal that sentenced them. In this context, then—and in a few others—the Tribunals' existence outside the framework of any state, and the fact that the Tribunals are therefore not subject to the authority of any state's executive, require the President of each Tribunal to assume executive-type duties in addition to the duties of a judge.

Having said that, the judges of the ad hoc Tribunals are not as insulated from politics as life-tenured American federal judges are. More problematic than the completion strategies—although less in terms of fairness than in terms of *perceived* fairness—is the fact that the judges of the ad hoc Tribunals must stand for re-election after a short four-year term. Although the United Nations' involvement in the selection of judges lends legitimacy to the Tribunals, its ability to send judges home at the end of their terms represents something of a threat to judicial independence—especially in light of how short these terms are. I understand that limits on judicial terms may be required in the international context. But perhaps a better solution would have been to adopt longer, non-renewable terms for judges, thus ensuring that judges do not feel threatened by reactions to unpopular decisions. While I am confident that my colleagues and I will take decisions that we believe to be just, even if we think they will provoke the ire of the Security Council or General

---

[8] Editor's note: The Tribunals' Appeals Chambers have ordered remand in two cases.

Assembly, the public's belief that we might be influenced could undermine the credibility of our decisions.

The ad hoc Tribunals' ability to accomplish so much is partly the result of the Tribunals' excellent staff, compromised largely of young lawyers who have excelled in their home countries, including, in so far as I am concerned, former clerks from the US Courts of Appeals and Supreme Court. The Tribunals have, in fact, served as a training ground for the next generation of leaders in the field of international criminal law.

♾

In sum, the ad hoc Tribunals are not perfect, but they have been a remarkably successful experiment. First, of course, they have had an immediate effect on the Balkans and Rwanda. In those regions, the Tribunals' judgments are increasingly accepted as historical records. They have given the victims of horrific crimes a chance to tell their stories. And they have contributed to stability by bringing to justice persons who might otherwise still be at large and even active in government, military, or social affairs.

Over the past decade, in dozens of trials and appeals, the ICTY and ICTR have shown that it is possible and practical to apply international criminal and humanitarian law in actual cases—not just a few times, as at Nuremberg and Tokyo, but repeatedly, and in a manner even more rigorous than that employed at the post-World War II trials. The Tribunals have also helped to instill the idea that justice, not retribution or impunity, should be the response to horrific crimes. And their jurisprudence will guide the next generation of international criminal courts, like the Special Court for Sierra Leone and the International Criminal Court, whose establishment was sparked, at least in part, by the success of the ad hoc Tribunals. Indeed, the ad hoc Tribunals have helped to create a whole new universe of international criminal justice in which an end to impunity and legal accountability for crimes are no longer just remote hopes but, increasingly, our reality.

10

THE PRINCIPLE OF LEGALITY IN INTERNATIONAL CRIMINAL LAW*

According to today's panel description, by some accounts, '[i]nternational criminal law judges have engaged in a full-scale—if unacknowledged—refashioning of international criminal law' in a number of different ways.[1] Reading this description, you might assume that as a judge sitting on the Appeals Chambers of the International Criminal Tribunals for the former Yugoslavia and Rwanda, I serve as the representative of judicial activists who delight in inventing retrospective sanctions, 'upset[ting] arrangements carefully negotiated between states', and potentially endangering the due process rights of defendants.[2]

I must take issue, however, with any imputation that international criminal tribunals are a laboratory for judges' legal experiments. A fair consideration of the work undertaken by the ad hoc Tribunals refutes this view. I will note for the record that my comments today reflect only my personal opinions and not my position as a judge on the Appeals Chambers of the ICTY and ICTR.

For the purposes of these remarks, I would propose the simple formulation of *nullum crimen sine lege*—'no crime without law'—as the definition of the principle of legality. I do, of course, accept that there could be considerable discussion of both my formulation and alternative definitions of the principle of legality.

---

* Delivered at the 103rd Annual Meeting of the American Society of International Law, Washington, DC, USA, on 26 March 2009. The text of these remarks first appeared as 'The Principle of Legality in International Criminal Law' (2010) 103 *American Society of International Law Proceedings* 107 (Remarks by Judge Theodor Meron), © The American Society of International Law; Theodor Meron. Used by permission and modified from that publication.

[1] American Society of International Law, 103rd Annual Meeting: International Law as Law, Program, available at ⟨http://am2009.asil.org/full-program-schedule.cfm⟩.

[2] Ibid.

With these preliminary observations, I turn to the question, implicit in the panel description, of whether the ICTY and ICTR have violated the principle of legality and thus denied defendants due process. To address this issue, I believe that we must answer two subsidiary questions:

(A) Did those convicted by the Tribunals understand that the relevant offenses were criminal at the time these offenses were committed?

(B) Have the Tribunals' procedures and legal formulations led to the conviction of individuals for actions that were excessively removed from the crimes of which they were found guilty?

With respect to my first sub-question, I can confidently state that those convicted by the Tribunals understood that the categories of behavior they were convicted of committing, promoting, or aiding and abetting were illegal. Even before the founding of the Tribunals, the defendants before the International Military Tribunal at Nuremberg argued that the tribunal's Charter—which was not in effect when the relevant crimes were committed—criminalized conduct retroactively. In short, these defendants urged that the crimes with which they were charged—murder, torture, and mass enslavement—were not criminal when committed. But the Nuremberg tribunal, recognizing that such acts were and are clearly criminal under every domestic legal system in the world, dismissed the challenge, rooting the legality principle not only in customary law, but also in treaties and general principles of criminal law.[3]

The same logic applies to the judgments of modern international criminal tribunals. The ICTY and ICTR, for example, convict individuals for crimes that are almost universally condemned by domestic legal systems and military codes—killings, sexual violence, mass deportation, and other crimes of this sort. The Tribunals target crimes recognized as unacceptable by a diverse array of legal systems, and it is of no import who commits these crimes.

It is true that many individuals convicted by the ICTY and ICTR did not understand that they might be prosecuted at all, given their positions of power and influence. Some of them may have believed that national and international collusion, apathy, corruption, and criminality would ensure that their misdeeds were not punished. But the international community's disapproval of this cynical expectation is not a due process violation; rather, it is a cause for celebration.

My second sub-question, concerning the Tribunals' processes and legal formulations, is harder to answer. But here, too, I believe that the

---

[3] International Military Tribunal (Nuremberg), 'Judgment and Sentences' (1947) 41 *AJIL* 172.

Tribunals' operations and jurisprudence have not led to violations of the principle of legality. Because my time is short, I will address only two relevant aspects of the Tribunals' work that are sometimes criticized: their categorization of certain actions and their use of customary law.

I. CATEGORIZATION OF CERTAIN ACTIONS

While those convicted by the ICTY and ICTR cannot credibly claim that the actions they were convicted of did not seem illegal, there is greater basis for claiming that they would not have been aware that certain criminal actions could constitute a particular type of offense. For example, prior to the ICTR's *Akayesu* judgment, which held that 'rape and sexual violence... constitute genocide in the same way as any other act as long as they were committed with the specific intent to destroy, in whole or in part, a particular group, targeted as such',[4] it might not have been clear to some defendants that rape could constitute an act of genocide. However, at the time the relevant offenses took place, it was already clear that, depending on context, rape could be a crime against humanity, a war crime, and a crime under domestic Rwandan law.

It does not appear to me to be a violation of the principle of legality for the ad hoc Tribunals to undertake additional legal interpretations, such as those in the *Akayesu* judgment, that involve categorizations of conduct generally acknowledged to be illegal. The jurisprudence of the Tribunals also directly refutes any suggestion that labeling a particular act as genocide as opposed to, for example, a war crime, automatically makes a defendant liable for a greater sentence.

II. CUSTOMARY LAW

The extensive reliance on customary law is a second controversial aspect of the jurisprudence of the Tribunals. But in this case as well, I would argue that there is very little basis on which to assert that the Tribunals' jurisprudence contravenes the principle of legality. With regards to the ICTY, for example, the UN Secretary-General noted that 'the application of the principle *nullum crimen sine lege* requires that the international tribunal should apply rules of international humanitarian law which are beyond any doubt part of customary law so that the problem of adherence of some but not all States to specific conventions does not arise'.[5] This

---

[4] *Prosecutor v Jean-Paul Akayesu* (Judgement) ICTR-96-4-T (2 September 1998), para 731.
[5] UNSC, 'Report of the Secretary-General Pursuant to Paragraph 2 of Security Council Resolution 808' (1993) UN Doc S/25704, para 34.

approach, which has been adopted by the ICTY despite not being explicitly a part of its Statute, prevents the Tribunal from imposing progressive development of customary international law, no matter how much its judges might believe that certain conduct deserves to be punished.

Some would ask whether individuals should be convicted for violating uncodified customary law at all. Codification of criminal prohibitions is the norm in modern domestic legal systems. However, I do not believe that the legality principle bars convictions under uncodified customary law, as a simple logical parallel can demonstrate. We do not really expect every citizen to read, understand, and commit to memory the thousands of pages of technocratic language defining codified domestic criminal law. But we choose to maintain the legal fiction that they have done so. By extension, it is no less realistic to hold that an accused should have been aware of well-established principles of the law of nations. After all, customary humanitarian law largely prohibits acts that everyone would assume to be criminal anyway: rape, murder, torture, attacking civilians, and so forth. Thus, in my view, customary law can provide a safe basis for a conviction—especially applying the ICTY and ICTR's requirement that a legal principle be firmly established as custom at the time of an alleged offense.

I would suggest that customary law, in fact, usually serves as the superimposition of a limiting factor on jurisprudence, rather than as an expansive one. The *Hadžihasanović* appeal judgment is an example of this limiting effect.[6] In that case, the ICTY Appeals Chamber found that the particular form of command responsibility for which Hadžihasanović had been convicted was not clearly established in customary international law at the time of the alleged offense, and it reversed the Trial Chamber's conviction. Similarly, in the *Kordić* case, the ICTY found that neither treaty nor international customary law criminalized attacks on civilians without serious result.[7] And in the *Stakić* case, the ICTY found that a Trial Chamber's definition of deportation was broader than could be supported under international customary law, and ruled that certain convictions for deportation should have been for forcible transfer instead.[8] More generally, in the *Galić* case, the ICTY Appeals Chamber explained that even when a relevant treaty provision exists, 'in practice

---

[6] *Prosecutor v Enver Hadžihasanović and Amir Kubura* (Judgement) IT-01-47-A (22 April 2008).
[7] *Prosecutor v Dario Kordić and Mario Čerkez* (Judgement) IT-95-14/2-A (17 December 2004).
[8] *Prosecutor v Milomir Stakić* (Judgement) IT-97-24-A (22 March 2006).

the International Tribunal always ascertains that the treaty provision in question is also declaratory of custom'.[9]

Of course, but for the strictures of time, there are many additional issues that I could discuss—especially the various modes of liability employed by the Tribunals. Still, I hope that I have given you some sense of why the painstaking jurisprudence of the ICTY and ICTR is a powerful antidote to doubts about the application of the principle of legality by international criminal tribunals.

In closing, I also believe it is important to discuss briefly the International Criminal Court (ICC), whose permanence makes its contribution to international law particularly significant. The ICC's Statute-based approach makes the principle of legality less of an issue in this tribunal. A major reason is the prohibition of retroactive application. The ICC was able to dismiss Democratic Republic of Congo warlord Thomas Lubanga's argument that child recruitment did not violate international customary law by pointing to the prohibition included in its 1998 Statute (and agreed with the Special Court for Sierra Leone's finding that child recruitment was an offense under customary law at least as of 1996).[10] The ICC Statute, in Article 21, opens the door widely to additional sources of international law, including custom as well as 'general principles'. In this latter regard, I believe it will be especially important for the ICC to draw on the practices and jurisprudence of other international criminal courts in matters of procedure, customary law, interpretation of relevant treaties, and the relationship between common and civil law. Starting *de novo* is not only inefficient; it might even clash with the principle of legality, given the extensive corpus of prior jurisprudence on these issues from earlier, ad hoc international criminal tribunals.

---

[9] *Prosecutor v Stanislav Galić* (Judgement) IT-98-29-A (30 November 2006), para 85.

[10] *Prosecutor v Thomas Lubanga Dyilo* (Decision on the Confirmation of Charges (Public Redacted Version)) ICC-01/04-01/06 (29 January 2007).

11

THE CHALLENGES FACING THE INTERNATIONAL CRIMINAL TRIBUNAL FOR THE FORMER YUGOSLAVIA*

The International Criminal Tribunal for the former Yugoslavia—often known by its English acronym ICTY—was established in 1993 and has undertaken the first international prosecutions of war crimes since Nuremberg. As was the case at Nuremberg, the Tribunal's creators hoped that it would do more than simply mete out justice to individual wrongdoers. They envisioned that it would also help to create an impartial record of atrocities committed during the Yugoslav conflicts and would offer victims a sense of vindication. And, by doing all of those things, they hoped that it would contribute to reconciliation and reconstruction in the republics of the former Yugoslavia.

To borrow a phrase from Justice Robert Jackson, the US Chief Prosecutor at Nuremberg, it has been our task to 'patiently and temperately disclose'[1] the record of the crimes that scarred the Balkans in the 1990s and devastated hundreds of thousands of lives. It would exceed the capacity of any single court to bring more than a partial reckoning to the vast scale of those crimes—the murders, rapes, and deportations; the acts of torture, destruction, and cruelty. But, if with painful slowness at first, this Tribunal has helped to bring to account a considerable number

---

* Delivered at the Lauterpacht Research Centre for International Law, University of Cambridge, Cambridge, United Kingdom, on 6 February 2004. Portions of the text of this speech have been published in 'Procedural Evolution in the ICTY' (2004) 2 *Journal of International Criminal Justice* 520, © Oxford University Press; Theodor Meron. Used by permission and modified from the original publication.

[1] Opening speech by Justice Robert H Jackson, Chief Prosecutor for the United States of America, in *The Trial of German Major War Criminals by the International Military Tribunal Sitting at Nuremberg Germany: Opening Speeches of the Chief Prosecutors* (Buffalo: William S Hein & Co, 2001), 3.

of accused of high rank, and is now doing so with growing confidence and efficiency.

These larger social and political goals are all vitally important, and one may, of course, debate how well the Tribunal has achieved them. But today, I would like to concentrate on what may seem like more mundane institutional and procedural problems that have arisen as the Tribunal has gradually developed into an experienced criminal court. In this gathering of jurists, I am sure that I need not belabor the point that structure and procedure are often as important in determining outcomes as substantive law. Without adequate solutions to structural questions, the Tribunal cannot hope to fulfill its larger missions.

The Tribunal represents an enormous experiment in international cooperation and legal institution building. It has sixteen permanent judges from sixteen countries and nine *ad litem* judges at this time. The judges sit in three Trial Chambers, with a total of six three-judge benches, and one Appeals Chamber. The Appeals Chamber is composed of seven judges, two of whom are appointed from the International Criminal Tribunal for Rwanda, and each appeal is decided by five Appeals Chamber judges.

At the moment, there are six trials being held in three courtrooms, and two of the trials involve two defendants. In its history, the Tribunal has held nearly thirty trials, including currently ongoing trials, involving forty-four defendants. Of the forty-four defendants who have been tried to final judgment, five were acquitted. As important as the Tribunal's ability to reach careful judgments of guilt for the terrible crimes within its jurisdiction, one of the essential tests of its fairness and legitimacy has been the Tribunal's insistence on acquitting defendants when the Prosecution has failed to meet its burden of proof.

After ten years in operation, the Tribunal's Chambers have handed down hundreds of decisions. For its substantive law, the Tribunal has numerous precedents—especially from Nuremberg, but also from national jurisdictions—upon which to draw. For its methods of organization and its rules of procedure, the Tribunal has had to rely much more on the creative work of its judges and staff. Let me outline for you seven institutional challenges the Tribunal has confronted and the solutions worked out so far.

CO

The first concerns the very method by which the Tribunal's procedures are established, which is determined by the fact that, unlike the International

Criminal Court, the ICTY is not the product of a treaty resulting from extended negotiations. Rather, the Tribunal was created by the Security Council of the United Nations pursuant to its powers under Chapter VII of the UN Charter to respond to threats to international peace and security.

Establishment by the Security Council had some clear advantages. For one, the refusal of the states of the former Yugoslavia to participate raised no obstacle to the Tribunal's creation. For another, the Tribunal's governing Statute could be drafted quickly. But without a treaty process, there was no assembly of state parties to serve as a legislature, as it were—a body that would assume functions such as the drafting of rules of procedure and evidence. In a sense, the Security Council was the legislature. It adopted the ICTY's Statute, and it could be called upon and is still called upon when major policy questions required. But, when it came to rules of procedure and evidence, it was left to the judges of the Tribunal to act as the legislators. And this secondary legislative activity has been substantial. The ICTY has about 154 Rules of Procedure and Evidence filling 120 pages of text.

I think this choice to entrust the judges of the ICTY with the authority to write their own Rules of Procedure and Evidence has largely proven a success. Admittedly, there have been many revisions. But the large number of revisions to the Rules reflects one of the main advantages of having judges do the rule-writing: the ability to quickly take into account lessons learned from concrete experiences in the courtroom.

◈

A second major institutional challenge, or set of challenges, for the Tribunal has arisen from the length and complexity of its trials. The average criminal trial in the United States is quite brief. Even for felonies, US trials rarely run longer than a few weeks. At the Tribunal, by contrast, the average length of our trials is more than sixteen months. This is due to a confluence of factors. The Tribunal's Statute restricts it to 'serious violations' of international humanitarian law,[2] and the Tribunal's Prosecutors have by and large concentrated on high-level perpetrators. Often, the crimes charged, connected to entire military campaigns, occurred over the course of months or years, across many

---

[2] Statute of the International Tribunal for the Prosecution of Persons Responsible for Serious Violations of International Humanitarian Law Committed in the Territory of the Former Yugoslavia since 1991 (1993) UN Doc S/25704 at 36, annex and S/25704/Add.1.

locations, and involved many defendants, requiring the parties and the judges to contend with a large quantity of evidence.

The *Slobodan Milošević* case offers one illustration. It is not typical, but it is not so far from the norm as one might think. Milošević is actually only one of four defendants who were originally indicted together. With sixty-six counts, hundreds of witnesses, tens of thousands of pages of documents—most of which must be translated from Serbo-Croatian into French and English, the Tribunal's working languages—the trial is extremely complex. It encompasses three separate indictments for Kosovo, Croatia, and Bosnia and Herzegovina. The defendant's health has led to a great number of delays and to a reduced schedule, in which the Trial Chamber sits only three days a week. Trials of this magnitude call for extraordinary energy and judicial skill.

Let me mention two implications of our trials' unusual length. First, many defendants remain in detention before judgment for years at a time. Many defendants, and a number of commentators, have questioned whether such lengthy detention is consistent with the presumption of innocence enshrined in Article 21 of the ICTY's Statute and Article 14 of the International Covenant on Civil and Political Rights, with the normative preference in many national jurisdictions (and, recently, in the ICTY) for provisional release pending trial and final judgment, and with international human rights entitlements to a speedy trial. This is a difficult question, made somewhat more difficult, on a practical level, because The Netherlands has not been willing to allow defendants to be provisionally released in The Netherlands, insisting instead that the persons who have been provisionally released be sent out of the country, thus increasing the uncertainty of whether they will return for trial. But, on balance, I think the Tribunal has reasonably found that such detention is not a violation of the Statute or international human rights standards—once a judge has confirmed that the evidence supporting an indictment shows a reasonable probability that the accused committed the offenses charged.

Above all, three factors lead me to that view. The crimes charged—genocide, crimes against humanity, and war crimes, such as grave breaches of the Geneva Conventions—are exceptionally serious. Unlike domestic courts, the ICTY lacks a police force to which it may turn to seek assistance in compelling the attendance of defendants. And, unfortunately, the governments which could most effectively supply that kind of policing assistance have often been less than cooperative.

A second implication of our trials' great length has been the need to craft a workable regime of interlocutory appeals—that is, appeals before the conclusion of the trial. In the United States, such appeals are exceptional. Normally, a defendant must wait until the issuance of the trial judgment, and then raise all his or her claims of error. Given the extraordinary duration of trials at the ICTY and the practice of detention during trial, it was initially thought that a more permissive system for interlocutory appeals was appropriate, particularly if a challenge to a Trial Chamber ruling might result in the dismissal of particular charges—and thus in the shortening of the trial—or even in the dismissal of the indictment. Moreover, since the Appeals Chamber of the ICTY started out with a limited caseload, it could render its decisions on such appeals quite quickly.

The initially generous rule on interlocutory appeals, designed in significant part as a response to long trials, unfortunately led to a flood of appeals, often of minor evidentiary rulings, that only delayed the progress of trials all the more. As a result, the Tribunal recently decided to restrict the possible grounds for interlocutory appeals and to require permission—or, in technical terms, certification—from the Trial Chamber before most issues could be raised in an interlocutory appeal. The regime of interlocutory appeals at the Tribunal is still probably more lenient than in most domestic systems, but it has moved back in the direction of domestic practices.

સ્જી

Judges writing the rules and trials lasting for years are not the only peculiarities of the ICTY. A third important cluster of differences between ICTY cases and typical domestic criminal prosecutions arises from the difficulties of gathering evidence from distant countries that have only recently emerged from armed conflict—without the assistance of an effective police force, and frequently without the full cooperation of the governments in the region. We do not have the advantages of the Nuremberg tribunals, which had police power to search for evidence in Germany and could benefit from the meticulous archives—a veritable paper trail—left behind by the Nazis. The ICTY must instead rely on the cooperation of supportive governments and of individuals who often may realistically fear reprisals if they cooperate openly.

Notably, governments are often willing to share information only if the sources of that information are kept confidential, a demand clearly in tension with the defendant's right to mount a full challenge to the evidence against him or her. The ICTY has had to devise a system—principally regulated by Rule 70 of our Rules of Procedure and Evidence—permitting confidential information-sharing at the investigative and pre-trial stages but requiring disclosure if information is actually used in evidence at trial. In recognition of the Tribunal's utter dependence on the assistance of states, however, states supplying confidential information are permitted to block the use at trial of the information they have provided.

The ICTY's dependence on courageous eyewitnesses from the former Yugoslavia has similarly required the creation of an elaborate system for protecting the identities of witnesses and the use, in quite a few cases, of testimony via video link, with the face of the witness blocked out and the voice modified. Unfortunately, despite these efforts, it seems clear that quite a few potential witnesses have been physically attacked—and many more threatened—to prevent their cooperation with the Tribunal.

In domestic criminal cases, it occasionally may turn out that important evidence is discovered late in the proceeding. At the ICTY the problem of an incomplete evidentiary base is much more common. There are even cases in which defendants have claimed that governments have deliberately withheld information to shield some defendants and implicate others. In order to cope with the problem of a shifting evidentiary foundation, the ICTY has adopted a rule permitting the admission of additional evidence even on appeal under some circumstances. But at some point, of course, criminal proceedings must reach a conclusion. Establishing the right balance between fairness (or should one say confidence in accuracy), on the one hand, and finality, on the other—a balance that all systems of criminal justice must strike—thus presents particular challenges to the ICTY.

⋄

A fourth institutional challenge faced by the ICTY has been the need to find a sensible combination of elements from different legal traditions.

As at Nuremberg, the structure of our trials draws more heavily on the common law adversarial model than on the civil law inquisitorial system. It is largely the responsibility of the parties to develop their cases—to collect and present documentary evidence, and to seek out and examine witnesses. The judges do not investigate and compile dossiers; rather, it is up to the Prosecutor and his or her assistants to compile the basic evidence supporting an indictment. This tilt toward the adversarial model may have several sources: the precedent of Nuremberg; the fact that the US Department of Justice made a detailed and comprehensive proposal concerning rules of procedure and evidence early on in the process of establishing the Tribunal's structure; and the perception that having judges stand between the parties (rather than being allied with the Prosecution) would help ensure the essential appearance of impartiality, particularly for a court whose cases are politically charged and whose judges, though of many nationalities, are not nationals of the same states as the defendants.

Another significant common law characteristic is the possibility of guilty pleas before the Tribunal. As of the beginning of this year, a total of sixteen defendants have pleaded guilty at the ICTY. I recognize that some observers are hesitant about this resort to plea agreements, in large measure because of the egregious nature of the crimes charged and because of the Tribunal's role in providing vindication for victims and contributing to the creation of an accurate record of terrible atrocities. This hesitancy regarding plea agreements is understandable and legitimate. Yet I believe that plea agreements can play a constructive role when defendants offer genuine expressions of remorse and properly detailed acknowledgment of their participation in the crimes for which they admit guilt.

In some cases, a forthright and specific acknowledgment of guilt may offer victims as much consolation as, or perhaps even more than, a conviction following repeated protestations of innocence. As a practical matter, the cooperation secured through plea agreements can also play an important role in securing convictions of more important participants in large-scale crimes. Moreover, the time and resources saved by avoiding trials in some cases contribute significantly to the Tribunal's ability to meet the deadlines indicated by the Security Council for the completion of its work and enable those in detention to have their cases heard more quickly. Guilty pleas may also bring to the victims a faster sense of vindication or justice.

Of course, plea agreements are not binding on the Tribunal, although in most cases the sentence pronounced by the Trial Chamber follows the range stipulated in the plea agreement. In the recent case of *Momir Nikolić*, the Trial Chamber found that egregious circumstances required a sentence of twenty-seven years, even though the Prosecutor recommended a range of fifteen to twenty years pursuant to the plea agreement.[3] Similarly, in the case of *Dragan Nikolić* the Trial Chamber pronounced a sentence of twenty-three years, despite the joint recommendation of the Prosecutor and the Defense for a sentence of fifteen

---

[3] *Prosecutor v Momir Nikolić* (Sentencing Judgement) IT-02-60/1-S (2 December 2003).

years.[4] In such cases, the convicted person may, of course, appeal—which both defendants in these cases have done. Their appeals are now pending before the Appeals Chamber.

If the Tribunal bears many characteristics of common law courts, civil law contributions are evident as well. First of all, the fact-finders are judges, not lay jurors. And although judges play a more passive role than do those, for example, in civil law countries, they take a more active part, particularly in examining witnesses, than do judges in criminal trials in common law jurisdictions. In the realm of appeals, where I work, the most striking civil law element is the provision for appeals by the Prosecution on equal terms with the Defense. In common law jurisdictions, the Prosecution's right to appeal is normally tightly circumscribed, and the Prosecution often cannot appeal factual determinations at all.

Although the first version of the Tribunal's Rules of Procedure and Evidence, adopted in February 1994, revealed a very strong common law influence, the extensive amendments since then show that the Rules have taken increasing guidance from the civil law system. With the aim of combining fairness and expeditiousness, the Tribunal's proceedings are now less adversarial in character, with the judges moving away from being the mere arbiters of trial proceedings, to playing a more active, managerial role in the judicial process. The change is affecting all phases of proceedings before the Tribunal and represents, in my view, an improvement over the Tribunal's rather exclusive reliance on common law sources during its early years.

I can offer a few examples from the pre-trial, trial, and appeal phases of a case where the civil law influence is apparent. In July 1998, Rule 65 *ter* established the functions of a pre-trial judge, whose role has only expanded since then. Today, the pre-trial judge coordinates communications between the parties during the pre-trial phase of a case, convening status conferences on a regular basis under Rule 65 *bis*. He or she ensures that proceedings are not unduly delayed and takes any measures necessary to prepare the case for a fair and expeditious trial. Such measures include ordering the parties to meet to discuss issues related to the preparation of the case; recording points of agreement and disagreement on matters of law and fact; and constituting files to be submitted to the Trial Chamber, including by compiling the list of witnesses called to testify (together with the facts to which they will testify), the corresponding points in the indictment, the estimated length of time required for each witness, and

---

[4] *Prosecutor v Dragan Nikolić* (Sentencing Judgement) IT-94-2-S (18 December 2003).

the anticipated length of the parties' cases. A similar procedure exists in the Appeals Chamber, where a pre-appeal judge convenes status conferences that allow persons in custody to raise issues in relation to the appeal proceedings and also enables the pre-appeal judge to monitor the status of the appeal and raise related issues with the parties, as needed.

The role of the trial judge has also changed considerably over time. In light of the documents received from the pre-trial judge, the Trial Chamber may determine the number of witnesses the Prosecutor may call and the time available to the Prosecutor for the presentation of evidence, sometimes requesting that the Prosecutor shorten the examination-in-chief for some witnesses. The Trial Chamber may intervene in a like manner in relation to the Defense case during the pre-defense conference under Rule 73 *ter*. Furthermore, pursuant to an amendment of July 2003, Rule 73 *bis* now allows the Trial Chamber to limit the Prosecution's evidence to a number of crime sites or incidents that are reasonably representative of the crimes charged.

The area where the blending of common law and civil law attributes is arguably most interesting is in the Tribunal's rules of evidence. Perhaps because our fact-finders are professional judges rather than lay jurors and perhaps because of the difficulties of collecting evidence of war crimes from a region still torn by bitter social and political divisions, our rules of evidence are quite liberal and not overly technical. In these respects, I think they draw more heavily on the civil law than on the common law model. The rules expressly provide that the Tribunal's judges are not bound by any national rules of evidence and, in Rule 89(C), that a Chamber 'may admit any relevant evidence which it deems to have probative value'. Thus, our rules do not incorporate the elaborate law of hearsay familiar in common law jurisdictions.

Along these same lines, Rule 92 *bis*, initially adopted in December 2000, allows a Trial Chamber to admit, in lieu of oral testimony, evidence of a witness in the form of a written statement. Such evidence may be used to prove the matter asserted in the testimony, so long as it is not an act or conduct of the accused as charged in the indictment. The Rule provides guidance for the Trial Chamber regarding the factors for and against admitting such evidence: namely, that the person making the statement must declare that its contents are true and correct, and that the declaration must be witnessed by an authorized person. The Trial Chamber may nonetheless require the witness to appear for cross-examination.

The Appeals Chamber also recently held, in an appeal in the *Milošević* case, that a Trial Chamber may permit a party to admit a written statement and forgo the examination-in-chief if the witness is present in court, available for cross-examination and questioning by judges, and attests that the statement accurately reflects the testimony he or she would give if examined.[5] The Trial Chamber may adopt this approach provided that it determines that this procedure would be in the interest of justice. Thus, while there are restrictions on the admission of evidence through written statements, they are much looser than those of many common law systems.

Still, the judges of the Tribunal have built at least some aspects of the common law world's hearsay concerns into the Rules. Rule 89(D) authorizes—but does not require—Chambers to 'exclude evidence if its probative value is substantially outweighed by the need to ensure a fair trial'. Under the rubric of that Rule, the ICTY's Appeals Chamber has instructed the Trial Chambers to consider the hearsay character of evidence as one factor possibly threatening the fairness of trials and, thus, a factor to be balanced against the evidence's probative value.[6]

If the roles of the parties suggest that our trial processes and procedures draw heavily on the common law adversarial model, our rules of evidence thus show a more complex mix and a greater indebtedness to civil law exemplars.

෦෯

A fifth interesting challenge facing the Tribunal is the task of construing the contours of a defendant's right to self-representation.

Two prominent accused currently being tried by the Tribunal have chosen to represent themselves. I refer to former President Slobodan Milošević and to Vojislav Šešelj, the leader of the Serbian Radical Party. Article 21 of the Tribunal's Statute, which enumerates the rights of the accused, provides that the accused shall be entitled 'to defend himself in person'. The Trial Chamber in the *Milošević* case has relied on this provision to reject, at least for the time being, the Prosecution's request to impose a counsel on Milošević.[7] Instead, the Trial Chamber appointed three lawyers as *amici curiae*, and instructed them to take any steps they

---

[5] *Prosecutor v Slobodan Milošević* (Decision on Interlocutory Appeal on the Admissibility of Evidence-in-Chief in the Form of Written Statements) IT-02-54-AR73.4 (30 September 2003).

[6] *Prosecutor v Dario Kordić and Mario Čerkez* (Decision on Appeal Regarding Statement of a Deceased Witness) IT-95-14/2-AR73.5 (21 July 2000).

[7] *Prosecutor v Slobodan Milošević* (Reasons for Decision on the Prosecution Motion Concerning Assignment of Counsel) IT-02-54-T (4 April 2003).

consider appropriate to secure a fair trial for the accused.[8] Pursuant to this mandate, the *amici* in the *Milošević* case have been filing briefs with the Trial Chamber and participating in the status conferences and questioning of the witnesses. The Trial Chamber in the *Šešelj* case took a somewhat different approach, appointing not an *amicus curiae* but a standby counsel.[9] The standby counsel may assist the accused in the preparation of his case when the accused so requests, but may not deprive the accused of the right to defend himself.

The issue of what steps a standby counsel is permitted to take will, I expect, continue to confront the judges of the Tribunal. Only recently, for example, the Appeals Chamber was faced with a question of whether the *amici curiae* in the *Milošević* case could bring an interlocutory appeal from a decision of the Trial Chamber.[10] The Appeals Chamber decided to hear the appeal, noting the close alignment of the *amici*'s arguments with those of the accused and the fact that the consideration of the appeal would further the interest of justice. This was not done without a dissent, and not without leaving open some questions as to how this issue will be handled in the future.

ය෴ා

A sixth live concern for our Tribunal is the problem of creating a coherent sentencing scheme, with sentences that reflect the gravity of the crimes committed without foreclosing the chance of rehabilitation.

Contrary to the practice of several countries, our Tribunal does not have a strictly defined sentencing regime or sentencing guidelines. The Tribunal's Statute provides only very general guidance on the issue. Article 24 of the Statute, which addresses the penalties the Tribunal may impose, states that the Trial Chambers shall 'take into account such factors as the gravity of the offence and the individual circumstances of the convicted person'. The Article directs the Trial Chambers to consider 'the general practice regarding prison sentences in the courts of the former Yugoslavia', but stops short of mandating an adoption of the region's sentencing regimes.

---

[8] *Prosecutor v Slobodan Milošević* (Order Inviting Designation of *Amicus Curiae*) IT-99-37-PT (30 August 2001).
[9] *Prosecutor v Vojislav Šešelj* (Decision on Prosecution's Motion for Order Appointing Counsel to Assist Vojislav Šešelj with his Defence) IT-03-67-PT (9 May 2003).
[10] *Prosecutor v Slobodan Milošević* (Decision on the Interlocutory Appeal by the *Amici Curiae* Against the Trial Chamber Order Concerning the Presentation and Preparation of the Defence Case) IT-02-54-AR73.6 (20 January 2004).

The Tribunal has taken a number of steps to study the problem, and to address the challenge of creating a well-structured sentencing regime. I have recently charged a working group of judges of the Tribunal to study our sentencing practices and to recommend ways to increase their fairness. Along similar lines, Trial Chamber II commissioned the Max Planck Institute for Foreign and International Criminal Law to conduct a study of the comparative law and practice of sentencing. This report, which was completed in October last year (and updated the following month), surveyed the sentencing regimes of the states of the former Yugoslavia, member states of the Council of Europe, and other major legal systems of the world. Trial Chamber II relied on the report in its recent sentencing judgment in the case of *Dragan Nikolić*, who is one of the accused I mentioned who pled guilty but received a higher sentence than the Prosecution had recommended. I expect that the Max Planck report, and similar expert studies, will further assist our Tribunal in fashioning a harmonious sentencing regime.

❧

The first institutional challenge I discussed concerned the Tribunal's birth. The last I would like to mention concerns its eventual demise.

Unlike the International Criminal Court, which is intended to be a permanent body, the ICTY is an ad hoc tribunal that was never intended to live forever. The Security Council has urged the Tribunal to conclude all trials by 2008 and all appeals by 2010. Given those deadlines, clearly the ICTY will only be able to take up the cases of a tiny fraction of those who committed war crimes during the Yugoslav conflict. Arrangements must be made for the orderly and fair prosecution of the many small-scale war criminals still at large in the region of the former Yugoslavia. I say 'small-scale', but by that I mean small as measured largely by the number of the victims, not by the gravity of the crime, which often involves murder, torture, rape, or other forms of terrible violence. Given the bitterness of the ethnic and political divisions that remain in the former Yugoslavia, establishing courts that are both effective and free from ethnic and religious bias presents an enormous challenge.

Some progress has been made on this front through the establishment of courts in the UN-administered areas of Kosovo. These courts, whose prosecutors and judges are a mix of local and foreign lawyers, have overseen a number of trials in the last few years. Even more recently, through the joint efforts of the Tribunal and the Office of the High Representative for Bosnia and Herzegovina, plans have been adopted for the establishment in Sarajevo of a special War Crimes Chamber within the State Court of Bosnia and Herzegovina. The War Crimes Chamber project was recently endorsed by a resolution of the UN Security Council. Initially, at least, this Chamber will consist of both local and foreign prosecutors and judges. How the financial support, the human talent, and the political will necessary to make these courts effective over the long run can be brought together is one of the principal projects I am working on now with representatives of the international community.

I look forward to the day when domestic war crimes trials that meet international human rights standards can be conducted throughout the region of the former Yugoslavia. One thing must be clear, however: once indictments have been submitted and confirmed by the judges of the ICTY, the legal process will have started and must run its course, in accordance with the governing law and the demands of due process. A strict application of the target dates for the completion strategy must not result in impunity, particularly for the most senior leaders suspected of being most responsible for the crimes within the Tribunal's jurisdiction. Nor should the approach of completion deadlines lead to a diminution in respect to the rights of the accused to a fair trial and to present a full defense.

⋙⋘

I have tried to review with you some of the challenges that the ICTY has faced, and some of the tentative solutions we have reached, as we have worked to create a fair and effective criminal court. I am sure that we have made some errors along the way. I am equally sure that we will continue to do our best to ensure that the cases that come before us are heard carefully and impartially.

By laying bare the consequences of ethnic and religious hatred, the trials held by the Tribunal have demonstrated the viciousness of those who built their power by encouraging their followers to embrace such hatred. The Tribunal has thus made a fundamental and lasting contribution to bringing justice to the peoples of the former Yugoslavia. And it is my belief that our jurisprudence will supply a foundation for all international criminal courts and tribunals and a model for national prosecutions of those who commit atrocities for years to come.

12

STATEMENT TO THE UN SECURITY COUNCIL*

Mr President, Excellencies: It is always a great honor for me to take the floor before the Council. That is more than ever the case today since it is the French presidency that is guiding the Council's work.

Mr President, your country has left a profound imprint on the history of democracy and is considered to be the homeland of human rights. As President of the International Criminal Tribunal for the former Yugoslavia, I believe that it is my duty to emphasize that France has also actively helped in setting up and developing the Tribunal and has played a key role in combating impunity.

Mr President, as the representative of a country that uses civil law, you are, of course, aware of the gradual development of our rules of procedure, in keeping with an ongoing concern to improve the effectiveness of our procedures without sacrificing the imperative need to safeguard the right of defense. Those changes have, in particular, transformed the role of judge from that of a neutral arbiter, as it is under common law, to that of a real participant in the procedure, both at the pre-trial preparation stage and during the trial itself. During the discussions which preceded and accompanied that development, French law and judicial practice were often a source of inspiration.

Mr President, it is with honor and pleasure that I address the Security Council as President of the International Tribunal for the former Yugoslavia under your presidency. Your country has been a steadfast supporter of the Tribunal, and that, Mr President, is very much appreciated.

This is the third report that I have presented to the Council since the adoption of Resolution 1534 in 2004, which requested the President and

---

* Delivered at the UN Security Council, UN Headquarters, New York City, New York, USA, on 13 June 2005.

Prosecutor of each ad hoc Tribunal to provide the Council with assessments every six months detailing the progress made towards the realization of their respective completion strategies. The written report is now before the Council in document S/2005/343.[1] Through both the narrative and the annexes, it is intended to provide the Council with a realistic picture of how the Yugoslavia Tribunal is grappling with the challenge of meeting the goals of the completion strategy. I shall try, in my oral statement, not to repeat the details of the report, but rather to highlight its salient features and to provide the Council with an update of the information provided therein.

Since the last report, submitted in November 2004, the Tribunal's three Trial Chambers and one Appeals Chamber have been working at maximum capacity, with the Trial Chambers handling six cases simultaneously. This means that, on average, six different cases are being tried by different benches of three judges each. The written report indicates that two judgments have been issued since the last report and predicts that, by the end of this November, four additional judgments will have been issued in cases involving an additional seven accused persons. That means, of course, that by the end of this year another batch of four cases will begin. The pace is unrelenting.

The new report also highlights the fact that twenty-two new accused persons have arrived at The Hague since the last full report was issued, meaning that there are now 50 percent more people awaiting trial than there were the last time I appeared before the Council. Obviously, that dramatic increase has significant implications for the completion strategy.

With those critical preliminaries out of the way, allow me to survey the major features of the report, and, in particular, to emphasize the relevant updates contained therein.

With regard to internal measures taken to implement the strategy, we have adopted significant amendments to our Rules of Procedure and Evidence, including one relating to judgment of acquittal—namely, Rule 98 *bis*—which mandates oral rather than written submissions. I am happy to report that this amendment has already had a salutary effect on speeding up our procedures to a few days or a few very short weeks, without sacrificing defendants' due process rights. Before the amendment,

---

[1] UNSC, 'Letter dated 25 May 2005 from the President of the International Tribunal for the Prosecution of Persons Responsible for Serious Violations of International Humanitarian Law Committed in the Territory of the Former Yugoslavia since 1991, addressed to the President of the Security Council' (2005) UN Doc S/2005/343, Annex I.

Rule 98 *bis* proceedings would likely have taken up several months of the Trial Chambers' time.

I have also appointed two working groups of judges for speeding up trials and appeals. The working group on trials, which is chaired by Judge Bonomy, has been exploring ways to speed up trials by, among other alternatives, finding additional courtroom space and streamlining our pre-trial and trial procedures. Those modalities were the subject of an in-depth and wide-ranging discussion among all the judges just a week ago.

The working group on speeding up appeals, which is chaired by Judge Mumba, has focused on the rules governing the admissibility of additional evidence at the appeals stage as well as on the procedures for translating decisions and judgments for appellants, which can have a major impact on the timely disposition of appeals. By the time the plenary of judges meets in July, I expect that both working groups will have presented concrete and actionable recommendations.

Turning now to *ad litem* judges, Mr President, I very much appreciate the adoption by the Council of Resolution 1597 (2005), which amended the Statute of the Tribunal to allow for the re-nomination and re-election of *ad litem* judges. Nonetheless, I am very concerned about the lack of a sufficient number of nominations. This has significantly delayed the election of a sorely needed new roster of *ad litem* judges. For new trials to be assigned to panels of judges without delay, it is absolutely imperative that the President have at his disposal a roster of distinguished jurists who are willing and able to serve the Tribunal, often on quite short notice, at this critical juncture. I appeal to all states that have not yet submitted nominations to nominate experienced jurists for that important position. It provides a unique opportunity for individuals to make a difference in advancing the cause of international justice.

I now come to a key component of the completion strategy, namely, the referral of cases involving intermediate and lower-rank accused persons to competent national jurisdictions. I should particularly like to highlight the opening of the War Crimes Chamber of the State Court of Bosnia and Herzegovina on 9 March 2005. After much time and effort devoted to making that event a reality—efforts in which I and my colleagues have been deeply involved—the Sarajevo War Crimes Chamber is now in a position to accept cases that the Tribunal's Referral Bench may decide to refer to the authorities of Bosnia and Herzegovina. The government and people of Bosnia and Herzegovina, the High Representative, donor governments, and the international community as a whole have made this possible, and the Tribunal and its staff are pleased to have been central to this endeavor.

The report notes that, so far, the Prosecutor has filed ten motions involving eighteen accused for such referrals under Rule 11 *bis* of our Rules of Procedure and Evidence. In enclosure V to the report, members of the Council will see that, of those ten motions, the Referral Bench has granted the motion in one case, referring the case to Bosnia and Herzegovina for proceedings before the Sarajevo War Crimes Chamber. However, that transfer must await the disposition by the Appeals Chamber of filed appeals. The Council will note that the Referral Bench has already held hearings in six other cases, involving thirteen accused persons. Future decisions on the Prosecutor's motions to refer cases to competent national jurisdictions are therefore expected in the very near future. In addition, as the Prosecutor points out in her assessments, she is considering filing additional Rule 11 *bis* motions for referral.

As for the cooperation of states in the region with the Tribunal, as I have already indicated, there has been a dramatic increase in the number of indictees and fugitives transferred to the Tribunal, mostly thanks to the efforts of the authorities of Serbia and Montenegro, sometimes together with the authorities of Republika Srpska. The impact of those new arrivals will be addressed later in my statement.

With regard to Croatia, while cooperation remains good in some areas, it is of major concern that the last remaining stumbling block to achieving full cooperation with the Tribunal is the continuing failure on the part of authorities in Croatia to apprehend Ante Gotovina and render him to The Hague.[2]

Concerning Republika Srpska, other than assistance with regard to the arrival of some indictees and fugitives, cooperation remains lacking in other areas, in particular with regard to the lack of any serious attempts to locate and arrest such notorious fugitives as Radovan Karadžić and Ratko Mladić.[3]

Cooperation has improved with Serbia and Montenegro with regard to the arrival of indictees and fugitives. During a meeting and in-depth discussion with Prime Minister Koštunica of Serbia and President Tadić of Serbia this March, I strongly encouraged them both to ensure the arrival of the remaining fugitives thought to be in Serbia and Montenegro or Republika Srpska. The largest impediment on that front is the continuing failure to apprehend and render to The Hague Ratko Mladić.

---

[2] Editor's note: Ante Gotovina was arrested and transferred to the ICTY in December 2005. His trial commenced in March 2008.

[3] Editor's note: Radovan Karadžić was arrested and transferred to the ICTY in July 2008. His trial commenced in October 2009.

Allow me to add, Mr President, that it goes without saying that when and if these three principal fugitives move across borders to avoid apprehension and arrest, the obligation to pursue and arrest them applies in full to the authorities of their temporary *séjour*. This also highlights the need for governments in the region to redouble their efforts to ensure judicial cooperation between their own authorities. I have consistently maintained that if the voluntary surrender of accused war criminals is not forthcoming, the international obligation of the states of the region is to arrest and transfer the accused without delay.

Distinguished members of the Council, as I have said many times, the Tribunal will not have fulfilled its historic mission—and it will not close its doors—until Karadžić, Mladić, and Gotovina have been arrested, brought to The Hague, and tried before the Tribunal in accordance with the full procedural protections recognized by our jurisprudence.

I now turn to the updated prognosis regarding implementation of the completion strategy. In my last assessments, I estimated that, by the end of 2008, the Tribunal could complete the trials of all accused in our custody at that time, including Gotovina if he arrived before 2006, but warned that any further growth of the trial docket would make achieving that target date entirely dependent on some cases being disposed of by guilty pleas. I also added that, if new indictees or fugitives were to arrive and require separate trials, it would become likely to take at least until the end of 2009 to complete the trials of all accused within the custody of the Tribunal.

As is evident from the report before the Council now, some of those factors bearing on the implementation of the strategy have come to pass and others must be addressed. Allow me to take them up one by one.

First, the number of new indictments: as the report indicates, seven new or amended indictments have been submitted since my November report. Five of the indictments will require new, separate trials. For two other cases involving five accused, I understand that the Prosecutor is considering whether to move the joinder of those cases with pre-existing cases.

Second, the number of Rule 11 *bis* motions for transfer granted: as I have mentioned, one of the ten outstanding motions has been granted by the Referral Bench and is currently on appeal. Six others have been the subject of hearings. While it might be anticipated that the Referral Bench will render more decisions by the end of this month, it would be neither possible nor appropriate for me to speculate about the ultimate disposition of those motions.

Third, the number of guilty pleas: on that score, I need only mention that there have been no new guilty pleas since my last report.

Fourth, I wish to refer to the arrival of new indictees and fugitives. With the arrival of twenty-two new indictees or fugitives, our projections must be adjusted, as I warned in my last report to the Council. As of now, we are working on the assumption that at least ten of the new accused will be the subject of seven new, separate trials. (Five trials will involve one individual accused; one will involve two accused; and another, three accused.) Of the remaining twelve accused, the Prosecutor has already moved to join three to a pre-existing case. I understand she is also considering moving the joinder of seven accused to another pre-existing case, which would result in a 'mega case' of eight or nine accused. Finally, two new arrivals are the subject of a Rule 11 *bis* motion for referral to a competent national jurisdiction. I cannot, of course, predict how Trial Chambers will decide on motions for joinder, or, indeed, anticipate the Prosecutor's ultimate decision about whether to move for joinders in the first place.

Turning to the ten fugitives who have still not arrived and the impact on the caseload should they arrive: six of the fugitives are on indictments with co-accused already in custody and therefore new, separate trials for them would not be required. Meanwhile, the Prosecutor is considering the suitability of two others for joinder. And the arrival of Karadžić and Mladić would entail a new, joint trial, provided they arrive more or less contemporaneously. We know that their trial will be lengthy and complex, but it is impossible to know how it will impact the timeline of the overall situation without knowing when they will arrive and when the trial could begin for both the Prosecution and Defense counsel. Obviously, for purposes of planning and enhancing the prospects of the Tribunal's completing its work sooner rather than later, the earlier they have been apprehended and transferred to The Hague, the better.

Fifth, the timing of the arrivals of remaining indictees and fugitives: this factor has a critical influence on the completion strategy, but it simply cannot be predicted with any degree of certainty. While it might be possible to estimate roughly the length of a trial prior to the arrival of an accused, we have to wait until the accused is actually in The Hague to assess a variety of factors—the readiness of both parties to proceed, whether joinder is possible, and the availability of courtrooms and judges to hear the case.

Sixth, the disposition of joinder motions: as I indicated earlier, the Trial Chambers are seized of several motions by the Prosecutor for joinder of cases, and she is considering filing further such motions.

Decisions are expected soon on the pending motions. If such motions are granted, there could be trials of up to eight or nine accused. Of course, such joinders are not a panacea, as additional time would be required to dispose of a given case, but they would clearly save time when compared to having separate trials for each of the accused. As my report indicates, I welcome any such major time-saving tactic that is consistent with due process and the rights of the accused.[4]

Mr President, allow me to mention another matter of importance. While the arrival of indictees and fugitives obviously complicates our completion strategy timetable, it goes without saying that the arrival of alleged war criminals can only be applauded. Persons accused of having committed war crimes must be brought to justice and cannot be allowed to hide, hoping that the Tribunal will close its doors before they are found and arrested. The arrival of such a substantial number of accused moves the Tribunal further towards the fulfillment of its mandate: prosecuting those accused of committing major war crimes in the former Yugoslavia.

Coming to the current estimate, I should preface my remarks with a cautionary word: any estimates are necessarily tentative, since they can only be based on assumptions subject to unpredictable factors. I could indicate, for instance, that if all possible Rule 11 *bis* motions are granted, if all possible motions for joinder are granted, if no new fugitives arrive, and if no guilty pleas are entered, the Tribunal could complete its current caseload some time in 2009. But all of those 'ifs' indicate that these estimates are based on assumptions that evolving reality will modify.

For example, if the Tribunal's three most notorious fugitives—Karadžić, Mladić, and Gotovina—are arrested in the near future, their cases would extend the time necessary to complete trials by an additional four to seven months, given the possible joinders. As a purely independent matter, if half of the pending and anticipated Rule 11 *bis* motions are denied, the trial completion date would slip an estimated nine months. Further, if one of the large joinder motions—the so-called mega cases—is denied, it could add another three months to the time required to try them all.

---

[4] Editor's note: Upon delivering a statement to the UN Security Council in 2004, Judge Meron emphasized that: 'We must be careful to ensure that our dedication to completing the Tribunal's mandate on time does not detract from the Tribunal's basic purposes, which are to administer justice even-handedly and to contribute to the restoration and maintenance of peace in the region. To depart from the Tribunal's mission to try those most responsible for alleged violations of international humanitarian law risks undermining the Security Council's decision to establish the Tribunal and does a disservice to the cause of international justice. A rigid and mechanistic pursuit of the completion strategy should be avoided, as it would lead to the espousal of trials that fall short of the guarantees of international human rights of which the United Nations is—and should be—protective and proud.' UNSC, '4999th Meeting' (29 June 2004) UN Doc S/PV.4999, 8.

Any combination of other contingencies—health-related trial interruptions, guilty pleas, *et cetera*—could also alter the outcome.

Knowing what we know now, the most that I can indicate is that trials will necessarily have to be conducted in 2009 and that they will most likely continue until the end of that year. When the next six-month report is presented, the President of the Tribunal should be able to provide an assessment that is based on more factual predictions. It is hoped that by next November, current and possible Rule 11 *bis* and joinder motions will have been disposed of. Arrivals of additional indictees will provide more data on the caseload and target dates. In addition, the judges will have considered recommendations for speeding up both trials and appeals.

Before concluding, I should like to raise another matter mentioned in my report: the possibility of adding a fourth courtroom. Such an additional courtroom would be very advantageous in my view and would make it possible for us to speed up trials and appeals. The report indicates the advantages to be derived from adding a fourth courtroom. Advantages would arise whether we maintain the existing six trials a day or—even more—if it were decided to allow three additional *ad litem* judges to serve so that a seventh trial bench could be established to help deal with the backlog. I wish to stress that I would not request that the cost of constructing such a courtroom be borne by the United Nations budget, but would rather approach possible donor countries which would see the long-term advantage of expediting trials and appeals through increased courtroom capacity.

This is a matter that we have just begun to explore, and no doubt the President of the Tribunal will return to the Council to discuss this subject once the possibilities have become clearer. We would welcome any comments that members of the Council might have regarding the matter and will count, as always, on the guidance and leadership of the Council as we pursue this question.

Before I conclude, Mr President, let me allude to the approaching tenth anniversary of an atrocity that, in its character and magnitude, was reminiscent of those committed during the Second World War. This July will mark ten years since the atrocities—the genocide—at Srebrenica. Let me quote the following from the 19 April 2004 *Krstić* Appeals Chamber judgment:

> By seeking to eliminate a part of the Bosnian Muslims, the Bosnian Serb forces committed genocide. They targeted for extinction the forty thousand Bosnian Muslims living in Srebrenica, a group which was emblematic of the Bosnian

Muslims in general. They stripped all the male Muslim prisoners, military and civilian, elderly and young, of their personal belongings and identification, and deliberately and methodically killed them solely on the basis of their identity. The Bosnian Serb forces were aware, when they embarked on this genocidal venture, that the harm they caused would continue to plague the Bosnian Muslims. The Appeals Chamber states unequivocally that the law condemns, in appropriate terms, the deep and lasting injury inflicted, and calls the massacre at Srebrenica by its proper name: genocide. Those responsible will bear this stigma, and it will serve as a warning to those who may in future contemplate the commission of such a heinous act.[5]

As we approach that commemoration, it is worth emphasizing that it is to the Security Council that the international community, the public, and, especially, the victims of atrocities turn for leadership and justice for the redress of atrocities. The Tribunal is one manifestation of the Council's commitment to international justice, the rule of law, and the struggle against impunity, as well as to peace and reconciliation. We are there to carry out the mission that the Council entrusted to us.

We commit ourselves to redouble our efforts to see that justice is done for victims and accused alike, that due process is honored, and that accused war criminals are not treated with impunity, but rather are afforded a fair trial. With the support of the members of the Council, I am confident that we can succeed in our difficult task in the remaining years of our mandate.

Mr President, I would now like to conclude by making some remarks in my personal capacity. Over the years, the Security Council has played a critical role by using its power and prestige to resist impunity, to establish individual criminal responsibility for perpetrators of atrocities, and to impose sanctions on those who violate human rights and humanitarian norms. The Council's decisions, taken under Chapter VII, to establish the ad hoc Tribunals in 1993 and 1994—half a century after Nuremberg—were seminal moments. They led not only to the trial and punishment of senior figures responsible for atrocities in the Balkans and Rwanda, but also to the creation of a whole new corpus of jurisprudence on international criminal law, procedure, and evidence—a body of law that will be the historic legacy of the ad hoc Tribunals. Of course, much remains to be done to combat impunity outside of the areas covered by the jurisdiction of the ad hoc Tribunals. The Council has the power and the responsibility to do all it can to advance those goals.

---

[5] *Prosecutor v Radislav Krstić* (Judgement) IT-98-33-A (19 April 2004), para 37.

I see the Council's referral under Chapter VII of the situation in Darfur to the International Criminal Court as a critical next step in the historic evolution of the anti-impunity principle. The referral underscores the world community's resolute commitment to the principle that the perpetrators of such crimes against humanity will be held to account. It also demonstrates the potential of Chapter VII and its beneficial uses in advancing accountability in all parts of the world. Speaking as a scholar of international humanitarian law, I congratulate the Council on its wise action this spring.

Finally, in mid-November, my presidency of the ICTY will come to an end and I will continue as an Appeals Chamber judge. This is thus my last appearance before the Council as Tribunal President. May I take this opportunity to express to you, Mr President, and to all the other members of the Council my deep gratitude for your steady support of the Tribunal and of international justice, and for the help you have generously given me in the performance of my duties.

13

DOES INTERNATIONAL CRIMINAL JUSTICE WORK? (ALEC ROCHE ANNUAL LECTURE IN PUBLIC INTERNATIONAL LAW)*

I. INTRODUCTORY REMARKS

As you have just heard, I serve as a judge and hear appeals on two international criminal courts: the International Criminal Tribunal for the former Yugoslavia, known as the ICTY, and the International Criminal Tribunal for Rwanda, known as the ICTR. I thus have strong incentives to tell you that the answer to the question 'Does international criminal justice work?' is 'Yes,' or at worst 'Yes, but...'. And I may well do so at the end. I am giving this talk strictly in my personal capacity, however, and in preparing it I have tried to put aside my biases and critically evaluate the system to which I belong.

This has not been an entirely comforting enterprise. Much as I would like to think that our system of international criminal justice works, and works well, the answer is much more mixed. While in some ways this system works very well indeed, in other ways it works poorly, or not at all. In still other ways, we lack a foundation for doing more than speculating, sometimes wistfully, on its effects.

II. THE RECENT EXPANSION OF INTERNATIONAL CRIMINAL JUSTICE

Before elaborating on these points, however, I wish to make a more fundamental one. It is noteworthy, and remarkable, that today we are

---

* Delivered as the Alec Roche Annual Lecture in Public International Law at the University of Oxford, Oxford, United Kingdom, on 7 November 2007.

asking questions like 'Does international criminal justice work?'. Twenty years ago, we would not have asked this question—we would have asked instead 'Will there ever be another international criminal tribunal?' or, in pessimistic moments, 'Is there such a thing as international criminal justice?'. This is because, twenty years ago, international criminal justice was largely a memory of Nuremberg. To understand where we are today—and to address the question posed in this lecture—we must consider the radical transformation that has since occurred.

Although today we take the International Military Tribunal at Nuremberg for granted, in its time it was, in the words of US Prosecutor Robert Jackson, both 'novel and experimental'.[1] It consciously broke from the approach taken at the end of World War I, when the prosecution of war crimes was left to the defeated nations with the result that very few individuals were tried and even fewer received meaningful punishments. Instead of leaving prosecutions to the defeated Germany after World War II, the Allied Powers therefore set up their own tribunal, composed of judges and prosecutors from the United Kingdom, the United States, France, and Russia, to try top Nazi leaders. In its single, year-long trial, the International Military Tribunal heard evidence in relation to a mind-boggling number of issues: from the planning and waging of aggressive war, to the deportation, forced labor, persecution, and annihilation of the Jewish people; to the atrocities committed against civilians and soldiers of the occupied countries; to the plunder of these occupied countries and crimes against culture; and to the inhumane treatment of prisoners of war. Ultimately, the International Military Tribunal convicted several organizations such as the SS and the Gestapo and nineteen of twenty-two individual defendants, with sentences for these individuals ranging from ten years in prison to death.[2] Three individual defendants were acquitted.

Of course, this was not all that the International Military Tribunal did. In the course of the trial and in the resulting judgment, it also developed and clarified many important issues of substantive law—especially crimes against humanity, with its citizen-to-citizen criminal liability. In addition, it also had to resolve differences between how the civil law courts of Continental Europe and the common law courts of the United States and Britain operate. Relatedly, the International Military Tribunal had to grapple with what due process rights defendants should receive—and

---

[1] Opening speech by Justice Robert H Jackson, Chief Prosecutor for the United States of America, in *The Trial of German Major War Criminals by the International Military Tribunal Sitting at Nuremberg Germany: Opening Speeches of the Chief Prosecutors* (Buffalo: William S Hein & Co, 2001) (Opening Statement), 3.

[2] International Military Tribunal (Nuremberg), 'Judgment and Sentences' (1947) 41 *AJIL* 172.

did a reasonable job in this regard, albeit one that was somewhat rudimentary by today's standards. Unlike the parallel Tokyo trials conducted by the International Military Tribunal for the Far East, the Nuremberg trial thus provided reassurance that there is some justice to victors' justice. It has generally been judged a success.

After the International Military Tribunal closed its doors in the fall of 1946, there were further trials conducted by individual Allied powers, particularly the United States, within their own zones of occupation in Germany. But there were no more international criminal tribunals. The enforcement of substantive international criminal law became very much a country-by-country affair rather than a matter for the international community more broadly. Although not framed or even intended this way, there was something of a compromise in the international community with regard to international criminal justice. The substance of international criminal law was able to develop through powerful and important treaties, including the Genocide Convention of 1948, the 1949 Geneva Conventions for the protection of victims of war, and the two Additional Protocols to the Geneva Conventions that were adopted in 1977. The *enforcement* of international criminal law at an international level, however, went nowhere. While there were calls as early as 1948 for the establishment of an international criminal court, the great powers seemed remarkably content to let the issue stall in committees.

This is why I say that, twenty years ago, international criminal justice was primarily a memory of Nuremberg—at least so far as its international practice was concerned. Back then, I do not think that even the most fervent advocates for the creation of international criminal tribunals could have predicted the explosion of courts that has since happened. Today we have the ICTY, the ICTR, and of course the International Criminal Court, or ICC. We also have several so-called hybrid courts and increased emphasis on the domestic prosecution of international war crimes. International criminal law is unquestionably the most dynamic branch of international law today.

How did this happen? How did we get from a dream of Nuremberg to a world where international criminal tribunals seem to be part of the international community's response to every conflict-related crisis that it addresses?

The establishment of the ICTY was crucial in this regard. The ethnically charged conflict in the former Yugoslavia sent shocks rippling through Europe, where nothing like it had occurred since World War II. At the same time, the political dynamics that followed the breakdown of the Soviet Union had loosened the Security Council, at least temporarily, from its traditional stand-off. As one of the modest measures it put in place in response to the conflict—and at the urging of NGOs and academic commentators—the Security Council established the ICTY in 1993. The ICTY has jurisdiction over genocide, war crimes, and crimes against humanity (which collectively I shall refer to as international crimes) that were committed in the former Yugoslavia from 1991 onwards.

In short, fourteen years ago, the Security Council gambled that the answer to the question 'Does international criminal justice work?' was 'Yes'. The gamble, admittedly, was a sensible one. At best, the ICTY would help bring justice, and possibly peace, to the region. At worst, the ICTY would simply be ineffective. This would lead to costs in terms of money and prestige, but these costs would be mitigated by the temporary and experimental nature of the Tribunal. And however it turned out, the ICTY could be considered a test case for an international criminal court.

This gamble was repeated in 1994 with the establishment of the ICTR. It would have been awkward, to say the least, for the Security Council to set up a tribunal in relation to a European conflict, but not to do the same with regard to the genocide in African Rwanda.

By 1998, it was clear that both the ICTY and ICTR were functioning institutions, although they had neither conducted many trials nor, in the case of the ICTY, gained custody over any particularly high-level indictees. Since then, however, international pressure has resulted in the arrival at The Hague of many senior accused. Despite slowness and expense, the Tribunal now conducts simultaneously seven trials of twenty-six persons, a situation inconceivable fifteen years ago.

The experiences of the ad hoc Tribunals may have helped encourage the renewed push for an international criminal court, which culminated in the Rome Statute in 1998. The ICC was officially established in July 2002, following the sixtieth ratification of the Rome Statute, and it is now beginning to find its feet.

In the last few years, the international community has also been experimenting with hybrid courts, namely, the Special Court for Sierra Leone, the Cambodia tribunal, and the proposed Lebanon tribunal.[3] These hybrids use a mix of domestic and international law and personnel. They either have jurisdiction over certain international or domestic crimes that occurred before the ICC came into effect or, as in the case

---

[3] Editor's note: The Special Tribunal for Lebanon began functioning on 1 March 2009.

of the Lebanon tribunal, over particular crimes that do not fall within the category of crimes over which the ICC can exercise jurisdiction.

Finally, there is increased emphasis on domestic prosecution of international war crimes, as exemplified by the domestic trials now underway in the states of the former Yugoslavia and in Rwanda, and, from time to time, in other countries under legislation reflecting the principle of universality of jurisdiction.

The establishment of the ICC created a mantra that the international community is tired of ad hoc criminal tribunals, which are, it has been argued, expensive, slow, and selective. The assumption was that the ICC would be less costly, more effective, and practically universal. It is not obvious, however, that these hopes about the ICC have not been rather rosy and that the ad hoc international criminal tribunals have had their day. States appreciate the work and the jurisprudence of the ad hoc and special tribunals. The jury is still out on the workload and the efficiency of the ICC.

This is where the practice of international criminal justice stands today. Now, for the question: does it work?

III. MEASURING SUCCESS

To address this question, I will set forth and evaluate four criteria: how successful we are in finding and trying suspected perpetrators of international crimes; the extent to which we are providing these accused a fair trial; whether and how we are deterring further international crimes; and whether and how effectively our actions are promoting peace and healing in the affected region.

A. Finding and trying alleged perpetrators

The first of my criteria—the most basic one—is the extent to which we are apprehending and trying the suspected perpetrators of international crimes.

On this front, international criminal justice works fitfully. I will begin with the problems. First, there are whole swathes of the world that remain out of the jurisdiction of any international criminal tribunal—including the United States, Russia, China, India, Indonesia, Pakistan, and most of the rest of Asia, the Middle East, and North Africa. In these countries, which account for over 70 percent of the world's population and are not state parties to the ICC, no international court has jurisdiction over international crimes committed by citizens of these countries on their soil. This means that to have an international institution with competence over the subject and the party concerned, it may be necessary to establish ad hoc international or hybrid tribunals in the future to coexist with the ICC. Short of a new international or hybrid tribunal, and setting aside the possibility of the exercise of jurisdiction by the courts of other states, such as through the principle of universal jurisdiction, we can rely only on these countries' own domestic courts for the enforcement of international criminal justice.

Sometimes, of course, the domestic courts do act. For example, the United States does a reasonable job of prosecuting rank-and-file members of its military who commit international crimes. Interestingly, one argument often brought in support of the American refusal to ratify the Rome Statute is precisely that US personnel suspected of having committed war crimes are already held accountable and tried before US courts-martial and that there is therefore no deficit of justice compelling the United States to enter the jurisdiction of the ICC. And despite the critiques made by many human rights defenders about the failure of the US military justice system to seriously investigate the responsibility of high-ranking military and security personnel for planning and implementing a policy of mistreatment of detainees in the 'War on Terror', some recent rulings rendered by US court-martials seem to indicate that an appreciable degree of progress has been achieved in the manner in which the United States is fulfilling its obligation to prosecute and punish perpetrators of the so-called grave breaches of the Geneva Conventions.

As some of you will remember, in the early seventies, the massacre of hundreds of civilians by US servicemen in the Vietnamese village of My Lai had resulted in only one conviction, that of 2nd Lt William Calley,[4] who eventually served only three and half years under a regime of house arrest. By contrast, a 2007 Kentucky court-martial has sentenced three US service members to sentences ranging from ninety years to 110 years of imprisonment for their participation in the rape and murder of a 14-year-old Iraqi girl and the murder of her entire family.[5] A fourth soldier is expected to be tried before a US federal court in the next few months and could face the death penalty for his alleged participation in the same crimes.[6]

More often than not, however, there is little domestic prosecution when international crimes are committed by members or affiliates of

---

[4] *United States v Calley* 46 CMR 1131 (1973).
[5] See Paul von Zielbauer, 'GI Gets 110 Years for Rape and Killing in Iraq' *The New York Times* (5 August 2007).
[6] See Associated Press, '110-year sentence in Iraq rape-killing' *USA Today* (5 August 2007).

the government in power, whether in the United States or elsewhere. With regard to Chechnya, the European Court of Human Rights recently observed that 'no meaningful result whatsoever has been achieved in the task of identifying and prosecuting the individuals who had committed the crimes' and that 'the astonishing ineffectiveness of the prosecuting authorities in this case can only be qualified as acquiescence in the events'.[7]

Similarly, the prosecutions in Indonesia with regard to international crimes committed by Indonesian forces in East Timor were, perhaps, as *pro forma* as were the German domestic prosecutions that followed World War I. A UN Commission of Experts report in 2005 observed that of the ten people charged with crimes against humanity, only one was convicted. And in the United States, I am not very confident that there have been real improvements in prosecuting persons involved in sanctioned, rather than rogue, operations. Nor is it clear whether the interrogation methods designed to extract security information from suspects have been significantly improved and whether personnel using authorized methods in conflict with the Geneva Conventions have been prosecuted.

Even where an international criminal tribunal has jurisdiction, it lacks police powers and it is entirely dependent on the cooperation of sovereign states. We thus have no certainty that indicted individuals will be apprehended and brought to trial.

Particularly in its early years, the ICTY had enormous difficulties getting Balkan governments to help apprehend indicted individuals. Although Radovan Karadžić and Ratko Mladić still remain at large, the situation is somewhat better now.[8] While NATO and UN forces were sometimes helpful in apprehending those indicted, their contribution was limited and uneven, depending in part on vagaries of mandate, leadership, and political will. After a change of government in Serbia in 2001, the ICTY managed to gain custody over Slobodan Milošević and other important leaders. Similarly, following significant incentives held out by the United States and, particularly, Europe to Croatia, the Croatian authorities assisted in the apprehension of former Croatian General Ante Gotovina in 2005.

The ICTR had fewer initial difficulties in apprehending suspects because of the change of regime in Rwanda. The Tutsi-led government has

---

[7] *Musayev and others v Russia* (App nos 57941/00, 58699/00, and 60403/00) ECHR (Judgment of 26 July 2007), para 164.

[8] Editor's note: Radovan Karadžić was arrested and transferred to the ICTY in July 2008. His trial commenced in October 2009.

unsurprisingly been quite willing to do what it can to help the ICTR prosecute prominent Hutu leaders accused of taking part in the genocide against the Tutsis. But the ICTR Prosecutor has not yet indicted any members of the RPF—the army associated with the Tutsis—and it is unclear whether cooperation from Rwanda would prove forthcoming were this to happen.

The ICC is also experiencing difficulties in apprehending suspects. Of the eight individuals for whom arrest warrants have been issued since the establishment of the ICC, only two have been apprehended. With regard to the other six, state cooperation is either unavailing or unforthcoming. While the government of Uganda would undoubtedly like to help the ICC gain custody over the five rebel leaders with regard to whom arrest warrants have been issued, it does not have the power to provide such help. Indeed, these rebel leaders have stated that the withdrawal of the ICC indictments is a necessary condition of any peace settlements they might consider. As to the other two indicted individuals, one is a Sudanese government official and the other is a Janjaweed militia leader with connections to the Sudanese government. Both are charged in relation to the conflict in Darfur. Since the ICC's jurisdiction over the Darfur situation comes from a referral by the Security Council—rather than through consent by Sudan—it has been particularly hard for the ICC to obtain cooperation from Sudan.

These difficulties in apprehending suspects often mean that trials occur years after the atrocities, if at all. In regard to these timing issues, I note that the recently established Cambodia tribunal, which is just beginning its first trial, deals with crimes that stem from the Khmer Rouge regime of the 1970s. Most of the Khmer Rouge genocidaires have died in the meantime with impunity. And few witnesses are still around and able to testify in the trials that are finally starting. With regard to the people of Cambodia, justice delayed is, for the most part, justice denied, although it is entirely possible that the tribunal will be able to indict and try a very limited number of leaders.

Each trial before an international criminal tribunal also takes enormous time and resources. Excluding guilty pleas, ICTY trials have lasted between six months and several years from the opening of trial to the delivery of judgment—and this excludes the often substantial time spent at the pre-trial phase and on appeal. Although the length of these trials has been criticized, I think that, realistically, international criminal trials will usually be long ones. Typically, they involve multiple crimes, committed over long periods of time and in many localities. They involve the travel of witnesses and translations of voluminous documents. In this regard, I note that while the mandate at the Special Court for Sierra Leone included a strong emphasis on efficiency, the shortest trial there has lasted over two years. Similarly, the ICC trial of a Congolese warlord charged with child recruitment is finally beginning after a few years of preparation. I note that the ICC budget is only slightly below that of the ICTY despite the tremendous difference in the caseload.

As a result, the number of suspects who can be tried is small. To date, the ICTY has completed proceedings involving 109 individuals out of the 161 who have been charged, and there are another fifty-two individuals whose cases remain pending at some stage before it. At the ICTR, the trials and appeals of twenty-seven individuals have been completed, and there are another fifty-nine individuals whose cases are at some stage of the pre-apprehension, pre-trial, trial, or appeal process. In large part, these trials involve top leaders or those who have committed particularly horrific crimes.

The reach of international criminal justice thus remains limited due to a number of different factors. Now, what can be counted on the positive side of the ledger? For one thing, we have succeeded in bringing a substantial number of high-level suspects in the former Yugoslavia and in Rwanda to justice. The experiences of the ICTY and ICTR have shown that where the international community provides sufficient resources and political support for tribunals, and where states, the European Union, the United Nations, and NGOs encourage or pressure recalcitrant but susceptible states to hand over suspects, we achieve results.

For another thing, we have increased domestic prosecution for international crimes, whether undertaken *sua sponte* or under pressure from the international community. The experiences of the ICTR and, particularly, the ICTY show us the importance of international encouragement and support for domestic prosecutions. In the former Yugoslavia, such cases have helped achieve and demonstrate governmental recognition of crimes committed by the government's own side in the conflict. The recent trial and conviction in Serbia of Serb paramilitary members who were video-taped killing Bosnian Muslim men in 1995 is an example of this. In this respect, I would also point towards the establishment—upon the initiative and with the support of the ICTY—of the special War Crimes Chamber in the State Court of Bosnia and Herzegovina, composed of both international and national judges and prosecutors. This court, which tries individuals under the national laws of Bosnia and Herzegovina, has become an important model for locally oriented rule of law projects in the Balkans.

The advantages of these internationally supported local courts in areas emerging from conflict are manifold. On a mundane level, they are less expensive and logistically complex than employing legions of international personnel who need translation of most evidence at locations which are often distant from witnesses and documents—the paradigm of many international criminal tribunals. In addition, these types of local courts serve as excellent training grounds for local judicial personnel and considerably simplify outreach and educational efforts through their location and, often, the language in which they take place.

Given the limited capacity of international criminal courts, it is reassuring that there is a significant trend to individual states' enforcing international law by holding accountable those who serve as accomplices to regimes that commit atrocities. The robust position taken by Belgium in this respect is well known. But also in The Netherlands, a Dutch businessman accused of selling raw materials for mustard gas to Saddam Hussein, used in the attacks against the Kurdish civilian population in mid-1980s, was sentenced at trial to no less than fifteen years' imprisonment for complicity in war crimes.[9]

B. Fair trial

My second criterion for measuring success is the extent to which we are giving a fair trial to the suspected perpetrators of international crimes. We do not want to create individual accountability for international humanitarian law at the expense of international human rights law.

A fair trial requires not only the application of advanced due process norms to the assessment of allegations involving genocide, crimes against humanity, and war crimes, but also the existence, at the time the offenses are committed, of substantive and detailed norms of international criminal law that satisfy the principle of legality and the prohibition of retroactive penal legislation. The Statutes of the ICC and the ad hoc Tribunals, together with customary norms which fill the interstices of the *lex scripta*, provide such a corpus of international criminal law. Additionally, the hundreds of decisions of the ad hoc Tribunals, on both substantive and procedural/evidentiary issues, demonstrate that war crimes law is finally coming of age.

With regard to this criterion, I believe that international criminal tribunals are doing very well indeed. We have certainly improved upon the protections available at Nuremberg. To give one example, I mentioned that there were three acquittals at Nuremberg—but I did not tell

---

[9] District Court of The Hague, Index No AU8685 (23 December 2005).

you that there was no provision protecting acquitted individuals from being tried again for the same crimes. These three men were seized and tried again by a German court. This cannot happen today. The guarantees now accorded to defendants in the foundational statutes of international criminal tribunals and in the case law are substantial, and the transparency with which international tribunals act provides a further safeguard.

The record is much more mixed in domestic fora trying individuals for international crimes. The proceedings—or lack of proceedings—with regard to the men held at Guantánamo Bay have rightly triggered international concerns. Concerns also exist with regard to the domestic court proceedings undertaken in Rwanda and the former Yugoslavia. I have just described these proceedings as an important complement to the work of the ICTR and ICTY, but they must be done fairly. This has not always proved the case. In an October 2004 report, for example, Human Rights Watch described troubling instances of anti-Serb bias in Croatian courts—including at least one decision where, in the course of convicting a defendant of Serb ethnicity for certain crimes, the court made reference to the prior five centuries in which 'the accused and his ancestors... were coming and destroying Croats'.[10] I should note that a retrial was ordered in this case. I will further say that with the recent establishment of a specialized War Crimes Chamber in Sarajevo—established and funded largely with assistance from the international community—we may hope for a fairer future. In Rwanda, which has undertaken domestic proceedings both through ordinary courts and through what are known as traditional gacaca courts, some commentators have expressed concern about the treatment of detainees and about the degree to which the proceedings respect international human rights law.

C. *Deterring international crimes*

My last two criteria have to do with the broader role of international criminal justice in promoting peace and healing—or at least in promoting the strictly lawful conduct of hostilities. This broader role is important to consider, not simply for its own sake but because international criminal justice is an expensive proposition. Since the ICTY began operating, the United Nations has budgeted a total of about $1.25 billion for it, with a budget of approximately $140 million for 2007 alone. The ICTR has cost somewhat less. While these expenses pale in comparison to, say, what

---

[10] Human Rights Watch, 'Justice at Risk: War Crimes Trials in Croatia, Bosnia and Herzegovina, and Serbia and Montenegro' (13 October 2004), 10 (internal quotation marks omitted).

NATO countries spent on the conflict in Kosovo—about $1.5 billion per month at its height, by one account—they make up a large chunk of the UN budget. In 2007, the combined budget for the ICTY and ICTR was about 14 percent of the regular UN budget. The ICC, which is funded by contributions from the 105 state parties, had a budget of about $114 million in 2006, even before trials have started. These costs are not that enormous when compared with the £60 million or so spent on the Lockerbie trial. Yet one can legitimately question whether these costs are worth it if the only benefit of international criminal justice is retribution.

So my third criterion is the extent to which international criminal justice deters the commission of international crimes. Unfortunately, there is very little hard evidence on this front. We do have a plethora of sweeping and anecdotal statements and guesses. The preamble to the Rome Statute speaks of state parties '[d]etermined to put an end to impunity for the perpetrators of [international] crimes and thus to contribute to the prevention of such crimes'.[11] Similar pronouncements exist with regard to the ICTY and ICTR. Nonetheless, I do have doubts about whether specific awareness of the existence of international criminal tribunals with jurisdiction will deter fanatical and genocidal leaders from committing international crimes. In this regard, I note that the genocide at Srebrenica occurred in 1995. The existence of the fledgling ICTY, established in 1993, plainly did not deter it. Perhaps, however, the fear of prosecutions is a bit more real now. Only the future will tell.

Then there is the question of generalized deterrence through norm-changing. I will not discuss this at length, but the basic idea is that the international criminal tribunals contribute to a culture in which humanitarian law and human rights law are better ingrained in the fabric of society and therefore adhered to more. At Nuremberg, Jackson referenced something along these lines in his opening remarks, when he told the International Military Tribunal that:

I am too well aware of the weaknesses of juridical action alone to contend that in itself your decision under this Charter can prevent future wars … But the ultimate step in avoiding periodic wars, which are inevitable in a system of international lawlessness, is to make statesmen responsible to law.[12]

In this regard, high hopes are pinned on the future of the ICC. Unfortunately, the two successful arrests in the Democratic Republic of Congo

---

[11] Emphasis omitted.
[12] Opening Statement, n 1 above, 45.

have made no dent in the continuing fighting and atrocities in that country.

Even today, however, the universe of the ICC and the ad hoc Tribunals creates a culture in which governments find it more and more difficult to openly tolerate impunity. In particular, armed forces the world over have taken note of the fact that those who bear the greatest responsibility for violations of international humanitarian law are increasingly facing justice. It is very difficult to establish a direct causal link between the verdicts of international criminal tribunals and increased respect for international humanitarian law. Nonetheless, I believe there is a correlation between the founding and work of the various international criminal tribunals in the 1990s and early 2000s and the increased attention given to international humanitarian law by armed forces. Western military forces certainly pay increased attention to the concept. For example, in a number of recent conflicts many military commanders both publicly accepted the importance of humanitarian law and engaged large teams of legal professionals to vet issues like targets and tactics. Complaints by military professionals about the 'excessive' restrictions on their freedom of action placed by lawyers is strong proof of the increased role that international humanitarian law plays in determining the tactics of such armed conflicts. This progress does not mean that armed forces, including those of western nations, have stopped violating international humanitarian law, but the increased attention and monitoring likely reduces the number and severity of violations, to very real effect.

D. *Promoting peace and healing*

My fourth criterion is the extent to which international criminal justice helps bring healing to the region at issue. There has been no shortage of expectations on this front. In establishing the ICTY in Resolution 827, for instance, the Security Council stated that it was:

Convinced that in the particular circumstances of the former Yugoslavia the establishment as an ad hoc measure by the Council of an international tribunal and the prosecution of persons responsible for serious violations of international humanitarian law... would contribute to the restoration and maintenance of peace....[13]

Once again, it is difficult to measure quantitatively whether and to what extent international criminal tribunals have had a positive influence on the establishment of regional peace. We can, however, try to draw some

---

[13] UNSC Res 827 (25 May 1993) UN Doc S/RES/827.

conclusions on this front from the experiences of the ICTY, the ICTR, and the ICC to date.

At the most basic level, these tribunals can contribute to regional peace by providing an internationally reputable mechanism for the removal of abusive leaders. Peace and ethnic harmony in the former Yugoslavia becomes much more of a possibility with removal from the region of the senior leadership suspected of international crimes against members of other ethnicities. Many commentators have made the point that the removal of Karadžić from power and his indictment was essential for the implementation of the Dayton agreements. The indictment of Charles Taylor had a similarly positive effect.

But there is a flipside to this point, which is that peace may also become *more* difficult to achieve if leaders know that they will face international criminal prosecutions once the hostilities are over. I have mentioned that the five Ugandan rebel leaders for whom the ICC has issued arrest warrants have suggested that they are willing to negotiate a peace settlement if granted immunity. Incidentally, I think the ICC is correct in refusing to grant such immunity. This is not to say that these considerations could have no part to play at the investigative stage—but once an arrest warrant has issued, the ICC should pursue its mission of justice unless directed otherwise by the Security Council.

So, while international criminal tribunals may make peace settlements initially more difficult, once a tenuous regional stability has been established they can further this stability by removing past alleged bad actors from the scene. What else can they do for regional peace and stability? A common claim is that in the course of holding wrongdoers accountable, international criminal tribunals break the cycle of vengeance and allow people to start moving forward. Again, it is hard to assess whether this happens in fact and, if so, on what timetable or scale. Moreover, as I have mentioned before, international criminal tribunals can bring only a small percentage of suspected perpetrators of international crimes to justice and, at least in the case of the ICTY and ICTR, they do so at locations removed from the region when the crimes occurred. This distance may diminish the value of international criminal tribunals and the resonance of their decisions to residents of the regions in question. A UN Development Program survey undertaken in Bosnia in June 2005 showed that while 60 percent of respondents thought the ICTY had done a good job, the majority of these same respondents thought that the ICTY was not necessary.

In order to have a stronger connection to the region, and thus to have a stronger likelihood of promoting regional healing, the ICTY has undertaken outreach efforts since 1999 to educate the people of the former Yugoslavia about its mission and accomplishments. The Special Court for Sierra Leone, which has the advantage of conducting three of its four trials in Sierra Leone itself, has likewise undertaken an outreach program—one which a UN independent expert deemed 'exceedingly effective' and 'exemplary'.[14] Among its outreach efforts have been joint projects with the International Committee of the Red Cross on explaining the role and importance of international humanitarian law, and activities stemming from this partnership have included the production of illustrated booklets providing visual representations of basic international humanitarian law tenets for the estimated 65 percent of Sierra Leone's population who are illiterate. Such culturally appropriate explanations provide a useful, comprehensible distillation of the principles that Sierra Leoneans can see being applied in the trials taking place at the Special Court. And with regard to both the former Yugoslavia and Rwanda, I have already mentioned the efforts to support and strengthen fair prosecutions of international crimes in the domestic justice systems. In my view, these efforts are essential if international criminal tribunals are to have any medium-term effect on promoting regional peace.

It will be interesting to see the extent to which the ICC can undertake similar efforts. While the ICC has an outreach program, the broader scope of its activities as compared with those of the ad hoc Tribunals will necessarily diminish the intensity with which outreach can be directed at any one community—at least in the absence of outside funding. Similarly, while the ICC must work to some extent with domestic courts in light of the principle of complementarity, it is unclear whether it or the international community will offer the same level of support to domestic courts that has accrued to those in the former Yugoslavia and in Rwanda. And although the wide geographic range of the ICC makes it the most likely of any international criminal tribunal to effect generalized deterrence through norm-changing, this same attribute may make it the least likely international criminal tribunal to further peace and healing in a particular region.

In short, while we have theories and some indications of how international criminal justice can best contribute to peace and healing, I believe we have a long way to go before we can speak with certainty on this issue. In this regard, I will briefly note that further assessment is needed with regard to the effectiveness of other mechanisms, such as truth and

---

[14] Antonio Cassese, 'Report on the Special Court for Sierra Leone, Submitted by the Independent Expert' (12 December 2006), para 30.

reconciliation commissions, or TRCs, and how such mechanisms can complement or conflict with the mechanism of international criminal justice. These types of mechanisms are very flexible and can be tailored to address specific situations much more readily and creatively than court procedures can. They are also able to engage in intensive educational activities, historical investigations, and traditional rituals of shaming and forgiveness without violating complicated procedural rules that typically bind national and international courts.

Before alternative transitional justice mechanisms operate alongside courts, however, it is important to set clear guidelines concerning the interactions of these different institutions. To date, the record of cooperation between courts of law and TRCs has been decidedly mixed. In Sierra Leone, for example, relations between the Special Court and the Sierra Leone TRC were notoriously poor, even though the two organizations operated only a few hundred meters from each other. Among other conflicts, stringent procedural rules at the Special Court interfered with the TRC's desire to elicit personal testimony from high-profile detainees.

However, I do not believe that this type of destructive relationship is preordained by any means. In South Africa, for example, the ability to grant amnesty from prosecutions gave the TRC more muscular powers of persuasion and added to public interest in its hearings. South Africa's case demonstrates the potential of court and non-court mechanisms to support rather than undermine each other. Particularly useful in encouraging such cooperation is a common legislative framework that unites different transitional justice institutions. These could also address complicated issues such as how evidence will be preserved for eventual use by courts in a way that does not render it 'contaminated'. Such an overarching legislative framework may be easier to implement for institutions such as the War Crimes Chamber of Bosnia and Herzegovina and other national courts than for international criminal tribunals.

IV. MOVING FORWARD

EM Forster famously gave two cheers for democracy: 'one because it admits variety and two because it permits criticism'.[15] He felt that it did not deserve three.

I too would give two cheers out of three to international criminal justice today. One cheer is for the fact that we have well-developed

---

[15] EM Forster, 'What I Believe', in *Two Cheers for Democracy* (New York: Harcourt Brace, 1951), 79.

standards under the statutes of international criminal courts and tribunals and under customary international law for what constitutes an international crime. This is no small feat. International conferences such as those that adopted the Additional Protocols to the Geneva Conventions could not reach agreement on a broad application of international humanitarian law to non-international armed conflicts. Yet following the ICTY's 1995 *Tadić* decision,[16] just such a broad application of these norms was accepted almost overnight. This development was later recognized in the ICC Statute and, surprisingly perhaps, is not even questioned by many of the governments that opposed a more expansive role for the Additional Protocols to the Geneva Conventions.

The second cheer is for the developments of the last twenty years—the increased commitment of the international community to international criminal justice, the concomitant rise of international criminal tribunals, and the rapid development of a corpus of substantive and procedural criminal law—which have demonstrated that international prosecution and trial are both feasible and credible.

I withhold the remaining cheer because large swathes of the world remain outside the reach of effective and timely international criminal justice and because we have a long way to go in demonstrating and strengthening the link between international criminal justice and either peace or, at the very least, the strictly lawful conduct of hostilities.

Now, how can we achieve the remaining cheer? I believe the answers are evident for the most part, and the challenge lies in implementing them. First, we must continue the good work that is ongoing. There must be sufficient international funding for existing international criminal tribunals, including the ICC, and there must be renewed emphasis on outreach. Where the ICC has issued arrest warrants, international pressure must be brought to bear to promote the apprehension of suspects and, more generally, to promote the cessation of international crimes. There must also be concomitant efforts to fund and strengthen domestic prosecutions in the countries treated as situations by the ICC—and monitoring by international institutions must be done to ensure that these prosecutions are free of partisan bias and fair.

Next, we must get more states on board. We must do what we can to make sure that the countries that are not state parties to the Rome Statute either join the ICC or take adequate steps domestically to promote the fair administration of international criminal justice. We must stress that

---

[16] *Prosecutor v Duško Tadić* (Decision on the Defence Motion for Interlocutory Appeal on Jurisdiction) IT-94-1-AR72 (2 October 1995).

international criminal justice is an apolitical issue of worldwide concern. Efforts by NGOs and committed states will be essential in this regard—particularly where the UN Security Council cannot take action due to one or more veto-wielding permanent members. And there are many small steps that would further a worldwide concept of international criminal justice. I, myself, would like to see a 'Top International Crime Suspects List' developed by reputable NGOs that uses objective criteria, such as the number and type of attributed atrocities, to identify top international suspects around the world.

Finally, with regard to the links between international criminal justice and peace, I doubt that any certain answers will emerge until much more time has passed since the recent resurgence of international criminal tribunals and the emergence of the broader international commitment to international criminal justice. The variety of tribunals and contexts in which they are deployed will hopefully provide fertile ground for comparisons and lessons to be learned.

In closing, I remind you of the words of Antarctic explorer Sir Ernest Shackleton—that 'optimism is true moral courage'. I strongly feel that, for all our recent achievements, continued—positive—change is possible. As Forster noted in the essay I just mentioned, the human spirit must snatch its opportunity while the going is good. Of course, we have a long way to go before we may claim an end to impunity for international crimes. But we have come a long way too, due to dedication and hard work, and the road before us lies clearly ahead.

14

THE ROLE OF THE ICC: ACCOUNTABILITY, PEACE, AND JUSTICE*

Today, I would like to focus on how the ICC should deal with the peace vs justice controversy, using the Uganda situation as an example to illustrate the challenges faced by the ICC as it seeks to end impunity and ensure accountability for 'the most serious crimes of concern to the international community as a whole'.[1] I hope to use this discussion to reflect on how the ICC can address these difficult issues, while retaining the integrity and credibility that are essential to any court of law.

I. THE PEACE VS JUSTICE CONTROVERSY

Let me begin by contextualizing the challenges that the ICC is facing within the context of the so-called peace vs justice controversy, which has had its roots in the expansion of international criminal law since the Nuremberg trials.

After World War I the prosecution of war crimes had been left to the defeated nations—with the result that very few individuals were tried and even fewer received meaningful punishments. The International Military Tribunal at Nuremberg consciously broke from this approach. Following in the tradition of Nuremberg, in 1993 the Security Council established the ICTY, which has jurisdiction over international crimes—genocide, war crimes, and crimes against humanity—that were committed in the former Yugoslavia from 1991 onward. This was followed, a year later, with the establishment of the ICTR, which has jurisdiction over international crimes committed in Rwanda in 1994.

---

* Delivered in Santorini, Greece, in July 2008.

[1] Rome Statute of the International Criminal Court (1998) 2187 UNTS 90 (Rome Statute), preamble.

This increasing preoccupation with ending impunity for the most serious crimes known to humanity highlighted the need for a permanent international criminal court, leading to the creation of the ICC. Today, we also have hybrid tribunals, namely, the Special Court for Sierra Leone, the Cambodia tribunal, the special War Crimes Chamber of the State Court of Bosnia Herzegovina, and the new Lebanon tribunal. Finally, there is also a greater emphasis on the domestic prosecution of international war crimes.

This increased focus on accountability has led some to claim that there is a divergence between international criminal lawyers' goal of ending impunity and conflict mediators' goal of resolving conflicts as quickly as possible. This is often referred to as the 'peace vs justice' controversy. Some argue that when achieving peace requires negotiating with the very people who are responsible for international crimes, insisting on prosecuting those people can prolong the conflict, resulting in further bloodshed. Others argue that there can be no true peace without accountability for these crimes.

I, myself, believe that the dichotomy between peace and justice is, in most cases, false. Justice is an essential element of peace and reconciliation. As Kofi Annan rightly said, 'there can be no healing without peace; there can be no peace without justice; and there can be no justice without respect for human rights and the rule of law'.[2]

Still, the tension between peace and justice can, in some situations, raise very difficult dilemmas for a court. For example, some people strongly criticized the ICTY Prosecutor's decision to issue indictments against Radovan Karadžić and Ratko Mladić—two Bosnian Serb leaders—while peace negotiations were ongoing. But many commentators believe these indictments actually helped make the Dayton Agreement possible. The existence of the ICC may also make peace more likely in some cases, by drawing increased international attention to a conflict and by acting as a deterrent to the warring parties.

Nevertheless, it is true that the ICC is likely to have to deal with the peace vs justice controversy more directly than the other international tribunals. Because it is a permanent court, the ICC's rulings may have an effect on the events on the ground—unlike some tribunals (such as the Cambodia tribunal) which were created after the conflicts ended. Already,

---

[2] UN Secretary-General, Press release, 'Secretary-General Welcomes Rwanda Tribunal's Genocide Judgment as Landmark in International Criminal Law' (2 September 1998) UN Doc SG/SM/6687L/2896.

all four situations before the ICC involve ongoing conflicts of varying degrees.

In particular, the ICC may have to address the legal effect of amnesties on its proceedings. Much of the peace vs justice debate has focused on the legality of using amnesties to persuade warring parties to sign a peace agreement. Of course, not all amnesties are problematic—in fact, to promote the ending of hostilities and peace-making, the Second Additional Protocol to the Geneva Conventions encourages amnesties wherever possible. The kind of amnesty that could raise problems for the ICC is the blanket amnesty that covers the very same international crimes over which the ICC has jurisdiction. Would such an amnesty prevent the ICC from investigating or prosecuting a case?

As yet, it remains unclear how the ICC will resolve this issue. The Rome Statute does not provide clear guidance for the Prosecutor or the Chambers. Some of the Statute's drafters believed that an amnesty similar to the one adopted in South Africa (where amnesty was only available following full disclosure to the Truth and Reconciliation Commission) would preclude admissibility. It is clear, however, that the legality of blanket amnesties is now highly contested.

In the context of the Lomé Peace Agreement in Sierra Leone, in 1999, for instance, the UN Secretary-General made it clear that the United Nations will not recognize amnesties for 'genocide, crimes against humanity, war crimes, and other serious violations of international humanitarian law'.[3] Later, in the *Kallon and Kamara* case, the Special Court for Sierra Leone found that the Lomé amnesty did not preclude its jurisdiction.[4] Other international courts have also expressed disapproval of amnesties for international crimes, including the ICTY in the *Furundžija* case[5] and the Inter-American Court of Human Rights in the *Barrios Altos* case.[6] State practice also appears to be moving away from blanket amnesties; for example, the Goma agreement, signed in the DRC on 23 January 2008 between the Congolese government and a number of rebel groups, provides for an amnesty law that explicitly does not cover war crimes, crimes against humanity, and genocide.

---

[3] UNSC, 'Report of the Secretary-General on the establishment of a Special Court for Sierra Leone' (4 October 2000), UN Doc S/2000/915, para 23.

[4] *Prosecutor v Morris Kallon and Brima Bazzy Kamara* (Decision on Challenge to Jurisdiction: Lomé Accord Amnesty) SCSL-2004-15-AR72(E) and SCSL-2004-16-AR72(E) (13 March 2004).

[5] *Prosecutor v Anto Furundžija* (Judgement) IT-95-17/1-T (10 December 1998).

[6] *Case of Barrios Altos et al. v Peru* (Judgment (Interpretation of the Judgment on the Merits)) Inter-American Court of Human Rights Series C No 83 (3 September 2001).

It is not only the ICC Chambers that will have to address the challenges raised by the peace vs justice controversy, nor are grants of amnesty the only context in which the ICC will confront the tensions of peace vs justice. The Prosecutor will also have to consider this dilemma in the exercise of his prosecutorial discretion.

Under the terms of the Rome Statute, the Prosecutor can decide not to prosecute in a given case if it 'is not in the interests of justice'.[7] The Prosecutor has made it clear that, once the requirements of jurisdiction and admissibility have been satisfied, he will only exercise his discretion not to prosecute in very 'exceptional' cases because the object and purpose of the Rome Statute create a presumption in favor of prosecution.[8] Still, as the Prosecutor has also acknowledged, the concept of the 'interests of justice' requires him to consider, in particular, the 'interests of victims'.[9] At first glance, it might appear obvious that victims have an interest in seeing justice done. But, in fact, in some cases, victims might prioritize peace over justice.

How both the Chambers and the Prosecutor will grapple with these difficult issues remains to be seen. Already, the Uganda case has raised some of these dilemmas very starkly. So, let me contextualize this as-yet abstract discussion of peace and justice by focusing in more detail on the Uganda case.

II. THE ICC AND THE UGANDA SITUATION

As you all know, in 2003, the government of Uganda referred crimes allegedly committed by the Lord's Resistance Army (or the LRA) to the ICC. The LRA has waged a notoriously bloody conflict in Northern Uganda for over twenty years in which countless human rights violations were committed. Consistent with the Rome Statute, the Prosecutor correctly construed the referral as requiring consideration of the entire situation in Northern Uganda—and thus of the conduct of all parties to the conflict, including the government.

In 2005, the ICC issued indictments and arrest warrants against five senior commanders of the LRA, including its leader, Joseph Kony. Although one of these warrants was withdrawn last summer following the death of the accused, the other four suspects remain at large.

---

[7] Rome Statute, n 1 above, art 53(2)(c).
[8] ICC Office of the Prosecutor, 'Policy Paper on the Interests of Justice' (September 2007) (Policy Paper), 3.
[9] Ibid., 5–6.

Initially, it appeared that the ICC warrants had a positive effect on the peace process, by pushing the LRA to resume the stalled peace talks. Since then, however, Kony has insisted that he will not sign a final peace agreement unless the ICC warrants are lifted. So, although the government and the LRA agreed on the text of a final peace agreement earlier this year, Kony has refused to sign it. In both April and May, he did not show up to the planned signing ceremonies.

For the moment, therefore, the peace negotiations appear to have stalled. Nevertheless, the peace process raised interesting peace vs justice issues for the ICC that are likely to resurface if negotiations resume and that are also likely to arise in other situations before the Court.

Indeed, during the peace negotiations, the government of Uganda began to speak of prioritizing ending the bloody conflict as quickly as possible, over supporting the ICC prosecutions. In March 2008, with the LRA insisting on scrapping the ICC indictments, the president of Uganda suggested that the rebel leaders should instead be allowed to atone through traditional justice methods. As a result, if peace negotiations resume, the government of Uganda may consent to provisions in the final peace agreement that effectively clash with the ICC indictments.

It is not difficult to imagine that other states with cases before the ICC might face a similar peace vs justice dilemma. It is therefore instructive to consider the challenges raised by the Uganda case in more depth, both on their own merits and as instructive guidance for future situations. How the ICC resolves these challenges will have a lasting impact on the young Court's credibility and its ability to play a real role in ending impunity for serious crimes.

III. HOW THE ICC SHOULD DEAL WITH THE PEACE VS JUSTICE CONTROVERSY IN THE UGANDA CASE

President Museveni of Uganda once stated that if the LRA leaders surrendered, he would withdraw the ICC referral. Clearly, this is not possible: there are no provisions under the Rome Statute for a state to withdraw a referral. Still, if the peace process resumes, there are three possible ways that the ICC may choose or be compelled to address the impact of its involvement on the peace process in Uganda.

First, Uganda could challenge admissibility under Articles 17 and 19 of the Rome Statute. Second, Uganda could request the Security Council to intervene and suspend proceedings under Article 16. Both of these options appear to be contemplated in the text of the most recent draft peace agreement. Finally, the Prosecutor himself could decide to suspend the case 'in the interests of justice' under Article 53. I want to discuss each of these possibilities and how I think the Court should respond to them in order to preserve its legitimacy and its effectiveness as a court of law.

A. The ICC should subject an admissibility challenge to the highest possible scrutiny

Under Article 17 of the Rome Statute, a case must be deemed inadmissible when a state that has jurisdiction over the case is investigating or prosecuting it—unless that state is unwilling or unable to genuinely investigate or prosecute. This is known as the complementarity principle. It means that national jurisdictions should always get the first shot at trying war criminals. The ICC Prosecutor has emphasized that the Office of the Prosecutor would take a 'positive approach to complementarity' and 'encourage national proceedings wherever possible'.[10]

Complementarity is both the great enabler and the great disabler of the ICC. It is the great enabler because, without granting states jurisdictional primacy in this way, there probably would have been no Rome Statute. It is also the great disabler, however, because it provides a ground for states like Uganda to bring their own national proceedings in order to render a case inadmissible before the ICC.

There are indications that this is exactly what Uganda was contemplating prior to the recent halt in the negotiations. The government and the LRA have signed several limited agreements that directly address the issue of accountability. In particular, on 29 June 2007, they signed an agreement on accountability and reconciliation. This agreement stated that Uganda was capable of addressing the crimes committed during the conflict. Subsequently, on 19 February 2008, the parties signed an annexure to this agreement. It provided both for the establishment of a special division of the High Court of Uganda to try individuals alleged to have committed serious crimes during the conflict and for a possible role for traditional justice mechanisms.

Moreover, under the terms of the draft peace agreement most recently on the negotiating table, the government of Uganda was obliged to urgently take all necessary steps to develop national mechanisms of accountability, to establish the special division of the High Court, and to begin investigations into crimes committed during the conflict. If

---

[10] Statement of the Prosecutor Luis Moreno Ocampo to Diplomatic Corps, The Hague, The Netherlands (12 February 2004), 1, available at <http://www.icc-cpi.int/NR/rdonlyres/0F999F00-A609-4516-A91A-80467BC432D3/143670/LOM_20040212_En.pdf>.

Uganda implements these steps, it could challenge the admissibility of the case currently before the ICC under Articles 17 and 19, arguing that it is investigating or prosecuting these matters, and therefore that the ICC case is inadmissible under the principle of complementarity.

The Court would then have to decide whether the processes established by Uganda amount to 'investigating or prosecuting'.[11] This is not a simple question to answer, especially if the government uses traditional justice methods instead of formal criminal trials. Even if the government uses formal criminal proceedings, the Court would still have to assess whether the government was genuinely 'willing and able' to investigate and prosecute. In particular, the Court would have to decide whether the proceedings were impartial and independent and whether they were initiated simply to shield the accused from a genuine trial before the ICC.

In making these assessments, the Court would have to ask itself the following question: is it a bad thing for these cases to be tried in Uganda instead of before the ICC? The answer, I believe, is: not necessarily. The principle of complementarity embodies the ideal that countries will themselves take direct responsibility for bringing to justice suspected war criminals within their jurisdictions. National prosecutions and trials conducted according to international standards would avoid many of the difficulties encountered with international proceedings conducted far away. They are also likely to resonate better with the victims and the local populations. And, of course, the capacity of international tribunals to prosecute war criminals will always be limited.

In addition, the Uganda situation suggests that the complementarity regime may have a trickle-down effect on domestic legal systems. The complementarity regime appears to motivate states to invest resources in their domestic judicial systems, reforming them to ensure that they are sufficiently independent, impartial, and capable to prevent admissibility before the ICC. This effect can be observed in the terms of the Ugandan peace agreement that I have just discussed.

But I must emphasize that these effects of the complementarity regime are only valuable if the reforms implemented are genuine and not used simply to shield suspected war criminals from real accountability. As a result, the ICC must subject this sort of admissibility challenge to the highest possible scrutiny. It must take into account the level of fear that these indictees induce within Uganda and the gravity and scale of the crimes alleged, which would make national trials politically and financially difficult. It

---

[11] Rome Statute, n 1 above, art 19(2)(b).

must also consider that Uganda has not yet implemented the Rome Statute into its domestic legislation. In fact, a recent study conducted by the Institute for Security Studies in South Africa suggests that only a handful of African states parties have adopted the necessary legislation for implementing the ICC Statute.

On this point, the practice of the ad hoc tribunals may provide the ICC with helpful guidance. In a number of cases, the Chambers of the ICTY have refused the Prosecutor's requests for referral to national jurisdictions.[12] Similarly, the ICTR Appeals Chamber has reversed the referral of a genocide case to Norway because Norway lacked legislation implementing the Genocide Convention.[13]

So, the ICC must carefully scrutinize any admissibility challenge by Uganda. Such careful scrutiny is required in order to ensure that the full benefits of the complementarity regime are achieved. It is also required in order to ensure that the ICC is respected as a court of law and not perceived of as a political tool of governments. Without such careful scrutiny, the ICC runs the risk that it will look as though Uganda manipulated the ICC into serving its political goals: namely, a peace agreement with the LRA. Such a perception would be detrimental for the Court's legitimacy and credibility.

Of course, denying the admissibility challenge and retaining the case would present the Court with new challenges. Primarily, the Court would struggle to gain custody over the suspects without Uganda's cooperation. Like its sister international tribunals, the ICC lacks police powers and is entirely dependent on the cooperation of sovereign states. Although Uganda is required to cooperate with the Court under Article 59 of the Rome Statute, it might prefer to violate its obligations rather than risk the resumption of the conflict that arresting the LRA leaders might entail. So far, in fact, none of the LRA leaders has been arrested. Similarly, neither of the two suspects indicted in the Darfur case has been taken into custody.

Here again, the ICC might draw useful guidance from our experience at the ICTY. Particularly in its early years, the ICTY had enormous difficulties getting some of the Balkan governments to help apprehend indicted individuals. During the lean years of the ICTY, Prosecutor Goldstone compensated for limited judicial activity by relentless use of

---

[12] See, eg, *Prosecutor v Milan Lukić and Sredoje Lukić* (Decision on Milan Lukić's Appeal Regarding Referral) IT-98-32/1-AR11*bis*.1 (11 July 2007).

[13] *Prosecutor v Michel Bagaragaza* (Decision on Rule 11*bis* Appeal) ICTR-05-86-AR11*bis* (30 August 2006).

the media—with considerable success. Today, the situation is much better, as practically all of the indictees have been transferred to The Hague—although, problematically, Karadžić and Mladić still remain at large.[14] Our experience at the ICTY has been that we only succeeded in obtaining the arrest of high level indictees when the international community, including the European Union and the United States, decided to exert intense pressure on the Balkan governments.

I believe that the ICC should take a hard look at these techniques and consider more vigorous, higher profile activities to mobilize support by governments and intergovernmental institutions. In fact, the ICC Prosecutor is already moving in this direction. And, of course, states and international organizations should do more to support the enforcement of the Court's decisions. In a candid statement in November 2007, ICC President Kirsch complained of the 'silence' of states and international organizations and its negative effect on the Court's work.[15]

B. *The Security Council should not defer the proceedings*

I want to move on now to discuss the second way that the government of Uganda might try to prevent the ICC from moving forward with this case. Under Article 16 of the Rome Statute, the Court may not proceed with a prosecution if the Security Council acts under Chapter VII of the UN Charter to request the Court to defer the prosecution for a period of twelve months. The draft peace agreement most recently on the negotiating table required the government of Uganda to request the Security Council to pass just such a resolution.

Of course, the government of Uganda cannot promise to deliver a Chapter VII resolution, and it is unclear whether there is the political will necessary among the state members of the Security Council to support such a resolution. Even if the Council passed such a resolution, it would only be a temporary deferral for twelve months. Although the Council can renew this deferral, it would be necessary for Uganda to build the political will to support such a renewal every year. Such support is unlikely if the LRA violates its obligations under the peace agreement. As a result, this approach might actually provide an incentive for the LRA to respect the peace.

---

[14] Editor's note: Radovan Karadžić was arrested and transferred to the ICTY in July 2008. His trial commenced in October 2009.

[15] UNGA, 'Report of the International Criminal Court' (1 November 2007) UN Doc A/62/PV.42, 25.

At a more general level, deciding whether deferring prosecutions is necessary to ensure peace is primarily a *political* assessment. As a result, the Security Council—as a political body—is better suited to make such a determination than the ICC, which is a court of law and which cannot afford to become politicized. In fact, I believe that the drafters of the Rome Statute included Article 16 not only because of deference to the Security Council in matters pertaining to peace and war, but also because they did not want the Court to become entangled in such assessments. That said, Article 16 sets the bar for deferral deliberately high. And it implicitly suggests, I believe, that investigations or proceedings should not be delayed in the absence of such a resolution.

C. *The Prosecutor should continue to refuse to suspend the investigation*

I will move on now to discuss the third and final way that the ICC could lose jurisdiction over this case.

Article 53(2)(c) allows the Prosecutor to determine that proceeding with a prosecution is not in the 'interests of justice'. In particular, Article 53(2)(c) provides that the Prosecutor may consider the interests of the victims in making this determination.

It appears possible that the Prosecutor could make a determination against proceeding with prosecution even at the current stage of the proceedings in the Ugandan situation. Under Article 53(4): 'The Prosecutor may, *at any time*, reconsider a decision whether to initiate an investigation or prosecution based on new facts or information.'[16] Although Article 53(4) does not explicitly refer to the 'interests of justice' standard, it must be read to include those interests, given the Article's place within the Rome Statute. While such a determination would effectively suspend the prosecution, the arrest warrants for the LRA leaders would remain in effect, under Article 58(4), 'until otherwise ordered by the Court'.

Nevertheless, the Prosecutor has consistently stated (most recently in March 2008) that he will not make this argument. He has made it clear that a Prosecutor's role is 'to apply the law without political considerations'.[17] I entirely support this position. First, it is not clear that suspending prosecution in this case would be in the interests of the victims. While

---

[16] Emphasis added.
[17] Address by Luis Moreno-Ocampo, Prosecutor of the International Criminal Court, at the International Conference on 'Building a Future on Peace *and* Justice' (25 June 2007), 3, available at <http://www.peace-justice-conference.info/download/speech%20moreno.pdf>.

some reports have questioned the victims' desire for prosecutions and found that many Ugandans prefer peace at all costs, even if it means that the LRA leaders will never be tried, it is important to remember that victims are not a single, homogenous group. Some victims have an interest in seeing their perpetrators tried. In fact, a survey conducted by the International Center for Transitional Justice and the Human Rights Center in 2005 found that 91 percent of Ugandans who were interviewed believed that prosecutions before the ICC would contribute to peace.

Moreover, it is not clear that achieving peace at all costs is necessarily conducive to building a durable peace in the long term. Accountability helps to weaken the culture of impunity that characterizes most conflicts and that often fuels conflicts in the first place. Without accountability, impunity reigns unchecked, undermining both justice and peace.

Above all, I want to emphasize—as the Prosecutor himself has done—that the 'interests of justice' cannot become a politicized standard. Prosecutors and judges alike must be guided at all times by the rule of law and, specifically in the case of the ICC, by the letter and the spirit of the Rome Statute. Politicizing the decision-making process can only weaken the Court's credibility and, in turn, its effectiveness.

IV. CONCLUSION

Focusing on the tension between peace and justice in the Ugandan context leads to one clear conclusion: the ICC must not allow itself to be manipulated by states. While the Court must respect the principle of complementarity, it is, as a court of law, an apolitical institution with a mandate of ending impunity. Its judicial integrity cannot be sacrificed to the peace-making process.

I began by saying that the ICC will have to face the peace vs justice challenge much more directly than other international tribunals have done so far. It is also true, however, that—as the first permanent international criminal court—the ICC has a unique opportunity to reframe the peace vs justice debate so that it is no longer a question of whether to pursue justice *or* peace, but instead a challenge of when and how to pursue *both*. The drafters of the Rome Statute were well aware of the potential for tension between the goals of justice and peace. I have every faith that they have equipped the Court with all of the tools necessary to address this challenge.

15

THE ICC'S RELATIONSHIP WITH NATIONAL JURISDICTIONS: WHAT FUTURE?*

The question at the heart of today's panel is 'What does the future hold for the ICC's relationship with national jurisdictions?'—a question that leaves open many avenues for exploration.

First, we must ask how the principle of complementarity will shape the future of the ICC's relationships with nations that have ratified the Rome Statute. In a 2004 statement, the Prosecutor of the ICC emphasized that the Office of the Prosecutor would take a 'positive approach to complementarity' and 'encourage national proceedings wherever possible'.[1] In making this statement, the Prosecutor might simply have been making the best of the situation before him. Given that the Rome Statute clearly grants national jurisdictions the first shot at trying war suspects, the Prosecutor will be more likely to be effective if he works closely with these jurisdictions from the start. Nonetheless, I think this statement on the part of the Prosecutor reflects more than simply the recognition of the realities at hand. It also reflects the ideal that countries themselves will take direct responsibility for bringing to justice suspected war criminals within their jurisdiction.

The ideal of states taking responsibility for the prosecution of war crimes is a valuable one; it was essential in the negotiations of the Rome Statute and remains essential in promoting adherence to the Statute. In

---

* Delivered in Trento, Italy, in June 2007. The text of this speech first appeared in 'Round Table', in Mauro Politi and Federica Gioia (eds), *The International Criminal Court and National Jurisdictions* (Farnham: Ashgate, 2008), 133–135, © Mauro Politi and Federica Gioia. Used by permission of the publishers and modified from the original publication.

[1] Statement of the Prosecutor Luis Moreno Ocampo to Diplomatic Corps, The Hague, The Netherlands (12 February 2004), available at <http://www.icc-cpi.int/NR/rdonlyres/0F999F00-A609-4516-A91A-80467BC432D3/143670/LOM_20040212_En.pdf>.

any event, international tribunals will never be able to try all the serious war crimes. The role of national courts will always be essential.

But what does the ideal of state responsibility mean for the ICC as an institution? Here, I think we must ask some rather hard questions, including whether there will be enough work left for the ICC. Obviously, the Office of the Prosecutor will always have work, whether investigating possible crimes or supporting domestic jurisdictions in their own investigations or prosecutions. But that work must include at least some prosecutions. I congratulate the ICC for its Darfur indictments and warrants of arrest and I hope and pray that they will lead to actual trials. For without a critical mass of actual cases, the ICC judges and Chambers will have little to do. This, in turn, may cause state parties and other actors to wonder whether the ICC is worth sustaining and funding. It may also make it difficult to attract judges of high caliber to the ICC in the future.

I do not wish to exaggerate this concern. Of course, the ICC will have cases where the national jurisdiction is unwilling or genuinely unable to prosecute. National jurisdictions may be unwilling where they resent the intervention of the ICC calling for such prosecution. National jurisdictions may also be unwilling to prosecute due to practical difficulties, such as the need or desire to devote their resources to other priorities. In such cases, these nations may refer matters to the ICC, as Uganda did. Finally, national jurisdictions may be genuinely unable to prosecute due to internal conflict, the danger of exacerbating domestic strife, or other reasons. Given all these possible ways for the ICC to end up with cases, perhaps my concern about the absence of a critical mass of work is overstated.

But I am not sure. For one thing, we face a problem of appearances. The states that lack the will, the resources, or the ability to prosecute war crimes suspects are likely to be overwhelmingly developing countries. Of course, some very wealthy states may lack the will to prosecute war crimes suspects. With regard to powerful non-party states, Security Council resolutions are unlikely. Thus, it seems likely that most or all of the ICC's cases will come from poor states or failed states—a situation that will give rise to considerable criticism. In cases of self-referral, where a state has asked the ICC to investigate a crime within the state's jurisdiction, there is an easy answer to charges of elitist imposition. But if the ICC's docket consists entirely or almost entirely of cases from poor states or from Africa, there may well be a groundswell of resentment— and if national jurisdictions stop cooperating with the ICC as a result, its work risks grinding to a halt.

One often hears suggestions that the Prosecutor should initiate cases by acting *proprio motu* and not only by accepting self-referrals or referrals of the Security Council. Given the geographically narrow confines of the areas from which self-referrals have originated, this may be an attractive idea. The question is whether the principle of complementarity would play out any differently from the cases where it was implicated in self-referrals. While in theory it would have the same force, in reality—and given the prospect that the Prosecutor would act *sua sponte* only in cases of major atrocities—it may be that the role of the complementarity principle in those cases would be diminished and the prospect for the successful involvement of the ICC enhanced. Nevertheless, in the case of Darfur, the government of Sudan is claiming that it has conducted its own investigations, suggesting that the principle of complementarity may remain a challenge to successful interventions by the ICC even in referral situations.

I offer these thoughts as concerns that the ICC and state parties should face openly and honestly so as to build a safer future and a more successful institution. Pursuant to Article 123, there will be a Review Conference seven years after the ratification of the Statute. It may be that the Conference will decide to revisit the overall statutory principle of complementarity—though I think that unlikely. Instead, I think it might be wise at the Conference to take up the question of whether the ICC needs any institutional reshaping in response to the realities arising from the principle of complementarity.

Now, and briefly, I wish to turn to the question of how the principle of complementarity will shape the future of the ICC's relationships with nations that have not ratified the Rome Statute. (Such states' nationals may now be subject to jurisdiction where crimes are committed on the territory of a state party.)

Will consideration of how the principle of complementarity has worked so far in practice encourage additional nations to ratify or accede to the Rome Statute, or at least not to oppose the ICC in the Security Council or other fora? On the one hand, to the extent that these non-state parties have concerns about their own sovereignty, the experience to date has shown that the principle of complementarity does, indeed, exercise a powerful check on the reach of the ICC. The principle of complementarity thus has helped put to bed some of the phobias associated with the creation of the ICC. On the other hand, to the extent that this principle exercises too powerful a check—so that the ICC is short on work, and thus is not a major, effective actor on the international scene—then these new nations may not deem it worth their while to join.

I hope that in the course of today's roundtable, we can reflect on these issues and others. Our object should be to provide, through frank discussion, an intellectual means for making the ICC a successful and vibrant instrument for justice and against impunity.

16

MAKING THE INTERNATIONAL CRIMINAL COURT A GLOBAL REALITY THROUGH COOPERATION*

I. INTRODUCTION

On the tenth anniversary of the Rome Statute, I think it is an auspicious time to reflect on how we can further facilitate the important work that it does. Our focus today is on cooperation, and I think it fitting because of the importance of cooperation to the ICC's task: 'to put an end to impunity for the perpetrators' of 'the most serious crimes of concern to the international community as a whole'.[1] Because these crimes 'threaten the peace, security and well-being of the world',[2] the ICC must necessarily have the support and assistance of as many states as possible. Of course, I am speaking purely in my personal capacity as a scholar and practitioner of international humanitarian and criminal law.

One of the ways to achieve the ICC's goal of ending impunity is to obtain greater cooperation from both state parties and non-party states. In the absence of police power, cooperation from states—in executing arrest warrants, in seizing and transferring evidence, and in logistics and the relocation of witnesses—is really the lifeline of international criminal tribunals. Although I will focus my comments primarily on cooperation by states, it should be noted that the experience of the ad hoc Tribunals, such as the International Criminal Tribunal for the former Yugoslavia,

---

* Delivered at an International Bar Association Roundtable Discussion held at the Peace Palace, The Hague, The Netherlands, on 12 November 2008.

[1] Rome Statute of the International Criminal Court (1998) 2187 UNTS 90, preamble.
[2] Ibid.

has demonstrated that relationships with other international institutions are extremely important as well.

I would like to begin by discussing what obligations states have to cooperate with the ICC, and then turn briefly to examining how states are living up to that duty in practice.

II. DUTY TO COOPERATE

As we all know, the principle of complementarity means that if a state that has jurisdiction over a case, is investigating or prosecuting it, the case is inadmissible before the ICC—unless that state is unwilling or unable to genuinely investigate or prosecute. However, complementarity also entails a duty of cooperation. If the ICC deems a case admissible, states have a duty to cooperate with the Court in its investigation and prosecution of that case.

This duty is found in Article 86 of the Rome Statute, which provides that 'States Parties shall, in accordance with the provisions of this Statute, *cooperate fully* with the Court *in its investigation and prosecution* of crimes'.[3] This duty includes, for example, a duty to cooperate in arresting indicted persons, gathering evidence, and protecting witnesses and victims. Most interestingly, this duty includes an explicit obligation, under Article 88 of the Rome Statute, for state parties to 'ensure that there are procedures available under their national law for *all* of the *forms of cooperation* which are specified under this Part'.[4] Thus, where such procedures are lacking, failure to enact implementing legislation is, in and of itself, a violation of the Rome Statute. This is very different from most treaties because, under the Vienna Convention on the Law of Treaties, there is no explicit duty to incorporate a treaty into domestic law.

Clearly, in this respect, the situation is very different for state parties, on the one hand, and non-party states, on the other. Non-party states do not have any treaty-based legal obligations to cooperate with the ICC, except in accordance with the terms of any Chapter VII referral resolutions by the Security Council under Article 13(b) of the Rome Statute. It is arguable, however, that non-party states may also have obligations stemming from general international law to investigate and prosecute these crimes, which may in turn create obligations to cooperate with the ICC.

In addition, it is becoming clear that non-party states may view cooperating with the ICC as in their best interests. A fight to end

---

[3] Emphasis added.   [4] Emphasis added.

impunity benefits all states, with its potential for enhancing peace and reconciliation. As a result, non-party states might want to enact legislation to be able to cooperate with the Court. At the very least, they might want to ensure that there is no legislation that would prevent this cooperation. In this context, the United States might wish to reflect on the continuing need for acts such as the American Service-Members' Protection Act.

Although the Rome Statute does not impose an explicit obligation on state parties to investigate and prosecute international crimes, such a duty can be implied from language in the preamble which recalls 'that it is the duty of every State to exercise its criminal jurisdiction over those responsible for international crimes'. Importantly, however, this implied duty applies equally to state parties to the Rome Statute and to non-party states. Notice the language of the preamble: 'it is the duty of *every State*'.[5] This language suggests a pre-existing duty flowing from other sources of international law, which may apply equally to states that are parties to the Rome Statute and to those that are not. For example, the United States is a party to the Genocide Convention and the Convention against Torture, which impose an obligation to prosecute genocide and torture, respectively. Moreover, all states have now ratified the four Geneva Conventions, which impose a duty to prosecute grave breaches. State parties and non-party states alike, therefore, often share the duty to investigate and prosecute many of the crimes that fall within the jurisdiction of the ICC.

III. COOPERATION: RATIFICATION AND ARRESTS

Even so, it is clear that the ICC is facing a dual problem of a lack of ratification and a lack of cooperation by states—by those not party to the Rome Statute and, most disturbingly, even by state parties.

Although 108 states have now ratified the Rome Statute, over 70 percent of the world's population still remains outside the ICC's jurisdiction. This is because seven of the world's ten most populated states, including China, India, and the United States,[6] as well as most of Asia, the Middle East, and North Africa, have not ratified.

This percentage, while dismaying, does not tell the full story. Because the Rome Statute provides for Security Council referral of cases, the

---

[5] Emphasis added.
[6] The seven countries, from the ten most populous states, that have not ratified the Rome Statute are: China, India, the United States, Indonesia, Pakistan, Bangladesh, and Russia (the three states that have ratified the Statute are: Brazil, Nigeria, and Japan). Editor's note: Bangladesh ratified the Rome Statute on 23 March 2010.

ICC's reach is potentially worldwide. Efforts to increase state cooperation, therefore, should include encouraging states to support Security Council referrals to the Court. Moreover, we must remember that while only sixty-five states have accepted the compulsory jurisdiction of the International Court of Justice (ICJ), other states have shown a willingness to refer cases to the ICJ through other means, resulting in a sustained or even increasing level of judicial activity for the ICJ.

The cooperation by states that have ratified the Rome Statute is not particularly encouraging, however. Take, for instance, the record of arrests. Of the ten individuals for whom arrest warrants have been issued, only four have been apprehended so far. States are not doing all that they can to ensure that the remaining individuals are taken into custody and that the necessary evidence is promptly provided to the ICC Prosecutor.

Experience from the other international criminal tribunals demonstrates that states can, and should, do more. For example, in its early years, the International Criminal Tribunal for the former Yugoslavia had enormous difficulties getting Balkan governments to help apprehend indicted individuals. After concerted pressure by the European Union and the United States, the situation is much improved. Out of 161 indictees, only two remain at large—an impressive record even for a national jurisdiction. Similarly, diplomatic pressure by states, in particular the United Kingdom and the United States, helped bring about the surrender of former Liberian president Charles Taylor for trial at the Special Court for Sierra Leone.

It bears noting that without a Chapter VII mandate from the Security Council, only state parties to the Rome Statute have an obligation to assist the Court in effecting arrests. This is a significant difference from the ICTY, which, as a subsidiary organ of the Security Council, can issue orders that are directly binding on all states. Of course, it is possible that when the Security Council refers a case to the ICC, as it did with Darfur, it could impose a binding obligation on all states, under Chapter VII, to cooperate with the ICC. But in the case of Darfur—the only Security Council referral to the ICC thus far—the Council appears to have done the exact opposite. The referral resolution imposed a cooperation obligation on the government of Sudan, but otherwise expressly recognized that states not party to the Rome Statute had no obligation under the Statute and only 'urge[d]' them to cooperate with the ICC.[7]

---

[7] UNSC Res 1593 (31 March 2005) UN Doc S/RES/1593, para 2.

I should also point out that the ad hoc Tribunals have occasionally been assisted by international peacekeepers to give effect to their warrants, which is an issue pertinent to the effective functioning of the ICC. The practice of using peacekeepers to arrest war criminals did not have a promising beginning. In 1993, UNOSOM II in Somalia was given the authority by the Security Council to arrest those responsible for armed attacks that had left twenty-four UN peacekeepers dead. As you all know, the subsequent operation to detain warlord Mohamed Farrah Aidid failed, with eighteen US soldiers killed, prompting the United States to withdraw all its forces from Somalia.

The legacy of Somalia has been a reluctance on behalf of troop-contributing nations to have their forces involved in similar arrest operations. For instance, NATO forces operating under a Security Council mandate in Bosnia and Herzegovina in the mid-1990s initially refused to arrest suspects located in the territory under their control. However, over time, NATO forces were persuaded to carry out arrests.

More recent examples also give hope that the ICC might be able to similarly rely on peacekeepers to effectuate arrests. The UN Mission in Liberia (UNMIL), for instance, was given an explicit mandate to apprehend and detain Charles Taylor and, acting in accordance with this mandate, UNMIL apprehended Taylor when he returned to Liberia from Nigeria in March 2006 and transferred him to the Special Court for Sierra Leone's custody.

In another example, the Security Council has authorized the UN Mission in the Democratic Republic of the Congo (MONUC) to 'cooperate in national and international efforts to bring to justice perpetrators of grave violations of human rights and international humanitarian law'.[8] This is particularly relevant because of the ICC's investigation into the situation in the DRC. Indeed, this spring, when the ICC made public the arrest warrant for Bosco Ntaganda, MONUC indicated its readiness to assist the Congolese government in arresting him.

If the Congolese government will be willing and able to arrest and transfer indictees to the ICC, MONUC's mandate allowing it to cooperate with the government in making these arrests may be sufficient, insofar as the ICC is concerned. The real problem arises in situations with uncooperative governments, such as Sudan, where the government has not cooperated with the ICC to arrest indictees Ahmad Harun and Ali Kushayb and is unlikely to become any more cooperative if the ICC's

---

[8] UNSC Res 1756 (15 May 2007) UN Doc S/RES/1756, para 3(c).

Pre-Trial Chamber grants the Prosecution's request for an arrest warrant for President Al-Bashir. As it presently stands, the UN Mission in Darfur (UNAMID) does not have a mandate that allows it to forcibly arrest persons indicted by the ICC. UNAMID is only authorized 'to take the necessary action' to protect its personnel and facilities and to protect civilians under imminent threat of violence.[9] Given the current political climate, it is unlikely that an attempt to expand UNAMID's mandate to include arrest powers would survive a veto in the Security Council.

The inability of the ICC to actually get its hands on accused has resulted, so far, in a low level of judicial activity by the Court. This undermines the Court's ability to build its institutional capacity and to achieve its goal of ending impunity for international crimes.

Fortunately, I believe the tide is shifting towards greater cooperation. In particular, the US decision not to block the Security Council's referral of the Darfur situation is a source of hope. Indeed, in a recent speech, John Bellinger, Legal Adviser of the US Department of State, concluded that the United States must recognize that 'in some cases such as Darfur, the ICC's success in investigating and prosecuting serious crimes may advance goals we share, and that in such cases we may have an interest in facilitating the ICC's work'.[10] This is a positive step in the right direction, as is the relationship agreement between the ICC and the United Nations, although a targeted Security Council mandate is still required for the use of UN peacekeepers for the execution of arrest warrants. Whenever the Council refers a situation to the ICC, it should lend its support through Chapter VII to executing arrest warrants of the Court.

IV. CONCLUSION

To conclude, let me say a few words about the need for greater cooperation and the need for greater efficacy in the way the Court operates.

First, these two goals are interrelated. Greater efficacy depends on increased cooperation, but greater cooperation is also likely to depend on the ICC being perceived as an effective institution. All persons interested in international criminal justice are closely watching how the Court handles the situations on its docket; if it is seen as effective, it will likely garner not only greater attention but greater cooperation as well.

---

[9] UNSC Res 1769 (31 July 2007) UN Doc S/RES/1769, para 15(a).
[10] John B Bellinger III, 'The United States and the International Criminal Court: Where We've Been and Where We're Going', Remarks to the DePaul University College of Law (25 April 2008), available at <http://2001-2009.state.gov/s/l/rls/104053.htm>.

Second, it is essential that the ICC receive greater cooperation from states that are not parties to the Rome Statute. We must do what we can to encourage these non-party states to join the ICC or, if they find it impossible, to take adequate steps domestically to promote the fair administration of criminal justice concerning the crimes identified in the ICC Statute, or their close equivalent. We must also encourage these states to facilitate the work of the Court whenever possible and we must stress that international criminal justice is—or at least should be—an apolitical issue of worldwide concern. The caliber of the judges and the other ICC actors, as well as the efficacy of the ICC, will be closely scrutinized, even as its politics may be becoming a non-issue.

Third, we must acknowledge that the ICC's effectiveness depends on greater cooperation not only by non-party states but by state parties themselves. The low number of state parties that have complied with their duty to enact implementing legislation to cooperate with the Court is particularly problematic. Many state parties, primarily in Asia and Africa but also in Latin America and Europe, are in violation of their obligation to enact national laws for cooperation with the Court. It is also distressing to note that so few of the persons indicted by the Court have been arrested and transferred into the Court's custody. Here again, state parties are not fulfilling their duties to cooperate with the Court.

Most importantly, however, the cooperation of the P-5—especially those which are not party to the Rome Statute—is needed to ensure that the Security Council refers new cases to the ICC. In this respect, US cooperation with respect to the Darfur situation is very welcome and hopefully the sign of a new trend of increased cooperation with the Court.

These are still early days for the ICC, but, as my reflections today suggest, I am confident that the ICC will make an invaluable contribution to ending impunity for the most serious crimes known to humanity. I have no doubt that the ICC, like its sister international tribunals, will successfully rise to the challenges inherent in administering a system of international criminal justice.

III

International Crimes and Jurisprudence of International Courts

17
HUMAN RIGHTS LAW MARCHES INTO NEW TERRITORY: THE ENFORCEMENT OF INTERNATIONAL HUMAN RIGHTS IN INTERNATIONAL CRIMINAL TRIBUNALS (MAREK NOWICKI MEMORIAL LECTURE)*

I am honored to have been invited to deliver this Marek Nowicki Memorial Lecture at the University of Warsaw, in the country of my birth. The object of my lecture is to highlight the increasing convergence between international human rights and international humanitarian law, and to show how international human rights are now being enforced in international criminal tribunals. It is particularly suitable that I am delivering this lecture in Warsaw, because no country more than Poland suffered from the atrocities of foreign occupation during World War II.

I. CHANGING LEGAL LANDSCAPE

But before I make my primary points, let me briefly examine the traditional relationship between human rights and humanitarian law. Human rights law has applied principally in times of peace and has protected individuals from their own governments, while humanitarian law has governed relations between states in time of war and protected individuals from enemy powers. Violations of human rights law resulted primarily in state responsibility, while violations of humanitarian law could lead not only to state responsibility and armed reprisals, but also

---

* Delivered at the University of Warsaw, Warsaw, Poland, on 27 November 2008 as one of two Marek Nowicki Memorial Lectures.

to individual criminal liability for the perpetrator. The reach of human rights law has been limited to the territory of the state concerned, while humanitarian law also applied extra-territorially, especially to situations of occupation or wherever an army found itself outside its national territory.

The traditional normative separation of human rights and international humanitarian law was mirrored by institutional divisions as well. The United Nations, human rights institutions, and human rights courts oversaw the applicability of human rights law, while the International Committee of the Red Cross (ICRC) and protecting states were the guardians of the Geneva Conventions and international humanitarian law.

All of these propositions have now undergone major change. The increasing symbiosis between human rights and humanitarian law was evident decades ago with the adoption of common Article 3 of the 1949 Geneva Conventions. Common Article 3 is a virtual mini-convention providing for the humane treatment of non-combatants and for the prohibition of their being murdered, mistreated, tortured, or unlawfully executed. Most importantly, perhaps, common Article 3 applies these protections to non-international armed conflicts. Thus, for the first time in an international treaty, humanitarian law projected into internal conflicts and imposed provisions that can be considered pure human rights law. This humanization of humanitarian law and its penetration into national armed conflicts has, in turn, influenced other developments, such as the expansion of prohibitions and restrictions on the use of certain weapons—especially those that make it impossible to distinguish between civilians and combatants—or weapons considered abhorrent to the public conscience, such as chemical and biological weapons.

With the drastic change in the nature of most armed conflicts from international to non-international and mixed conflicts, humanitarian law has been further pulled in the direction of human rights. At the same time, human rights bodies have been confronted with situations in which humanitarian law is central, and have thus been compelled to apply that law, at least to some extent.

The role of the International Court of Justice (ICJ) in developing this new theory of the place of international humanitarian law and human rights in contemporary conflicts has been critical. In the *Nuclear Weapons* advisory opinion[1] and the *Construction of a Wall* advisory

---

[1] *Legality of the Threat or Use of Nuclear Weapons* (Advisory Opinion) [1996] ICJ Rep 226.

opinion,[2] the ICJ made it clear that human rights continued to apply in time of war, even outside of national territory—subject to the *lex specialis* status of international humanitarian law with regard to the right to life and lawful derogations.

The most dramatic change, however, occurred as a result of the establishment of the international criminal tribunals. Although mandated to apply humanitarian law, in practice the UN ad hoc Tribunals have been instructed by human rights as well. This jurisprudential move was motivated in part in order to apply due process norms. However, because of the tremendous similarity between the normative content of common Article 3 and crimes against humanity, on the one hand, and human rights, on the other, international criminal tribunals have also had recourse to human rights law with respect to the material elements of substantive crimes.

These developments have enhanced the protective character of both humanitarian law and human rights law. Thus, due to the reliance on human rights in international criminal tribunals, gross violations of human rights are now prosecuted with violations of humanitarian law for the first time.

The object of this lecture is to discuss these developments, particularly in the context of the jurisprudence of the International Criminal Tribunal for the former Yugoslavia (ICTY) and the International Criminal Tribunal for Rwanda (ICTR). I hope to show how tightly interwoven these legal regimes have become and how, as a consequence, for the first time, human rights violations are subject to criminal enforcement.

II. JURISDICTION OF THE TRIBUNALS

When the ICTY was established, the Secretary-General of the United Nations explicitly directed the Tribunal to take international human rights into account by stating that 'the International Tribunal must fully respect internationally recognized standards regarding the rights of the accused at all stages of its proceedings'.[3] He went on to note that those internationally recognized standards were, in particular, those contained in Article 14 of the International Covenant on Civil and Political Rights (Political Covenant).

---

[2] *Legal Consequences of the Construction of a Wall in the Occupied Palestinian Territory* (Advisory Opinion) [2004] ICJ Rep 136.

[3] UNSC, 'Report of the Secretary-General Pursuant to Paragraph 2 of Security Council Resolution 808' (1993) UN Doc S/25704, para 106.

The Secretary-General's focus, then, was on the procedural or fair trial rights of the accused, such as the right to be informed of the case against him or her and the right to be tried without undue delay. And, in fact, Article 14 of the Political Covenant was the source of Article 21 of the Statute of the ICTY and of Article 20 of the Statute of the ICTR, which provide minimum judicial guarantees to the accused.

However, the Tribunals have gone much further than instructed. Undoubtedly, human rights have been a vital source of the procedural protections the Tribunals enforce. But what is more striking is that the Tribunals have also relied on human rights principles to define, elaborate, and interpret substantive humanitarian law. I will discuss each form of reliance—procedural and substantive—in turn.

III. DUE PROCESS AND PROCEDURAL RIGHTS

The Secretary-General's emphasis on procedural rights is, of course, not misplaced, because it is critically important for international criminal tribunals to ensure fair trials. Indeed, trial fairness could plausibly be argued to be the foremost criterion for measuring the success of international criminal justice. The notion of a fair trial encompasses a bundle of protections and requirements, but at the very least requires the application of due process norms and respect for the principle of legality.

To determine what those due process norms are, and what they require, the Tribunals have frequently turned to international human rights. For instance, in the *Janković* referral decision, the ICTY determined that, for its purposes, fair trial requirements included the guarantees enshrined in both Article 14 of the Political Covenant and Article 6 of the European Convention on Human Rights, as reflected in Article 21 of the ICTY Statute.[4] This position—that the fair trial standards of the Tribunal must accord with international standards evinced by human rights instruments—has been reiterated numerous times by the ICTY as well as the ICTR.

In the first case before the ICTY, *Tadić*, the Trial Chamber discussed the Tribunal's relationship to human rights law as a result of a request by the Prosecution for protective measures for witnesses.[5] The Tribunal held that human rights instruments such as the Political Covenant must be 'interpreted within the context of the "object and purpose" and unique

---

[4] *Prosecutor v Gojko Janković* (Decision on Referral of Case under Rule 11 *bis*) IT-96-23/2-PT (22 July 2005).
[5] *Prosecutor v Duško Tadić* (Decision on the Prosecutor's Motion Requesting Protective Measures for Victims and Witnesses) IT-94-1-T (10 August 1995).

characteristics of the [ICTY's] Statute'.[6] Further, decisions by other domestic and international judicial bodies interpreting human rights would be 'only of limited relevance'.[7]

For a tribunal that had been explicitly directed to take human rights into account, this might be seen as a fairly surprising statement. However, I think the Trial Chamber was guided by the unique context in which the Tribunal operates. At the time of the decision, the conflict in the former Yugoslavia was ongoing and the Tribunal had no witness protection program. The Trial Chamber noted that the Tribunal is, 'in certain respects, comparable to a military tribunal, which often has limited rights of due process and more lenient rules of evidence'.[8]

Although the ICTY has held that international human rights must conform to its Statute's context, the Tribunals have not been hesitant to borrow human rights principles developed by other judicial bodies in construing various fair trial requirements. Moreover, in the Tribunals' developing jurisprudence, human rights norms are now more readily accepted on their face.

A. Lawfulness of arrests

An illustration of the Tribunals' reliance on human rights norms is the ICTY's review of arrests made by states to ensure that they comply with international human rights and due process standards. In these cases, the question is not only whether the states at issue made the arrest in a way that violated the accused's rights, but also whether any such violation taints the Tribunal's jurisdiction.

In the *Nikolić* case, for instance, the accused claimed that he had been illegally arrested and abducted by unknown persons in the territory of the former Yugoslavia and then transferred to the territory of Bosnia and Herzegovina, where he was arrested and detained by NATO forces.[9] In his view, his arrest violated internationally recognized human rights, was a breach of the fundamental principles of due process of law, and thus imperiled his right to a fair trial.

In analyzing his claims, the Trial Chamber recognized its 'paramount duty'[10] to respect human rights norms and noted that 'due process of law encompasses more than merely the duty to ensure a fair trial' for the accused—it also includes considerations such as how the parties

---

[6] Ibid., para 26.   [7] Ibid., para 27.   [8] Ibid., para 28.
[9] *Prosecutor v Dragan Nikolić* (Decision on Defence Motion Challenging the Exercise of Jurisdiction by the Tribunal) IT-94-2-PT (9 October 2002).
[10] Ibid., para 110.

have conducted themselves in the case and how the accused has been brought into the jurisdiction of the Tribunal.[11] In that respect, the Trial Chamber reviewed several decisions of the Human Rights Committee relating to forced abductions in the 1980s in Latin America. In these cases, the allegations of human rights violations were made against the state, which was itself involved in the abduction of the victims. This was, of course, a different context than that before the Tribunal, because the accused's alleged abduction was not attributable to the Prosecution or even to NATO forces. The Trial Chamber was thus hesitant to apply these decisions mechanically to the accused's claims. Still, the Trial Chamber held that there may well be situations 'where an accused is very seriously mistreated...before being handed over to the Tribunal, [which] may constitute a legal impediment to the exercise of jurisdiction over such an accused'.[12] And as the Appeals Chamber later noted, 'the correct balance must...be maintained between the fundamental rights of the accused and the essential interests of the international community in the prosecution of persons charged with serious violations of international humanitarian law'.[13]

Similarly, in the *Barayagwiza* case before the ICTR, the Tribunal turned to human rights jurisprudence to judge various aspects of the accused's detention.[14] The accused had been arrested and detained in Cameroon, but was only informed of the charges against him after eleven months in detention. He was held in Cameroon for a total of nineteen months before being transferred to the Tribunal, during which time he filed a writ of habeas corpus which was never adjudicated. The Appeals Chamber recognized that Mr Barayagwiza's detention implicated several basic rights enumerated in the Tribunal's Statute and provided in international instruments, and held that accused were entitled to these protections when detained at the behest of the Tribunal. Although the rights at issue are generally uncontroversial—such as the right to be informed promptly of the reasons for arrest and the nature of the charges—the Appeals Chamber turned to the jurisprudence of the Human Rights Committee and the European Court of Human Rights to flesh out what practical requirements these rights impose.

---

[11] Ibid., para 111.   [12] Ibid., para 114.
[13] *Prosecutor v Dragan Nikolić* (Decision on Interlocutory Appeal Concerning Legality of Arrest) IT-94-2-AR73 (5 June 2003), para 30.
[14] *Jean-Bosco Barayagwiza v Prosecutor* (Decision) ICTR-97-19-AR72 (4 November 1999).

B. Right to self-representation

1. At trial

Another procedural right that the Tribunals have interpreted with the aid of human rights norms is the accused's right to self-representation. Article 21 of the Statute of the ICTY and Article 20 of the Statute of the ICTR provide that the accused has a right to defend himself or herself in person, although the rules of both Tribunals provide that: 'The Trial Chamber may, if it decides that it is in the interests of justice, instruct the Registrar to assign a counsel to represent the interests of the accused.'[15]

Although the right to self-representation may seem straightforward, given the size and complexity of the cases before the Tribunals, and because accused are occasionally obstructive, the Tribunals have been confronted with challenges concerning the scope of this right a number of times, and have typically answered with reference to international human rights standards. While propositions developed under human rights law have been foundational, given the distinctive circumstances of the work of the Tribunals, the ICTY and ICTR have explored the contours of the right to self-representation more fully than many human rights bodies and have adapted the right to the international criminal law context.

In the *Slobodan Milošević* case, for instance, the Prosecution argued repeatedly for counsel to be imposed on Mr Milošević.[16] Noting his serious health problems, the Prosecution argued that the public interest demanded a comprehensive prosecution of Mr Milošević and that the international community would not accept the curtailment of the case in a situation where the accused, by insisting on representing himself, had exacerbated his health problems. In considering the matter, the Trial Chamber started from the proposition that a plain reading of Article 21 of the ICTY Statute prevents the imposition of counsel on an accused. The Trial Chamber sought confirmation of this principle from international and regional human rights conventions and found that the human rights regime also 'plainly articulate[s] a right to defend oneself in person', although that right is subject to exceptions.[17] The Trial Chamber found the decisions of the Human Rights Committee especially pertinent, as the

---

[15] ICTY, Rules of Procedure and Evidence, Rule 45 *ter*; ICTR, Rules of Procedure and Evidence, Rule 45 *quater*.
[16] *Prosecutor v Slobodan Milošević* (Reasons for Decision on the Prosecution Motion Concerning Assignment of Counsel) IT-02-54-T (4 April 2003).
[17] Ibid., para 36.

Political Covenant is not only a convention of widespread acceptance, but also provides the foundation for Article 21 of the Statute.

However, in the face of Mr Milošević's serious and persistent health problems, and the resultant extreme delays in the pace of the trial, the Trial Chamber later returned to the matter to consider whether the right to self-representation is subject to qualification, and if so, what circumstances would justify the imposition of counsel.[18] The Trial Chamber observed that the notion that a trial should be fair is a fundamental, universally recognized human right, and that it is under the ambit of trial fairness that a number of rights, including the right to self-representation, fall. As such, the right to self-representation may have to 'yield to the overarching right to a fair trial' if its exercise undermines the integrity of the trial.[19] Indeed, the Trial Chamber noted, in *Barayagwiza* before the ICTR and in *The Prosecutor v Norman* before the Special Court for Sierra Leone, international criminal tribunals have recognized that there may be situations 'where it is... appropriate for a Trial Chamber to insist that the defence is presented by counsel'.[20]

The Trial Chamber therefore imposed counsel on Mr Milošević and proceeded to outline the working relationship between assigned counsel and Mr Milošević, thus articulating when Mr Milošević would be entitled to participate personally in the proceedings. On appeal, the Appeals Chamber agreed that the Trial Chamber was entitled to impose counsel, but held that any restrictions on Mr Milošević's right to represent himself must be limited to the minimum extent necessary to protect the Tribunal's interest in assuring a reasonably expeditious trial.[21] The Appeals Chamber adopted the basic proportionality principle employed in human rights jurisprudence which dictates that when restricting a fundamental right, such restriction must be in service of a sufficiently important objective and must impair the right no more than is necessary to accomplish that objective. The Appeals Chamber thus found that, in sharply restricting Mr Milošević's ability to participate in the conduct of the case, the Trial Chamber did not sufficiently protect his fundamental right to participate in his defense.

---

[18] *Prosecutor v Slobodan Milošević* (Reasons for Decision on Assignment of Defence Counsel) IT-02-54-T (22 September 2004).
[19] Ibid., para 33.   [20] Ibid., para 38.
[21] *Slobodan Milošević v Prosecutor* (Decision on Interlocutory Appeal of the Trial Chamber's Decision on the Assignment of Defense Counsel) IT-02-54-AR73.7 (1 November 2004).

2. On appeal

The *Krajišnik* case has added a further element to the Tribunals' consideration of the right to self-defense, namely whether individuals possess a right to self-representation during appeals from judgment.[22] The Appeals Chamber noted its prior jurisprudence, which held that 'the drafters of the Statute clearly viewed the right to self-representation as an indispensable cornerstone of justice, placing it on structural par with defendants' right to remain silent, to confront the witnesses against them, to a speedy trial, and even to demand a court-appointed attorney if they cannot afford one themselves'.[23] Because no distinction is made in the Statute between trial and appeal, there was no textual basis for the Appeals Chamber to restrict the right to self-representation on appeal. As established previously, however, this 'cornerstone' right is not unqualified at the Tribunal.

Human rights law has thus shaped the parallel provisions of humanitarian law. Conversely, this jurisprudence will no doubt have an impact on the consideration of the right to self-representation by human rights bodies and will be one more example of the increasing convergence of humanitarian law and human rights.

IV. SUBSTANTIVE NORMS

As I hope these few examples have demonstrated, human rights norms have been vital to the development of procedural rights before the Tribunals. But what about the substantive norms governing culpability? How have the Tribunals used human rights with respect to the substantive aspects of international humanitarian law?

As I will attempt to illustrate, the Tribunals have relied on human rights instruments and norms to interpret and lend greater specificity to the prohibitions contained in international humanitarian law. As the Trial Chamber observed in *Kunarac*, because of the paucity of precedent in the field of international humanitarian law, the Tribunals have often resorted to human rights norms in interpreting the content of customary international humanitarian law.[24]

---

[22] *Prosecutor v Momčilo Krajišnik* (Decision on Momčilo Krajišnik's Request to Self-Represent, on Counsel's Motions in Relation to Appointment of *Amicus Curiae*, and on the Prosecution Motion of 16 February 2007) IT-00-39-A (11 May 2007).

[23] Ibid., para 9 (quotation marks and citation omitted).

[24] *Prosecutor v Dragoljub Kunarac et al.* (Judgement) IT-96-23-T & IT-96-23/1-T (22 February 2001) (*Kunarac* Trial Judgement).

While noting the similarity of these bodies of law in terms of goals, values, and terminology, the Trial Chamber in *Kunarac* also underscored that such reliance must be undertaken cautiously, given the crucial differences between the two. The Trial Chamber noted, in particular, that the law applied by the Tribunals constitutes a 'penal...regime', concerned with individual criminal responsibility, whereas the human rights regime is focused on the state, as both the guarantor and abuser of human rights protections.[25]

A. Torture

An example of how this different focus is pertinent to international humanitarian law is the Tribunals' consideration of torture. Although torture is universally condemned and prohibited under both conventional and customary law and in times of peace as well as during armed conflict, arriving at a definition of torture has been difficult. While several human rights conventions provide such a definition, international humanitarian law does not. As a result, the Tribunals have turned to human rights instruments and jurisprudence to determine when an act constitutes torture in the particular context of international humanitarian law.

In *Kunarac*, the Trial Chamber started with the definition of torture provided in the Torture Convention, but held, after reviewing several human rights decisions, that this definition was not reflective of customary international humanitarian law. The Torture Convention provides that torture comprises four main elements, namely, the severity of treatment, the deliberate nature of the act, the specific purpose of the act, and that the act is committed by or at the instigation of a public official. While the first three elements are present in other human rights instruments, such as the 1950 European Convention for the Protection of Human Rights, the final element—the involvement of an authority or state action—is controversial.

The Trial Chamber reasoned that this additional element is a result of the context in which the Torture Convention operates—at the inter-state level or with states as respondents—and is therefore directed only to states' obligations. For the purposes of the Tribunal, however, 'the involvement of the state does not modify or limit the guilt or responsibility of the individual who carried out the crimes in question'.[26] On that basis, the Trial Chamber held that the involvement of a state official or other authority is not necessary for the act to be regarded as torture under

[25] Ibid., para 470.   [26] Ibid., para 493.

international humanitarian law, or for the personal culpability of the perpetrator to be assessed.

This development has the potential of strengthening the force of the prohibition against torture. And this decision demonstrates once again that the Tribunals, in their enthusiasm for human rights, have not wholly or mechanically adopted the human rights regime. Indeed, as I have noted, the Tribunals have been cautious to ensure that when transplanting human rights norms, the particularities of international humanitarian law as a legal regime have been respected.

B. *Rape*

Thus far we have been considering acts which are prohibited by both human rights and international humanitarian law. What happens when human rights law differs from international humanitarian law?

Rape, for instance, is an unusual crime in that it has been specifically prohibited under international humanitarian law and the statutes of all international criminal tribunals and courts, but not explicitly under human rights treaties—perhaps because it was thought that in normal situations, rape would be dealt with by the criminal law of the land. In *Furundžija*, the ICTY Trial Chamber noted that although rape is specifically prohibited by the Geneva Conventions and the Additional Protocols, prohibited in armed conflict by customary law, and expressly classified as a crime against humanity under (post-World War II occupation era) Control Council Law No 10—and although convictions were entered for rape and sexual assaults as violations of the laws or customs of war by the Tokyo Tribunal, while more recent jurisprudence recognizes even 'genocidal rape'—no international human rights instrument specifically prohibits rape or other serious sexual assaults.[27] However, the Trial Chamber reasoned that these offenses are implicitly prohibited by treaty provisions safeguarding physical integrity.

In order to establish the material elements of rape, the ICTY in *Furundžija* and in the later case of *Kunarac*[28] turned instead to the general principles of criminal law common to the major legal systems of the world. The *Furundžija* Trial Chamber also evoked human rights norms, such as human dignity and physical integrity, in its discussion. Similarly, the ICTR Trial Chamber in *Akayesu*—the first case to define rape in international law—drew analogies with the treatment of torture under the Torture Convention and concluded that rape, like torture,

---

[27] *Prosecutor v Anto Furundžija* (Judgement) IT-95-17/1-T (10 December 1998).
[28] See *Kunarac* Trial Judgement, n 24 above.

is a violation of personal dignity used for such purposes as 'intimidation, degradation, humiliation, discrimination, punishment, control or destruction of a person'.[29]

This demonstrates just how important human rights have become to the development of humanitarian law. At the very least, the Tribunals want to ensure that the norms developed under humanitarian law conform to those contained in human rights law. Further, the jurisprudence affects the definition of rape in customary law and, as such, it is sure to eventually shape the definition of rape in human rights law as well—thus promoting once again the convergence between these two regimes.

C. Crimes against humanity and other crimes

The delicate interplay between international human rights and international humanitarian law can also be seen in the Tribunals' elucidation of crimes against humanity and certain other crimes. Crimes against humanity are inhumane acts of a very serious nature—such as willful killing, torture, or rape—which are committed as part of a widespread or systematic attack against a civilian population.

1. Enslavement

The *Kunarac* case concerned the abduction, confinement, rape, and forced labor of several women and girls after the city of Foča was taken over by Serb forces in April 1992. One of the questions for the Trial Chamber was whether such treatment constituted enslavement as a crime against humanity.[30]

In order to answer this question, the Trial Chamber undertook an extensive examination of international law. Although slavery has long been prohibited, and indeed the legal struggle against slavery was one of the most important forerunners to the international protection of human rights, the definition of slavery in international criminal law has not been clear. When crimes against humanity were first codified in the Nuremberg Charter, enslavement was proscribed, but not defined. Nor did the Nuremberg judgment provide a definition or draw a distinction between deportation to slave labor and enslavement. The Geneva Conventions and Additional Protocols provided some guidance by outlining who may be required to perform what kinds of work under what conditions in armed conflict, but they stopped short of providing a definition. While international human rights treaties routinely prohibit slavery, they too

---

[29] *Prosecutor v Jean-Paul Akayesu* (Judgement) ICTR-96-4-T (2 September 1998), para 597.
[30] See *Kunarac* Trial Judgement, n 24 above.

fail to offer a definition. Nonetheless, human rights jurisprudence provides assistance by interpreting the relevant provisions, thus elucidating the distinction between servitude and forced labor, for instance.

Drawing on this jurisprudence, the norms of human rights treaties, and other international law precedents, the Trial Chamber in *Kunarac* held that 'enslavement as a crime against humanity in customary international law consisted of the exercise of any or all of the powers attaching to the right of ownership over a person'.[31] The Trial Chamber observed that this definition may be broader than the traditional definition provided in the 1926 Slavery Convention, in that elements of enslavement include not only control or ownership, but also exploitation, the extraction of forced or compulsory labor or service, sex, prostitution, and human trafficking. It should be noted that Article 7 of the Statute of the International Criminal Court prohibits enslavement pursuant to this same definition, a fact that assisted the Trial Chamber in concluding that the definition it articulated was reflective of customary international law.

2. Persecution, 'inhuman treatment', and other inhumane acts

While most crimes against humanity listed in the Statutes of the Tribunals are relatively clear, the crimes against humanity of persecution and 'other inhumane acts' as well as inhuman or cruel treatment under Articles referencing the 1949 Geneva Conventions were empty shells which the Tribunals had to fill with content in their case law.

Persecution, other inhumane acts, and inhuman or cruel treatment are often referred to as 'residual' or 'umbrella' crimes because these crimes encompass a broad range of conduct. Again, they are virtually indistinguishable from parallel prohibitions in human rights law. In light of this definitional indeterminacy and the wide range of possible prohibited acts, these crimes initially gave rise to a concern that they did not meet the need for specificity in criminal law or respect the principle of legality. However, by turning to international human rights, the Tribunals have been able not only to provide further precision to these crimes, but also to identify a commonly accepted basic set of rights, the infringement of which may amount to a crime against humanity. In other words, the human rights regime has provided the Tribunals with the legal foundations necessary to protect the rights of the accused, while also punishing serious violations of both human rights and international humanitarian law.

---

[31] Ibid., para 539.

For example, in *Čelebići*, the Trial Chamber relied on human rights law to define inhuman treatment prohibited in Article 2 of the ICTY's Statute and cruel treatment prohibited in Article 3 of that Statute.[32] The Trial Chamber defined both offenses as an intentional act or omission that, 'judged objectively, is deliberate and not accidental [and] which causes serious mental or physical suffering or injury or constitutes a serious attack on human dignity'.[33] This definition reflects human rights jurisprudence, which has tended to define inhuman treatment in relative terms—that is, as an act or omission that deliberately causes mental and physical suffering, but falls short of the severe mental and physical suffering required for the offense of torture. The Appeals Chamber upheld this finding, noting that the material elements of cruel treatment and inhuman treatment are the same.[34]

With respect to persecution, in *Kupreškić* the Trial Chamber held that persecution is 'the gross or blatant denial, on discriminatory grounds, of a fundamental right, laid down in international customary or treaty law, reaching the same level of gravity as the other acts prohibited' as crimes against humanity.[35] Turning to the Universal Declaration on Human Rights, the two UN covenants on human rights of 1966, and other international instruments on human rights or humanitarian law, the Trial Chamber held that it was possible to identify a set of fundamental rights, the gross infringement of which may amount to persecution as a crime against humanity. Thus, the definition of persecution necessarily implicates international human rights.

In *Brđanin*, the ICTY Appeals Chamber dismissed the argument that the denial of certain human rights—including the rights to employment, freedom of movement, proper judicial process, and proper medical care— do not rise to the level of serious violations of international humanitarian law and therefore do not come within the jurisdiction of the Tribunal.[36] The Chamber noted that, according to settled jurisprudence, the crime of persecution includes not only the acts in the Statute, but also acts which are not listed in the Statute altogether. Further, acts underlying persecutions need not even necessarily constitute a crime in international law. Rather, an act must be 'of equal gravity' to the crimes against humanity

---

[32] *Prosecutor v Zejnil Delalić et al.* (Judgement) IT-96-21-T (16 November 1998) (*Čelebići* Trial Judgement).

[33] Ibid., paras 543, 552.

[34] *Prosecutor v Zejnil Delalić et al.* (Judgement) IT-96-21-A (20 February 2001) (*Čelebići* Appeal Judgement).

[35] *Prosecutor v Zoran Kupreškić et al.* (Judgement) IT-95-16-T (14 January 2000) (*Kupreškić* Trial Judgement), para 621 (emphasis omitted).

[36] *Prosecutor v Radoslav Brđanin* (Judgement) IT-99-36-A (3 April 2007).

listed under Article 5 of the Statute when considered in isolation or in conjunction with other acts.[37] Determining whether the acts *actually* constitute persecution is a fact-specific exercise. Ultimately, in light of the facts of the case, the Tribunal criminalized violations of the rights to employment, to freedom of movement, proper judicial process, and proper medical care—all of which could be considered human rights violations—as crimes against humanity.

In *Simić*, the ICTY Trial Chamber reviewed a number of acts alleged to amount to persecution.[38] It began by noting that persecution can involve a number of discriminatory acts, involving violations of political, social, or economic rights. For instance, the Nuremberg tribunal found that the requirement that the members of a group mark themselves by wearing a yellow star amounted to persecution. The Trial Chamber then consulted human rights instruments to help define unlawful arrest and determine whether unlawful arrest could constitute the underlying act of persecution as a crime against humanity. While unlawful detention and confinement had each been considered persecutory acts, the Tribunal had not yet considered whether unlawful arrest may also constitute persecution. The Trial Chamber noted that international human rights conventions enshrine the right to be free from arbitrary arrest and imprisonment, and consequently defined unlawful arrest as the apprehension of a person without due process of law. The Trial Chamber found that unlawful arrest, without more, did not constitute a gross or blatant denial of a fundamental right reaching the same level of gravity as the other acts prohibited by Article 5. However, 'when considered in context, together with unlawful detention or confinement', unlawful arrest may reach this standard and therefore constitute persecution as a crime against humanity.[39]

The Trial Chamber further held that a decision adopted by the Republika Srpska requiring political parties to freeze their activities did not constitute persecution. First, all parties, without discrimination, were subject to the decision, and second, such a decision may be legitimate under international law. In fact, '[t]he suspension of the activity of political parties, if required by special circumstances', is contemplated by both the Political Covenant and the European Convention on Human Rights.[40] Freedom of association is a right expressly subject to derogation in a time of armed conflict under

---

[37] Ibid., para 296.
[38] *Prosecutor v Blagoje Simić et al.* (Judgement) IT-95-9-T (17 October 2003).
[39] Ibid., para 62.
[40] Ibid., para 507.

both of these treaties, which demonstrates that although international human rights law is particularly important to the development of international humanitarian law, these two regimes remain different in important respects. Indeed, as the Trial Chamber in *Kupreškić* noted, although every crime against humanity can be described as a gross violation of human rights, 'not every denial of a human right may constitute a crime against humanity'.[41]

The Tribunals therefore need to ensure not only that rights, the violation of which is subject to criminal prosecution, are truly fundamental, universally recognized human rights, but also that any violations of these rights are acts which constituted a violation of the law at the time of their commission.

D. *Common Article 3 of the Geneva Conventions and the principle of legality*

This brings me to the principle of legality. Respect for the principle of legality is particularly important when the Tribunals borrow from human rights norms to inform the substantive crimes of international humanitarian law.

The issue was discussed extensively in the *Čelebići* case with respect to common Article 3 of the Geneva Conventions. The Defense argued that to punish breaches of common Article 3 would violate the principle of legality in that it would amount to the creation of *ex post facto* law, clearly contrary to basic human rights, as articulated in Article 15 of the Political Covenant.[42] The ICTY Appeals Chamber first considered whether common Article 3 was customary law, and therefore applied to international conflicts, rather than only internal conflicts as provided in the Geneva Conventions. The Appeals Chamber noted that common Article 3 reflects 'fundamental humanitarian principles which underlie international humanitarian law as a whole'.[43] Indeed, the norms in common Article 3 were customary even before being codified in the Geneva Conventions, as the most universally recognized humanitarian principles. This conclusion was confirmed by a consideration of human rights law, which shares with the Geneva Conventions 'a common "core" of fundamental standards... applicable at all times, in all circumstances and to all parties, and from which no derogation is permitted'.[44] As such, the Appeals Chamber

---

[41] *Kupreškić* Trial Judgement, n 35 above, para 618.
[42] See *Čelebići* Trial Judgement, n 32 above.
[43] *Čelebići* Appeal Judgement, n 34 above, para 143.
[44] Ibid., para 149.

concluded that it would be 'legally and morally untenable' to hold that common Article 3, which constitutes mandatory minimum rules, would not be applicable to international conflicts.[45] Indeed, the ICJ's holding in the *Nicaragua* judgment that common Article 3 is a 'minimum yardstick'[46] makes this conclusion compelling.

The Appeals Chamber held that, although not expressly provided in the Geneva Conventions, violations of common Article 3 undoubtedly give rise to individual criminal liability. The purpose of the principle of legality is to prevent the prosecution and punishment of an individual for acts which he or she reasonably believed to be lawful at the time of their commission. Notice is thus of the essence. As codified in Article 15 of the Political Covenant, the principle does not prevent the criminalization of acts which are proscribed according to the general principles of law recognized by the community of nations. As the Trial Chamber noted, it is undeniable that acts such as murder, torture, and inhuman treatment prohibited by common Article 3 are criminal according to this standard. It would strain credulity 'to contend that the accused would not recognise the criminal nature' of these acts.[47]

V. CONCLUSIONS

As I hope this discussion has demonstrated, by turning to internationally recognized human rights to inform the procedural and substantive provisions of international humanitarian law, the Tribunals have enhanced both the scope and legitimacy of international humanitarian law. The application of human rights norms in the ad hoc Tribunals ensures that accused are accorded the due process and fair trial protections necessary to show that international accountability can be achieved without violating an accused's rights. Further, by drawing on fundamental human rights to inform the substantive crimes of humanitarian law, the Tribunals have ensured that serious violations of international humanitarian law do not go unpunished because of lack of precedent, while also respecting the principle of legality.

But what is most important is this: by criminalizing violations of the provisions of common Article 3 of the Geneva Conventions as well as crimes against humanity, both with content identical to human rights norms, the Tribunals have enhanced the bite of human rights law.

---

[45] Ibid., para 150.
[46] *Military and Paramilitary Activities in and against Nicaragua (Nicaragua v United States of America)* (Merits: Judgment) [1986] ICJ Rep 14, para 218.
[47] *Čelebići* Trial Judgement, n 32 above, para 313.

Although victims of human rights violations were once confined to seeking redress from states through civil remedies, by importing human rights norms into the courtroom, the Tribunals are providing additional powerful enforcement mechanisms for human rights abuses committed by individual actors.

Quietly, almost unnoticed, fundamental principles of human rights have become values protected and enforced by international criminal law. The entire international community may take pride in this development.

18

THE PROTECTION OF CIVILIANS IN THE JURISPRUDENCE OF THE ICTY AND ICTR*

It is a great pleasure for me to speak to you today about the jurisprudence concerning the protection of civilians of the International Criminal Tribunal for the former Yugoslavia (ICTY) and the International Criminal Tribunal for Rwanda (ICTR), which I will refer to collectively as the Tribunals. The Tribunals' interpretation of customary international and treaty law and elucidation of specific norms have played an important role in increasing civilians' protection in times of conflict.

I will note that though I serve as a judge on the Appeals Chambers of both Tribunals, I speak to you today only in my personal capacity rather than as a representative of the ICTY or ICTR.

Before addressing aspects of the Tribunals' jurisprudence that explicitly discuss the protection of civilians, I want to offer some preliminary remarks on the underlying bases of that protection, and also on the Tribunals' general jurisprudence. After that I would like to discuss the protection of civilians in the context of Tribunal jurisprudence concerning both crimes against humanity and war crimes—focusing especially on the definitions of the terms 'civilian' and 'civilian population' with regard to crimes against humanity—and the parameters of specific crimes explicitly directed against a civilian population, especially the war crime of terror. Finally, I hope to offer some concluding thoughts on the

---

* Delivered at the twenty-seventh annual ICRC-NYU Law Seminar for Diplomats on International Humanitarian Law (for diplomats accredited to the United Nations), in New York City, New York, USA, on 4 March 2010.

application of the norms established and clarified by the Tribunals' jurisprudence.

☙❧

The Tribunals' jurisprudence concerning the protection of civilians has not, of course, appeared in a vacuum. Already in the Middle Ages societies recognized the importance of protecting civilians in times of armed conflict. In more recent times, civilians have gradually received additional protections from various treaties, including The Hague Conventions, the Geneva Conventions of 1949, and the Additional Protocols of 1977.

The gradually expanding body of treaties to which I have just referred constitutes a central corpus of international humanitarian law, which I will refer to henceforth as IHL, and which governs the conduct of armed conflict. At the core of this body of law is what the ICTY Appeals Chamber has termed the 'absolute prohibition on the targeting of civilians in customary international law'.[1] This unequivocal interpretation of the protections provided by international law, repeated and echoed in other judgments of the ICTY Appeals Chamber,[2] underscores that no justification for the explicit targeting of civilians—including military necessity—can be read into customary international law.

As IHL has developed, however, it has gradually grappled with additional issues that arise from this prohibition on attacks against civilians, including questions of proportionality, distinction, and collateral damage. These questions have also been a major focus of those interpreting the parameters of customary international law.

Prior to the creation of the Tribunals, and with the exception of certain post-World War II trials, addressing violations of both treaty-based and customary international law was considered to be the responsibility of individual states, which could hold individuals criminally responsible for breaches of these rules through their domestic legal systems. The establishment of the Tribunals, and eventually other international criminal courts such as the International Criminal Court (ICC), allowed individual criminal responsibility to be assessed at an international as well as a domestic level. In particular, the Tribunals have provided authoritative interpretations relating to the crime of genocide, war crimes, and crimes

---

[1] *Prosecutor v Tihomir Blaškić* (Judgement) IT-95-14-A (29 July 2004) (*Blaškić* Appeal Judgement), para 109.

[2] See, eg, *Prosecutor v Dragomir Milošević* (Judgement) IT-98-29/1-A (12 November 2009) (*Dragomir Milošević* Appeal Judgement); *Prosecutor v Stanislav Galić* (Judgement) IT-98-29-A (30 November 2006) (*Galić* Appeal Judgement).

against humanity, and these efforts have significantly clarified the parameters of civilian protection in conflict.

༺༻

In order to understand the Tribunals' roles in protecting civilians, it is important to turn first to their founding documents as well as their interpretive practice.

Article 2 of the ICTY Statute, for example, grants the ICTY the power to prosecute grave breaches of the 1949 Geneva Conventions, such as those concerned with torture, deprivation of fair trial rights, deportation, confinement, and hostage-taking. Article 4, the corresponding part of the ICTR's Statute, grants it jurisdiction over violations of common Article 3 of the 1949 Geneva Conventions and Additional Protocol II, reflecting the non-international nature of the Rwanda conflict. Article 5 of the ICTY Statute and Article 3 of the ICTR Statute, meanwhile, grant the power to prosecute a long list of crimes against humanity during both international and non-international armed conflicts. And Article 4 of the ICTY Statute and Article 2 of the ICTR Statute give the respective Tribunals jurisdiction over genocide.

Despite these explicit statutory grants of jurisdiction, however, in practice the Tribunals, and in particular the ICTY, convict for crimes that were part of customary international law at the time they were committed, in order to avoid any risk of violating the principle of legality. In accordance with this approach, many of the Tribunals' judgments have devoted careful attention to The Hague Conventions, the Geneva Conventions and the Additional Protocols, and other relevant treaties, and their relationship to customary international law.

Thus, for example, the ICTY extensively addressed the Genocide Convention in convicting General Radislav Krstić for aiding and abetting genocide at Srebrenica,[3] and the ICTR, in its 1998 *Akayesu* trial judgment, found, inter alia, that rape and sexual violence can constitute genocide under the Genocide Convention, which is declaratory of customary law.[4] Judgments of both Tribunals also deal with a variety of other potential violations of the Geneva Conventions and Additional Protocols, and many of these address issues of direct concern to civilians, such as whether and when plunder and destruction of property and

---

[3] *Prosecutor v Radislav Krstić* (Judgement) IT-98-33-A (19 April 2004).
[4] *Prosecutor v Jean-Paul Akayesu* (Judgement) ICTR-96-4-T (2 September 1998) (*Akayesu* Trial Judgement).

cultural artifacts can be prosecuted.[5] For the purposes of this lecture, however, I will focus on crimes against humanity and violations of the laws and customs of war involving direct civilian casualties.

◯З○

To begin, I turn to the issue of crimes against humanity. Because the ICTY's jurisprudence on this issue is so extensive, I will begin by focusing on that Tribunal's case law.

Article 5 of the ICTY Statute, which addresses crimes against humanity, explicitly prohibits civilians' murder, extermination, enslavement, deportation, imprisonment, torture, rape, persecution on political, racial, and religious grounds, and other inhumane acts. Article 5 specifies, however, that the ICTY may only hear cases involving crimes against humanity when they are committed in an international or internal armed conflict and are directed against any civilian population.

In interpreting the text of Article 5, one of the central questions facing the ICTY has been defining the terms 'civilian' and 'civilian population'. Through numerous judgments, the ICTY has addressed these questions and developed robust case law concerning both the status of individuals who are not civilians but are *hors de combat* and present within a given civilian population, and the status of populations into which some combatants are mixed.

In its 2002 *Kunarac* judgment, the ICTY Appeals Chamber specified that a Chamber must be satisfied that 'the attack was in fact directed against a civilian "population", rather than against a limited and randomly selected number of individuals'.[6] Moreover, 'the expression "directed against" is an expression which "specifies that in the context of a crime against humanity the civilian population is the primary object of the attack"'.[7] This analysis eliminated the possibility of arguing that the presence of certain non-civilian individuals among members of a civilian population could excuse an attack primarily directed at that population.

The ICTY Appeals Chamber further developed this point in its 2004 *Blaškić* judgment, where it concluded that, 'in order to determine whether the presence of soldiers within a civilian population deprives the population of its civilian character, the number of soldiers, as well as whether

---

[5] See, eg, *Prosecutor v Dario Kordić and Mario Čerkez* (Judgement) IT-95-14/2-A (17 December 2004) (*Kordić and Čerkez* Appeal Judgement).

[6] *Prosecutor v Dragoljub Kunarac et al.* (Judgement) IT-96-23&23/1-A (12 June 2002), para 90.

[7] Ibid., para 91.

they are on leave, must be examined'.⁸ The identification of these more specific criteria helped to provide bases by which courts and armed forces lawyers, among others, could identify what constitutes a 'civilian population'—ensuring that this crucial distinction can more easily be applied in future trials and 'on the ground' during particular military operations.

In its 2008 *Martić* judgment, the Appeals Chamber formalized its previous approaches by holding that 'the definition of civilian contained in Article 50 of Additional Protocol I reflects the definition of civilian for the purpose of applying Article 5 of the [ICTY] Statute'.⁹ The Appeals Chamber explained that individuals who were not civilians, but were *hors de combat*, were not included in the definition of 'civilian' in Article 5 of the ICTY Statute. However, the Appeals Chamber went on to hold that individuals who were *hors de combat* but not civilians, yet were present within a civilian population, could still be the victim of a crime against humanity directed at that civilian population.

The conclusions of these appeal judgments were reaffirmed and extended in the ICTY Appeals Chamber's 2009 *Mrkšić and Šljivančanin* judgment, over which I presided.¹⁰ Noting its previous *Kordić and Čerkez*, *Blaškić*, and *Martić* judgments, among others, the Appeals Chamber explained that 'the civilian status of the victims, the number of civilians, and the proportion of civilians within a civilian population are factors relevant to the determination of whether' a population qualifies as civilian for purposes of Article 5, but that 'there is no requirement nor is it an element of crimes against humanity that the victims of the underlying crimes be "civilians"'.¹¹ An attack aimed at a civilian population can thus be prosecuted even if none of the casualties falls within the ICTY's definition of 'civilian'.

The ICTR has been less focused on the definition of a 'civilian population' than the ICTY. This is primarily because the armed conflict in Rwanda was internal, as opposed to the international aspects of the Yugoslavia conflict, and thus governed by a different set of international laws, especially common Article 3 of the Geneva Conventions and Additional Protocol II. Consequently, the definition of 'civilian population' adopted by certain ICTR Trial Chambers with regards to crimes against humanity under Article 3 of the ICTR Statute has been more expansive

---

⁸ *Blaškić* Appeal Judgement, n 1 above, para 115. See also *Galić* Appeal Judgement, n 2 above, para 137.
⁹ *Prosecutor v Milan Martić* (Judgement) IT-95-11-A (8 October 2008), para 302.
¹⁰ *Prosecutor v Mile Mrkšić and Veselin Šljivančanin* (Judgement) IT-95-13/1-A (5 May 2009) (*Mrkšić and Šljivančanin* Appeal Judgement).
¹¹ Ibid., para 32.

than that of the ICTY Appeals Chamber, reflecting the fact that in internal armed conflict, the key distinction in terms of international law is not between civilians and combatants, but between persons that directly participate in hostilities and those that do not.

More specifically, the ICTR's 1998 *Akayesu* trial judgment explained that:

> Members of the civilian population are people who are not taking any active part in the hostilities, including members of the armed forces who laid down their arms and those persons placed *hors de combat* by sickness, wounds, detention or any other cause. Where there are certain individuals within the civilian population who do not come within the definition of civilians, this does not deprive the population of its civilian character.[12]

Under this definition, unlike that of the ICTY's *Martić* appeal judgment, a group of combatants temporarily *hors de combat* would qualify as a civilian population. The *Akayesu* definition was echoed in the 1999 *Rutaganda* and 2000 *Musema* trial judgments.[13]

The differences between the *Akayesu*-based ICTR definition of 'civilian population' and that of recent ICTY Appeals Chamber judgments might lead to some questions of whether there was a more general difference in the approaches of the two Tribunals. However, judges at the two Tribunals are acutely aware of the differences between the two conflicts, and of the different legal regimes that apply to each. Indeed, the ICTR's 2008 *Bagosora* trial judgment acknowledged the ICTY's *Martić* appeal judgment's definition of civilian population in cases of international armed conflict.[14] Thus, I would suggest that though there may be some facial differences between the jurisprudence of the two Tribunals, there is, in fact, little substantive conflict.

೧೮೦

The ICTY has also given special care to interpreting Article 3 of its Statute, which gives it jurisdiction over violations of the laws or customs of war.

On a general level, the law of war crimes often addresses certain types of violence against military personnel, who do not benefit from the more

---

[12] *Akayesu* Trial Judgement, n 4 above, para 582 (internal citations omitted).

[13] *Prosecutor v Alfred Musema* (Judgement and Sentence) ICTR-96-13-T (27 January 2000); *Prosecutor v Georges Anderson Nderubumwe Rutaganda* (Judgement and Sentence) ICTR-96-3-T (6 December 1999).

[14] *Prosecutor v Théoneste Bagosora et al.* (Judgement and Sentence) ICTR-98-41-T (18 December 2008).

general protections provided to civilians. Thus, for example, the torture and murder of a group almost exclusively composed of Croat soldiers who were prisoners of war resulted in convictions for murder and torture as war crimes, rather than crimes against humanity, in the ICTY's *Mrkšić* judgments.[15]

With regard to civilians, ICTY judgments addressing war crimes laws have effectively confirmed that warfare itself is not prohibited under IHL, and that certain types of civilian casualties are lawful if they are proportionate and the incidental result of attacks on military objectives. In line with this principle, the 2008 *Strugar* appeal judgment reiterated that in order to establish a violation of common Article 3, and thus commission of a war crime, a court must be satisfied that there was no nexus between a victim and acts of war intended to harm opponents' personnel or equipment.[16] Such a nexus might legalize the act of war concerned.

In addition to underscoring the basic standards that are needed to sustain convictions for violations of the laws or customs of war, the ICTY Appeals Chamber has also elucidated the elements of a number of war crimes directed against civilians. Among the most basic of these is the prohibition of attacks on civilians. Thus, for example, the *Strugar* appeal judgment reiterated that attacks 'wilfully directed at civilians', whether deliberately or through reckless disregard for the civilians' safety, are illegal.[17] The *Strugar* appeal judgment also provided a list of factors that may be relevant to determining whether an attack was directed against civilians.

In addition to discussing attacks on civilians, the ICTY's judgments have also addressed a number of other relevant issues under the rubric of Article 3 of the Statute. Among these is the unlawful confinement of civilians, which the *Kordić and Čerkez* appeal judgment explained was illegal if there are no reasonable grounds for believing that the security of the detaining power makes such confinement necessary, or if procedural safeguards elucidated in Article 43 of Geneva Convention IV are not followed.[18]

Another issue addressed in an Article 3 context is forced labor by civilians. The ICTY's 2004 *Blaškić* appeal judgment confirmed that

---

[15] *Prosecutor v Mile Mrkšić et al.* (Judgement) IT-95-13/1-T (27 September 2007); *Mrkšić and Šljivančanin* Appeal Judgement, n 10 above. Editor's note: One of the convictions, for aiding and abetting murder, was later vacated. *Prosecutor v Veselin Šljivančanin* (Review Judgement) IT-95-13/1-R.1 (8 December 2010).

[16] See, eg, *Prosecutor v Pavle Strugar* (Judgement) IT-01-42-A (17 July 2008).

[17] Ibid., para 270.

[18] See *Kordić and Čerkez* Appeal Judgement, n 5 above, para 73.

forced labor by civilians was not necessarily a violation of IHL; relying on Geneva Conventions III and IV, however, it held that forced labor related to military activities or as part of a military or semi-military operation was prohibited. The Appeals Chamber also found that orders to build fortifications (such as trenches) for use against enemy forces with which the civilian forced laborers sympathized caused serious mental or physical suffering and constituted an attack on human dignity. This finding parallels Article 6 of the 1907 Hague Convention (No IV), which prohibits the use of prisoner of war labor in connection with the operations of a war.

Recently, some of the most significant ICTY jurisprudence regarding civilians and violations of the laws or customs of war has involved the crime of terror. This issue is directly addressed by two cases relating to events accompanying the siege of Sarajevo.

As all of you will recall, the Bosnian capital was besieged by Serbian military forces between 1992 and 1996, a campaign that became emblematic of Yugoslavia's break-up. Elements of the siege included sniper attacks, shelling, and the use of modified air bombs. These last consisted of explosives normally launched from the air, modified to allow deployment by ground forces using rockets. Large numbers of civilians residing in Sarajevo were killed or injured in these attacks.

Two of the Generals who consecutively commanded the forces besieging Sarajevo, Generals Stanislav Galić and Dragomir Milošević, were found guilty by the ICTY of various crimes in relation to the siege, including murder and inhumane acts as crimes against humanity, and were ultimately sentenced to life and twenty-nine years of imprisonment, respectively. The Appeals and Trial Chamber judgments in these cases engaged in a reasoned judicial dialogue that both established that the crime of terror was prohibited under customary international law and clarified the elements required to sustain a conviction for the crime of terror.

More specifically, in its 2006 *Galić* appeal judgment, the ICTY Appeals Chamber took the view that 'the prohibition of terror against the civilian population[,] as enshrined in Article 51(2) of Additional Protocol I and Article 13(2) of Additional Protocol II, was a part of customary international law from the time of its inclusion in those treaties'.[19] (I would note at this juncture that the crime of terror is distinct from the separate crime of terrorism of the al-Qaeda type, which is not my subject in this lecture.)

---

[19] *Galić* Appeal Judgement, n 2 above, para 86.

The 2009 *Dragomir Milošević* appeal judgment followed the *Galić* appeal judgment's conclusion that the crime of terror was part of customary international law, and further delineated the specific elements that underpin the crime. The Appeals Chamber confirmed that, in order to be convicted for the crime of terror, a defendant must be shown to have intended 'to make the civilian population or individual civilians not taking direct part in hostilities the object of... acts of violence or threats thereof'.[20] It also required the 'specific intent to spread terror among the civilian population'.[21] The Appeals Chamber underscored that, to sustain a conviction, the Tribunal must find that 'the *primary* purpose' of a given act or threat of violence is the spread of terror, but that this does not need to be its sole purpose.[22]

With regard to the *actus reus* or 'unlawful act' requirement of the crime of terror, the *Dragomir Milošević* appeal judgment explained that, in order for the crime of terror to fall under the jurisdiction of the Tribunal, victims must have 'suffered grave consequences resulting from the acts or threats of violence; such grave consequences include, but are not limited to[,] death or serious injury to body or health'.[23] The Appeals Chamber underscored that 'the nature of the acts of violence or threats thereof constitutive of the crime of terror can vary',[24] but that it was unquestionable that in the context of Sarajevo—with its numerous civilian casualties and injuries—this threshold was met.

The Appeals Chamber also emphasized two additional points concerning the *actus reus* of the crime of terror. Making reference to the *travaux préparatoires* of Additional Protocol I, the Appeals Chamber rejected the Prosecution's contention that a conviction for the crime of terror was possible independent of showing any particular injury to body or health—however, it left open the exact scope of impact that might constitute sufficient justification to convict for the crime of terror. The Appeals Chamber also noted that, while the actual terrorization of a population was not an element of the crime of terror that needed to be proved, evidence of such terrorization could contribute to establishing other elements of the crime of terror. The Appeals Chamber concluded that, in the context of the case against General Dragomir Milošević, the Trial Chamber's findings on the psychological impact of Serbian attacks

---

[20] *Dragomir Milošević* Appeal Judgement, n 2 above, para 37.
[21] Ibid.
[22] Ibid. (emphasis in original).
[23] Ibid., para 33 (internal citation omitted).
[24] Ibid.

on Sarajevo's civilian population were sufficient to satisfy the gravity threshold requirement of the crime of terror.

It is noteworthy that, in defining the elements of the crime of terror, the Appeals Chamber has not attempted to delimit every aspect of the crime. In particular, the Appeals Chamber has left somewhat open the exact scope of the serious injuries to body and health that are required for a conviction. It has also underscored that the list of factors identified in the *Galić* appeal judgment as helpful in identifying whether individual threats and attacks were aimed at terrorizing a civilian population—including the attacks' nature, timing, manner, and duration—were not 'mandatory considerations' but were, instead, indicators of potential means of interpreting intent.[25] This reluctance to delimit recognizes that the crime of terror can take many forms, depending on its context, and that the Tribunal is not in a position to foresee all future iterations of the crime.

In addition to providing for the explicit protection of civilians in all circumstances, and identifying the parameters of the crime of terror, the Tribunals have also underscored the importance of distinguishing between civilian and combatant populations when planning and carrying out attacks. The *Galić* and *Dragomir Milošević* appeal judgments are again instructive in delineating the ICTY's jurisprudence on this issue, which relies heavily on Article 51(2) of Additional Protocol I and which states that civilians and civilian populations should not be subject to attack, making no exemptions even for exigencies such as military necessity.

More specifically, the *Galić* appeal judgment underscored that 'a fundamental principle of international humanitarian law, the principle of distinction,... obliges warring parties to distinguish *at all times* between the civilian population and combatants and between civilian objects and military objectives and accordingly to direct their operations only against military objectives'.[26] The *Dragomir Milošević* appeal judgment further explained that there was no basis for arguing that particular geographical zones of the city of Sarajevo could be distinguished as civilian or military, with free-for-all attacks allowed in the latter; instead, it required that case-by-case distinctions be made in order to avoid civilian populations and targets. This clarification strongly suggests that many Allied

---

[25] Ibid., para 37.
[26] *Galić* Appeal Judgement, n 2 above, para 191 (internal quotation marks omitted, emphasis in original).

tactics during World War II, such as the mass bombing of Dresden, would not be permissible under customary law today.

༄༅།

As I come to the close of my remarks, I acknowledge that my review of the Tribunals' jurisprudence has necessarily been brief. Still, it should already be obvious that the Tribunals have done far more than merely repeat legal truisms—instead, in the limited period of their existence, they have played a significant role in translating generalized international prohibitions into workable rules that are not just recited with approbation in conference halls or the pages of law journals but can be practically applied by courts of law.

As you consider the Tribunals' work, I would underscore again that the protection of civilians is not a unitary field of law in the jurisprudence of the Tribunals, but instead constitutes distinct strands of protections emerging from the separate legal settings of crimes against humanity and war crimes. Crimes against humanity are comparatively straightforward to assess once an attack against a civilian population is established. For civilian casualties to be classified as war crimes, however, requires a more delicate assessment. This reflects the uncomfortable fact that IHL does not prohibit war and its attendant violence—it only seeks to regulate the conduct of war, by means that include prohibiting deliberate or indiscriminate attacks on civilians and imposing proportionality rules, codified in Article 51(5) of Additional Protocol I. Thus, civilian casualties will only constitute a war crime when courts are able to conclude beyond reasonable doubt that individuals were not combatants, and that their deaths or injuries were not an acceptable by-product of a legitimate military action.

Views on this last issue are almost inevitably subjective at the margins, and the Tribunals have not established—nor will they be able to establish—definitive criteria for uniformly calculating 'acceptable' levels of civilian casualties. Instead, this is a question that will continue to be ripe for dialogue, not just among lawyers, but also among philosophers, literary scholars, military personnel, and, indeed, all educated persons.

As the sun slowly sets on the time-limited ad hoc Tribunals, I have great confidence that the ICC, as a permanent court, will both benefit from the Tribunals' labors and continue their work of elucidating customary international law, even as the ICC operates in a functionally distinct way, relying primarily on its Statute rather than on customary law.

The post hoc efforts of the Tribunals, the ICC, and other international judicial institutions to assess and assign individual criminal responsibility have been, and will continue to be, significant—but, of course, they are only one of the ways these institutions help to ensure the protection of civilian populations. The ultimate hope of the international community in creating international criminal tribunals is that combatants—both organized and irregular—will take note of and conform to the norms these institutions enforce. The Tribunals' elaboration of the full panoply of protections that civilian populations are due thus not only serves as a more detailed rendering of the treaty elements and customary law constituting international prohibitions, but also stands as a warning and interpretive guide to combatants the world over.

While it is hard to point to individual cause-and-effect relationships between particular judgments and subsequent military actions, I have been encouraged by the increased emphasis in a variety of militaries on distinguishing between civilians and combatants, and on providing appropriate protections to civilian populations. I have no illusions that these protections are as complete as they should be, nor do I claim any specific credit for particular judgments of the Tribunals. But I am convinced that the Tribunals' convictions of high-ranking military officers for crimes against civilian populations have not passed unnoticed, and am equally sure that the details of the Tribunals' judgments are carefully studied by military lawyers.

Ultimately, the creation of international criminal tribunals is a solemn undertaking by the international community that there will be no impunity for genocide, war crimes, and crimes against humanity. The judgments of the Tribunals offer both a warning signal to combatants and a guide for other courts about the parameters of the law. I believe the carefully delineated protections for civilian populations that I have discussed today will serve important roles in future prosecutions and, most encouragingly, be respected by future military lawyers, strategists, and combatants. In this sense, the Tribunals' judgments constitute another step towards Henry Dunant's and the ICRC's goal of a world where the worst excesses of warfare are eliminated.

19

DELIVER US NOT TO EVIL: KEEPING POWS SAFE*

Few groups of individuals are more vulnerable and more in need of protection than prisoners of war (POWs) who have been captured by their enemy or by other hostile actors. All too often, they are mistreated, tortured, or even killed by those who have taken them captive or to whom they have surrendered.

But for all of the risks of mistreatment that arise when POWs are taken into custody by an opposing force or other hostile group, a host of additional dangers emerge when the custody of POWs is transferred from that first entity to another. Often the individuals or groups that assume custody of POWs through such transfers are harder to locate, less accountable, and less likely to provide POWs with the protections to which they are entitled. And sometimes such transfers even lead to the death of the POWs. This was the situation in *Prosecutor v Mile Mrkšić and Veselin Šljivančanin*, a case before the International Criminal Tribunal for the former Yugoslavia (ICTY) involving one of the most terrible massacres of POWs during the Yugoslavia conflicts. The ICTY's 2009 appeal judgment in this case, and, in particular, the Appeals Chamber's delineation of the law related to POWs, will be the subject of my talk today.[1]

Although I serve as a judge of the ICTY, I will note for the record that my comments reflect only my personal opinions.

ଔଓ

The problems posed by the transfer of custody of POWs are not new. During World War II, for example, Wehrmacht authorities would, from

---

* Delivered at the International Criminal Tribunal for the former Yugoslavia, The Hague, The Netherlands, in December 2010.

[1] *Prosecutor v Mile Mrkšić and Veselin Šljivančanin* (Judgement) IT-95-13/1-A (5 May 2009) (*Mrkšić and Šljivančanin* Appeal Judgement).

time to time, pass POWs into the custody of the SS or the Gestapo, from whom the prisoners received much worse treatment. Likewise, the Soviet army would sometimes transfer custody of POWs to the NKVD (the Soviet secret police), as at Katyn. Such transfers of custody remain a persistent practice even today, and for the International Committee of the Red Cross (ICRC) and others in the humanitarian sector, transfers of POWs can create difficult, if not insurmountable, challenges in tracing and protecting individual prisoners. These humanitarian tasks are rendered all the more difficult when—as is increasingly the case in modern conflicts—POWs are transferred to the custody of non-state actors. Grave humanitarian difficulties are also caused by the so-called extraordinary renditions of detainees by one state to another state where mistreatment is expected.

The escalating involvement of non-state actors in armed conflicts around the world poses a number of challenging legal questions for those who wish to ensure that POWs are protected, because non-state actors typically do not consider themselves bound by—and often operate without regard to—the requirements of international humanitarian law, including the protections enshrined in the 1949 Geneva Conventions. Even when applying the Geneva Conventions, however, difficult questions still arise.

ೞ

For example, the Third Geneva Convention—the quintessential international treaty for the protection of POWs—states that POWs 'must at all times be humanely treated'[2] and enumerates various ways in which POWs shall be protected. Yet, the provisions of the Third Geneva Convention—common Article 3 excepted—apply in a clear and uncontroversial way only when the conflict at issue is international in character, or when the parties to the conflict have agreed that the Convention or its provisions will apply. Where a conflict is not international in character, it must therefore be determined whether the warring parties have explicitly or implicitly agreed that POWs should be afforded the protections guaranteed by the Third Geneva Convention. Just such an issue was presented on appeal in the *Mrkšić and Šljivančanin* case.

---

[2] Geneva Convention relative to the Treatment of Prisoners of War (Third Geneva Convention) (1949) 75 UNTS 135, art 13.

The events giving rise to that case took place in the autumn of 1991 in and around the municipality of Vukovar, in present-day Croatia. Serb forces had laid siege to Vukovar from August until November of 1991, during which time the city was largely destroyed by shelling and hundreds of people were killed. In the final days of the siege, several hundred people sought refuge at the Vukovar hospital in the hope that it would be evacuated in the presence of international observers. Those who took shelter in the hospital were ultimately captured by advancing Serb forces. The Trial Chamber found that 194 such people—the majority of whom were Croatian POWs—were taken from the Vukovar hospital to Ovčara, where they were mistreated and, after the withdrawal of the last troops of the Yugoslav Peoples' Army (JNA), killed by members of the Territorial Defense (TO) and Serb paramilitaries.[3]

On appeal, the ICTY's Appeals Chamber observed that the Trial Chamber had made no finding as to whether the armed conflict in the municipality of Vukovar was international in nature. The Appeals Chamber did not make any such finding itself. It concluded, however, that certain orders and instructions of Serb military leaders, as well as the provisions of the Zagreb Agreement (reached between representatives of the Republic of Croatia and the JNA concerning the evacuation of the sick and wounded from the Vukovar hospital), extended the protections of the Third Geneva Convention to POWs captured at the hospital. As the Appeals Chamber explained, 'these documents provide sufficient evidence to conclude that the JNA had agreed that the Croat forces were to be considered prisoners of war and that Geneva Convention III was to apply'.[4]

But what if such documents had not been in evidence? Would the Appeals Chamber have been forced to conclude that the POWs captured at the Vukovar hospital were devoid of protection under the Geneva Conventions? The answer, quite simply, is no.

It is well established—including by the ICTY's own jurisprudence—that common Article 3 of the Geneva Conventions, which is applicable to both international and non-international armed conflicts, is part of customary international law and therefore binds all parties to a conflict. Common Article 3, as the *Mrkšić and Šljivančanin* appeal judgment explains, 'enshrines the prohibition against any violence against the life and person of those taking no active part in the hostilities, including members of armed forces who have laid down their arms and those placed *hors de combat* by

---

[3] *Prosecutor v Mile Mrkšić et al.* (Judgement) IT-95-13/1-T (27 September 2007).
[4] *Mrkšić and Šljivančanin* Appeal Judgement, n 1 above, para 69.

sickness, wounds, detention, or any other cause'.[5] The Appeals Chamber accordingly reasoned that common Article 3 'reflects the same spirit of the duty to protect members of armed forces who have laid down their arms and are detained' as the specific protections provided for POWs in the Third Geneva Convention, viewed as a whole.[6]

This conclusion, which turns on customary law, was not unprecedented. During World War II, well before the adoption of common Article 3 in the 1949 Geneva Conventions, the 1929 Geneva Convention on POWs—the predecessor of the Third Geneva Convention—was not applicable on the eastern front because Stalin had made the grave mistake of not ratifying it. Yet, both the International Military Tribunal established in the wake of the war and the follow-on Nuremberg tribunals did not hesitate to regard the 1929 Geneva Convention as a reflection of long-established principles of customary humanitarian law concerning the treatment of POWs—and to convict Nazi war criminals on that basis.[7] Of course, the customary law character of the Third Geneva Convention, and of its third Article, are no longer questioned. But the Nuremberg jurisprudence was seminal in establishing the customary law character of the main provisions of its predecessor—the 1929 Geneva Convention.

෴

Even if there is a growing jurisprudence concerning the universality of certain duties to protect POWs, there is—or, at least, there was, before the *Mrkšić and Šljivančanin* appeal judgment—considerably less guidance concerning if and when those duties may cease to apply. This question was squarely presented by the facts in the *Mrkšić and Šljivančanin* case because the Trial Chamber acquitted Veselin Šljivančanin of the murder of the POWs at Ovčara on the basis that his responsibility for the welfare and security of the POWs ended with the withdrawal of the last JNA troops at Ovčara. The Prosecution appealed this aspect of the Trial Chamber's judgment, arguing, in essence, that Šljivančanin—who had command authority over the JNA troops involved in evacuating POWs from the Vukovar hospital—had a continuing legal duty under international humanitarian law to protect the POWs, even after Šljivančanin's

---

[5] Ibid., para 70.
[6] Ibid.
[7] International Military Tribunal (Nuremberg), 'Judgment and Sentences' (1947) 41 *AJIL* 172; *United States v Wilhelm von Leeb et al. (The High Command Case)*, reprinted in *Trials of War Criminals Before the Nuernberg Military Tribunals Under Control Council Law No 10*, Vol X–XI (Buffalo: William S Hein & Co, 1997).

co-accused, Mile Mrkšić, ordered the JNA troops' withdrawal from Ovčara. The Appeals Chamber agreed with the Prosecution, and I would like to take a few minutes to explain why.

First, let us recall that the fundamental principle enshrined in the Third Geneva Convention is that POWs shall be treated humanely and protected from physical and mental harm. As I have already explained, the Appeals Chamber concluded that this basic principle mirrors the protective principle found in common Article 3 of the Geneva Conventions and is non-derogable. Under the Third Geneva Convention, this fundamental principle applies from the time POWs fall into the power of the enemy until their final release and repatriation or transfer to another unit capable of ensuring their protection and welfare.

This means that it is the obligation of each agent in charge of the protection or custody of POWs to ensure that their transfer to another agent will not diminish the protection to which the prisoners are entitled. That obligation is so well established that it appears in both Articles 12 and 46 of the Third Geneva Convention, concerning the transfer of POWs to another state party to the Convention and the transfer of POWs to other locations by a detaining power, respectively. The Appeals Chamber therefore made plain in its appeal judgment that, before transferring custody of the POWs at Ovčara, the JNA troops should have satisfied themselves of the willingness and ability of the members of the TO—like the JNA, a constituent element of the armed forces of the former Yugoslavia and subordinated to the Supreme Defense Council—to apply the principle enshrined in the Third Geneva Convention.

The Appeals Chamber also made clear that, although the Third Geneva Convention places the responsibility for POWs squarely on the detaining power, this is not to the exclusion of individual responsibility. Drawing upon the text of the Third Geneva Convention, ICRC commentaries, and the regulations of the JNA itself, the Appeals Chamber concluded that individuals are personally accountable when they have breached the law governing the treatment of POWs. It follows from this that agents of detaining powers need not be specifically invested with authority over POWs to be subject to international obligations concerning POWs' protection. Thus, in the view of the Appeals Chamber,

all state agents who find themselves with custody of prisoners of war owe them a duty of protection regardless of whether the investment of responsibility was made through explicit delegation such as through legislative enactment or a superior order, or as a result of the state agent finding himself with *de facto* custody over prisoners of war such as where a prisoner of war surrenders to that agent.[8]

Based upon these considerations, the Appeals Chamber concluded that the Trial Chamber erred in finding that Šljivančanin's duty to protect the POWs held at Ovčara pursuant to the laws and customs of war ended upon Mrkšić's order to withdraw. Šljivančanin was under a duty to protect the POWs evacuated from the Vukovar hospital and taken to Ovčara, and this duty included an obligation not to allow the transfer of custody of the POWs to anyone without first assuring himself that they would not be harmed. Put differently, Mrkšić's order to withdraw the JNA troops did not relieve Šljivančanin of his position as an officer of the JNA. As such, Šljivančanin remained an agent of a detaining power—and thus continued to be bound by the Third Geneva Convention not to transfer the POWs to another agent who would not guarantee their safety.

෴

The *Mrkšić and Šljivančanin* appeal judgment thus has seminal importance for the proposition that the captor retains responsibility for the protection and welfare of the POWs in his or her custody until their transfer to another unit with the capability of ensuring such protection and welfare.

Although certain aspects of the Appeals Chamber's judgment have been vacated following review proceedings conducted in 2010, nothing in the Appeals Chamber's review judgment[9] undermines the logic of the Chamber's earlier delineation of 'the legal responsibilities that Šljivančanin bore, and agents of Detaining Powers continue to bear, with respect to [POWs] in their custody',[10] including the obligation to ensure that the transfer of POWs to another agent will not diminish or detract from their protection. 'No matter what other procedures might be bypassed in times of stress and conflict, these responsibilities are neither vague nor elective, and the *Mrkšić and Šljivančanin* Appeal Judgement's careful guidance on this subject remains valid.'[11]

---

[8] *Mrkšić and Šljivančanin* Appeal Judgement, n 1 above, para 73.
[9] *Prosecutor v Veselin Šljivančanin* (Review Judgement) IT-95-13/1-R.1 (8 December 2010).
[10] Ibid., Separate Opinion of Judge Meron, para 3.
[11] Ibid., Separate Opinion of Judge Meron, para 4.

20

INTERNATIONAL AND NON-INTERNATIONAL CONFLICTS IN THE JURISPRUDENCE OF THE ICTY AND ICTR*

In this lecture I will discuss with you some of the jurisprudence of the international criminal tribunals for the former Yugoslavia and Rwanda on international and non-international armed conflicts. I will begin by focusing on the seminal interlocutory decision of the ICTY Appeals Chamber in the *Tadić* case, which involved a challenge to the Tribunal's jurisdiction.[1] I will then proceed to discuss some of the important ways in which the *Tadić* decision, presided over by the visionary scholar and judge Antonio Cassese, has influenced the jurisprudence of the ad hoc Tribunals and the development of international humanitarian law more generally.

Although I serve as a judge on the Appeals Chambers of the ICTY and ICTR, I will note that I am speaking with you today strictly in my personal capacity.

I. THE TADIĆ DECISION

As you are all, of course, aware, prior to the 1949 Geneva Conventions, there were hardly any rules in international law governing non-international armed conflicts. Internal conflicts were seen, with few exceptions, as matters of sovereign or domestic concern, falling outside the scope of international law.

---

* Delivered at the twenty-eighth annual ICRC-NYU Law Seminar for Diplomats on International Humanitarian Law (for diplomats accredited to the United Nations), in New York City, New York, USA, on 17 March 2011.

[1] *Prosecutor v Duško Tadić* (Decision on the Defence Motion for Interlocutory Appeal on Jurisdiction) IT-94-1-AR72 (2 October 1995) (*Tadić* Decision).

This began to change in the 1930s and then, more dramatically, in 1949 with the introduction of common Article 3 of the Geneva Conventions, which calls for state parties to provide certain minimum protections in the context of non-international armed conflicts. But while the Geneva Conventions' grave breaches regime (applicable to international armed conflicts) contains penal provisions, common Article 3 does not explicitly criminalize conduct in breach of its requirements. Additional Protocol II, which expanded the protections announced in common Article 3, also stopped short of assigning individual criminal responsibility. Although the frequency and exceptional brutality of internal conflicts have only increased over time, as recently as the early 1990s violations of common Article 3 and Additional Protocol II were still not regarded as amounting to criminal conduct under international law.

It was in 1995, just a few months before the *Tadić* decision was issued, that I published in the *American Journal of International Law* an article entitled 'International Criminalization of Internal Atrocities'.[2] In this article, I tried to supply theoretical foundations for the extension of the concept of international criminality to violations of common Article 3 and of Additional Protocol II—that is, to violations committed in non-international armed conflicts. My task was, of course, facilitated by the fact that in 1986 the International Court of Justice held in the *Nicaragua v USA* case that common Article 3 contains rules that constitute a minimum yardstick, or a normative floor, for all conflicts—whether international or non-international in character.[3] You can imagine how pleased I was that just a few months after my article's publication, a similar approach received a judicial imprimatur in the *Tadić* decision.

In *Tadić*, as you may recall, the accused claimed on appeal that the ICTY lacked subject-matter jurisdiction over the crimes he was alleged to have committed. Specifically, the accused asserted that Articles 2 and 3 of the ICTY's Statute applied only to crimes committed in the context of an international armed conflict—and that the alleged crimes, even if proven, had occurred in the context of an internal armed conflict, and thus fell outside of the Tribunal's jurisdiction. In response, the Prosecution maintained that the UN Security Council had, by adopting the Tribunal's Statute, already determined that the conflicts in the former Yugoslavia were international.

---

[2] Theodor Meron, 'International Criminalization of Internal Atrocities' (1995) 89 *AJIL* 554.
[3] *Military and Paramilitary Activities in and against Nicaragua (Nicaragua v United States of America)* (Merits: Judgment) [1986] ICJ Rep 14.

In its decision, the Appeals Chamber rejected the Prosecution's argument that the situation as a whole should be treated as an international armed conflict. Instead, the Appeals Chamber decided that the conflicts in the former Yugoslavia since 1991 had both international and internal aspects, that the members of the UN Security Council took into account both aspects of the conflicts in adopting the Tribunal's Statute, and that the Security Council members intended to empower the Tribunal to adjudicate violations of humanitarian law that occurred in either context. The Appeals Chamber then proceeded to explain how the Tribunal's Statute provided jurisdiction over crimes committed in both contexts. The Appeals Chamber left the ICTY's Trial Chambers to decide whether individual cases involved an international or an internal conflict.

Let us pause and consider that the Appeals Chamber could, of course, have decided to consider the entire situation in the former Yugoslavia as an international armed conflict. This would have enabled the Tribunal to apply the totality of international humanitarian law regulating such conflicts, including the provisions governing grave breaches. But that route would have deprived the Tribunal of the opportunity to consider those aspects of the Yugoslav conflict that were internal, and to affirm that serious violations of international law committed in internal wars are crimes under international customary law, thereby consolidating humanitarian law for the most frequent—and often the most cruel—of conflicts: non-international armed conflicts.

Instead, the Appeals Chamber interpreted Article 3 of the ICTY's Statute—which provides for the prosecution of '[v]iolations of the laws or customs of war'—in such a way that the words 'laws or customs of war' would cover both international and non-international armed conflicts. As the Appeals Chamber explained:

Article 3 is a general clause covering all violations of humanitarian law not falling under Article 2 or covered by Articles 4 or 5, more specifically: (i) violations of the Hague law on international conflicts; (ii) infringements of provisions of the Geneva Conventions other than those classified as 'grave breaches' by those Conventions; (iii) violations of common Article 3 and other customary rules on internal conflicts; (iv) violations of agreements binding upon the parties to the conflict, considered *qua* treaty law, *i.e.*, agreements which have not turned into customary international law....[4]

---

[4] *Tadić* Decision, n 1 above, para 89.

In other words:

Article 3 functions as a residual clause designed to ensure that no serious violation of international humanitarian law is taken away from the jurisdiction of the International Tribunal. Article 3 aims to make such jurisdiction watertight and inescapable.[5]

Article 3 of the Statute would thus encompass violations of both Hague Law and Geneva Law (except for grave breaches)—including, most notably, violations of common Article 3 of the Geneva Conventions, which thereby assumes the mantle of international criminal law.

II. THE IMPACT OF THE TADIĆ DECISION

In the jurisprudence of the Tribunal, the *Tadić* decision has taken on a life of its own. Although Article 3 of the Tribunal's Statute—the residual clause—was supposed to apply to situations not covered by other Articles of the Statute, in the practice of the Tribunal it has been applied as an autonomous provision, invocable even when other Articles cover the same criminal acts. Moreover, *Tadić* has been construed to authorize the importation not only of common Article 3, but of the entirety of customary law applicable in non-international armed conflict, and thus even the customary law governing offenses not explicitly mentioned in common Article 3, such as rape.

The *Tadić* decision has also encouraged the blurring of the distinction between international and non-international conflicts. Indeed, what strikes one about the jurisprudence of the ICTY is that often there is no need to determine whether a conflict is international or not, and that, except for the applicability of grave breaches provisions, the same normative rules govern both kinds of conflict.

An example of this approach is found in the ICTY appeal judgment in the case of *Dragomir Milošević*.[6] In considering the characterization of the conflict, the Appeals Chamber noted that the Trial Chamber's judgment had not established the nature of the armed conflict at issue in the indictment. Indeed, although the indictment charged Milošević under Article 51(2) of Additional Protocol I and, in the alternative, Article 13(2) of Additional Protocol II, the Trial Chamber's judgment cited both Protocols without specifying which of them applied to the conflict at issue. Let me read to you what the Appeals Chamber wrote:

---

[5] Ibid., para 91.
[6] *Prosecutor v Dragomir Milošević* (Judgement) IT-98-29/1-A (12 November 2009).

Although the Appeals Chamber considers that the Trial Chamber should have made a clear finding as to the nature of the armed conflict or the applicability of the Additional Protocols, the Appeals Chamber finds the references to the relevant provisions of both Additional Protocols permissible given that they form part of customary international law and apply both in international and internal armed conflicts.[7]

This blurring of the distinction between international and non-international armed conflicts is not simply a matter of judicial expediency. To the contrary, as the ICTY Appeals Chamber explained in the *Tadić* decision, a continued emphasis on the distinction between international and non-international conflicts makes little sense, particularly in light of the human rights revolution:

Why protect civilians from belligerent violence, or ban rape, torture or the wanton destruction of hospitals, churches, museums or private property, as well as proscribe weapons causing unnecessary suffering when two sovereign States are engaged in war, and yet refrain from enacting the same bans or providing the same protection when armed violence has erupted 'only' within the territory of a sovereign State? If international law, while of course duly safeguarding the legitimate interests of States, must gradually turn to the protection of human beings, it is only natural that the aforementioned dichotomy should gradually lose its weight.[8]

As the distinction between international and non-international conflict has grown increasingly irrelevant, it is not surprising that a growing number of rules and principles long applicable to international wars have been recognized as extending to non-international conflicts. One example of this move to elaborate rules for non-international conflict is found in the law governing means and methods of warfare. As the *Tadić* decision itself recognized, while most early prohibitions on the use of weapons governed only international armed conflict, those narrow prohibitions make little sense today:

Indeed, elementary considerations of humanity and common sense make it preposterous that the use by States of weapons prohibited in armed conflicts between themselves be allowed when States try to put down rebellion by their own nationals on their own territory. What is inhumane, and consequently proscribed, in international wars, cannot but be inhumane and inadmissible in civil strife.

This fundamental concept has brought about the gradual formation of general rules concerning specific weapons, rules which extend to civil strife the sweeping

---

[7] Ibid., para 23 (internal citation omitted).
[8] *Tadić* Decision, n 1 above, para 97.

prohibitions relating to international armed conflicts. By way of illustration, we will mention chemical weapons.[9]

Largely as a result of *Tadić*, there has thus been a broadening of international humanitarian law applicable to non-international armed conflicts, often through the elimination of distinctions between international and non-international armed conflicts. This trend was evident in the International Committee of the Red Cross (ICRC) study on the rules of customary humanitarian law published soon after the *Tadić* jurisdictional decision.[10] The study made only the basic distinction between international and non-international armed conflicts. It did not adopt the three-tiered approach of the Geneva Conventions and Additional Protocols, namely: international armed conflicts, non-international armed conflicts under common Article 3, and the more rigorous and restrictive definition of non-international armed conflicts under Additional Protocol II, Article 1. Moreover, the ICRC study recognized that many rules are applicable to both international and non-international conflicts.

This trend is also evidenced by the remarkable progress that has been made in recent years in both the identification of customary rules—attributable in large part to the establishment of the two ad hoc Tribunals and the direction of their jurisprudence—and the increased willingness of states to recognize the extension of rules elaborated with regard to international armed conflicts to non-international armed conflicts. In this regard, the fact that the Statute of the International Criminal Court lists serious violations of common Article 3 and some provisions of Hague Law as war crimes applicable in non-international armed conflicts is a signal achievement, as is the codification in that Statute of the principle that crimes against humanity can be committed in all situations—not only in furtherance of state policy, but also in furtherance of the policy of non-state entities. (On this latter point, I should note that Article 5 of the ICTY's Statute explicitly provides for jurisdiction over crimes against humanity 'when committed in armed conflict, whether international or internal in character'. However, the ICTY Appeals Chamber made clear in the *Tadić* decision that customary international law may not require any connection or nexus between such crimes and the conflict itself.)

---

[9] Ibid., paras 119, 120.
[10] Jean-Marie Henckaerts and Louise Doswald-Beck (eds), *Customary International Humanitarian Law*, Vols I-II (Cambridge: Cambridge University Press, 2005).

These developments are particularly noteworthy because, as recently as 1977, the diplomatic conference in Geneva that adopted the Additional Protocols to the Geneva Conventions voted down proposals by Norway and others to enhance Additional Protocol II by making most protective rules applicable to international conflicts cover non-international conflicts as well. Yet, perhaps indicating the influence of international judicial rulings, there has been hardly any opposition from states to the *Tadić* jurisdictional decision.

III. BEYOND THE TADIĆ DECISION

Of course, neither the *Tadić* decision nor the increased willingness of states to accept the extension of rules elaborated with regard to international armed conflicts to internal conflicts has put an end to all questions regarding the nature of international and non-international conflicts or what rules are applicable in assessing violations of common Article 3. I will spend my remaining time with you today outlining a few such questions that have arisen in the jurisprudence of the ICTY and ICTR, and how the ad hoc Tribunals have addressed these questions.

A. *Internationalizing internal conflicts*

As I mentioned earlier, in the *Tadić* decision the ICTY Appeals Chamber left it for Trial Chambers to determine whether individual cases involved an international or non-international conflict. This is not as straightforward a question as one might assume, as evidenced by the Appeals Chamber's judgment issued in the *Tadić* case several years after the decision on jurisdiction.

In 1999, during the merits phase of the *Tadić* case, the ICTY Appeals Chamber had to establish on what legal conditions armed forces fighting in a *prima facie* internal armed conflict may be regarded as fighting on behalf of a foreign power, thus internationalizing the conflict.[11] On the basis of the evidence produced, the Appeals Chamber found that, at least between 1992 and 1995, overall political and military authority over the Republika Srpska was held by the Federal Republic of Yugoslavia (FRY), including with regard to participation in the planning and supervision of military operations. The Chamber concluded that, during the relevant period in 1992, the armed conflict in Bosnia and Herzegovina between the Bosnian Serbs and the central authorities of Bosnia and Herzegovina must be classified as an international armed conflict.

---

[11] *Prosecutor v Duško Tadić* (Judgement) IT-94-1-A (15 July 1999).

Similarly, in the 2004 *Kordić and Čerkez* appeal judgment, the Appeals Chamber found that at the relevant time, Croatia exercised overall control over the Croatian Defense Council (HVO), including through logistic support and leadership in planning, coordination, and organization.[12] The Appeals Chamber therefore upheld the Trial Chamber's finding that the armed conflict between the HVO and the Bosnian Muslim Army (ABiH) was international in character.

B. *Public agents*

Another interesting question came up in the appeal judgment in the ICTR case of *Akayesu*, namely: whether only persons belonging to a particular category of public agents could be held criminally responsible for violating common Article 3, breaches of which may be prosecuted under Article 4 of the ICTR's Statute.

The *Akayesu* Trial Chamber answered this question in the affirmative. While acknowledging that the Geneva Conventions and their Additional Protocols had an overall protective and humanitarian purpose, which counseled against restricting the category of persons bound by the provisions in common Article 3 and Additional Protocol II too narrowly, the Trial Chamber nevertheless found that the category of persons likely to be held responsible for violations of Article 4 of the ICTR's Statute was limited. Specifically, the Trial Chamber concluded:

> The duties and responsibilities of the Geneva Conventions and the Additional Protocols ... will normally apply only to individuals of all ranks belonging to the armed forces under the military command of either of the belligerent parties, or to individuals who were legitimately mandated and expected, as public officials or agents or persons otherwise holding public authority or *de facto* representing the Government, to support or fulfil the war efforts.[13]

The Trial Chamber explained that its approach would allow application of the provisions of the ICTR's Statute in the manner that corresponds best with the underlying protective purpose of both the Geneva Conventions and the Additional Protocols.

Was this interpretation consistent with the Statute and with humanitarian law? The Appeals Chamber thought not. In reviewing the Trial Chamber's conclusions in this regard, the Appeals Chamber first held that common Article 3 seeks to extend to non-international armed conflicts

---

[12] *Prosecutor v Dario Kordić and Mario Čerkez* (Judgement) IT-95-14/2-A (17 December 2004).
[13] *Prosecutor v Jean-Paul Akayesu* (Judgement) ICTR-96-4-T (2 October 1998), para 631.

the protection contained in the provisions of the Geneva Conventions that apply to international armed conflicts. And I quote:

> Its object and purpose is to broaden the application of the international humanitarian law by defining what constitutes minimum humane treatment and the rules applicable under all circumstances. Indeed, '[i]n the words of ICRC, the purpose of common Article 3 [is] to ensure respect for the few essential rules of humanity which all civilized nations consider as valid everywhere and under all circumstances and as being above and outside war itself. These rules may thus be considered as the *quintessence* of humanitarian rules found in the Geneva Conventions as a whole.'[14]

Put most simply, the core notion of common Article 3 is the protection of victims.

The Appeals Chamber was therefore of the view that the minimum protection provided for victims under common Article 3 necessarily implies the need for effective punishment of all persons who violate it—without distinctions as to rank or categories of person. In other words:

> [S]uch punishment must be applicable to everyone without discrimination, as required by the principles governing individual criminal responsibility as laid down by the Nuremberg Tribunal in particular... [I]nternational humanitarian law would be lessened and called into question if it were to be admitted that certain persons be exonerated from individual criminal responsibility for a violation of common Article 3 under the pretext that they did not belong to a specific category.[15]

The Appeals Chamber acknowledged that, in actuality, authors of violations of common Article 3 will likely fall into one of the categories identified by the Trial Chamber, namely: commanders, combatants, and other members of armed forces. According to the Appeals Chamber:

> This stems from the fact that common Article 3 requires a close nexus between violations and the armed conflict. This nexus between violations and the armed conflict implies that, in most cases, the perpetrator of the crime will probably have a special relationship with one party to the conflict. However, such a special relationship is not a condition precedent to the application of common Article 3 and, hence[,] of Article 4 of the Statute.[16]

The Appeals Chamber therefore overruled the Trial Chamber, concluding that the latter had 'erred in requiring that a special relationship

---

[14] *Prosecutor v Jean-Paul Akayesu* (Judgement) ICTR-96-4-A (1 June 2001), para 442.
[15] Ibid., para 443.
[16] Ibid., para 444.

should be a separate condition for triggering criminal responsibility for a violation of Article 4 of the Statute'.[17]

C. Nexus

I have already discussed the nexus between the applicability of the statutory provision on crimes against humanity and the nature or existence of a conflict in light of customary law. I will now address the question of the nexus between the alleged offense itself and armed conflict, which requires some additional comments. Let me start by recalling that while the Statute of the ICTY applies to both international and non-international armed conflicts, the Statute of the ICTR applies only to non-international armed conflicts. Although the nexus question is relevant to both, it is particularly important for non-international armed conflicts, where the need to distinguish between violations of humanitarian law and 'ordinary' crimes frequently arises. Indeed, the jurisprudence of the ICTR is particularly rich in its articulation of the nexus requirement.

As I have already mentioned, in the 2001 *Akayesu* appeal judgment, the ICTR Appeals Chamber held that common Article 3 requires a close nexus between the violations of humanitarian law at issue and the armed conflict. The *Akayesu* appeal judgment did not, however, adopt a particular definition of the nexus requirement. This occurred two years later in the ICTR's 2003 appeal judgment in the *Rutaganda* case (over which I presided),[18] when the Appeals Chamber embraced the standard articulated in the ICTY's *Kunarac* appeal judgment.[19] Let me first read to you what the *Kunarac* appeal judgment had to say about the nexus requirement:

> What ultimately distinguishes a war crime from a purely domestic offence is that a war crime is shaped by or dependent upon the environment—the armed conflict—in which it is committed.... The armed conflict need not have been causal to the commission of the crime, but the existence of an armed conflict must, at a minimum, have played a substantial part in the perpetrator's ability to commit it, his decision to commit it, the manner in which it was committed or the purpose for which it was committed. Hence, if it can be established ... that the perpetrator acted in furtherance of or under the guise of the armed conflict, it would be sufficient to conclude that his acts were closely related to the armed conflict.[20]

---

[17] Ibid.
[18] *Georges Anderson Nderubumwe Rutaganda v Prosecutor* (Judgement) ICTR-96-3-A (26 May 2003) (*Rutaganda* Appeal Judgement).
[19] *Prosecutor v Dragoljub Kunarac et al.* (Judgement) IT-96-23&23/1-A (12 June 2002).
[20] Ibid., para 58.

The *Rutaganda* appeal judgment specifically endorsed this explanation of the nexus requirement. It also endorsed *Kunarac*'s non-exhaustive list of factors that a Trial Chamber may take into account in determining whether or not the act in question is sufficiently related to the armed conflict. These factors include:

the fact that the perpetrator is a combatant; the fact that the victim is a non-combatant; the fact that the victim is a member of the opposing party; the fact that the act may be said to serve the ultimate goal of a military campaign; and the fact that the crime is committed as part of or in the context of the perpetrator's official duties.[21]

However, the ICTR Appeals Chamber added two important glosses to the explanation of the nexus requirement found in the *Kunarac* appeal judgment:

First, the expression 'under the guise of the armed conflict' does not mean simply 'at the same time as an armed conflict' and/or 'in any circumstances created in part by the armed conflict'. For example, if a non-combatant takes advantage of the lessened effectiveness of the police in conditions of disorder created by an armed conflict to murder a neighbour he has hated for years, that would not, without more, constitute a war crime under Article 4 of the Statute....Second,...the determination of a close relationship between particular offences and an armed conflict will usually require consideration of several factors, not just one. Particular care is needed when the accused is a non-combatant.[22]

Applying this articulation of the nexus requirement to the facts of the case, the Appeal Chamber recalled that the Trial Chamber had found that Rutaganda participated in the underlying attack on Tutsi refugees; that he exercised de facto influence and authority over the *Interahamwe*; that the *Interahamwe* were armed with guns, grenades, and clubs; that the *Interahamwe*, alongside the soldiers of the Presidential Guard, entered the compound where the attack occurred throwing grenades, firing guns, and killing the refugees with machetes and clubs; and that the victims of the killings were persons protected under common Article 3 of the Geneva Conventions and Additional Protocol II. Taking all of these circumstances into account, the Appeals Chamber concluded that 'no reasonable trier of fact could have failed to find that a nexus between the armed conflict and Rutaganda's participation in the particular killings charged...had been established beyond a reasonable doubt'.[23]

---

[21] Ibid., para 59.
[22] *Rutaganda* Appeal Judgement, n 18 above, para 570.
[23] Ibid., para. 577.

D. Lingering distinctions between international and non-international armed conflicts

I have spent a good deal of time today talking about how the distinction between international and non-international armed conflicts is being eroded and how, often as a matter of customary law, rules traditionally applied in the international context are being applied to the non-international context as well. However, an interesting and not always easy question is whether all of the normative principles and doctrines of international humanitarian law applicable to international conflicts are necessarily relevant to non-international conflicts. Such a question arose in the 2003 interlocutory appeal challenging jurisdiction in the *Hadžihasanović* case.[24]

In that case, it was not contested that serious violations of humanitarian law committed in internal armed conflicts incur individual criminal responsibility under customary international law. Nor was it disputed that the doctrine of command responsibility was part of customary international law relating to international armed conflicts. The question on which the parties disagreed was whether the command responsibility doctrine applies, as customary international law, in a non-international armed conflict.

It was by drawing on basic principles of humanitarian law that the Appeals Chamber derived an affirmative answer to this question. I will read to you what the Appeals Chamber wrote:

Prohibitions on the doing of certain acts in the course of an internal armed conflict are imposed by Article 3 common to the Geneva Conventions of 1949, which has long been accepted as having customary status. In the *Tadić* Jurisdiction Decision, the Appeals Chamber found that 'customary international law imposes criminal responsibility for serious violations of common Article 3, as supplemented by other general principles and rules on the protection of victims of internal armed conflict, and for breaching certain fundamental principles and rules regarding means and methods of combat in civil strife'. Likewise, at all times material to this case, customary international law included the concept of command responsibility in relation to war crimes committed in the course of an international armed conflict. Thus, the concept would have applied to war crimes corresponding to the prohibitions listed in common Article 3 when committed in the course of an international armed conflict. It is difficult to see

---

[24] *Prosecutor v Enver Hadžihasanović et al.* (Decision on Interlocutory Appeal Challenging Jurisdiction in Relation to Command Responsibility) IT-01-47-AR72 (16 July 2003).

why the concept would not equally apply to breaches of the same prohibitions when committed in the course of an internal armed conflict.[25]

Indeed, as the Appeals Chamber proceeded to explain, whether Article 3 of the ICTY's Statute—the Statute's residual clause—is referring to war crimes committed in the context of international conflicts or to war crimes committed in the context of non-international conflicts (under common Article 3), it assumes that there is an organized military force. This is key, as the Appeals Chamber noted, because:

> It is evident that there cannot be an organized military force save on the basis of responsible command. It is also reasonable to hold that it is responsible command which leads to command responsibility. Command responsibility is the most effective method by which international criminal law can enforce responsible command.[26]

Thus, the fact that it was in the context of a non-international armed conflict that a war crime was about to be committed or was committed may be relevant to the characteristics of the particular crime—but it is simply not relevant to the responsibility of the commander.

It is important to note that the *Hadžihasanović* decision does not suggest or assume that all of the rules and doctrines of international humanitarian law applicable to international armed conflicts should automatically be considered applicable to non-international armed conflicts. Indeed, according to the Appeals Chamber, it would be incorrect to make such an assumption. However, the Appeals Chamber also emphasized that where a principle can be shown to have been established as part of customary international law, 'it is not an objection to the application of the principle to a particular situation to say that the situation is new if it reasonably falls within the application of the principle'.[27] Thus, I think it is fair to say that while the decision does not endorse a notion of automatic applicability, it creates a certain presumption in that direction, even as it suggests that the question of the applicability of other specific humanitarian law doctrines will have to be decided on an ad hoc basis and in context.

IV. CONCLUSION

Despite the salutary rapprochement between the rules of international humanitarian law governing international and non-international armed

---

[25] Ibid., para 13 (internal citations omitted).
[26] Ibid., para 16.
[27] Ibid., para 12.

conflicts, it would be wrong to assume that all of the rules of international humanitarian law now apply to both kinds of conflicts without distinction. As already mentioned, the grave breaches provisions of the Geneva Conventions continue to apply to international armed conflicts alone. Only in international armed conflicts do captured combatants benefit from the status and entire panoply of protections to which prisoners of war are entitled under international law. And while many of the rules pertaining to the use of weapons and methods of warfare are now regarded as applying in both international and non-international armed conflicts, this topic must still be approached with considerable caution, as there may well be some weapons and means of warfare that are still regulated in international armed conflicts alone. Moreover, Geneva Convention IV's protective provisions on the treatment of detainees do not apply, as such, to non-international armed conflicts.

As the President of the ICRC stated in his important address last September concerning the ICRC's new study on the current state of international humanitarian law, for all that has been achieved in the field of humanitarian law in recent years—including in the area of non-international armed conflicts—humanitarian law 'does not always respond fully to actual humanitarian needs'.[28] There are still inadequate protections for persons deprived of liberty in non-international armed conflicts. Humanitarian law must also be reinforced—particularly in the context of non-international armed conflicts—to ensure that there are mechanisms to monitor and halt potential violations of humanitarian law, to prosecute violations, and to provide reparations to victims where such violations have occurred. With regard to internally displaced persons, it is imperative that additional legal protections be developed. And the law governing the protection of the natural environment during armed conflicts must be strengthened.

These are not easy tasks. But I hope that, as we look ahead to what we would like humanitarian law to achieve in the coming decades, we can take no small amount of pride and courage from the important ways it has developed and strengthened in the past two decades alone, thanks in part to the jurisprudence of the ICTY and ICTR and to the sustained efforts of the ICRC.

---

[28] Dr Jakob Kellenberger, President of the ICRC, 'Strengthening legal protection for victims of armed conflicts' (21 September 2010), available at <http://www.icrc.org/eng/resources/documents/statement/ihl-development-statement-210910.htm>.

21

THE ICJ'S OPINION IN *BOSNIA AND HERZEGOVINA V SERBIA AND MONTENEGRO**

Let me begin with one general observation. The finding by the ICJ that genocide has occurred in Srebrenica[1] is of fundamental importance, especially following upon the ICTY judgment in the *Krstić* case concerning genocide and the events of Srebrenica, over which I presided.[2] It is important from a symbolic standpoint, both for the people affected by events at Srebrenica and, as I will discuss in a moment, for the ICTY. And it is important from a legal perspective, for a number of different reasons. For instance, the fact that the Court and the Tribunal have aligned their findings that genocide can occur in a quite circumscribed geographic area puts an end to any lingering debate on this issue.

Having said that, I wish to focus in these remarks on some more specific aspects of the ICJ decision and, in particular, on its connections with criminal law and the specific synergies it has created or enhanced between the ICJ and the ICTY.

CR&O

This is a civil case, but it is striking how much it draws from criminal law and issues of criminal responsibility. The subject matter, genocide, is one

---

* Delivered at the 101st Annual Meeting of the American Society of International Law in Washington, DC, USA, on 29 March 2007. The text of this speech first appeared as 'Breaking Developments in International Law: A Conversation on the ICJ's Opinion in *Bosnia and Herzegovina v Serbia and Montenegro*' (2007) 101 *American Society of International Law Proceedings* 215 (Introductory Remarks by Theodor Meron), © The American Society of International Law. Used by permission and modified from the original publication.

[1] *Application of the Convention on the Prevention and Punishment of the Crime of Genocide (Bosnia and Herzegovina v Serbia and Montenegro)* (Merits: Judgment) [2007] ICJ Rep 43 (*Genocide Case*).

[2] *Prosecutor v Radislav Krstić* (Judgement) IT-98-33-A (19 April 2004).

traditionally developed under criminal law. The Genocide Convention under which this case was brought does, indeed, touch upon relations between states and confer jurisdiction on the ICJ, but it is primarily a treaty about individual criminal responsibility for genocide. It is a treaty developed in the wake of World War II—a period in which individuals were held criminally responsible for genocide (under the rubric of crimes against humanity), but when Germany itself was never held so responsible. This nexus with criminal law has given the case several notable features.

First, like most criminal cases, this case proved to be a primarily fact-intensive undertaking, in which the result was largely determined by the evidence presented to the Court. There were two components to the evidence needed for Bosnia to prove its case: first, the evidence to establish whether genocide had occurred; and second, the evidence to establish Serbia's awareness and support. Notably, knowledge or *mens rea*—inherent in both components—is not an issue that the ICJ is often called upon to adjudicate. Intent is not normally a matter of relevance for treaty interpretations. It is also particularly hard to prove without subpoena power, especially when one must find evidence of knowledge and intent at the highest levels of government in order to establish state responsibility. This is especially true when the level of intent required is something as specific as an 'intent to destroy' a group or knowledge of such intent.

From our experience at the ICTY, we have learned how difficult it is, even for a court established under Chapter VII of the UN Charter, to obtain the full cooperation of states with regard to the production of evidence. Such difficulties are enhanced in the case of the ICJ. The problem lies not only in the ICJ's soft statutory language (Article 49), which contrasts sharply with the ICTY's peremptory language permitting orders to states to produce documents, subject to the designation of protective orders concerning national security. (Paradoxically, because the ICJ is not concerned with individual accused persons, the conclusions it may draw from any state's refusal to cooperate are not limited, as they would be in the ICTY.) The problem is more that the ICJ is dealing with sovereign governments and that, in doing so, it employs a certain degree of caution and self-restraint. This is demonstrated by the tradition constraining questions from the bench—an approach that is necessarily somewhat rigid and structured with the ICJ bench of fifteen or more judges and is not helpful in elucidating matters of criminal responsibility, at least in the absence of a 'smoking gun'.

Second, the close nexus to criminal law also shows itself in another area: the standard of proof applied by the ICJ. In the case under discussion, the ICJ, invoking its opinion in *Corfu Channel*, determined that claims against a state involving charges of exceptional gravity must be proved by evidence that is 'fully conclusive' and that the crime of genocide as well as the attribution of that crime must have been 'clearly established'.[3] Interestingly, while the ICJ states that it has 'long recognized' the need for 'evidence that is fully conclusive',[4] the page it cites from *Corfu* in relation to this proposition only speaks of the need for 'conclusive' evidence.[5]

In any event, I am not sure how the ICJ's chosen standard in the case at hand differs from the reasonable doubt standard applied in criminal law. At one point, the ICJ talks about how, 'for a pattern of conduct to be accepted as evidence of [genocidal intent], it would have to be such that it could *only* point to the existence of such intent'.[6] This sounds a lot like the reasonable doubt standard and the requirement that guilt be the *only* reasonable inference from the facts. Indeed, in one instance the Court remarks that certain facts have not been 'established beyond any doubt in the argument between the Parties'.[7]

The ICJ's decision to apply such a high standard of proof is noteworthy. Because of the egregious criminality of genocide and the serious implications of a determination that a state is responsible for genocide, it is, perhaps, reasonable for the Court to apply standards of proof that are rather higher than the normal standard of the balance of probabilities. But should the Court apply standards as high as in a criminal case? These higher standards will make it particularly hard for applicant states to succeed in such cases in the future, especially given that the 'fully conclusive' evidence requirement will be applied in assessing attribution to the state as well—including with respect to state actors at the highest levels.

In this regard, it is worth noting that the Court applied the high standard of conclusiveness to the charge of complicity, but not to the claims pertaining to the non-prevention of genocide. To the non-prevention of genocide the Court applies 'proof at a high level of certainty appropriate to the seriousness of the allegation',[8] a standard that may be lower than 'fully conclusive'.

---

[3] *Genocide Case*, n 1 above, para 209.
[4] Ibid.
[5] *Corfu Channel Case (United Kingdom of Great Britain and Northern Ireland v Albania)* (Merits: Judgment) [1949] ICJ Rep 4, 17.
[6] *Genocide Case*, n 1 above, para 373 (emphasis added).
[7] Ibid., para 422.
[8] Ibid., para 210.

But if the Court should apply something short of the standards used in criminal cases, what standards should these be? If the balance of probabilities or preponderance of the evidence tests might be considered to set too low a threshold, would the test of clear and convincing evidence, such as that followed by the Inter-American Court of Human Rights in the *Velásquez Rodríguez* merits judgment,[9] not better serve the objects of the Genocide Convention? Or perhaps the Court's own standard of 'proof at a high level of certainty'[10] would suffice in assessing all of the questions arising in what is, after all, a *civil* case—including the questions of committing genocide, complicity for genocide, non-prevention of genocide, and, more generally, attribution? Would the result of the case have been different had different and consistent standards been employed? On these complex issues, I am afraid I can offer only questions.

One of the problems here is that the ICJ has no provision in its Statute or Rules on the burden of proof and the Court's shaping of evidentiary rules as it goes along with a particular case does not give parties advance notice as to what is expected of them.

◌8◌

This case has also proved groundbreaking for its development of a synergy of cooperation between international courts and tribunals.

Much ink has been spilt lamenting the danger of fragmentation of international law as a result of the establishment of myriad international courts. I must admit that this is a question about which I have never been much troubled. There is still a deficit, not surplus, in international judicial institutions and I have confidence that judges will take seriously their responsibility to maintain the integrity and a holistic perception of international law.

Here, the coexistence with the ICJ of a competent UN criminal tribunal proved beneficial for both institutions. I mentioned earlier the evidentiary difficulties presented in this case. These were made much less, however, because the ICJ could rely on competent fact and law determinations in the judgments of the ICTY, a reliance which proved essential to the Court's conclusions. Without the relevant ICTY judgments, it would have been even harder for Bosnia to argue its case.

---

[9] *Case of Velásquez Rodríguez v Honduras* (Judgment (Merits)) Inter-American Court of Human Rights Series C No 4 (29 July 1988).
[10] *Genocide Case*, n 1 above, para 210.

I note here that the ICTY judgments to which I refer go primarily to the first evidentiary issue—whether genocide, in fact, occurred with the involvement of Bosnian Serb officials—and not to the second issue, namely, the extent to which Belgrade knew this. The ICTY had held that downstream leaders such as Radislav Krstić had knowledge of Ratko Mladić's alleged plan at Srebrenica, but the ICTY has never held upstream Serbian leaders responsible. In the absence of ICTY convictions of top Serbian leaders, the ICJ thus had little to use from the ICTY on this latter issue and the ICJ declined to attribute knowledge of the genocide to Serbia (although it did find the genocide foreseeable in its findings on prevention). We can speculate, of course, as to what would have happened had Slobodan Milošević not died, but we will never know.

The ICTY's legitimacy and international reputation are enhanced by this significant, repeated—and mostly very positive—reliance on its decisions by the ICJ. But this is not the only way that the ICJ's opinion bolsters the work of the ICTY. Also groundbreaking was the finding by the Court that Serbia has violated its obligations under the Genocide Convention towards the ICTY by failing to transfer Mladić, indicted for genocide and complicity in genocide, for trial by the ICTY, and thus having failed fully to cooperate with the Tribunal. In the same vein, the Court ordered Serbia to take immediate steps under the Genocide Convention to transfer to the ICTY individuals accused of crimes under the Convention. Here the ICJ demonstrated its role as the principal judicial organ of the United Nations.

⋘⋙

In light of all these factors, should this case have been brought to the ICJ? As international lawyers, and setting aside political calculations to focus on the likelihood of success, would we have advised a party to bring it?

Where the subject matter is quasi-criminal, where evidence is unlikely to be in the public domain, and where proof of intent is required, there may be few successful suits and expectations should not be excessive. This is particularly true for litigation in a court as cautious as the ICJ. So, answering the question of whether the case should have been brought depends on one's expectations, ie whether—despite the challenges just mentioned—one expects the Court to confirm that genocide has occurred, or, rather, to recognize the responsibility of the respondent and grant remedies, or to do all of the above.

IV

Responsibility and the Role of the Judge

22

JUDGE THOMAS BUERGENTHAL AND THE DEVELOPMENT OF INTERNATIONAL LAW BY INTERNATIONAL COURTS*

It gives me great pleasure to speak on this occasion honoring my very close friend, and one of the greatest international jurists of our time, Judge Thomas Buergenthal.

Through his contributions as a scholar and a judge, Tom Buergenthal has played a critical role at the juncture of the two most important international law developments of the last half a century. The first is the human rights revolution, where he has attained a unique status. The second is the establishment and growth of international courts and tribunals and their role in the normative development of international law. It is with this latter development that I would like to begin my remarks today.

I. INTERNATIONAL COURTS AND TRIBUNALS AND THE DEVELOPMENT OF INTERNATIONAL LAW

One of the most notable changes in the international legal landscape over the last two decades has been the significant increase in the number of international courts and tribunals. In addition to the ICJ, international courts include the European Court of Justice, the European, American, and African Courts of Human Rights, the Hamburg Law of the Sea Tribunal, the International Criminal Court, and multiple ad hoc and hybrid international criminal tribunals. With this critical mass of tribunals and the resulting case law, it is not surprising that we have entered a new and dynamic stage in the development, interpretation, and clarification of

---

* Delivered at the Peace Palace, The Hague, The Netherlands, on 25 May 2010.

the law by international courts, one to which Tom Buergenthal—who has served as a judge of various international courts and tribunals for more than a quarter century—has made important contributions.

For example, the jurisprudence of international tribunals increasingly encompasses reasoning based on cross-institutional judicial dialogue and fertilization, demonstrated by the ICTY's and other tribunals' citations to the ICJ. The ICJ too has relied on the ICTY with regard to factual and legal findings on the law of genocide. I am convinced that the creation of additional international courts, far from fragmenting international law as some skeptics have suggested it might, has, in fact, led to its invigoration.

The recently increasing importance of customary international law is another example of the dynamism fostered by international courts, and this trend has most obviously been driven by the jurisprudence of the ad hoc criminal tribunals: the ICTY and ICTR. As criminal tribunals, they are bound to respect the principle of *nullum crimen, nulla poena sine lege* (or the legality principle), which they commonly ground in customary law. Nowhere is the new centrality of customary law more important than in these courts, which have developed a rich jurisprudence elucidating customary principles of humanitarian law.[1]

The ad hoc Tribunals' achievements, grounded on customary law, are manifold. They have created a set of evidentiary and procedural rules that the Nuremberg tribunals did not bequeath, as well as a corpus of substantive law expressed in detailed jurisprudence and hundreds of judicial decisions. They have also enshrined individual criminal liability for an increasing number of norms previously only applied to states as a matter of civil responsibility. Most fundamentally, they have laid to rest the age-old question of whether international law really is law. The direct application of international law to individuals by international courts and tribunals leaves no doubts that it is.

In my own work, moreover, I have come to realize that statements regarding a criminal norm in statutory or treaty provisions are often not detailed enough for application in a case, and that a carefully developed judicial gloss is required for a court to perform its role. The same is true of many other rules of international law. Thus, in recent years, international courts ranging from the ICJ, to the Iran-United States Claims Tribunal and arbitral tribunals, to the regional human rights courts

---

[1] Editor's note: For a detailed discussion of why customary law is critically important for the ad hoc criminal Tribunals, see Ch 3 above, 'Customary Humanitarian Law: From the Academy to the Courtroom'.

have pronounced on important issues of customary or general international law.

The *Nicaragua* case is an example of the ICJ's approach.[2] In that case, the Court held that common Articles 1 and 3 of the Geneva Conventions constitute general principles of humanitarian law that are binding on the United States—in other words, that they are customary law. Equally importantly, the Court described common Article 3, which explicitly applies to non-international armed conflict, as establishing rules which, as a minimum yardstick, are also applicable to international armed conflicts. The Court thus paved the way for the recognition, in the ICTY's *Tadić* interlocutory appeal of 1995, of the principle that most of the protective rules of international humanitarian law apply both to international and non-international armed conflict.[3] This conclusion is particularly noteworthy because it was rejected by the diplomatic conference of 1977 on the Additional Protocols to the Geneva Conventions.

The impact of *Nicaragua* on the subsequent development of the law was such that the customary law character of practically the entire corpus of the Geneva Conventions—including common Articles 1 and 3 and the minimum yardstick feature—is now taken for granted and virtually never questioned. (The same is true, under the influence of the Nuremberg tribunals, of Hague Convention No IV of 1907.)

In these developments, one can discern the outlines of an informal *stare decisis* principle. Courts and governments increasingly rely on precedent rather than repeatedly engaging in *de novo* detailed analysis of whether particular principles enjoy the status of customary law. It is significant that in both the ICJ and the ICTY, the sources most relied on are their own precedents. As the corpus of international jurisprudence grows, this practice will become even more prominent.

International courts' judicial decisions thus appear to be gaining greater weight than that accorded by Article 38 of the ICJ Statute. Indeed, in his 2009 talk at the annual meeting of the American Society of International Law, Judge Buergenthal spoke of the law-making role and authority of international and regional courts achieved in the context of non-criminal tribunals—a role and authority achieved through acts of clarification and interpretation which result in normative accretion. Even in the criminal field, it has been held that the *nullum crimen* principle does

---

[2] *Military and Paramilitary Activities in and against Nicaragua (Nicaragua v United States of America)* (Merits: Judgment) [1986] ICJ Rep 14.
[3] *Prosecutor v Duško Tadić* (Decision on the Defence Motion for Interlocutory Appeal on Jurisdiction) IT-94-1-AR72 (2 October 1995).

not prevent a court from assessing an issue through a process of interpretation and clarification; nor does that principle prevent a court from relying on previous decisions regarding the particular ingredients of a given norm.[4]

The increasing trend of international courts relying on precedents they themselves set, together with those precedents' quick acceptance by the international community, illustrates what I would describe as the validation function by international courts. In my experience, legal principles whose maturation into customary law has long been in dispute become accepted as customary law by the international community very rapidly after they have been given the imprimatur of adoption by an international tribunal. The existence and widespread recognition of legal precedent by the principal judicial organ of the United Nations, the ICJ, or by other international courts, usually suffices to demonstrate the binding character of the norm concerned.

II. JUDGE BUERGENTHAL'S PERSONAL CONTRIBUTIONS

Turning now to Tom Buergenthal's personal contribution to international law, I want to discuss two areas where his scholarly writings have significantly impacted the development of international law by international courts, and, in particular, the advancement of human rights law.

The first such area concerns the normative status of the American Declaration of the Rights and Duties of Man. The American Convention on Human Rights and the revised Charter of the Organization of American States are treaties which create binding international obligations on the states concerned. The Charter did not, however, define the term 'human rights' or its scope; these were defined in the Declaration of the Rights and Duties of Man of 1948 which was proclaimed by the International Conference of American States.

Based only on the texts of the relevant documents, it was unclear whether the Declaration is normative or merely programmatic. However, in a seminal article published in the *American Journal of International Law* in 1975, well before the entry into force of the Convention, Judge Buergenthal first articulated an influential and original theory regarding the normative character of the Declaration.[5]

The importance of this interpretation did not end with the entry into force of the American Convention. Writing in the *American Journal of*

---

[4] *Prosecutor v Zlatko Aleksovski* (Judgement) IT-95-14/1-A (24 March 2000). Editor's note: For a discussion of this case, see Ch 3 above, 'Customary Humanitarian Law: From the Academy to the Courtroom'.

[5] Thomas Buergenthal, 'The Revised OAS Charter and the Protection of Human Rights' (1975) 69 *AJIL* 828.

International Law in 1985, Judge Buergenthal underscored the reasons why, although the Declaration was not a treaty, it was binding on members of the Organization of American States, and he urged the Inter-American Court to view its power to interpret the Charter as giving it the power to interpret the Declaration as well.[6] The Court, which by then included Judge Buergenthal, eventually accepted his logic in its advisory opinion of 14 July 1989.[7] The opinion was clearly influenced by his writings, and echoed the construction advanced in his articles in the *American Journal of International Law*. In particular, the Court accepted that, by virtue of Article 29(d) of the Convention, state parties would continue to be bound by the requirements of the Declaration. The opinion of the Court is important to this very day because the Declaration empowers the Organization of American States and the Inter-American Commission to deal with large-scale violations, whereas the Convention addresses only violations of individual human rights.

My second example of Judge Buergenthal's influence relates to the extraterritorial applicability of the International Covenant on Civil and Political Rights. As you all know, Article 2(1) of the Covenant governs the obligation of each party to respect and to ensure to all individuals within its territory and subject to its jurisdiction the rights recognized in the Covenant. The question is thus whether the requirements for the application of the Covenant are cumulative, namely that the person concerned has to be both within the territory and subject to the jurisdiction of a state party. In a 1981 article published in a major volume on the Covenant edited by Professor Louis Henkin, Judge Buergenthal wrote:

> Article 2(1) permits and requires a different construction. Clearly, the phrase 'within its territory and subject to its jurisdiction' should be read as a disjunctive conjunction, indicating that a state party must be deemed to have assumed the obligation to respect and to ensure the rights recognized in the Covenant 'to all individuals within its territory' *and* 'to all individuals subject to its jurisdiction.'
>
> ...
>
> It would follow that a state party to the Covenant which maintains actual civil or military control over a given territory is under an obligation to ensure in that territory the rights the Covenant guarantees....[8]

---

[6] Thomas Buergenthal, 'The Advisory Practice of the Inter-American Human Rights Court' (1985) 79 *AJIL* 1.

[7] *Interpretation of the American Declaration of the Rights and Duties of Man Within the Framework of Article 64 of the American Convention on Human Rights* (Advisory Opinion) Inter-American Court of Human Rights Series A No 10 (14 July 1989).

[8] Thomas Buergenthal, 'To Respect and to Ensure: State Obligations and Permissible Derogations', in Louis Henkin (ed), *The International Bill of Rights: The Covenant on Civil and Political Rights* (New York: Columbia University Press, 1981), 74, 77.

Judge Buergenthal was the first to advance this interpretation of the Covenant. His lead was followed by the Human Rights Committee in the 1980s and, after Buergenthal joined the Court in 2000, by the ICJ in the 2004 advisory opinion on *Construction of a Wall in the Occupied Palestinian Territory*[9] as well as in the 2005 *Democratic Republic of the Congo v Uganda* judgment.[10] Judge Buergenthal's reasoning regarding the concept of extraterritorial applicability of the Covenant played a critical role in the United Nations' and international courts' acceptance of the extraterritorial applicability of the Covenant.

III. THE INVISIBLE COLLEGE

As I conclude, I would be remiss if I did not reflect on the extraordinary authority and influence of Tom Buergenthal in what Oscar Schachter called the 'invisible college of international lawyers'[11] and in the international community at large.

Any appreciation of Judge Buergenthal must start with the unique quality of his writings. Analytical, precise, clear, concise, humane, steering clear of trendy concepts and catchy phrases, Judge Buergenthal has grounded his enlightened ideas in the very highest standards of scholarship and discerning analysis. The integrity that characterizes Judge Buergenthal's personality permeates all of his writings, giving them unique credibility.

Although my focus in this talk has been Judge Buergenthal's contribution to international law, it would be remiss if I were to say nothing about his impact on the teaching of human rights in American and foreign universities. He published in 1973, with Professor Louis Sohn, the first US casebook on the international protection of human rights.[12] This book resulted in a dramatic increase in the teaching of human rights as a separate course in American law schools.

In addition to his impressive scholarship, Judge Buergenthal's hard work and readiness to serve have been recognized by his appointment and election to a wide variety of academic and public posts. I hold particularly significant Judge Buergenthal's unique record of judicial,

---

[9] *Legal Consequences of the Construction of a Wall in the Occupied Palestinian Territory* (Advisory Opinion) [2004] ICJ Rep 136.

[10] *Case Concerning Armed Activities on the Territory of the Congo (Democratic Republic of the Congo v Uganda)* (Merits: Judgment) [2005] ICJ Rep 168.

[11] Oscar Schachter, 'The Invisible College of International Lawyers' (1977) 72 *Northwestern University Law Review* 217.

[12] Louis B Sohn and Thomas Buergenthal (eds), *International Protection of Human Rights* (Indianapolis: Bobbs-Merrill Co, 1973).

quasi-judicial, and investigatory functions, through which he has advanced his inspiring vision of human rights and international law. These latter roles are so numerous I mention them only briefly. They include, apart from his service on the bench of the ICJ, service as Judge, Vice President, and President of the Inter-American Court of Human Rights (I note that he was the first American to be elected to this court, first nominated by Costa Rica and, for re-election, by Costa Rica and Colombia); Judge, Vice President, and President of the Administrative Tribunal, Inter-American Development Bank; Member of the United Nations Truth Commission for El-Salvador; Member of the United Nations Human Rights Committee (I note, again, that he was the first American elected to this Committee); Vice-Chairman of the Claims Resolution Tribunal for Dormant Accounts in Switzerland; and Member of the Ethics Commission of the International Olympic Committee.

Judge Buergenthal is retiring from the Court. For very many years he has been my friend and role model. I will miss him greatly.

23

FAIRNESS IN SENTENCING (SEPARATE AND PARTIALLY DISSENTING OPINION, *PROSECUTOR V STANISLAV GALIĆ*)*

1. I agree with the reasoning of the Appeals Chamber with regard to Galić's Appeal. I write separately for two reasons: first, to add a brief thought on why acts or threats of violence the primary purpose of which is to spread terror among the civilian population are criminal violations of customary international law; and second, to dissent from the decision to grant the Prosecution's Appeal as to the sentence.

I

2. The Appeals Chamber explains why criminal responsibility attaches to acts or threats of violence the primary purpose of which is to spread terror among the civilian population. I believe this conclusion also follows logically from the ban, present at least since the Fourth Hague Convention on the Laws and Customs of War, on 'declar[ing] that no quarter will be given.'[1] It is a crime to violate principles of customary international law identified in the Fourth Hague Convention.[2] And if threats that no quarter will be given are crimes, then surely threats that a party will not respect other foundational principles of international law—

---

* Rendered as part of *Prosecutor v Stanislav Galić* (Judgement) IT-98-29-A (30 November 2006). Citations and abbreviations not explained here are defined elsewhere in the Judgement.

[1] Regulations Respecting the Laws and Customs of War on Land, annexed to Hague Convention IV, art 23.

[2] See, eg, 1 Trial of the Major War Criminals Before the International Military Tribunal 220 (1947) (Nuremberg Judgement) ('The Hague Convention of 1907 prohibited resort to certain methods of waging war... [S]ince 1907, [these prohibitions] have certainly been crimes, punishable as offenses against the laws of war.').

such as the prohibition against targeting civilians—are also crimes. The terrorization at issue here is exactly such a threat.

II

3. I respectfully dissent from the Appeals Chamber's decision to increase Galić's sentence from 20 years to life imprisonment. In my view, this increase is incompatible with the standard of review that we have applied in the past.

4. 'Sentencing is essentially a discretionary process on the part of a Trial Chamber.'[3] Our jurisprudence makes this very clear. We have recognized in numerous cases that 'Trial Chambers are vested with broad discretion in determining an appropriate sentence'.[4] We have similarly emphasized that '[a]ppeals against sentence, as appeals from a trial judgement, are appeals *stricto sensu*; they are of a corrective nature and are not trials *de novo*.'[5] Our obligation to give broad deference to the Trial Chamber stems from the standard set forth in Article 25 of the Statute.[6] As the court most familiar with the particulars related to the defendant and his crime, the Trial Chamber is best positioned to identify the proper sentence.[7] Accordingly, our precedents make clear that we can reverse a sentence imposed by the Trial Chamber only where we identify a 'discernible error'.[8]

5. As the Prosecution concedes, there is no discernible error in the Trial Chamber's factual findings.[9] The Trial Chamber fully acknowledged the

---

[3] *Kvočka et al.* Appeal Judgement, para 669.
[4] *Babić* Judgement on Sentencing Appeal, para 7; see also, eg, *Naletilić and Martinović* Appeal Judgement, para 593; *Deronjić* Sentencing Appeal Judgement, para 8; *Momir Nikolić* Judgement on Sentencing Appeal, para 8; *Krstić* Appeal Judgement, para 242.
[5] *Momir Nikolić* Judgement on Sentencing Appeal, para 7 (footnotes and accompanying citations omitted); see also, eg, *Babić* Judgement on Sentencing Appeal, para 6.
[6] *Momir Nikolić* Judgement on Sentencing Appeal, para 7.
[7] Cf. *Attorney-General's Reference No 4 of 1989*, 11 Cr App R (S) 517, 521 (Lane, CJ) ('[I]t must always be remembered that sentencing is an art rather than a science; that the trial judge is particularly well placed to assess the weight to be given to various competing considerations; and that leniency is not in itself a vice').
[8] *Krstić* Appeal Judgement, para 242; see also *Naletilić and Martinović* Appeal Judgement, para 593; *Momir Nikolić* Judgement on Sentencing Appeal, para 8; *Prosecutor v Miodrag Jokić*, Case No IT-01-42/1-A, Judgement on Sentencing Appeal, 30 August 2005, para 8; *Deronjić* Sentencing Appeal Judgement, para 8; *Babić* Judgement on Sentencing Appeal, para 7; *Kvočka et al.* Appeal Judgement, para 669; *Kordić and Čerkez* Appeal Judgement, para 1047; *Blaškić* Appeal Judgement, para 680; *Vasiljević* Appeal Judgement, para 9; *Dragan Nikolić* Appeal Judgement, para 9; *Krnojelac* Appeal Judgement, para 253; *Kunarac et al.* Appeal Judgement, para 33; *Kupreškić et al.* Appeal Judgement, para 408; *Jelisić* Appeal Judgement, para 99; *Čelebići* Appeal Judgement, para 725; *Furundžija* Appeal Judgement, para 239; *Aleksovski* Appeal Judgement, para 187; *Tadić* Sentencing Appeal Judgement, para 22.
[9] See Prosecution Appeal Brief, para 2.3.

gravity of Galić's crimes in its discussion of the sentence.[10] It also noted his 'very senior position' in aggravation,[11] and his 'exemplary behaviour... throughout the proceedings before the International Tribunal' in mitigation.[12] Taking into account all these factors, the Trial Chamber imposed a single sentence of 20 years imprisonment.[13] The Appeals Chamber now overturns this sentence and imposes a life sentence on the grounds that a 'sentence of only 20 years was so unreasonable and plainly unjust, in that it underestimated the gravity of Galić's criminal conduct.'[14]

6. I must dissent from the Appeals Chamber's decision to treat the Trial Chamber's chosen sentence as outside its broad discretion. For where a Trial Chamber properly identifies the relevant factors that should govern its decision and where no new convictions are entered on appeal, I would increase its chosen sentence only if one of two conditions is met: either the sentence is clearly out of proportion with sentences we have given in similar situations, or the sentence is otherwise so low that it demonstrably shocks the conscience. Any more stringent review denies the Trial Chamber the broad discretion vested in it.

7. Neither of these two conditions is satisfied here. As to the first condition, our case law indicates that 'in principle, [a sentence] may be thought to be capricious or excessive if it is out of reasonable proportion with a line of sentences passed in similar circumstances for the same offences.'[15] This principle is of limited use, given the 'multitude of variables, ranging from the number and type of crimes committed to the personal circumstances of the individual,' and '[o]ften too many variables exist to be able to transpose the sentence in one case *mutatis mutandis* to another.'[16] Nonetheless, an 'overview of the International Tribunal's cases' can be helpful in assessing whether the sentence was disproportionate.[17]

8. The ICTR Appeals Chamber has applied a comparative analysis in one case: in *Gacumbitsi* it increased a sentence from thirty years to life in

---

[10] Trial Judgement, para 764 (recognizing the 'scale, pattern and virtually continuous repetition, almost daily, over many months' of Galić's offenses, and stating that '[i]nhabitants of Sarajevo—men, women, children, and elderly persons—were terrorized and hundreds of civilians were killed and thousands wounded during daily activities such as attending funerals, tending vegetable plots, fetching water, shopping, going to the hospital, commuting within the city, or while at home'); see also ibid., para 584.
[11] Trial Judgement, para 765.
[12] Trial Judgement, para 766.
[13] Trial Judgement, para 769.
[14] See Appeal Judgement, *supra*, para 455.
[15] *Jelisić* Appeal Judgement, para 96.
[16] *Kvočka et al.* Appeal Judgement, para 227.
[17] *Kordić and Čerkez* Appeal Judgement, para 1064.

keeping with a line of life sentences given in ICTR genocide cases in which there were 'no especially mitigating circumstances.'[18] The ICTY, however, lacks a comparable line of genocide cases and so *Gacumbitsi* is not applicable here.[19] Indeed, the ICTY Appeals Chamber has been reluctant to apply a comparative analysis.[20]

9. Perhaps partly in consequence of the ICTY's emphasis on individualized sentencing, the final sentences imposed upon convicted individuals have ranged widely. Of the convictions which have become final,[21] 15 individuals have received sentences of less than 10 years;[22] 19 have

---

[18] See *Gacumbitsi* Appeal Judgement, para 204. The ICTR Trial Chambers had previously issued life sentences, affirmed on appeal, in genocide cases to Jean-Paul Akayesu *(Akayesu* Appeal Judgement, para 421), Jean Kambanda *(Kambanda* Appeal Judgement, para 126), Jean De Dieu Kamuhanda *(Prosecutor v Kamuhanda*, Case No ICTR-99-54A-A, Judgement, 19 September 2005, para 364), Clément Kayishema *(Kayishema and Ruzindana* Appeal Judgement, para 371), Alfred Musema *(Musema* Appeal Judgement, para 399), and Eliézer Niyitegeka *(Niyitegeka* Appeal Judgement, paras 266–9). Georges Anderson Nderubumwe Rutaganda also received a life sentence, which the Appeals Chamber did not reconsider. See *Rutaganda* Appeal Judgement, para 592. The Appeals Chamber in *Gacumbitsi* distinguished those ICTR genocide convictions in which a life sentence was not given. *Gacumbitsi* Appeal Judgement, fn. 446.

[19] Contrary to the suggestion of my learned colleague, see Separate Opinion of Judge Shahabuddeen, para 44, I do not distinguish *Gacumbitsi* on the ground that 'life sentences have been handed down by the ICTR but not by the ICTY.' Instead, I show that *Gacumbitsi* rests on a comparative analysis of genocide sentences that is entirely inapplicable here—as demonstrated by the majority's opinion's failure to provide *any* discussion of *any* prior cases in its analysis, see *supra* paras 454–5.

[20] See, eg, *Kvočka et al.* Appeal Judgement, paras 682, 690; *Naletilić and Martinović* Appeal Judgement, para 616. While the Prosecution urges that convictions for crimes involving murder should generally lead to 'sentences at the high end of the sentencing spectrum', see Prosecution Appeal Brief, para 2.19(1), this principle cannot be deduced from our case law. To the contrary, we have found 'the view that crimes resulting in loss of life are to be punished more severely than those not leading to loss of life' to be 'too rigid and mechanistic.' *Furundžija* Appeal Judgement, para 246. See also *infra* fns 22–4 (demonstrating that murder-related convictions are not strongly correlated with high-end sentences in ICTY jurisprudence).

[21] In identifying the length of sentences given, I mention only the longest single sentence where concurrent sentences are given.

[22] Dragan Kolundžija received 3 years for persecution of detainees at the Keraterm camp *(Prosecutor v Sikirica et al.*, Case No IT-95-8-S, Sentencing Judgement, 13 November 2001, paras 1, 241–3); Damir Došen received 5 years for persecution of detainees at the Keraterm camp *(Prosecutor v Sikirica et al.*, Case No IT-95-8-S, Sentencing Judgement, 13 November 2001, paras 1, 237–9); Dražen Erdemović received 5 years for murdering Bosnian Muslim civilian men from Srebrenica *(Prosecutor v Erdemović*, Case No IT-96-22-T*bis*, Sentencing Judgement, 5 March 1998, paras 13, 23); Dragoljub Prcać received 5 years as a co-perpetrator of murder, persecution, and torture at the Omarska camp *(Kvočka et al.* Appeal Judgement, para 5 & p 243); Milan Simić received 5 years for two counts of torture which he personally participated in while holding a high-ranking civilian position *(Prosecutor v Simić*, Case No IT-95-9/2-S, Sentencing Judgement, 17 November 2002, paras 10, 11, 64, 122); Milojica Kos received 6 years for his role as a co-perpetrator of murder, torture, and persecution, all encompassing large numbers of victims, at the Omarska camp *(Prosecutor v Kvočka et al.*, Case No IT-98-30/1-T, Judgement, 2 November 2001, paras 504, 729, 735); Mario Čerkez received 6 years for persecution, imprisonment, and unlawful confinement of civilians *(Kordić and Čerkez* Appeal Judgement, para 1070 & p 302); Simo Zarić received 6 years for persecution of non-Serb civilians *(Prosecutor v Simić et al.*, Case No IT-96-9-T, Judgement, 17 October 2003, paras 1123–6); Miroslav Kvočka received 7 years as a co-perpetrator of persecution, murder, and torture at the Omarska camp *(Kvočka et al.* Appeal Judgement, para 3 & p 242); Miodrag Jokić received 7 years as a co-perpetrator for unlawful shelling, murder of civilians, and destruction of buildings of significance *(Prosecutor v*

received sentences of 10–19 years;[23] and only 12 have received sentences

Jokić, Case No IT-01-42/1-A, Judgement on Sentencing Appeal, 30 August 2005, paras 2, 31); Zlatko Aleksovski received 7 years for, among other things, violent mistreatment of detainees (*Aleksovski* Appeal Judgement, paras 36, 37, 191); Miroslav Tadić received 8 years for aiding and abetting persecution based on his direct participation in preparation for the deportation and forcible transfers of civilians (*Prosecutor v Simić et al.*, Case No IT-95-9-T, Judgement, 17 October 2003, paras 1119–22); Pavle Strugar received a sentence of 8 years for attacks on civilians and the destruction of buildings of significance (*Prosecutor v Strugar*, Case No IT-01-42-T, Judgement, 31 January 2005, paras 481, 478); Pedrag Banović received 8 years for persecution based on excessive violence to detainees at the Keraterm camp, such as the beating to death of 5 detainees (*Prosecutor v Banović*, Case No IT-02-65/1-S, Sentencing Judgement, 28 October 2003, paras 90, 91, 93, 95); Zdravko Mucić received 9 years for, among other things, superior responsibility for murder, torture, and sexual assault (*Prosecutor v Mucić et al.* ('*Čelebići*'), Case No IT-96-21-A*bis*, Judgement on Sentence Appeal, 8 April 2003, paras 1, 5). A sixteenth individual, Timohir Blaškić, received 9 years for various crimes (*Blaškić* Appeal Judgement, p 258), but a motion for reconsideration in his case is pending.

[23] Miroslav Deronjić received 10 years for persecutions based on his ordering an attack on a Bosnian Muslim village that led to the deaths of 64 civilians, destroyed much of the town, and caused the forcible displacement of residents (*Deronjić* Sentencing Appeal Judgement, paras 2, 4 & p 56); Anto Furundžija received 10 years for torture (*Furundžija* Appeal Judgement, para 216 & p 79); Stevan Todorović received 10 years for persecution involving murder, beatings, and sexual coercion of various non-Serbs (*Prosecutor v Todorović*, Case No IT-95-9/1-S, Sentencing Judgement, 31 July 2001, paras 5, 9, 117); Biljana Plavšić received 11 years for persecution of non-Serbs in 37 municipalities including killings, forced deportations, and plunder (*Prosecutor v Plavšić*, Case No IT-00-39&40/1-S, Sentencing Judgement, 27 February 2003, paras 8, 15, 132); Drago Josipović received 12 years for persecution, murder, and inhumane acts related to attacks on certain Bosnian Muslim homes and the murder of their inhabitants (*Kupreškić et al.* Appeal Judgement, paras 15–17 & p 170); Zoran Vuković received 12 years for the torture and rape of a fifteen-year-old (*Kunarac et al.* Appeal Judgement, paras 21, 395, 414); Ivica Rajić received 12 years for, among other things, wilful killing (*Prosecutor v Rajić*, Case No IT-95-12-S, Sentencing Judgement, 8 May 2006, paras 5, 9, 184); Milan Babić received 13 years as a co-perpetrator of persecutions that included the extermination or murder of hundreds of non-Serb civilians, deportation of thousands of non-Serb civilians, and deliberate destruction of non-Serb homes and other establishments (*Babić* Judgement on Sentencing Appeal, para 3 & p 47); Esad Landžo received 15 years for various crimes related to killing, torture, sexual assault, and beating of detainees in the Čelebići camp (*Prosecutor v Mucić et al.* ('*Čelebići*'), Case No IT-96-21-A*bis*, Judgement on Sentence Appeal, 8 April 2003, paras 1, 61); Blagoje Simić received 15 years for aiding and abetting persecutions of non-Serb civilians through, among other things, confinement under inhumane conditions and forcible displacements (*Prosecutor v Blagoje Simić*, Case No IT-95-9-A, Judgement, 28 November 2006, para 301); Mitar Vasiljević received 15 years as an aider and abettor to persecution and murder related to the shooting of seven Muslim men (*Vasiljević* Appeal Judgement, paras 148, 182); Duško Sikirica received 15 years for persecution of detainees at the Keraterm camp, at which he had a position of responsibility, and for personally murdering one detainee (*Prosecutor v Sikirica et al.*, Case No IT-95-8-S, Sentencing Judgement, 13 November 2001, paras 1, 233–5); Milorad Krnojelac received 15 years for multiple counts of murder, torture, persecution, and cruel treatment committed over an extended stint as a camp warden (*Krnojelac* Appeal Judgement, para 255 & pp 113–14); Darko Mrđa received 17 years for crimes related to the massacre of two busloads of non-Serb civilians (*Prosecutor v Mrđa*, Case No IT-02-59-S, Sentencing Judgement, 31 March 2004, paras 1, 5, 10, 129); Dragan Obrenović received 17 years for persecutions related to the murder of thousands of Bosnian Muslims at Srebrenica (*Prosecutor v Obrenović*, Case No IT-02-60/2-S, Sentencing Judgement, 10 December 2003, paras 11, 29, 156); Ranko Češić received 18 years for ten murders and for forcing two brothers to commit a sex act upon each other (*Prosecutor v Češić*, Case No IT-95-10/1-S, Sentencing Judgement, 11 March 2004, paras 3–4, 17, 111); Hazim Delić received 18 years for wilfully killing one detainee, wilfully causing great suffering to another, raping two victims, and committing several other crimes (*Prosecutor v Mucić et al.* ('*Čelebići*'), Case No IT-96-21-A*bis*, Judgement on Sentence Appeal, 8 April 2003, paras 40–7); Vladimir Šantić received 18 years for persecution, murder, and inhumane acts related to attacks on certain Bosnian Muslim homes and the murder of their inhabitants (*Kupreškić et al.* Appeal Judgement, paras 19–20 & p 171); Vinko

of 20 years or more.²⁴ In no case has an ICTY defendant ended up with a life sentence. This is not to say such a sentence cannot be given. To the contrary, the Appeals Chamber in *Stakić* acknowledged that a life sentence for a 'co-perpetrator of extremely serious crimes, including an extermination campaign that the Trial Chamber estimated killed approximately 1,500 people in the Prijedor municipality' fell 'within the Trial Chamber's discretion,' though the Appeals Chamber did not suggest that such a life sentence was compelled.²⁵ But in the absence of any ICTY case where a defendant has ended up with a life sentence after appeal, a comparative analysis gives us no basis for finding that the Trial Chamber was obligated to impose a life sentence on Galić. This is true even if, as the Prosecution claims, Galić's 'crimes are among the worst that come before the Tribunal.'²⁶

Martinović received 18 years for various crimes related to events at Mostar, including persecution, murder, wilful killing, and plunder (*Naletilić and Martinović* Appeal Judgement, para 6 & p 280).

²⁴ Momir Nikolić received 20 years for persecution related to his role in Srebrenica, including the murder of thousands of Bosnian Muslim civilians and the cruel treatment of many others (*Momir Nikolić* Judgement on Sentencing Appeal, paras 2–3 & p 48); Dragan Nikolić received 20 years for persecutions, including murder, rape, and torture, from which he derived enjoyment (*Dragan Nikolić* Appeal Judgement, paras 4, 30 & p 44); Radomir Kovač received 20 years for outrages on personal dignity, rape, and enslavement (*Kunarac et al.* Appeal Judgement, paras 11, 367, 394); Duško Tadić received 20 years for nine counts, (*Tadić* Sentencing Appeal Judgement, para 76); Mladen Naletilić received 20 years for persecution, torture, and multiple other offenses based upon his role as a Croat commander at Mostar (*Naletilić and Martinović* Appeal Judgement, paras 3–4 & p 207); Mlao Radić received 20 years for persecution, murder, and torture at the Omarska camp, where he personally raped or committed sexual violence on 4 victims (*Kvočka et al.* Appeal Judgement, paras 6, 393 & p 243); Dario Kordić received 25 years for a multitude of horrific crimes committed in many locales over many months (*Kordić and Čerkez* Appeal Judgement, para 1070 & p 302); Zoran Žigić received 25 years for persecution, murder, and torture at three camps, one of which he entered for the sole purpose of abusing detainees (*Kvočka et al.* Appeal Judgement, paras 7, 716 & p 243); Dragoljub Kunarac received 28 years for various counts of torture, rape, and enslavement (*Kunarac et al.* Appeal Judgement, paras 5, 336, 366); Radislav Krstić received 35 years for his role in aiding and abetting genocide, extermination, and persecution with regard to the massacres of Bosnian Muslims at Srebrenica (*Krstić* Appeal Judgement, paras 237, 275); Goran Jelisić received 40 years for 31 counts, among them murder, which he had undertaken enthusiastically (*Jelesić* Appeal Judgement, paras 86, 93 & p 41); Milomir Stakić received 40 years for extermination, murder, and persecution committed in the Prijedor Municipality, where he was a Serbian leader (*Stakić* Appeal Judgement, para 3 & p 141–2).

²⁵ *Stakić* Appeal Judgement, para 375. The Appeals Chamber reduced this life sentence to 40 years for other reasons. See ibid., paras 393, 428.

²⁶ Prosecution Appeal Brief, para 2.3. The Prosecution does not suggest that this is *the* worst case to come before the Tribunal. Nor does the Prosecution explain why a life sentence is warranted here when it has not been given in other cases. Even in the case involving an authority figure in arguably the most horrific incident in the entire conflict—the massacre of 7000–8000 Bosnian Muslim civilians at Srebrenica—the Trial Chamber did not impose a life sentence on Radislav Krstić. Like the Prosecution, the Appeals Chamber does not even attempt to show that Galić's crimes can be considered graver than Krstić's.

I also note another illogical aspect of the Prosecution's submission. The Prosecution both suggests that there was 'a discretionary range which was available to the Trial Chamber' and that the only

10. Turning to the second condition I identified, I cannot conclude that a 20-year sentence is so low that it demonstrably shocks the conscience.[27] The war crimes and crimes against humanity committed by Galić are grave indeed. He commanded a lengthy campaign that led to deaths and serious injuries of civilians of all ages and that sought to terrorize countless more. Yet his sentence is hardly insubstantial. It is not a two-and-a-half-year slap-on-the-wrist,[28] but rather a term of 20 years—a sentence that is as long as or longer than the vast majority of sentences imposed by the ICTY to date.[29] And as noted by the Trial Chamber, this sentence is as long as was the longest prison sentence that could be imposed in the former Yugoslavia.[30] The Trial Chamber fully considered the awful nature of Galić's crimes and the individual considerations pertinent to him in meting it out.

11. Reasonable minds can disagree about this sentence, just as they can disagree about whether there was enough evidence to support all the convictions in the first place. Just as we review the convictions on the merits to see whether any reasonable trier of fact could have found the defendant guilty beyond a reasonable doubt rather than considering whether we ourselves would have entered such a conviction, so we review the sentence to see whether a Trial Chamber could reasonably impose it—rather than whether we ourselves would have done so. Had I sat as a Trial Judge, I might not have found Galić guilty beyond a reasonable doubt of the shelling of Markale market, but I cannot say that all reasonable triers of fact had to reach this conclusion. Similarly, had

---

sentence the Trial Chamber could have imposed was a life sentence. Prosecution Appeal, para 2.3; see also Separate Opinion of Judge Shahabuddeen, *supra*, para 35 (apparently endorsing this reasoning). This cannot be. If the Trial Chamber was indeed compelled to impose a life sentence, then it had no discretion at all.

[27] Only once has the ICTY Appeals Chamber arguably revised a sentence upward for such reasons. In *Aleksovski*, the Appeals Chamber concluded that the sentence of two-and-a-half years was too low and raised it to 7 years instead. Aleksovski had been the commander of the Kaonik prison, and in that capacity he had, among other crimes, 'aid[ed] and abett[ed] the mistreatment of detainees during body searches'; 'order[ed], instigat[ed] and aid[ed] and abett[ed] violence on Witnesses L and M, who were beaten regularly during their detention (sometimes four to six times a day)… [and] order[ed] the guards to continue beating them when they stopped'; and 'aid[ed] and abett[ed] the use of detainees as human shields'. *Aleksovski* Appeal Judgement, para 175. In rejecting the two-and-a-half year sentence as unduly low, the Appeals Chamber provided extensive reasoning. See ibid., paras 183–8. Although the Appeals Chamber's decision emphasized the disparity between the crimes and the sentence, it also identified at least one discernible error made by the Trial Chamber. Specifically, the Trial Chamber erred in failing to treat Aleksovski's superior role as an aggravating factor. See ibid., para 183. The Appeals Chamber also noted that under the law of the former Yugoslavia, Aleksovski could not have received a sentence of less than five years. See ibid.

[28] Compare *Aleksovksi*, discussed in the preceding footnote.

[29] See *supra* fns 22–4. Of the 46 sentences that have become final, 40 have been for 20 years or less.

[30] Trial Judgement, para 761. The law of the former Yugoslavia permitted a death sentence, but did not permit a prison term of more than 20 years.

I sat as a Trial Judge, I might have called for a sentence of a longer term than 20 years, but I cannot say that all reasonable triers of fact were obligated to do the same. The need for a consistent standard of review is particularly high in cases like this one, where the scope of the defendant's guilt presents a close question. Judge Nieto-Navia, for example, would have found Galić responsible for fewer incidents than did the majority of the Trial Chamber; would have found him guilty only of failing to restrain his subordinates from unlawful conduct that he had reason to know was occurring; and would have sentenced him to ten years.[31] It is most unfair to affirm Galić's convictions by genuinely deferring to the findings of the Trial Chamber majority, and yet to increase Galić's sentence by not deferring (or only nominally deferring) to the Trial Chamber's choice of sentence.

12. Finally, I see no meaningful difference between the Prosecution's appeal in this case and its appeal in *Kordić and Čerkez*.[32] There, the Prosecution called for us to increase the 25-year sentence imposed by the Trial Chamber on Dario Kordić, who was held responsible for, among other crimes, the persecution of Bosnian Muslims, the murder or wilful killing of hundreds of civilians, inhumane acts, wanton destruction, and plunder committed in and around at least 17 towns and villages in three municipalities of Bosnia-Herzegovina.[33] As in this case, the Prosecutor did 'not argue that the Trial Chamber erred in failing to take into account factors that would have called for a longer sentence.'[34] Rather, and again parallel to this case, the Prosecution claimed that 'the sentence of 25 years' imprisonment is manifestly inadequate in relation to (i) the magnitude, scope—geographic and temporal—and extremely grave nature of the offences, the attacks being committed against defenceless civilians; [and] (ii) Kordić's position, powers, responsibilities as the highest Bosnian Croat political leader in Central Bosnia at the time.'[35] We readily held that 'The Prosecution has not shown that the Trial Chamber handed

---

[31] Separate and Partially Dissenting Opinion, paras 17–102; 120, 123. Judge Nieto-Navia was influenced in part by the fact that Galić 'personally instructed his troops in writing to respect the Geneva Convention and other instruments of international humanitarian law.' Ibid., para 116; see also Trial Judgement, para 708.

[32] Regrettably, I have no guidance on this matter from the majority opinion or the separate opinions of my distinguished colleagues. None of these opinions even acknowledges the Appeals Chamber's decision in *Kordić and Čerkez*, let alone attempts to show that Galić's crimes are graver than Kordić's.

[33] See generally, *Kordić and Čerkez* Appeal Judgement; see also ibid. paras 1057–65.

[34] *Kordić and Čerkez* Appeal Judgement, para 1063.

[35] Ibid., para 1058.

down a sentence which did not reflect the gravity of Kordić's conduct.'[36] For the same reasons, we should reach the same conclusion in this case.

13. The majority's decision to increase Galić's sentence to life imprisonment may satisfy our sense of condemnation. But this increase disserves the principles of procedural fairness on which our legitimacy rests. As the highest body in our court system, we are not readily accountable to any other authority and thus have a particular obligation to use our power sparingly. We should not substitute our own preferences for the reasoned judgement of a Trial Chamber. A sound method for assuring that we have not fallen prey to such preferences is to measure our choices fully and comprehensively against those made in prior cases. Although precise comparisons may be of limited value, the radically different approach adopted by the majority in this case requires at least some explanation. Rather than undertaking such an analysis, however, the majority simply offers conclusory statements. I cannot accept the majority's approach. No matter what he has done, Galić is entitled to due process of law—including a fair application of our standard of review. I respectfully dissent.

[36] Ibid., para 1065.

24

JUDICIAL INDEPENDENCE AND JUDICIAL IMPARTIALITY*

My distinguished co-panelists, Justice O'Connor and Lord Chief Justice Woolf, have presented an illuminating overview of the long and sophisticated tradition of judicial independence and judicial impartiality in the United States and England. I would like to emphasize a few themes that I think are crucial to the notions of judicial independence and impartiality. I will draw in part on the experience of judges in international courts and, of course, on my own experience. I will also refer, however, to the general experience of judges in national courts of the United States and Europe. The themes which I will mention will no doubt resonate with those Justice O'Connor and Lord Woolf have already discussed, but I hope to provide some additional perspective to the points they made.

I. WHY JUDICIAL INDEPENDENCE MATTERS

As is clear from their remarks, and from those made by Justice Kennedy and Judge Higgins yesterday, judicial independence is crucial for the rule of law. Most obviously, when judges are independent from political or other pressures, they will resolve the disputes brought to them fairly, with an eye to the guiding legal principles and without any undue influence. This will solidify public respect for the courts, and lead people to turn to the courts more often for the settlement of their disputes.

The ability to resolve disputes fairly has a wider social consequence: it is essential for a stable economy and polity. Economic and political actors need to know that there is an impartial arbiter who will administer the

---

* Delivered at a training conference for Iraqi judges in The Hague, The Netherlands, in May 2004. Portions of the text of this speech have been published in Editorial Comment, 'Judicial Independence and Impartiality in International Criminal Tribunals' (2005) 99 *AJIL* 359, © The American Society of International Law; Theodor Meron. Used by permission and modified from the original publication.

rules of the game and that their expectations based on existing laws and regulations will be honored. Independent judges play a critical role in this regard. Judges, when they resolve disputes, also explain and clarify the existing laws and regulations. When judges are independent and behave in a rule-based way, their explanations have a certain predictability, because they are based on existing laws, on the prior judicial precedent, and on logic. This predictability allows political and economic actors to plan their behavior accordingly. This contributes greatly to the political stability and economic prosperity of a society.

Judicial independence is also necessary to effectively protect individual rights, which are the bedrock of any free society. These rights may be enshrined in the country's constitution or laws, but there must exist an authority, such as the courts, which can review—independently and impartially—a citizen's complaint and, if necessary, order that his or her improperly infringed rights be vindicated. To do so effectively, judges must be assured that, irrespective of their ruling, there will be no unpleasant repercussions to them in terms of salary diminution or threats of dismissal.

This brings me to the final, and most important, role played by judicial independence. Independent courts are the indispensable means of constraining the government by law. The government is often a party to a lawsuit, as in the example of alleged infringement of individual rights I just mentioned. One of the most fundamental principles of the rule of law is that no one should be the judge of his or her own case. There must therefore exist an independent entity, such as the courts, which has the power to determine when the government has violated the legal constraints upon it.

This conclusion has implications not only for the protection of individual rights, but also for the maintenance of separation of powers and of federalism. In a system with competing authorities—be they the executive and the legislature, or the national government and the regional government—there are bound to be frictions and even outright conflicts. Some of these frictions can, and often will, resolve themselves through political mechanisms. It is unrealistic, however, to expect that all of these conflicts will solve themselves in this manner. The reliance on political mechanisms alone is, moreover, a potentially dangerous one. While some conflicts may be easily solved through the legislative process, through elections, or through other political means, some conflicts may polarize the society and produce either an intractable stalemate or a bitterly divisive polity. The existence of a neutral, respected, and independent arbiter, such as the courts, provides an alternative way of resolving political (and sometimes social) disputes.

II. ENSURING AN INDEPENDENT JUDICIARY

What, then, is necessary to ensure an independent judiciary? While there are many necessary elements, I would suggest that two of the most crucial are the public's respect for the courts and the judge's own self-perception as an independent and impartial arbiter. These two factors are closely related, for if the courts are viewed as impartial, they will be respected; and a court which enjoys public respect will find it easier to display independent judgment and confront, if necessary, powerful government or social interests. I would like to spend the remainder of my time with you today discussing different ways in which judicial impartiality and the perception of such impartiality may be threatened, and how these threats may be addressed.

A. Judicial selection

Yesterday, Chief Justice Medhat asked a very good question of whether the involvement of the US President and Congress in the selection and appointment of judges endangers the principle of the separation of powers, and thereby the independence of the judiciary. A somewhat analogous question is often asked with respect to judges who are selected to sit on international courts, such as my own. In the case of my court, the judges are nominated by member-states of the United Nations and are then elected by the UN General Assembly; in the case of the International Court of Justice, on which Judge Buergenthal and Judge Higgins sit, they must be elected by both the General Assembly and the Security Council. Unlike judges in the United States, we do not hold tenure for life, nor, unlike in England, until a mandatory retirement age. Instead, we are elected for a specified term—in my own case, four years, and in the case of the ICJ judge, nine years—with the possibility of re-election. It is possible that overt campaigning by judges may create a perception of inappropriate politicization, not to mention distraction from the work at hand. I have thought at times that a ban on direct electioneering by judges might well be attractive. It would certainly raise some practical problems—campaigning by judges might simply be replaced by proxy campaigns, for example—but, in principle at least, keeping judges at one remove from the political process might be beneficial both to the perceived impartiality of the international court, and to the efficiency and effectiveness of the individual judges.

There is often a concern expressed that a judge on an international court who is focused on the prospects of re-nomination by his or her government or re-election may decide cases in such a way as not to antagonize powerful member states of the United Nations and, especially, his or her own state. Let me first underscore that I have no doubt that any conscientious judge sitting on an international court will decide cases before him or her only in accordance with the law and his or her judicial conscience. But the possibility of public perception that a judge may be biased because of extra-judicial considerations—particularly if these considerations appear self-serving—counsels strongly for international judges to be scrupulously impartial in their decision-making. This is especially so when a judge on an international court makes a ruling or writes an opinion in favor of his or her own member state or a member state that strongly supported that judge's candidacy. I am not suggesting, of course, that a judge should alter his or her view as to the legal outcome in such a case; I only suggest the importance of being sensitive to the possibility of the public perception of bias.

The judges of international courts, as a rule, do not explain their rulings in press interviews, and so cannot respond directly to public criticism or to allegations of partiality in the media. Instead, international judges put their effort into producing a reasoned and persuasive opinion, which explains, in language understandable both to lawyers and to the general public, the reasons why the court reached a particular outcome. If an opinion is persuasive and clearly explains why the decision was a correct one in terms of law, it will resonate as such with the public, and go a long way to counter possible allegations of bias.

B. Judicial assignments

A subtler concern about influence presents itself in the ICTY President's power over the make-up of judicial panels. At the ICTY, in my role as President, I assign the full panel of judges for both trials and appeal proceedings. So when a defendant is brought before the Tribunal, it is up to me to determine which three judges will decide his or her fate at the trial level. Similarly, when a verdict has been entered at the trial level and the defendant or prosecutor files an appeal or appeals, I am responsible for naming the bench of appeals judges who will decide the appeal. It is worth noting that the ICC has a similar, but not identical system of panel appointments, in which the ICC Presidency selects the judges that make up both Pre-Trial Chambers and the Trial Chambers themselves.

How much discretion does this add up to in practice? Well, in terms of raw numbers, the structure of the ICTY leaves me much less leeway at the appeals level: I must select a five-judge panel from a total of seven judges in the Appeals Chamber. But at the trial level, the leeway is much broader: I appoint trial panels of three judges from among a pool of eighteen trial judges (although at least one judge on each panel must be a permanent judge, of which there are only nine at the trial level, and all of the selected judges must already belong to one of three pre-established Trial Chambers).

The self-regulating culture of the Tribunal, I suppose, constrains my discretion to some extent, since transparent workload surveys show how the work is allocated among judges. There is also an essentially political check on my activities, since I serve as President only at the sufferance of the other judges of the Tribunal. Under our system, the Tribunal must rely on the conscientious goodwill of the President, as monitored by his or her colleagues, to avoid inappropriate ideological control over panel memberships. But ultimately the integrity of the system rests on the integrity of all judges, such that the composition of the bench should have no predictable effect on the judicial result. In some ways, this last reflection holds true for judicial impartiality more generally: the best defense of that principle lies in the culture of judicial independence and integrity that must be fostered at the Tribunal and in legal settings throughout the world.

As a second, and in some ways even more important, example of this power of judicial selection, the Yugoslavia and Rwanda Tribunal Presidents actually control the permanent make-up of the Appeals Chamber itself—the body that has the final say on the law that governs both Tribunals. The mechanics of this require some explanation. The two Tribunals actually share a single seven-judge Appeals Chamber, of which only one member is defined by statute: the Yugoslavia Tribunal President. So there are six judges left. Four of them are named by the Yugoslavia Tribunal President, and two of them by the Rwanda Tribunal President (although they must choose from among the permanent judges elected to their respective Tribunals), after both Presidents have consulted with the other judges of their Tribunal. In theory, then, the Yugoslavia Tribunal President could stack the decks in the Appeals Chamber to lock in ideological uniformity. As evidenced by the dissents and vigorous debate on the Appeals Chamber, this does not seem to have happened because of the prevailing culture of judicial integrity, but it is nonetheless a structural element that, in theory, could be seen to undercut judicial independence.

The Rwanda Tribunal President's power in this regard is even more striking, since the Rwanda Tribunal's Statute has been interpreted to allow mid-term transfers. So, for example, part-way through a judicial term, the Rwanda Tribunal President may remove one of his or her appointees from the Appeals Chamber and replace that judge with a judge from the Rwanda Tribunal's Trial Chamber. Would this implicate judicial independence? It depends. Periodic replacements shifting judges between the Trial Chamber and the Appeals Chamber on a pre-set schedule strike me as acceptable from the perspective of judicial independence. Random replacements, on the other hand, could be problematic. The appropriateness of an exercise of this power also depends on the motives of the President. If the President shifts judges from one Chamber to another in order to stifle dissent, then that is clearly inappropriate. I am confident that shifting for such reasons has never occurred. But if the President shifts judges with an eye to balancing the make-up of the appellate chamber (in terms of countries of origin, for example, or in terms of the varying experience of the judges), then it presents less of a problem.

C. *Judicial bias and recusal*

There is another form of possible bias that may also endanger the public perception of impartiality of the judiciary. It is the danger of a preconceived notion in favor of a particular outcome. Judges are expected to approach any case brought before them with an open mind, with the willingness to listen to the parties' arguments, and with the intention to decide the case only after they have heard from all parties and have reviewed the facts of the case and the applicable law. This open-mindedness is crucial to solidifying public respect for the courts. It indicates to every litigant that he or she will have a fair day in court because the judges are willing to listen to the litigant's arguments and, should they have merit, hold for him or her.

Of course, judges are not empty vessels that the litigants fill with content. Judges are appointed, at least in the international courts and in many countries, such as the United States and the United Kingdom, from among prominent members of the legal profession. These individuals already have a wealth of experience, as practitioners or academics, or, in some cases, as government officials. At some point in their judicial career, they will be called upon to decide cases raising issues with which they have dealt as practicing lawyers or civil servants, or on which they have written as academics. These situations raise the question of whether a judge should abstain from deciding that case and recuse him- or herself, on the basis either that the judge cannot be impartial or that his or her impartiality can be questioned by a reasonable observer.

These are two related, but separate considerations. In the first scenario, if a judge concludes that he cannot be impartial because he had already formed an irreversible opinion on the issue, he must, of course, recuse himself. In this situation, he is unable to act as a judge: weighing competing legal positions and assessing the merits of each party's case.

The second scenario is more complicated. There, a judge actually concludes that she can act impartially in the case, but that others may reasonably perceive her as partial. In such a situation, a judge recuses herself not because she is unable to exercise her judicial function, but in order to preserve the integrity of her court and of the concept of law. A well-known British jurist, Lord Hewart, famously remarked eighty years ago, in a case named *Ex parte McCarthy*, that: 'Justice must not only be done, but should manifestly and undoubtedly be seen to be done.'[1] There are situations where the reputation of the judiciary may be compromised if there is even an appearance of bias, and in these situations caution and concern for the reputation of the court often counsel that a judge recuse him- or herself from deciding that particular case.

What are such situations? The easiest one is where a judge may have a financial or similar stake in the outcome. Even though that personal interest may be unimportant to the judge, the public may justly question the impartiality of a judge who stands to profit from his or her own decision.

A more difficult situation is where a judge has a strong personal connection to one of the parties. If this connection is such that it may indicate to an outside observer that a judge is likely to be swayed by the personal bond, the judge should recuse him- or herself. Care must be taken, however, that judges do not feel forced to step aside from deciding cases where they are either acquainted with some of the litigants or connected to them in some way, but the connection is not so strong as to call into question their ability to render an impartial judgment.

A third, and perhaps the most difficult, question is whether a judge should recuse him- or herself if the judge has previously publicly expressed an opinion that can be viewed as pre-judging the case now before him or her. My own Tribunal faced this issue a few years ago. In a case called *Furundžija*, the defendant on appeal sought the disqualification of

---

[1] *R v Sussex Justices, Ex parte McCarthy* [1924] 1 KB 256, 259.

the presiding trial judge (and the vacatur of the judgment in which this judge participated) because the judge was previously a member of the UN Commission on the Status of Women, which investigated allegations of mass and systematic rape in the former Yugoslavia and called for their prosecution by our Tribunal.[2] The defendant, who had been convicted of committing rape as a war crime, argued that having this judge preside over his trial created an appearance of partiality because a reasonable observer could have concluded that the judge used the trial and the judgment to promote the legal and political agenda of the Commission on the Status of Women that she had helped to create.

The Appeals Chamber of my Tribunal rejected the defendant's claim, and elaborated what I believe is a workable rule for deciding when a judge should disqualify him- or herself. This principle covers the examples of bias—real or perceived—which I gave earlier. We explained that a judge is not impartial and should recuse him- or herself if there is a showing of actual bias. We also stated that a judge should recuse him- or herself if there is an 'unacceptable appearance of bias'.[3] This appearance can be manifested in two ways. First, a judge should recuse him- or herself if the judge 'is a party to the case, or has a financial or proprietary interest in the outcome of a case, or if the Judge's decision will lead to the promotion of a cause in which he or she is involved, together with one of the parties'.[4] Second, a judge should disqualify him- or herself if 'the circumstances would lead a reasonable observer, properly informed, to reasonably apprehend bias'.[5]

I say this rule is workable because recently it was followed by another international court, the Special Court set up to prosecute atrocities committed during the civil war in Sierra Leone. That Court had a request from the defense to disqualify the Court's President because, in a book he had previously published, he had written that the armed organization to which the defendants belonged was guilty of crimes against humanity. The President of the Sierra Leone Court refused to disqualify himself, but his colleagues disagreed and ordered his recusal.[6] They concluded that a reasonable bystander could, reading the passages in question, have a legitimate reason to fear that the judge who wrote them lacked impartiality. Notably, the recused judge accepted the decision and the rationale. He stated that, while he holds no preconceived

---

[2] *Prosecutor v Anto Furundžija* (Judgement) IT-95-17/1-A (21 July 2000).
[3] Ibid., para 189.
[4] Ibid.   [5] Ibid.
[6] *Prosecutor v Issa Hassan Sesay* (Decision on Defence Motion Seeking the Disqualification of Justice Robertson from the Appeals Chamber) SCSL-2004-15-AR15 (13 March 2004).

views on the guilt or innocence of the defendants, his earlier criticisms of the organization to which they belonged could give rise to a perception that he could not judge them with an open mind.

Also worth mentioning in the recusal context is one interesting and, generally speaking, rare issue that presented itself at the Yugoslavia Tribunal in the *Čelebići* case (so named because of the location where the crimes at issue were committed). Judge Odio Benito, who was on the trial panel in *Čelebići*, was elected as the Second Vice-President of Costa Rica partway through the trial, but continued to serve on the trial panel. On appeal in *Čelebići*, the defendants made several arguments that she should not have continued to sit on the trial panel after her election as Second Vice-President.[7] Most relevantly for present purposes, they contended that her position in domestic government meant that she no longer possessed the necessary judicial independence required by international law.

In its ruling, the Appeals Chamber appeared to acknowledge that active service as a member of a national executive branch might be incompatible with service in the Yugoslavia Tribunal. In the circumstances of Judge Odio Benito's case, however, the Appeals Chamber noted that she had declined to assume any vice-presidential functions until completing her duties as a member of the trial panel in *Čelebići*. If she had been serving in an active capacity as Second Vice-President while still actively serving on the *Čelebići* bench, presumably the Appeals Chamber would have been much more likely to find an appearance of impropriety. In such a case, her dual loyalties—as a political representative of her nation and a member of its political hierarchy, on the one hand, and as an impartial judge whose positions on the case before her had nothing to do with her nationality, on the other—might well have appeared to be a conflict of interest to a reasonable observer.

A lesson that can be derived from these cases is that while the judge whose impartiality is challenged should be the first one to assess whether to recuse him- or herself, there may also be situations where, should the judge refuse to stand aside, the other members of the court may re-visit this question and rule on whether it would be proper for that judge to participate. Care, of course, must be taken to ensure that such a decision is taken in the proper spirit of collegiality.

These kinds of issues are likely to recur at international tribunals. The judges on these tribunals come from academic backgrounds or from

---

[7] *Prosecutor v Zejnil Delalić et al.* (Judgement) IT-96-21-A (20 February 2001) (*Čelebići*).

careers in other sectors of public life, legal practice, or the judiciary, and they have usually been chosen precisely because of their expertise in international or criminal law, typically evidenced by a lengthy publication trail. So the fact that judges will have spoken or written on some of the issues that come before them in their role as judges is to be expected. Usually, when previous writings have not been with reference to specific individuals or specific defendants, I would think that a judge's prior analysis of a legal problem in an academic context should not be an issue worthy of recusal—certainly not where the judge has the openness of mind to be willing to reconsider his or her prior position. But drawing lines may be somewhat difficult: when does an expression of a purely academic view about a legal issue in international law raise an appearance of partiality?

My own Tribunal is currently striving to determine the best way to resolve such questions where they arise after a judge declines to step down of his or her own accord. Our rules provide that all such issues are resolved by the Bureau, a five-judge body that is composed of the President and Vice-President of the Tribunal along with the Presiding Judges of the three Trial Chambers. In an instance where there may be a genuine appearance of bias, but where the judge in question rejects the challenge to his or her impartiality, the Presiding Judge of the Chamber first attempts to resolve the issue through informal consultation with the judge whose impartiality has been challenged. If a mutually satisfactory resolution cannot be reached, the question is then referred to the Bureau, which is charged with deciding whether the judge must be excluded from the case. The decision of the Bureau is not subject to appeal.

As you might imagine, there are differing opinions about who should be the ultimate authority on this matter. Some judges feel that, notwithstanding the fact that all five of its members are judges of the Tribunal, the Bureau acts as a quasi-administrative body and therefore should not be involved in the judicial question of assessing impartiality. There has therefore been a proposal that, in recusal cases, the President should appoint a separate three-judge panel to determine the question of impartiality. That panel's decision could then be appealed to the Appeals Chamber, which would have the final say on the matter.

The difficulty with that approach, some believe, is that (similar to the issues discussed above) it may vest excessive power in the President over one of the most delicate issues we face as a Tribunal. It would also raise some hierarchical complexities in the case of a challenge to a judge on the Appeals Chamber, since Trial Chamber judges would be determining his or her suitability to decide a case. My point here is not to suggest which of these alternatives is the best, but to underscore how complex is the task of referring recusal challenges to a higher authority than the judge whose impartiality has been questioned.[8]

D. *Institutional design and management*

This brings me to another point I would like to make. To maintain the judiciary's reputation for impartiality, it must have a variety of internal mechanisms to either filter out potential bias or to correct it before the result becomes final. One such mechanism is multi-judge panels. In my Tribunal, all trials are conducted by a bench of three judges and all appeals by a bench of five. A majority of these judges must agree on the outcome and the rationale. This prevents a single member who may be biased from influencing the result. The judges, moreover, discuss the case among themselves prior to agreeing on a decision, and this discussion helps to correct any latent biases, because a judge is confronted with, and has to respond to, the logical arguments of his or her colleagues.

Another mechanism is appellate review. In my Tribunal, as I have already mentioned, there is a right of appeal granted to both parties. This right is also recognized by many international instruments, although with some limitations. Appellate review ensures that decisions of lower courts are accurate and uniform, and that injustice is not committed. Allegations of bias by trial judges can be raised at this stage. Appellate review also enhances judicial independence in another way: by correcting the judicial error internally, it reduces the need for other institutions to step in and deal with abuses or mistakes within the court system.

The last mechanism I would mention is internal committees and guidelines which ensure compliance with the code of judicial ethics. The importance of judicial ethics has been comprehensively addressed this morning by Justice Kennedy, Chief Justice Davids, and Professor Gurule, so I need not mention it further.

E. *Communicating with the public*

Lastly, let me speak briefly about the courts' relationship with the public. As the courts decide an increasing number of important issues in public life, they become more visible in the eyes of the public and, of course, the media. When the courts render a decision of which certain sections of the

---

[8] Editor's note: Pursuant to a July 2005 amendment to Rule 15 of the ICTY's Rules of Procedure and Evidence, the Bureau is no longer tasked with determining applications for a judge's disqualification and withdrawal. Instead, where necessary, the President of the Tribunal appoints a three-judge panel to decide the merits of the application.

government or society disapprove, these latter often express their criticism publicly. Of course, the right to publicly express disagreement with a judicial decision is an integral element of a free society and a free press. Courts are public institutions and should not be immune from criticism. Indeed, there are occasions when such criticism is beneficial. Constructive criticism facilitates self-examination and self-improvement of the judiciary. In addition, in the instances where a judicial decision interpreting a particular law is being criticized, that criticism may motivate the legislature to review the law and change it.

There are occasions, however, when criticism goes too far. This happens when criticism is motivated solely by the dislike of a particular result reached by a court, without any regard to the underlying reasoning or the supporting law, or when particular judges are targeted for criticism for reasons unrelated to their professional performance. The judges, of course, cannot cave in under this pressure, for it would be an abandonment of their judicial function. The judges are also, as I already mentioned, limited in their means of responding to this criticism.

But there are certain things that judges can do to promote a better understanding on the part of the public of the work they do. One solution is to recruit media and public affairs officers to the service of the courts. In my Tribunal, we have a special public affairs office which provides the media with weekly briefings about the work of the Tribunal and its judges, answers questions from journalists, and disseminates a variety of information both to the press and to any interested researcher. Of course, the Tribunal's public affairs officers do not interpret judicial decisions to the media; that would be an unacceptable encroachment upon the judicial function. But what they do is help journalists—who often work under strict deadlines—to report important court decisions accurately. The public thereby becomes better informed about our work, and that, I hope, increases appreciation of the important work we perform.

III. CONCLUSION

Judicial independence is indispensable for a law-based society. There are many important structural safeguards that facilitate judicial independence, such as lifetime tenure or non-removability until a certain retirement age. But judicial independence also depends on the public support for the judiciary as an institution, and to earn that support, the judiciary must appear scrupulously impartial in its decision-making. Along with fidelity to the law, impartiality is a means of ensuring the accountability of an independent judiciary.

25
THE ROLE OF JUDGES IN PUBLIC LIFE*

I would like to lay out a framework for considering different aspects of public life, and identify considerations that should attend judges' participation in these.

As an initial point, I note that my examples derive primarily from my knowledge of the International Criminal Tribunals for the former Yugoslavia and Rwanda (ICTY and ICTR, respectively) and US federal and state courts. Nonetheless, I believe that the broad concepts of judicial independence I will discuss are applicable to judges in both common and civil law systems, and at all levels of the judiciary. I would also observe that my discussion deals with judges' public actions—and thus will not address fascinating questions relating primarily to the private internal workings of courts, such as those addressed by the European Court of Human Rights in *Kress v France*.[1] Finally, I underscore that I speak in my private capacity, not as a representative of the ICTY or ICTR.

I. JUDICIAL INDEPENDENCE

Before addressing judges' participation in specific aspects of public life, I will briefly consider the question of judicial independence and the justifications that underlie this concept.

As I have previously stated in the *American Journal of International Law*, I believe that judicial independence is critical to the rule of law, instrumental in the protection of individual rights, and an indispensable means of holding a government or community to its laws.[2] As a judge of the

---

* Delivered at the Brandeis Institute for International Judges in Salzburg, Austria, on 29 July 2010.

[1] *Kress v France* (App no 39594/98) ECHR 2001-VI 41. In this judgment, the ECHR addressed, inter alia, the role of the Advocate-General in the private deliberations of judges.

[2] Theodor Meron, Editorial Comment, 'Judicial Independence and Impartiality in International Criminal Tribunals' (2005) 99 *AJIL* 359 (Judicial Independence Article), 359.

ICTY and ICTR Appeals Chambers, I have come to appreciate the particular significance of judicial independence when considering the gravest of crimes, such as genocide. Legal judgments on serious issues such as these can be particularly controversial, and it is especially important that they not be tainted by any suggestion of impropriety or inappropriate influence.

My remarks today presuppose that judicial independence is an accepted norm for judges in any democracy. Even if the value of judicial independence is not disputed, however, achieving it is not easy, and the specifics of how it is expressed partially depend on the context of a judge's court and locale. Despite the diversity of courts and locales, I believe that four factors can be identified as particularly important in assuring the judicial independence of almost all judges: public respect for the courts and judges' conduct; judges' self-perception as independent and impartial agents; the judicial process's transparent nature; and the provision of reasoned judicial decisions.[3]

Judges' public actions affect popular respect for the judiciary, the first factor just mentioned, and it is especially for this reason that restrictions on particular public activities—both individually assumed and externally imposed—are appropriate. I believe that in order to maintain public respect, judges must continuously act and appear to act in a manner consonant with their rendering decisions in an impartial, transparent, and reasoned manner. Because of the importance of appearances, every public activity that judges undertake is thus subject to justified scrutiny. I will focus my remarks today on activities where judges could justifiably feel that their judgment is not impaired, but there is a risk that the public might reach a different conclusion.

II. PARTICIPATION IN PUBLIC LIFE

Judges' participation in public life can be divided into three broad categories. The first category involves public activity that is directly related to a judge's judicial position. This includes, most basically, their actions and demeanor in the courtroom, as well as their legal opinions and activities related to their selection for or election to judicial office. The second category involves public activity that is separate from an individual's role as a judge. This includes teaching and academic and other writings and speeches; affiliations with for-profit and non-profit organizations, and activities on behalf of these organizations; and political

---

[3] See ibid., 360.

activities, broadly defined (other than a judge's own judicial election or confirmation processes). Finally, the third category of participation in public life includes nominally private activities that, if brought to the attention of the public, could undermine the public's belief in the independence and transparency of the judicial process.

A. *Judicial conduct and selection*

Turning to my first category, I note that judges' important role in resolving all manner of civil and criminal issues makes it natural that their work and selection should, in many instances, take on a prominent public profile. Because this type of engagement with public life is inevitable and expected, it is also the most likely to be heavily regulated by written rules and to be subject to explicit checks and balances.

1. Judicial conduct

The regulatory frameworks influencing judges' conduct vary, of course, depending on jurisdiction. Some, such as the Judicial Conference's code of judicial conduct in the United States, are particularly detailed. Others, such as Article 18 of the ICJ Statute—which allows dismissal of a judge based on a unanimous vote of the other judges—are much less specific.

Still, even when judges' specific behavior is not regulated in detail, the very structure of almost all court systems effectively imposes limitations on judges. Thus, the selection of judges—whether through an administrative procedure or by an executive, a legislative body, or voters themselves—is typically subject to official rules, as is any subsequent re-appointment, where that is permitted. Following selection, judges' oral comments and written decisions in the context of cases before them are generally subject to review and appeal, with the exception of the highest level courts in any given system.

Given this relatively significant regulation of judges' actions, and its public nature, it appears at first glance that judges' only concern in these situations should be to follow the letter of rules that govern their conduct and professional activity. Indeed, in many cases, judges are able to avoid undermining a sense of judicial independence simply by obeying rules and judicial canons.

The presence of relatively detailed regulations does not, however, absolve judges of the need to pay careful attention to their own conduct. This is recognized by the official commentary of Canon 2A of the Judicial Conference's code of judicial conduct in the United States, which requires judges to avoid impropriety and the appearance of impropriety. The official commentary accompanying the Canon recognizes that the Canon's prohibitions are 'cast in general terms that extend to conduct by judges that is harmful although not specifically mentioned in the Code'.[4] Ironically, detailed regulation of judges' professional actions is not a guarantee of judicial propriety. There is always a danger that individual judges will interpret a regulation as allowing behavior that is not explicitly prohibited but still very problematic.

For example, whatever one's opinion about public election to judicial office, I believe all of us could agree with the US Supreme Court's recent holding in *Caperton v Massey*.[5] In this case, the Supreme Court ruled that Justice Brent Benjamin of the West Virginia Supreme Court, who had received massive but legal campaign contributions from one party to a case that would soon come before him, should have recused himself, despite feeling himself impartial. Even though the campaign contributions were lawful, the Supreme Court justifiably found the facial probability of bias was too high to be constitutionally tolerable.

Beyond their insufficiency as an absolute guide to behavior, official rules are also inadequate in certain extraordinary situations, such as the trial of uncooperative defendants—especially those who are self-represented. This latter issue has been particularly difficult in the context of international criminal tribunals such as the ICTY, where certain defendants refuse to recognize the legitimacy of the tribunals and feel they have nothing to gain from cooperating with the tribunals' procedures. In the trial of former Yugoslav President Slobodan Milošević, for example, ICTY judges were forced to engage with a self-represented defendant who explicitly embraced obstructive behavior, ignoring courtroom rules and deadlines while harassing witnesses, judges, and others in the courtroom.

In cases like that of Slobodan Milošević, where rules fail, judges' demeanor and intelligence becomes essential to guaranteeing that a trial resembles neither a circus nor a kangaroo court. The judges must ensure that they remain in control of the courtroom while avoiding offering any impression that they are giving in to anger at personal insults or frustration at disruptive behavior. Achieving this balanced approach is certainly challenging, but absolutely necessary to preserving the sense that a trial is proceeding in an impartial and appropriate manner.

---

[4] Administrative Office of US Courts, *Code of Conduct for United States Judges* (2009), Canon 2A cmt.
[5] *Caperton v AT Massey Coal Co*, 556 US ___, 129 SCt 2252 (2009).

In all courts, judges are frequently accused of favoritism or prejudice towards one party or another. In international criminal tribunals, where the crimes at issue are typically committed in an inter-ethnic context, such accusations are routine. Judges must exercise special caution to remain fair, but, at the end of the day, must understand that being subjected to even the harshest criticism is a part of the job.

2. Judicial selection

As I have underscored, while the performance of official public duties by judges is usually supported by relatively voluminous and clear guiding regulations, it is essential that judges continuously exercise independent judgment even with regard to authorized action. It is also clear, however, that in certain cases—especially those related to judicial appointment—official regulations can effectively force judges into very problematic situations with regard to judicial independence. Partisan judicial elections, such as those in many US states (where significant amounts are spent on campaigns by parties with large financial interests at stake), are the most egregious example of this type of Catch-22 situation. But even in international courts the process of judicial appointment and re-appointment can be problematic. In the ICTY, for example, permanent judges depend on votes in the UN General Assembly for election and re-election, and it is standard practice for judges to visit various delegations to 'lobby' for their votes.

It is obvious that elections such as those of ICTY and ICJ judges at least raise the possibility of inappropriate influence, especially as the time for re-election draws near. Judges face a potential conflict when their professional views in a particular case are contrary to those of the General Assembly majority. At the ICTY, such a scenario could involve both substantive issues of guilt or innocence or procedural concerns such as the advisability of remand, decisions on which can create additional expenses for the international community. At the ICJ, I could imagine that a judge working on an advisory opinion relating to an issue on which most UN members have a specific position might be aware that taking a position different from that of a majority of UN members would be unpopular. In both scenarios, judges will no doubt be cognizant that taking the more criticized route could have negative consequences for their efforts to secure re-election. This is especially the case when an unpopular decision is temporally proximate to a vote on re-election. I would hope that judges' sense of professionalism would prevail in these scenarios, but litigants before international courts may be reluctant to rely on faith in judges' better natures.

This type of conflict is perhaps even more of a potential problem in domestic jurisdictions with non-electoral judicial confirmation processes. In these jurisdictions, judges, especially on appellate and supreme courts, routinely rule on crucial policy questions of great concern to the government that is also charged with appointing, potentially re-appointing, and promoting members of the judiciary. As a result, in the United States, nominees to federal courts are routinely screened by the government to identify their opinions on particular issues, such as the scope of Presidential power, abortion, and criminal sentencing.

To address the potential conflict of interest posed by government or voter input on the selection of judges, I would suggest exploring policy solutions that make judges more independent from these groups' specific policy preferences. I am on record as preferring longer, single, non-renewable terms for judges at international tribunals,[6] and even with regard to first selection, I would prefer that a non-political committee of experts vet judges—perhaps in conjunction with subsequent legislative, General Assembly, or executive approval—for both international and national courts. Such an approach removes explicit threats to judicial independence while still allowing judges and potential judges to be held accountable for their performance.

Of course, governments have a critical responsibility to nominate for international judgeships the most highly qualified candidates. A good practice is for a government to submit two or even more candidates, as is already the practice with regard to WTO panels and the European Court of Human Rights. It is unfortunate that during the political process in the institution electing the judges, governments often resort to bargaining or the trading of votes, which is not commensurate with the high standards of behavior that should instruct such voting.

B. *Non-judicial actions and engagements*

My second category of participation in public life involves actions and engagements that are not essential to judges' judicial positions. This is a very broad field, and one where there can be considerable divergence of opinion on the levels of appropriate conduct. The more extensive judges' permitted non-judicial engagements, the higher the likelihood that they will comment on or otherwise be involved with an issue that will eventually appear before them, increasing the number of recusal decisions and potentially the suspicion of a non-independent judiciary. However, restricting

---

[6] Judicial Independence Article, n 2 above, 362.

these commitments too drastically risks both discouraging multi-talented individuals from considering a career in the judiciary and depriving society of the fruits of judges' experiences and intellect.

1. Public speaking and publications

In regulating external commitments, I believe that there is a significant difference between judges' teaching, speaking, and publishing, on the one hand, and their association with political parties, on the other. In the former case, I believe judges should be relatively free to publish and speak about issues that are not immediately before them. This respects the important value of freedom of expression. More to the point, in cases where recusal may be required, the parameters of a judge's comments and expressed opinions are usually clear and transparent, making it easier to assess where recusal is appropriate or, in extreme cases, should be required. Under this standard, prolific public intellectuals, such as Judge Posner of the US Court of Appeals for the Seventh Circuit, or former Chief Justice Barak of the Israeli Supreme Court, can continue to contribute to public discourse without having to continually avoid any topic that may come before a court. They can make their own decision about the risk of speaking so specifically about a given issue that recusal may later be necessary if the subject comes before them as judges.

Judges do not usually arrive on the bench as virgins to public life, and, especially in the common law tradition, often have a considerable record of publications and activities during their pre-judicial life. I do not feel that writings and opinions expressed before an individual becomes a judge should necessarily preclude him or her from addressing related issues on the bench. However, whether or not a judge should recuse him- or herself in this situation depends very much on the level of generality of previous writings.

A less common problem than judges' writings and speeches are those by litigants. What would be the effect if these explicitly attack individual judges, either before or after the judges' elevation to judicial office? Much caution should accompany any consideration of recusal in these circumstances, in order to avoid giving parties an incentive to force the recusal of particular judges by launching public attacks against them.

2. Political parties and non-profit organizations

I believe that judges' involvement and official affiliation with political parties should be subject to considerably greater restrictions than their speech and writings. This is because of the vagueness inherent to this type of affiliation, where a wide array of opinions could be ascribed to a judge. While it is difficult for litigants to demonstrate that mere affiliation implies espousal and pre-consideration of particular legal positions, suspicions concerning lack of independence can remain concerning a very large range of potential issues. I understand that in certain jurisdictions—regions of the United States, for example—affiliation with a political party is a basic requirement for office, as judges are selected through partisan votes. I would reiterate, however, that in such cases I would support changing such a selection system to ensure it requires less active political participation on the part of judges. With regard to international judges, I note that I am not inherently opposed to their taking non-partisan, oversight positions in some political processes. However, such positions should only be undertaken if permitted within the letter and spirit of their institutions' statutes.

Judges' involvement in less political, non-profit organizations can also prove problematic, but less so than their affiliation with explicitly political groups. I would be inclined to permit judges' affiliations with non-profit organizations such as bar associations or civil improvement organizations, but only on the understanding that judges would recuse themselves from any cases involving these organizations and refrain from becoming too involved in advocacy or fundraising activities, where a judge's judicial and organizational identities could become confused. I would also note that judges should be particularly wary of formal affiliation with officially 'non-political' organizations that are clearly linked with particular political agendas. On a personal level, I believe that this avoidance should be mandatory in the case of organizations advocating invidious discrimination against particular groups of individuals. I also believe that caution should extend to affiliations with organizations campaigning on controversial questions, such as the environment, if those organizations work on issues that might result in litigation before the judge concerned.

3. For-profit organizations and arbitration

As regards for-profit organizations, I believe the public appearance of divided loyalties—especially where a large or politically sensitive corporation is involved—is problematic enough to make most potential associations with for-profit enterprises ill-advised for judges. There could be obvious exceptions to this rule for certain types of for-profit enterprises, such as family businesses or farms.

Can judges serve as commercial arbitrators without compromising their judicial role, given the close similarity between serving as a judge and as an arbitrator? Most international tribunals do not create a blanket prohibition on judges serving as arbitrators, even when states involved in the tribunals' work are parties. However, certain institutions insist that judges not serve as party-nominated arbitrators.

I would add that in agreeing to serve as arbitrators, judges should be keenly aware of the precedence that their primary institutional affiliations must both take and appear to take. Routine participation by judges in arbitration may create the impression that their courts have little work—or that, for courts with full dockets, that work is being neglected. I would also note that judges should exercise special caution before participating in more politically sensitive arbitrations, especially those involving states. Participation in such interstate arbitrations may raise questions concerning whether the judges will be able to remain impartial—and maintain the appearance of impartiality—if one or more of the state parties to the arbitration later bring cases before the judges' court. Similar questions may arise concerning judges' independence if they are appointed as arbitrators by one of the state parties to the earlier arbitration.

More broadly, it may be time for international institutions to consider the value of standardizing the rules on judges accepting commercial arbitration assignments, in order to increase transparency and reduce the possibility that judges are perceived to be using a public position to obtain private benefits.

C. *Other affiliations and contacts*

My third category of involvement in public life revolves around affiliations or contacts that do not, in the normal course of events, involve the public, but which could, if they became widely known, give the impression that judges were not independent or justice not transparent. These could include interactions with personal friends who are litigants or lawyers in cases before a judge, privately circulated commentary on controversial issues, and other private business. My definition of this category is deliberately vague and partially overlaps with my first two categories of activities that qualify as 'public life'. But in discussing this third category, I am attempting to capture my sense that in becoming a judge, an individual perforce sacrifices some of the private space that others can take for granted.

While the exact scope of my third category of activities is not fully defined, I believe that there would be general consensus that certain types of behavior are inappropriate. In particular, private meetings or cohabitation with litigants or attorneys involved in cases before a judge, even if details of a case are not discussed, seem outside the bounds of the acceptable. The exact parameters of such a prohibition could certainly be subject to debate, especially in the case of high public officials, such as the President and Vice President of the United States, who are sometimes targeted, in their official capacities, by lawsuits against government action. In cases involving these high public officials, a blanket prohibition on private meetings with judges may be excessive, given the officials' essential non-involvement in most cases. Still, even in these situations, I believe judges should act very cautiously. Justice Scalia, for example, found it unnecessary to recuse himself from a case involving Vice President Dick Cheney even though the two flew on a duck hunting expedition together, using the Vice President's Gulfstream jet, after the case was filed before the US Supreme Court.[7] I can understand why this close level of interaction could have been disquieting for the litigants opposing the Vice President in that case.

There might be greater agreement that judges should refrain from most other types of potentially compromising behavior—such as the distribution or creation of privately circulated materials disparaging categories of people on the basis of protected categories such as race, sex, religion, or sexual orientation. In such circumstances, and if the private materials are leaked, there are clear opportunities for litigants to feel that a judge will not treat them impartially or fairly. But a strong official rule might also mean judges feel unable to express themselves on matters of private concern, or even that judges would be prevented from expressing personal religious convictions. Given these concerns, and the difficulty of creating a workable rule in any event, it is probably best left to individual judges to weigh the importance of private actions against the potential damage to their office should a putatively private action become public.

III. CONCLUSION

One conclusion from these reflections on various types of public activity is that judges are called on to exercise continuous discretion in preserving a sense of judicial independence and impartiality. I underscore again that outside influences and rules, such as those involved in the process of judicial appointment or election, can also heavily impact the ability of a judge to behave in an impartial and independent manner. The level of

---

[7] *Cheney et al. v US Dist Ct for the Dist of Columbia et al.*, Memorandum of Justice Scalia, 541 US 913 (2004).

detail that these rules go into, or should go into, and when it is better to rely instead on judges' personal sense of what is appropriate, are subjects on which there can be many views. Whatever the ideal level of detail for rules affecting their conduct, I believe that judges are entitled—and, in fact, should lobby—to ensure that these rules are formed or amended to promote judicial independence. But in the final analysis, it is always the individual judge, whatever the context, who remains responsible for acting in a way that reflects the significance of the office he or she holds.

26

DECISION-MAKING IN INTERNATIONAL CRIMINAL TRIBUNALS*

My specific knowledge about decision-making processes in arbitrations and in international tribunals other than those on which I serve is somewhat limited, so I will leave commenting on these areas to my fellow panelists, who are leading experts and practitioners in their respective fields and far more qualified than I to speak on these matters. I will instead focus my remarks on decision-making in the ICTY and ICTR—which I will refer to as the 'Tribunals'—and, in particular, on the context in which, and processes by which, decisions are reached at the Tribunals. I recognize that decision-making could also be addressed in terms of judges' differing attitudes towards evidence, customary international law, or the principle of legality. I will not be addressing these issues in my comments today. I emphasize that I speak to you today in my personal capacity, rather than in my position as a judge on the Appeals Chambers of the two Tribunals.

As you all know, the ICTY and ICTR are an experiment by the international community to end impunity for those responsible for the most serious of crimes. The success of this experiment depends in no small part on the transparency of our proceedings.

Transparency is essential to building public confidence in the fair administration of justice—and public confidence is, in turn, essential to fostering a broad understanding of and support for the Tribunals' work. Transparency in court proceedings also serves as an important safeguard against judicial arbitrariness and helps to ensure not only the fairness of the proceedings but the independence and impartiality of the bench and

---

* Prepared for delivery at the 105th Annual Meeting of the American Society of International Law, Washington, DC, USA, on 24 March 2011. A version of these remarks will be published in *American Society of International Law Proceedings* (forthcoming), © The American Society of International Law; Theodor Meron. Used by permission.

the predictability of judicial decisions. And transparency is, perhaps, particularly vital in criminal courts like the Tribunals, where the issues at stake—including horrific alleged crimes and determinations of the guilt or innocence of an accused—make it all the more imperative to have clear and visible adherence to internationally recognized standards of due process.

This commitment to transparency in court proceedings is not absolute, however. It is limited by other factors, such as the importance of protecting witnesses and victims and the requirement that certain information be kept confidential, such as that provided conditionally by a state to the Prosecutor. Our commitment to maximum transparency is also limited by the sacrosanct principle of the secrecy of judicial deliberations, and judges must reach their decisions in the shadow of this tension between transparency and secrecy. (My remarks to you today are also influenced by this tension, as I must adhere to the principle that judicial deliberations are secret, even as I attempt to make the Tribunals' decision-making processes a bit more transparent.)

The tension between transparency and secrecy is not unique to international tribunals, of course. It also exists in national courts. The difference is that in an international tribunal this tension between the transparency of process and the secrecy of judicial decision-making is negotiated through a powerful dialectic of differing legal cultures and systems of law. This dialectic, in turn, plays an important role in shaping not only the Tribunals' substantive legal decisions, but also their approach to decision-making more generally.

In identifying factors of particular import to decision-making at the Tribunals, I would highlight four specific issues: (i) the uniqueness of the Tribunals; (ii) the diversity of decision-makers at the Tribunals, including judges, the President, and the Registrar; (iii) the diverse backgrounds of the Tribunals' judges and staff; and (iv) the ways in which judicial decisions are reached at the Tribunals. I will address each of these issues in turn as well as certain broader conclusions concerning the nature of decision-making at the Tribunals.

I. THE UNIQUENESS OF THE TRIBUNALS

The Tribunals were created in the early 1990s, after a long period following the Nuremberg trials during which the enforcement of international criminal law did not take place at the international level. The end of the Cold War and the televised atrocities of the Yugoslavia conflict, along with the increasing power of NGOs, convinced the Security Council to set up the ICTY, and later, the ICTR.

In some ways, the Tribunals may appear to operate like a domestic criminal court—trying individual defendants charged with killing, rape, and other offences. However, in many respects, the Tribunals' mission and their approach are unique. At the most basic level, the criminal cases tried before the Tribunals are unprecedented in scope and scale, and involve crimes almost never prosecuted on a national level, such as genocide. In trying these cases, moreover, the Tribunals do not simply refer to a penal code of long standing or rely on a pre-approved statute, as the ICC does; in addition to applying their Statutes, they, and in particular the ICTY, ensure that convictions involve violations of customary international law at the time the offences took place and thus respect the principle of legality—a not altogether straightforward task at any time. (Despite the somewhat indeterminate nature of customary international law, international criminal judges must be seen to *apply* the law, not make it, and doing so cogently and carefully is far from easy. Of course, judicial discretion inevitably involves a certain measure of judicial creativity, but judges must restrain themselves from any tendency to drift toward law-making.)

When they were established the Tribunals also had little procedural precedent on which to depend, and had to create many of their procedural rules based on diverse national precedents from different legal traditions. Administrative structures and processes were likewise developed based on a variety of models, both international and domestic. Finally, and fundamentally, the Tribunals operate in the context of the traumatic time-periods and locations over which they possess jurisdiction—and while defendants are tried in their individual capacities, their fates are often seen by outside commentators as emblematic of broader geopolitical concerns.

All of these factors, along with the lofty expectations of the international community, make it particularly important for the Tribunals to render judgments that are carefully wrought, based on the law, and scrupulously solicitous of the rights of the accused. And all of these factors impact the ways in which decisions are reached at the Tribunals and who is tasked with making decisions.

II. DIVERSE DECISION-MAKERS

In considering decision-making at the Tribunals, it is necessary to remember that important decisions emanate not just from Trial and

Appeals Chamber panels, but also from various other sources, including regular plenaries of the Judges; the President; the Registrar; and, as regards overall administration, various sub-groupings, including the Bureau (consisting of the President, the Vice-President, and the Presiding Judges of the Trial Chambers) and the Coordination Council (consisting of the President, the Prosecutor, and the Registrar).

Substantive legal decisions obviously rest with the Trial and Appeals Chambers, as do many decisions concerning procedural issues. However, many other decisions which can significantly impact the lives of accused and convicted individuals are made through other channels. Thus, for example, certain procedural decisions—such as routine pre-appeal questions, issues of pre-trial management, and urgent matters arising during judicial recess—are often decided by a single judge. By contrast, the Tribunals' Rules of Procedure and Evidence, which govern core aspects of trials' conduct, are adopted and subject to change based on decisions taken by judges at their plenaries.

The President also plays a very significant role in deciding particular issues, including by: responding to requests for early release from individuals serving their sentences; addressing requests for the disqualification of judges; monitoring the enforcement of sentences; appointing appeal and trial benches; and adjudicating complaints from detainees at the United Nations Detention Units. The Registrar, in turn, is responsible for decisions on a variety of other important issues, such as the remuneration of defense counsel and the conditions under which detainees are held, including their access to media, protective measures, and other issues. And some decision-makers within the Tribunals review the decisions reached by others; thus, for example, the President may review certain decisions of the Registrar.

Of course, the most fundamental questions of guilt and innocence and the status of customary international criminal law are decided by panels of judges. But as my brief survey hopefully demonstrates, other decision-making bodies and Tribunal officers are responsible for a great many decisions too—including amendments to the Tribunals' Rules of Procedure and Evidence—and these decisions may have a profound impact not simply on a given case but on the Tribunals' operations more generally.

III. DIVERSE BACKGROUNDS

All of the decision-makers I have just discussed are, of course, individuals, and individuals who bring a wealth of different training and experiences to their work. The diversity of the Tribunals' staff and judges is one of the

Tribunals' sources of strength—but can also pose a challenge in terms of reaching decisions.

On a basic level, permanent judges at each Tribunal must be of a different nationality from each other. Staff recruitment efforts also emphasize diverse representation, complying with the general aim of representing the world's legal systems. The diversity in judges' and staff members' backgrounds helps bring different perspectives to assessing the status of customary international law and the types of procedural rules that should be adopted. This diversity also underscores the Tribunals' reliance on international precedents, and increases its public legitimacy.

But this diversity in backgrounds creates certain challenges. For instance, not all judges speak the same languages, requiring interpretation and making easy, informal communication somewhat more difficult to achieve. Diversity in backgrounds also means that judicial decisions must be reached in the context of an interplay between different legal cultures and legal systems. For example, in the Appeals Chamber—the Chamber that lays down the binding law for the Trial Chambers—four of the seven judges come from civil law countries. However, both the Tribunals' Statutes and their Rules of Procedure and Evidence are—despite various adjustments and a general rapprochement—still primarily a product of the common law.

More broadly, discussions of legal and procedural issues often begin from first principles, because in some cases basic understandings—often universally shared by individuals operating within national legal systems—are not common to the Tribunals' staff and judges. Basic approaches to judicial precedents may also vary. Speaking generally, common law-trained staff and judges are typically interested in situating proposed decisions in the context of precedents, and they will usually make an effort to distinguish any case that does not follow such precedent. Civil law-trained staff and judges, on the other hand, may often refer to past decisions, but they may be less systematic in canvassing existing precedent. They may, instead, take steps to situate their decision in a general theory of law, whether international or not.

Even among judges from similar legal systems there may be variation in how they approach decision-making, including the degree to which they are inclined to express their views in separate or dissenting opinions. In the United States, for instance, panels of appellate judges generally issue a decision in the form of a single text that may reflect compromises among the judges, with individual judges occasionally adding concurring or dissenting opinions. In the United Kingdom, meanwhile, I understand that it is not uncommon for each judge on a panel to issue an opinion explaining how he or she reached a particular legal conclusion, even if there is general agreement among the judges as to the outcome of the case.

IV. THE PROCESS OF JUDICIAL DECISION-MAKING

So far in my remarks, I have focused on the background to decision-making at the Tribunals, rather than the technical means by which decisions are reached. I would like to turn now to the decision-making process at the Tribunals, with a special emphasis on the areas with which I am most familiar: namely, the judicial decision-making process and the process within the Appeals Chamber in particular.

Generally, a team of legal staff considers the issues that arise with respect to particular motions or appeals and provides judges with helpful briefing papers and notes to assist in their decision-making. This assistance is essentially the same as that provided by judicial clerks in the United States, but involves a larger number of staff, reflecting the complexity and scale of the cases before the Tribunals, which can often involve dozens of crime sites, thousands of victims, and enormous volumes of written materials.

With regard to many decisions and contempt judgments before the Appeals Chamber, the official communications among judges are conducted by means of exchanged memoranda, usually on the basis of a draft decision prepared by a presiding judge. For most judgments and some decisions, judges on the Appeals Chamber meet for formal deliberations, assisted in most cases by legal staff (although sentencing deliberations are conducted by judges alone). It is during deliberations that judges typically vote by simple majority on all parts of the disposition of an appeal. These formal exchanges are supplemented by extensive conversations between judges and the staff who assist them, as well as by conversations among judges. While the complexities of judicial decision-making discussions are often not apparent in the Tribunals' judgments and decisions, by reading concurring and dissenting opinions one may glean some perspective on judges' different views.

Not having served on the trial level of the Tribunals, I will refrain from commenting at length about the decision-making process at that level. I will note, however, that unlike in many national jurisdictions, Trial Chambers at the Tribunals consist of three-judge panels. This situation yields its own specific dynamics, as it requires the panel to deliberate, unlike in those countries where a single judge may hear and decide a case.

I will also note that reserve judges in the Trial Chambers have gradually expanded their role. Originally meant to function simply as potential replacements if one member of a trial panel is unable to continue in his or her position, reserve judges are now generally well integrated into deliberations, though they do not, of course, have a vote.

One final note about the decision-making process at the Tribunals: While I have tried to offer you some insight into the technical decision-making process at the Tribunals and the judicial decision-making process in particular, I must emphasize that the specifics of judicial decision-making discussions are kept secret—and rightfully so.

Of course, I am aware of Judge Posner's perhaps somewhat cynical perspective that secrecy in judicial deliberations is 'an example of professional mystification' which helps to promulgate the notion that judicial decisions are 'unmarred by wilfulness, politics, or ignorance'.[1] It may very well be that some judges do, indeed, enjoy this element of mystification, which gives judicial deliberations the appearance of a consecrated, secret rite. Nevertheless, in my opinion, judges sitting as part of a panel must be free to discuss, develop, and sometimes even change their views without fear of repercussions, either personal or for the institution of which they are a part, and the principle of secrecy in judicial deliberations makes this possible. In other words, secrecy in judicial deliberations plays a crucial role in ensuring the independence and impartiality of the bench during the decision-making process. It also lends greater authority to the ultimate decision that the judges pronounce. As a recent commentator has suggested, '[t]he decisions of an appellate court are more authoritative when we know the legal reasoning behind a decision, but not the personal or institutional dynamics'.[2]

Seen in this light, it becomes clear that secrecy in judicial deliberations and transparency in court proceedings—however antithetical they may first appear—actually foster the same goals: independent and impartial decision-making and, as a result, greater public confidence in the Tribunals and in their administration of justice.

V. CONCLUSIONS

I began my comments today by noting that the Tribunals' success depends in no small part on the transparency of their proceedings. As I hope I have made clear, the Tribunals' success also depends in no

---

[1] Richard A. Posner, *How Judges Think* (Cambridge: Harvard University Press, 2008), 3.
[2] Paul R. Bernard, 'Transparency and Authority in Appellate Decision-Making' (February 2008) 87:2 *Michigan Bar Journal* 44, 46.

small part on effective and, where necessary, confidential decision-making at all levels.

To be sure, the diverse expectations of and roles played by the Tribunals—as well as the institutional and logistical challenges they face—sometimes make their decision-making processes slower and more formal than those in national jurisdictions. However, the diversity of the Tribunals' judges and staff, and the careful scrutiny that the Tribunals' decisions are subjected to before being issued, are a necessary accompaniment to the Tribunals' historic mission of ending impunity. And these decisions—substantive, procedural, and administrative—have laid the groundwork for broader enforcement of international criminal law, as exemplified by institutions such as the ICC and increased domestic prosecutions.

27
JUSTICE AND LEADERSHIP DILEMMAS IN SHAKESPEARE*

Ben Jonson said that Shakespeare was a man 'not of an age, but for all time'.[1] My talk will suggest some ways in which that is certainly true in Shakespeare's penetrating depictions of leaders who commit or tolerate crimes and how they do so.

Time and again, Shakespeare's work—and, in particular, his history plays—illustrates the ambiguous netherworld of compulsion, indirection, and diffusion of responsibility that make assessing culpability for war crimes a vexing question to the present day. We see in his work the intellectual and moral compromises made by legal advisers faced with a national leader's determined political will to undertake acts of dubious legality. He illustrates the recurrent effort by rulers to preserve plausible deniability in the face of subsequent inquiry—while nonetheless making their intentions perfectly clear to those who will execute them. He shows us the underpinnings of the instinct that leads to the contemporary doctrine of command responsibility. By connecting these and other themes to contemporary currents in the international jurisprudence of the law of war—from Nuremberg to the International Criminal Tribunal for the former Yugoslavia—I will seek to further illuminate certain overarching themes of leaders' responsibility and the subtle synergy between the soldier and the leader.

---

* Delivered at the Mid-Year Meeting of the American Society of International Law in Miami, Florida, on 12 November 2010. These remarks will be published in *American Society of International Law Proceedings* (forthcoming), © The American Society of International Law; Theodor Meron. Used by permission.

[1] Ben Jonson, 'To the memory of my beloved, the Author Master William Shakespeare, and what he hath left us', reprinted in Stanley Wells and Gary Taylor (eds), *William Shakespeare: The Complete Works* (Compact edn, Oxford: Oxford University Press, 1988), xlv. All citations to Shakespeare in this lecture are drawn from this edition.

I. ADVISERS AND LEADERS

But, first, let me briefly discuss the role of the adviser, who, in Shakespeare's time, often enjoyed ecclesiastical authority, and the justness *vel non* of resort to war. In the fifteenth-century *Book of Fayttes of Armes and of Chyvalrye*, one of the first and rare medieval feminists, Christine de Pisan, urged that a prince consult impartial advisers before deciding whether the war under consideration was just. Humanists, especially Thomas More, also bared open the adviser's dilemma. The temptation to enter into a prince's service was great, since the humanists aspired to reform the political system through educating the rulers. But the danger, as the fictional Raphael Hythlodaeus warns in More's *Utopia*, is that the independent expert is bound to lose his independence; that the career-oriented councilor is bound to tell the prince what he wants to hear; that the adviser is likely to sink into sycophancy; and that tampering with truth is the very condition of service in the councils of the mighty. How little have things changed since the early sixteenth century.

We certainly see self-serving advice in Shakespeare's Archbishop of Canterbury, whose desire to please the King and protect the interests of his Church from expropriations led him to make categorical, though patently dubious, assurances to Henry V that the latter's claim to the crown of France was just and was not barred by the Salic law, which disqualified women and the female line. Changing the King's focus to foreign wars was the central interest of Canterbury, who doubled as the King's principal adviser and the most senior English ecclesiastic. Obviously, the rules on conflict of interest had not yet been invented. But even in the twentieth century, as Professor Vagts has shown, some legal academics under the Third Reich were only too eager to develop tortured arguments justifying Hitler's actions under international law.[2] Indeed, throughout history, and all the way to present-day capitals, the responsibility of advisers for unprincipled advice on the law governing resort to war, the conduct of the war, and the interpretation of the governing texts has been a heavy one.

Of course, the leader often does not need a lot of prompting to resort to questionable behavior. Lady Macbeth reminds her husband that his superior forces offer ample protection from accountability: 'What need we fear... when none can call our power to account?' (*Macbeth*, V.i.35–36). And another not very nice person, King Lear's Goneril, makes the

---

[2] Detlev F Vagts, 'International Law in the Third Reich' (1990) 84 *AJIL* 661.

ultimate claim of the absolute ruler: 'the laws are mine, not thine. / Who can arraign me for't?' (*The Tragedy of King Lear*, V.iii.149–150).

But competing with such considerations of realpolitik is the awareness of Shakespeare's monarchs that they bear a special responsibility for what occurs on their watch. In *The Rape of Lucrece*, Lucrece pleads with Tarquinus to spare her from rape, invoking in vain his special responsibility as a leader, and both Cleopatra in *Antony and Cleopatra* and especially Henry V (in his famous soliloquy on the eve of the battle of Agincourt, 'Upon the King', which concerns spiritual responsibility for the death of many innocent soldiers) engage in royal self-pity as they rail against their special responsibility.

Leaders' awareness of responsibility leads to whole arrays of strategies for avoiding accountability and diffusing responsibility. Thus, for instance, to justify the catalogue of atrocities, including rape, pillage, and murder, with which he threatens the besieged population of Harfleur, Henry V claims that he will bear no personal responsibility for the actions of his troops—who will be uncontrollable with blood lust after the coming victory—and that, instead, it is the leaders of Harfleur, because of their refusal to surrender, on whose heads will rest the true responsibility for their people's suffering.

II. ORDERS AND EXECUTIONS

Let me now turn to the responsibility for and the articulation of an order to commit a crime. The need to communicate murderous purpose has clashed with the desire to avoid a record of illegal orders from antiquity to Nazi Germany and beyond. Even the Nazi leaders resorted to euphemisms in referring to the Holocaust. No explicit written order from Hitler to carry out the final solution has ever been found. At the height of their power, the Nazis treated the data on the killing of Jews as top secret.

I start from a relatively obscure play, *King John*, concerning the brother of the glamorous Richard the Lionheart and the eventual signer of the Magna Carta. King John was also involved in brutal conflicts on legitimacy and succession. The play presents a fascinating portrayal of the deniability minuet.

Consider King John's order to his servant Hubert to eliminate Prince Arthur, who, as the son of John's brother Geoffrey, presents a risk to John's entitlement to the crown of England. In enlisting Hubert, King John tells him that Arthur is a serpent in his way, who merits death. There is no order, no direct incitement. But when Hubert reports to the

King that he had killed Arthur, John, characteristically for Shakespeare's kings, disowns the order, complaining that 'It is the curse of kings to be attended / By slaves that take their humours for a warrant' (*King John*, IV. ii.209–210) and act on the mere 'winking of authority' (*King John*, IV. ii.212), without ever trying to discourage the King from pursuing his purpose. To mount a barrier of deniability and significantly shift the responsibility to his adviser, King John hypocritically tells Hubert that had Hubert advised the King not to proceed with his murderous design, or even asked for more explicit language, he would have desisted from his purpose of eliminating Arthur.

But Hubert surprises us, showing the King a warrant of execution, bearing the King's signature. Hubert must have been ready to confront a denial. Legal form is thus adhered to. Typically for the ambivalence of Shakespeare's kings, John does not reward Hubert, but banishes him from the Court.

It is worth observing, as a side note, that in *King John*, Hubert takes pity on Arthur and does not kill him. Particularly interesting is the exchange between the two men during their encounter, in which Hubert invokes the need to comply with orders even if they are unlawful, while Arthur argues that orders to commit murder may not be obeyed, and that orders of execution are only valid when issued in compliance with both the substance and the form of law. In an exchange set in the Middle Ages, Shakespeare thus squarely prefigures the twentieth-century debates about the Nuremberg defense.

Now consider the killing of Richard II. Forced to abdicate in favor of Henry Bolingbroke, who becomes Henry IV, the imprisoned Richard, like all deposed monarchs, presents a danger so long as he breathes. Henry wants Richard assassinated by one of his courtiers, Sir Piers Exton. The order to kill is never explicitly stated. It is the courtiers who transform Henry's desire into an operational order. Exton: 'Didst thou not mark the King, what words he spake? / "Have I no friend will rid me of this living fear?"...Come, let's go. / I am the King's friend, and will rid his foe' (*Richard II*, V.iv.1–2, 10–11). Henry's words closely resemble the statement attributed by oral tradition to Henry II in 1170 before the murder of Thomas à Becket in the Canterbury Cathedral: 'Will no one rid me from this turbulent priest?'

After Exton and his men assassinate Richard, Henry disowns the act and punishes Exton with exile. Exton's fate is reminiscent of the complaint voiced by the Second Knight, one of the murderers of Archbishop Thomas à Becket, in TS Eliot's *Murder in the Cathedral*: 'King Henry— God bless him—will have to say, for reasons of state, that he never meant this to happen;... and at the best we shall have to spend the rest of our lives abroad.'[3]

I now turn to a play with which you all are familiar: *Richard III*, the Shakespearean quintessence of evil and state terror.

Take this episode: Richard III gives two murderers a written order to deliver to Brackenbury, the Lieutenant of the Tower of London, ordering Brackenbury to hand the Duke of Clarence over to Richard's minions. The submissive Brackenbury chooses not to question the purpose of the order, but engages instead in a deliberate self-deception. Famously, he says, 'I will not reason what is meant hereby, / Because I will be guiltless of the meaning' (*Richard III*, I.iv.90–91). Even in the terrifying murder scene, when Clarence invokes protection of both the secular and the religious law, the murderers claim authority resulting from the King's warrant.

Can Brackenbury be compared to another type of collaborator—for example, a French policeman in July 1942 executing written Nazi orders to round up Jews and deliver them for deportation to the Vel d'Hiv? He, too, chooses not to question the orders and thus to remain 'guiltless of the meaning'. By agonizing over his 'guiltlessness', Brackenbury is aware of his moral dilemma, which the strength of his defense of superior orders cannot resolve. Brackenbury's options were more limited than those of the French policeman, as non-compliance would bring about Brackenbury's own death, while the policeman would face only disciplinary Vichy measures. Under the utilitarian view of moral responsibility, Brackenbury may be justified in turning over the keys. If he refuses, Clarence will be killed anyway and he will die as well. Under the absolutist theory of moral responsibility, however, murder can never be allowed.

Consider now the dilemma of Drazen Erdemović, a soldier in the army of Republika Srpska, who was ordered to participate in the executions of Muslim males in the Srebrenica massacre. Here is his duress plea before an ICTY Trial Chamber:

Your Honour, I had to do this. If I had refused, I would have been killed together with the victims. When I refused, they told me: 'If you are sorry for them, stand up, line up with them and we will kill you too'. I am not sorry for myself but for my family [,] my wife and son who then had nine months, and I could not refuse because then they would have killed me.[4]

---

[3] TS Eliot, *Murder in the Cathedral* (London: Faber and Faber Ltd, 1935), pt II, 77.
[4] *Prosecutor v Dražen Erdemović* (Transcript) IT-96-22-PT (31 May 1996), 32.

The Tribunal's test for the defense of superior orders and of duress is whether moral choice was, in fact, possible, and, in the absence of evidence supporting the claim of extreme necessity, the Trial Chamber did not accept Erdemović's claim.[5] On appeal, the Appeals Chamber rejected duress as a complete legal defense for crimes against humanity and war crimes involving the killing of innocent persons.[6] Following his appeal, Erdemović was sentenced to just five years' imprisonment.[7]

III. COMMAND RESPONSIBILITY

Finally, let us turn to *Antony and Cleopatra*—not for romance, but for a stark statement of the issues underlying (to this very day) questions of command responsibility. Let us consider the overlapping issues of responsibility for the acts of subordinates and responsibility for actions a leader had the power to prevent.

The following episode from *Antony and Cleopatra* is not purely fictional. Like many other events drawn from the Chroniclers, Shakespeare borrowed this story from Plutarch's *Parallel Lives*. And here it is: The triumvirs of Rome—Mark Anthony, Octavius Caesar, and Lepidus—are dining and drinking heavily on the boat of their former competitor, Sextus Pompey. The scene presents an unparalleled opportunity for eliminating competitors to supreme power. Menas, Pompey's friend, urges him to let Menas kill the visiting leaders so that Pompey may become the ruler of Rome. Pompey desires nothing more than to remove the triumvirs, provided that his honor is not soiled, and his responsibility is not involved. But once he is apprised of the plot, he is forced to forbid the assassination: 'Being done unknown, / I should have found it afterwards well done, / But must condemn it now. Desist, and drink' (*Antony and Cleopatra*, II.vii.77–79). He leaves his friend with a message for next time, however: '[T]his thou shouldst have done / And not have spoke on't. In me 'tis villainy, / In thee 't had been good service' (*Antony and Cleopatra*, II.vii.72–74). 'Repent', Pompey says (*Antony and Cleopatra*, II.vii.76), not for having considered the murder but for having told me of your intent.

Pompey's episode illustrates the concept of command responsibility, or the Yamashita principle. Yamashita, the commander of the Japanese forces in the Philippines, was charged after the war with having failed to prevent his troops from committing massacres, murder, pillage, and rape. While he protested that he had not personally directed the commission of

---

[5] *Prosecutor v Dražen Erdemović* (Sentencing Judgement) IT-96-22-T (29 November 1996).
[6] *Prosecutor v Dražen Erdemović* (Judgement) IT-96-22-A (7 October 1997).
[7] *Prosecutor v Dražen Erdemović* (Sentencing Judgement) IT-96-22-T*bis* (5 March 1998).

these atrocities, the US Supreme Court held that commanders must be responsible for their subordinates if they fail to employ due diligence to prevent such war crimes.[8] The Yamashita principle was the first authoritative articulation of the modern rule of command responsibility: if a superior knew, or had information that would have enabled him or her to conclude, that his or her subordinates were about to commit, or had already committed, a breach of the law of war, and if the superior did not accordingly take all feasible measures to prevent or punish the breach, he or she would be deemed responsible for the subordinates' crimes. Pompey is both the host and the commander of his troops and of the pirates on board. Since Menas informs Pompey of his criminal purpose, Pompey is put on notice, and acquiescence would make him criminally responsible.

The Yamashita principle was not incorporated in the Geneva Conventions of 12 August 1949 but was codified as what appears to be a due diligence standard in Article 86(2) of the Additional Protocol I to the Geneva Conventions and in the Statutes of the International Criminal Tribunals for the former Yugoslavia and Rwanda. The case law of the Tribunals has further clarified the place of the Yamashita principle in international law. In the leading case of *Čelebići*, which involved the question of the responsibility of leaders of a concentration camp in Bosnia/Herzegovina, the ICTY's Appeals Chamber drew on the Nuremberg jurisprudence, the Yamashita principle, the US Army Field Manual, and Additional Protocol I to conclude that the principle of superior responsibility encompasses not only senior military officers but also political leaders and other civilian superiors in positions of authority, that the term superior includes authority based on de facto powers, and that command responsibility is not a form of strict liability.[9] Resonating with Menas' statement to Pompey, the Appeals Chamber concluded that the test of 'had reason to know'—used to establish the responsibility of the superior—would apply only if information was available to that superior which would have put him or her on notice of offenses committed by subordinates.

The case of General Radislav Krstić illustrates some of the complexities, and the pitfalls, of command responsibility. The General, who became commander of the Drina Corps of the Serbian army on the eve of Srebrenica, had knowledge of the genocidal intent of some of the members of the army's Main Staff, but there was no evidence that he

---

[8] *In re Yamashita*, 327 US 1 (1946).
[9] *Prosecutor v Zejnil Delalić et al.* (Judgement) IT-96-21-A (20 February 2001) (*Čelebići*).

shared their genocidal intent, that he ordered any of the murders, or that he directly participated in them. The evidence established only that Krstić knew the murders were occurring but nonetheless permitted the Main Staff to use personnel and resources under his command to facilitate them. On the basis of these findings, the Appeals Chamber reversed the General's conviction as a participant in a joint criminal enterprise to commit genocide, and entered, instead, a conviction for aiding and abetting genocide.[10]

The reasons why the Appeals Chamber did not enter a conviction based on the General's command responsibility are noteworthy. The Chamber found that the most Krstić could have done was to report the use of his assets in facilitating the killings to the Main Staff and to his superior, General Mladić—the very people who allegedly ordered the executions and allegedly were active participants in them. Although Krstić could have tried to punish his subordinates for their participation, as the Appeals Chamber noted, 'it is unlikely that he would have had the support of his superiors in doing so'.[11] The feasibility of prevention and punishment is thus central to the command responsibility case law of the Tribunal.

My comparison between Shakespeare's depictions of leader–subordinate interaction and modern cases dealing with command responsibility suggests the extent to which the existence and basic form of certain principles of humanitarian law have long been appreciated by advisers, soldiers, and even leaders intent on doing something that runs afoul of these laws. Indeed, the present system of humanitarian law—which has The Hague and the Geneva Conventions as its base, was enforced in Nuremberg, and is now enforced at The Hague—is derived from the medieval rules of chivalry, with their emphasis on honor as the underlying value ensuring respect for the rules. This is the ideal articulated in Shakespeare's dramas.

The system worked reasonably well in Christian Europe, but its scope was narrow. It did not protect peasants or commoners. Knights or 'gentlemen' were careful not to surrender to commoners because they expected no mercy, nor did they give any to captured commoners. The system also did not apply in the relations between Christian and non-Christian states, or between Christians and others. Thus, it was a crime to deny quarter to a Christian knight. It was a crime to rape a Christian woman. But it was not a crime to massacre and to rape the entire Muslim

---

[10] *Prosecutor v Radislav Krstić* (Judgement) IT-98-33-A (19 April 2004).
[11] Ibid., fn. 250.

and Jewish population of Jerusalem during the First Crusade. Thankfully, our current jurisprudence has come a long way since the moral framework of the Crusades.

Shakespeare's plays were not intended to be a code of conduct for Christian princes and their advisers. But his leadership dilemmas clearly give the impression that chivalry and honor imply an important code of behavior for the honorable person in a civil society and suggest answers to the choice between good and evil. Their legacy still shapes our contemporary values.

Epilogue

28
ADDRESS AT MEMORIAL CEMETERY AT POTOČARI, SREBRENICA*

It is with honor and humility that I stand today at the Potočari Memorial Cemetery. This place is a daily reminder of the horrors that visited the town of Srebrenica during the war in Bosnia and Herzegovina. The crimes committed there have been well documented and have been recognized—and roundly and appropriately condemned—by the United Nations, by the international community in general, and by the people of the region of the former Yugoslavia. These crimes have also been described in detail and consigned to infamy in the decisions rendered by the court over which I preside, the International Criminal Tribunal for the former Yugoslavia.

I have had a special wish to visit the Potočari Memorial Cemetery because earlier this year I had the privilege of sitting as the Presiding Judge in the appeal which, for the first time, judicially recognized the crimes committed against the Bosnian Muslims in Srebrenica in 1995 as genocide.

In that case, named *Prosecutor* versus *Radislav Krstić*, the Appeals Chamber of our Tribunal convicted one of the leaders of the Bosnian Serb assault on Srebrenica, General Radislav Krstić, for aiding and abetting genocide.[1] The Appeals Chamber also found that some members of the Main Staff of the Bosnian Serb Army harbored genocidal intent against the Bosnian Muslim people who sought safety in the enclave of Srebrenica, and that these officials acted upon that intent to carry out a deliberate and massive massacre of the Muslims in Srebrenica.

The judgment which the Appeals Chamber has pronounced will be of importance not only in acknowledging the crime committed in

---

* Delivered at Srebrenica, Bosnia and Herzegovina, on 23 June 2004.
[1] *Prosecutor v Radislav Krstić* (Judgement) IT-98-33-A (19 April 2004).

Srebrenica for what it is, but also in developing and enhancing international criminal law's understanding of genocide. By discussing and elaborating the legal requirement of genocide, and by explaining how it applied that legal requirement in the circumstances of Srebrenica, the Appeals Chamber has facilitated the recognition—and, I hope, the prevention—of this horrible crime.

Many victims of this crime lie here, in this cemetery. In honor of their memory, I would like to read a brief passage from the judgment in *Krstić*, the passage which discusses the gravity and the horrific nature of the crime of genocide, and states unhesitantly that its perpetrators will unfailingly face justice.

Among the grievous crimes this Tribunal has the duty to punish, the crime of genocide is singled out for special condemnation and opprobrium. The crime is horrific in its scope; its perpetrators identify entire human groups for extinction. Those who devise and implement genocide seek to deprive humanity of the manifold richness its nationalities, races, ethnicities and religions provide. This is a crime against all of humankind, its harm being felt not only by the group targeted for destruction, but by all of humanity.

The gravity of genocide is reflected in the stringent requirements which must be satisfied before this conviction is imposed. These requirements—the demanding proof of specific intent and the showing that the group was targeted for destruction in its entirety or in substantial part—guard against a danger that convictions for this crime will be imposed lightly. Where these requirements are satisfied, however, the law must not shy away from referring to the crime committed by its proper name. By seeking to eliminate a part of the Bosnian Muslims, the Bosnian Serb forces committed genocide. They targeted for extinction the forty thousand Bosnian Muslims living in Srebrenica, a group which was emblematic of the Bosnian Muslims in general. They stripped all the male Muslim prisoners, military and civilian, elderly and young, of their personal belongings and identification, and deliberately and methodically killed them solely on the basis of their identity. The Bosnian Serb forces were aware, when they embarked on this genocidal venture, that the harm they caused would continue to plague the Bosnian Muslims. The Appeals Chamber states unequivocally that the law condemns, in appropriate terms, the deep and lasting injury inflicted, and calls the massacre at Srebrenica by its proper name: genocide. Those responsible will bear this stigma, and it will serve as a warning to those who may in future contemplate the commission of such a heinous act.[2]

Those who drafted, on the heels of World War II and the Holocaust, the Convention for the Prevention and Punishment of the Crime of Genocide were animated by the desire to ensure that the horror of a

---

[2] Ibid., paras 36, 37.

state-organized, deliberate, and massive murder of a group of people purely because of their identity would never recur in the history of humankind. The authors of the Convention hoped that by encapsulating the crime of genocide, by declaring unambiguously that it would not go unpunished, and by requiring the international community to do the utmost to prevent it, they would forestall forever attempts to annihilate any national, ethnic, or religious group in the world.

As the graves in this cemetery testify, the struggle to make the world free of genocide is not easy and is not one of uninterrupted victories. But I would like to think that by recognizing the crimes committed here as genocide, and by condemning them with the utmost force at our command, we have helped to make the hope of those who drafted the Genocide Convention into an expectation and perhaps even a reality. As I stand here today, I can do little better than to repeat the solemn warning sounded by the Appeals Chamber of our Tribunal that those who commit this inhumane crime will not escape justice before the courts of law and the court of history.

TABLE OF CASES

EUROPEAN COURT OF HUMAN RIGHTS

Al-Adsani v United Kingdom (App no 35763/97) (2001) 34 EHRR 11 30
Assanidze v Georgia (App no 71503/01) (2004) 39 EHRR 32 30
Ilaşcu and others v Moldova and Russia (App no 48787/99) (2004)
    40 EHRR 46 30
Korbely v Hungary (App no 9174/02) (2008) 50 EHRR 48 .... 30, 56
Kress v France (App no 39594/98) ECHR 2001-VI 41 267
Musayev and others v Russia (App nos 57941/00, 58699/00, and
    60403/00) (2007) ECHR 144

INTER-AMERICAN COMMISSION OF HUMAN RIGHTS

Juan Carlos Abella et al. v Argentina (Merits: Report no 55/97)
    Inter-American Commission on Human Rights Case 11.137
    (18 November 1997) 57
Salas et al. v United States (Admissibility: Report no 31/93)
    Inter-American Commission on Human Rights Case 10.573
    (14 October 1993) 57

INTER-AMERICAN COURT OF HUMAN RIGHTS

Case of Almonacid-Arellano et al. v Chile (Judgment (Preliminary
    Objections, Merits, Reparations and Costs)) Inter-American Court of Human
    Rights Series C No 154 (26 September 2006) 30
Case of Barrios Altos et al. v Peru (Judgment (Interpretation of the Judgment
    on the Merits)) Inter-American Court of Human Rights Series C No 83
    (3 September 2001) 159
Case of Velásquez Rodríguez v Honduras (Judgment (Merits))
    Inter-American Court of Human Rights Series C No 4 (29 July 1988) 29, 234
Interpretation of the American Declaration of the Rights and Duties
    of Man Within the Framework of Article 64 of the American Convention
    on Human Rights (Advisory Opinion) Inter-American Court of Human Rights
    Series A No 10 (14 July 1989) 243

INTERNATIONAL COURT OF JUSTICE

Application of the Convention on the Prevention and Punishment of the
    Crime of Genocide (Bosnia and Herzegovina v Serbia and Montenegro)
    (Merits: Judgment) [2007] ICJ Rep 43 .... 30, 31, 231, 233, 234
Armed Activities on the Territory of the Congo (New Application: 2002)
    (Democratic Republic of the Congo v Rwanda) (Jurisdiction and
    Admissibility: Judgment) [2006] ICJ Rep 6 26

Case Concerning Armed Activities on the Territory of the Congo
    (Democratic Republic of the Congo v Uganda) (Merits: Judgment) [2005]
    ICJ Rep 168 244
Case Concerning Oil Platforms (Islamic Republic of Iran v United States
    of America) (Merits: Judgment) [2003] ICJ Rep 161 10
Case Concerning the Aerial Incident of July 27th, 1955 (Israel v Bulgaria)
    (Preliminary Objections: Judgment of May 26, 1959) [1959]
    ICJ Rep 127 5
Corfu Channel Case (United Kingdom of Great Britain and
    Northern Ireland v Albania) (Merits: Judgment) [1949] ICJ Rep 4 233
Legal Consequences of the Construction of a Wall in the Occupied
    Palestinian Territory (Advisory Opinion) [2004]
    ICJ Rep 136 .... 27, 59, 183, 244
Legality of the Threat or Use of Nuclear Weapons (Advisory Opinion)
    [1996] ICJ Rep 226 .... 26, 58, 182
Military and Paramilitary Activities in and against Nicaragua
    (Nicaragua v United States of America) (Merits: Judgment) [1986]
    ICJ Rep 14 .... 23, 25, 29, 57, 197, 218, 241
North Sea Continental Shelf Cases (Federal Republic of
    Germany v Denmark; Federal Republic of Germany v Netherlands)
    (Merits: Judgment) [1969] ICJ Rep 3 .... 30, 32

INTERNATIONAL CRIMINAL COURT

Prosecutor v Thomas Lubanga Dyilo (Decision on the Confirmation of
    Charges (Public Redacted Version)) ICC-01/04-01/06
    (29 January 2007) 40, 114

INTERNATIONAL CRIMINAL TRIBUNAL FOR RWANDA

Prosecutor v Jean-Paul Akayesu (Judgement) ICTR-96-4-T
    (2 September 1998) 112, 192, 201, 204, 224
Prosecutor v Jean-Paul Akayesu (Judgement) ICTR-96-4-A
    (1 June 2001) 225, 226, 249
Prosecutor v Michel Bagaragaza (Decision on Rule 11bis Appeal)
    ICTR-05-86-AR11bis (30 August 2006) 163
Prosecutor v Théoneste Bagosora et al. (Judgement and Sentence)
    ICTR-98-41-T (18 December 2008) 204
Jean-Bosco Barayagwiza v Prosecutor (Decision) ICTR-97-19-AR72
    (4 November 1999) 186
Sylvestre Gacumbitsi v Prosecutor (Judgement) ICTR-2001-64-A
    (7 July 2006) 89, 249
Jean Kambanda v Prosecutor (Judgement) ICTR-97-23-A
    (19 October 2000) 249
Jean de Dieu Kamuhanda v Prosecutor (Judgement) ICTR-99-54A-A
    (19 September 2005)
Prosecutor v Clément Kayishema and Obed Ruzindana
    (Judgement (Reasons)) ICTR-95-1-A (1 June 2001) 249
Prosecutor v Alfred Musema (Judgement and Sentence) ICTR-96-13-T
    (27 January 2000) 204, 249

Prosecutor v Alfred Musema (Judgement) ICTR-96-13-A
(16 November 2001) 249
Prosecutor v Ferdinand Nahimana et al. (Judgement and Sentence)
ICTR-99-52-T (3 December 2003) 39
Eliézer Niyitegeka v Prosecutor (Judgement) ICTR-96-14-A (9 July 2004) 249
Prosecutor v Georges Anderson Nderubumwe Rutaganda
(Judgement and Sentence) ICTR-96-3-T (6 December 1999) 204
Georges Anderson Nderubumwe Rutaganda v Prosecutor
(Judgement) ICTR-96-3-A (26 May 2003) 226, 227, 249

INTERNATIONAL CRIMINAL TRIBUNAL
FOR FORMER YUGOSLAVIA

Prosecutor v Zlatko Aleksovski (Judgement) IT-95-14/1-A
(24 March 2000) 35, 37, 53, 242, 247, 250, 252
Prosecutor v Milan Babić (Judgement on Sentencing Appeal) IT-03-72-A
(18 July 2005) 247, 250
Prosecutor v Predrag Banović (Sentencing Judgement) IT-02-65/1-S
(28 October 2003) 250
Prosecutor v Tihomir Blaškić (Judgement) IT-95-14-A
(29 July 2004) 200, 203, 247, 250
Prosecutor v Radoslav Branin (Judgement) IT-99-36-A (3 April 2007) 194, 195
Prosecutor v Ranko Češić (Sentencing Judgement) IT-95-10/1-S
(11 March 2004) 250
Prosecutor v Zejnil Delalić et al. (Čelebići) (Judgement) IT-96-21-T
(16 November 1998) 194, 196, 197
Prosecutor v Zejnil Delalić et al. (Čelebići) (Judgement) IT-96-21-A
(20 February 2001) 34, 53, 194, 196, 197, 247, 263, 292
Prosecutor v Miroslav Deronjić (Judgement on Sentencing Appeal) IT-02-61-A
(20 July 2005) 247, 250
Prosecutor v Dražen Erdemović (Transcript) IT-96-22-PT (31 May 1996) 290
Prosecutor v Dražen Erdemović (Sentencing Judgement) IT-96-22-T
(29 November 1996) 291
Prosecutor v Dražen Erdemović (Judgement) IT-96-22-A (7 October 1997) 291
Prosecutor v Dražen Erdemović (Sentencing Judgement) IT-96-22-Tbis
(5 March 1998) 249, 291
Prosecutor v Anto Furundžija (Judgement) IT-95-17/1-T
(10 December 1998) 89, 158, 191
Prosecutor v Anto Furundžija (Judgement) IT-95-17/1-A
(21 July 2000) 247, 249, 250, 262
Prosecutor v Stanislav Galić (Judgement and Opinion) IT-98-29-T
(5 December 2003) 33, 248, 252, 253
Prosecutor v Stanislav Galić (Judgement) IT-98-29-A
(30 November 2006) 33, 114, 200, 203, 206, 208, 246, 248
Prosecutor v Enver Hadžihasanović et al. (Decision on Interlocutory
Appeal Challenging Jurisdiction in Relation to Command Responsibility)
IT-01-47-AR72 (16 July 2003) 34, 228, 229
Prosecutor v Enver Hadžihasanović and Amir Kubura (Decision on
Joint Defence Interlocutory Appeal of Trial Chamber Decision on Rule
98bis Motions for Acquittal) IT-01-47-AR73.3 (11 March 2005) 38

TABLE OF CASES 303

Prosecutor v Enver Hadžihasanović and Amir Kubura (Judgement)
IT-01-47-A (22 April 2008) 113
Prosecutor v Gojko Janković (Decision on Referral of Case under Rule 11 bis)
IT-96-23/2-PT (22 July 2005) 184
Prosecutor v Goran Jelisić (Judgement) IT-95-10-A (5 July 2001) 247, 248, 251
Prosecutor v Miodrag Jokić (Judgement on Sentencing Appeal)
IT-01-42/1-A (30 August 2005) 250
Prosecutor v Dario Kordić and Mario Čerkez (Decision on
Appeal Regarding Statement of a Deceased Witness) IT-95-14/2-AR73.5
(21 July 2000) 124
Prosecutor v Dario Kordić and Mario Čerkez (Judgement) IT-95-14/2-A
(17 December 2004) 113, 202, 205, 224,
247, 248, 249, 251, 253, 254
Prosecutor v Momčilo Krajišnik (Decision on Momčilo Krajišnik's
Request to Self-Represent, on Counsel's Motions in Relation to
Appointment of Amicus Curiae, and on the Prosecution Motion of
16 February 2007) IT-00-39-A (11 May 2007) 37, 189
Prosecutor v Milorad Krnojelac (Judgement) IT-97-25-A
(17 September 2003) 247, 250
Prosecutor v Radislav Krstić (Judgement) IT-98-33-A
(19 April 2004) 11, 136, 201, 231,
247, 251, 293, 297, 298
Prosecutor v Dragoljub Kunarac et al. (Judgement) IT-96-23-T & IT-96-23/1-T
(22 February 2001) 189, 190, 191, 192, 193
Prosecutor v Dragoljub Kunarac et al. (Judgement) IT-96-23&23/1-A
(12 June 2002) 11, 36, 89, 202, 226, 227, 247, 250, 251
Prosecutor v Zoran Kupreškić et al. (Judgement) IT-95-16-T
(14 January 2000) 194, 196
Prosecutor v Zoran Kupreškić et al. (Appeal Judgement) IT-95-16-A
(23 October 2001) 247, 250, 251
Prosecutor v Miroslav Kvočka et al. (Judgement) IT-98-30/1-T
(2 November 2001) 249
Prosecutor v Miroslav Kvočka et al. (Judgement) IT-98-30/1-A
(28 February 2005) 247, 248, 249, 251
Prosecutor v Milan Lukić and Sredoje Lukić (Decision on Milan
Lukić's Appeal Regarding Referral) IT-98-32/1-AR11bis.1 (11 July 2007) 163
Prosecutor v Milan Martić (Judgement) IT-95-11-A (8 October 2008) 203
Prosecutor v Dragomir Milošević (Judgment) IT-98-29/1-A
(12 November 2009) 200, 207, 208, 220, 221
Prosecutor v Slobodan Milošević (Order Inviting Designation of Amicus
Curiae) IT-99-37-PT (30 August 2001) 125
Prosecutor v Slobodan Milošević (Reasons for Decision on the
Prosecution Motion Concerning Assignment of Counsel) IT-02-54-T
(4 April 2003) 124, 187
Prosecutor v Slobodan Milošević (Decision on Interlocutory Appeal on the
Admissibility of Evidence-in-Chief in the Form of Written Statements)
IT-02-54-AR73.4 (30 September 2003) 124
Prosecutor v Slobodan Milošević (Decision on the Interlocutory
Appeal by the Amici Curiae Against the Trial Chamber Order
Concerning the Presentation and Preparation of the Defence Case)
IT-02-54-AR73.6 (20 January 2004) 125

Prosecutor v Slobodan Milošević (Reasons for Decision on Assignment
of Defence Counsel) IT-02-54-T (22 September 2004) 188
Slobodan Milošević v Prosecutor (Decision on Interlocutory Appeal
of the Trial Chamber's Decision on the Assignment of Defense Counsel)
IT-02-54-AR73.7 (1 November 2004) 188
Prosecutor v Milan Milutinović et al. (Judgement) IT-05-87-T
(26 February 2009) 86
Prosecutor v Darko Mra (Sentencing Judgement) IT-02-59-S
(31 March 2004) 250
Prosecutor v Mile Mrkšić et al. (Judgement) IT-95-13/1-T
(27 September 2007) 205, 213, 214
Prosecutor v Mile Mrkšić and Veselin Šljivančanin (Judgement) IT-95-13/1-A
(5 May 2009) 203, 205, 211, 213, 216
Prosecutor v Zdravko Mucić et al. (Čelebići) (Judgement on Sentence Appeal)
IT-96-21-Abis (8 April 2003) 250
Prosecutor v Mladen Naletilić and Vinko Martinović (Judgement) IT-98-34-A
(3 May 2006) 247, 249, 251
Prosecutor v Dragan Nikolić (Decision on Defence Motion Challenging
the Exercise of Jurisdiction by the Tribunal) IT-94-2-PT
(9 October 2002) 185, 186
Prosecutor v Dragan Nikolić (Decision on Interlocutory Appeal
Concerning Legality of Arrest) IT-94-2-AR73 (5 June 2003) 186
Prosecutor v Dragan Nikolić (Sentencing Judgement)
IT-94-2-S (18 December 2003) 121, 122
Prosecutor v Dragan Nikolić (Judgement on Sentencing Appeal) IT-94-2-A
(4 February 2003) 247, 251
Prosecutor v Momir Nikolić (Sentencing Judgement) IT-02-60/1-S
(2 December 2003) 121, 122
Prosecutor v Momir Nikolić (Judgement on Sentencing Appeal)
IT-02-60/1-A (8 March 2006) 106, 247, 251
Prosecutor v Dragan Obrenović (Sentencing Judgement) IT-02-60/2-S
(10 December 2003) 250
Prosecutor v Momčilo Perišić (Decision on Motion to Appoint
Amicus Curiae to Investigate Equality of Arms) IT-04-81-PT
(18 June 2007) 37
Prosecutor v Biljana Plavšić (Sentencing Judgement) IT-00-39&40/1-S
(27 February 2003) 250
Prosecutor v Ivica Rajić (Sentencing Judgement) IT-95-12-S (8 May 2006) 250
Prosecutor v Vojislav Šešelj (Decision on Prosecution's Motion
for Order Appointing Counsel to Assist Vojislav Šešelj with his Defence)
IT-03-67-PT (9 May 2003) 125
Prosecutor v Duško Sikirica et al. (Sentencing Judgement) IT-95-8-S
(13 November 2001) 249, 250
Prosecutor v Milan Simić (Sentencing Judgement) IT-95-9/2-S
(17 November 2002) 249
Prosecutor v Blagoje Simić et al. (Judgement) IT-95-9-T
(17 October 2003) 195, 247, 250
Prosecutor v Blagoje Simić (Judgement) IT-95-9-A (28 November 2006) 250
Prosecutor v Veselin Šljivančanin (Review Judgement) IT-95-13/1-R.1
(8 December 2010) 205, 216

Prosecutor v Milomir Stakić (Judgement) IT-97-24-A
(22 March 2006) 36, 113, 251
Prosecutor v Pavle Strugar (Judgement) IT-01-42-T (31 January 2005) 250
Prosecutor v Pavle Strugar (Judgement) IT-01-42-A (17 July 2008) 37, 205
Prosecutor v Duško Tadić (Decision on the Prosecutor's Motion
  Requesting Protective Measures for Victims and Witnesses)
  IT-94-1-T (10 August 1995) 184
Prosecutor v Duško Tadić (Decision on the Defence Motion
  for Interlocutory Appeal on Jurisdiction) IT-94-1-AR72
  (2 October 1995) 32, 51, 53,
                                    90, 154, 184, 185, 217, 219, 220, 221, 222, 241
Prosecutor v Duško Tadić (Judgement) IT-94-1-A (15 July 1999) 53, 223
Prosecutor v Duško Tadić (Judgement in Sentencing Appeals) IT-94-1-A
  & IT-94-1-Abis (26 January 2000) 247, 251
Prosecutor v Stevan Todorović (Sentencing Judgement) IT-95-9/1-S
  (31 July 2001) 250
Prosecutor v Mitar Vasiljević (Judgement) IT-98-32-A
  (25 February 2004) 247, 250

SPECIAL COURT FOR SIERRA LEONE

Prosecutor v Morris Kallon and Brima Bazzy Kamara (Decision on Challenge
  to Jurisdiction: Lomé Accord Amnesty) SCSL-2004-15-AR72(E) and
  SCSL-2004-16-AR72(E) (13 March 2004) 158
Prosecutor v Sam Hinga Norman (Decision on Preliminary Motion
  Based on Lack of Jurisdiction (Child Recruitment)) SCSL-2004-14-AR72(E)
  (31 May 2004) 39
Prosecutor v Issa Hassan Sesay (Decision on Defence Motion Seeking
  the Disqualification of Justice Robertson from the Appeals Chamber)
  SCSL-2004-15-AR15 (13 March 2004) 262

UNITED NATIONS ADMINISTRATIVE TRIBUNAL

Dauchy v Secretary-General of the United Nations (Judgement No 492)
  Administrative Tribunal of the United Nations Case No 548
  (2 November 1990) 10

UNITED NATIONS HUMAN RIGHTS COMMITTEE

Lilian Celiberti de Casariego v Uruguay, UNHRC Communication
  No 56/1979 (29 July 1981) UN Doc CCPR/C/13/D/56/1979 59

NATIONAL COURTS

Netherlands
District Court of The Hague, Index No AU8685 (23 December 2005) 147

United Kingdom
R v Sussex Justices, Ex parte McCarthy [1924] 1 KB 256 261

Attorney-General's Reference No 4 of 1989, 11 Cr App R (S) 247

United States

Caperton v AT Massey Coal Co, 556 US __, 129 SCt 2252 (2009) 270
Cheney et al. v US Dist Ct for the Dist of Columbia et al., Memorandum of
    Justice Scalia, 541 US 913 (2004) 276
In re Yamashita, 327 US 1 (1946) 292
United States v Calley, 46 CMR 1131 (1973) 143

POST-WORLD WAR II MILITARY TRIBUNALS

International Military Tribunal

International Military Tribunal (Nuremberg), 'Judgement and
    Sentences'(1947) 41 AJIL 172 .... 22, 28, 29, 31, 32, 38, 44, 76-78,
        83-85, 87-102, 108, 109, 111, 115, 116, 119, 120, 136, 139, 140, 147, 149,
                156, 192, 195, 214, 225, 240, 241, 246, 279, 292, 293

International Military Tribunal for the Far East

Judgement of the International Military Tribunal for the Far East,
    reprinted in BVA Röling and CF Rüter (eds), The Tokyo Judgment:
    The International Military Tribunal for the Far East, 29 April 1946-12
    November 1948, Vols I-II (Amsterdam: University Press
    Amsterdam BV, 1977) 77, 78, 83, 85, 87,
                                        89-92, 98, 99, 109, 140, 191

Trials Under Control Council Law No 10

United States v Wilhelm von Leeb et al. (The High Command Case),
    reprinted in Trials of War Criminals Before the Nuernberg Military
    Tribunals Under Control Council Law No 10, Vols X-XI (Buffalo:
    William S Hein & Co, 1997) 93, 214
United States v Wilhelm List et al. (The Hostage Case), reprinted in
    Trials of War Criminals Before the Nuernberg Military Tribunals Under
    Control Council Law No 10, Vol XI (Buffalo: William S Hein & Co, 1997) 94

TABLE OF INSTRUMENTS

Additional Protocols I and II – *See* Geneva Conventions (1949)
Allied Control Council Law No 10, Punishment of Persons Guilty
 of War Crimes, Crimes Against Peace and Against Humanity (1945) 3
 Official Gazette of the Control Council for Germany 50 (1946) 85, 191
American Convention on Human Rights (1969) reprinted in Basic
 Documents Pertaining to Human Rights in the Inter-American System,
 OAS/Ser.L/V/I.4 rev. 13 (2010) 242
American Declaration of the Rights and Duties of Man (1948) reprinted
 in Basic Documents Pertaining to Human Rights in the Inter-American
 System, OAS/Ser.L/V/I.4 rev. 13 (2010) 242, 243

Berlin Resolution on the Application of International Humanitarian Law and
 Fundamental Human Rights in Armed Conflicts in which Non-State Entities
 are Parties (Berlin Resolution of the Institute of International Law) (1999)
 reprinted in Dietrich Schindler and Jiri Toman (eds), *The Laws of Armed
 Conflicts: A Collection of Conventions, Resolutions, and Other Documents*
 (Fourth rev edn Leiden: Martinus Nijhoff Publishers, 2004) 67
Biological Weapons Convention – *See* Convention on the Prohibition of the
 Development, Production and Stockpiling of Bacteriological (Biological)
 and Toxin Weapons and on their Destruction ....

Charter of the International Military Tribunal – Annex to the Agreement
 for the prosecution and punishment of major war criminals of the European
 Axis (London Charter) (1945) 82 UNTS 284 .... 87–91, 94, 111, 192
Charter of the International Military Tribunal for the Far East
 (Tokyo Charter) (1946) TIAS No. 1589 90
Charter of the Organization of American States (1948) reprinted in
 Basic Documents Pertaining to Human Rights in the Inter-American System,
 OAS/Ser.L/V/I.4 rev. 13 (2010) 242, 243
Charter of the United Nations (1945) 59 Stat 1031 .... 20, 27, 40, 44, 69, 71,
88, 100, 117, 164, 232
Chemical Weapons Convention – *See* Convention on the Prohibition
 of the Development, Production, Stockpiling and Use of Chemical Weapons
 and on their Destruction
Convention against Torture and Other Cruel, Inhuman or Degrading
 Treatment or Punishment (Torture Convention) (1984) 1465 UNTS
 85 .... 173, 190, 191
Convention for the Amelioration of the Condition of the Wounded in Armies
 in the Field (Geneva Convention of 1864) (1864) 22 Stat 940 .... 20, 46, 79
Convention for the Amelioration of the Condition of the Wounded and Sick
 in Armies in the Field (Geneva Convention of 1906) (1906) 35 Stat 1885 46
Convention for the Amelioration of the Condition of the Wounded
 and Sick in Armies in the Field (Geneva Convention of 1929) (1929)
 118 LNTS 303 .... 22, 46

Convention for the Protection of Cultural Property in the Event of
  Armed Conflict (1954) 249 UNTS 240 24
Convention on Prohibitions or Restrictions on the Use of Certain
  Conventional Weapons which May be Deemed to be Excessively Injurious
  or to Have Indiscriminate Effects (Conventional Weapons Convention)
  (1980) 1342 UNTS 137
    Protocol on Prohibitions or Restrictions on the Use of Mines,
      Booby-Traps and Other Devices (Protocol II) (1996) 2048 UNTS 93 .....24, 51
Convention on the Non-Applicability of Statutory Limitations to War
  Crimes and Crimes Against Humanity (1968) 754 UNTS 73 ....89, 90
Convention on the Prevention and Punishment of the Crime of Genocide
  (1948) 78 UNTS 277.........20, 30, 44, 87, 140, 163, 173, 201, 232, 234, 235, 298, 299
Convention on the Prohibition of the Development, Production and
  Stockpiling of Bacteriological (Biological) and Toxin Weapons and on their
  Destruction (Biological Weapons Convention) (1972) 1015 UNTS 163...................51
Convention on the Prohibition of the Development, Production, Stockpiling
  and Use of Chemical Weapons and on their Destruction (Chemical Weapons
  Convention) (1993) 1974 UNTS 45 51
Convention on the Prohibition of the Use, Stockpiling, Production and
  Transfer of Anti-Personnel Mines and on their Destruction (Mine
  Ban Treaty) (1997) 2056 UNTS 211 51
Convention on the Rights of the Child (1989) 1577 UNTS 3...27
Convention relative to the Treatment of Prisoners of War (Geneva POW
  Convention of 1929) (1929) 118 LNTS 343.................. 22–25, 28, 46, 52, 93, 94, 214
Convention respecting the Laws and Customs of War on Land (Hague
  Convention IV) (1907) 36 Stat 2277 .... 31, 48, 49, 79, 93, 94, 206, 241
    Regulations concerning the Laws and Customs of War on Land (Hague
      Regulations) (1907) 36 Stat 2277...21, 22
Convention with respect to the Laws and Customs of War on Land and
  its annex: Regulations concerning the Laws and Customs of War on Land
  (Hague Convention II) (1899) 32 Stat 1803...48, 79
Conventional Weapons Convention - *See* Convention on Prohibitions or
  Restrictions on the Use of Certain Conventional Weapons which May be
  Deemed to be Excessively Injurious or to Have Indiscriminate Effects

Dayton Agreement – *See* General Framework Agreement for Peace
  in Bosnia and Herzegovina
Declaration of Amnesty and Protocol (1923) 36 LNTS 145 82
Declaration of German Atrocities (Moscow Declaration) (1943) 9
  Dep't. St. Bull. 310...83
Declaration of Minimum Humanitarian Standards (Turku Declaration)
  (1995) UN Doc E/CN.4/1995/116...8, 9, 33, 67
Declaration Respecting Maritime Law (Paris Declaration) (1856) 115 Parry 1 79
Declaration Renouncing the Use, in Time of War, of Explosive Projectiles
  Under 400 Grammes Weight (St. Petersburg Declaration) (1868) 138 Parry
  297 79
Draft Articles on Responsibility of States for Internationally Wrongful
  Acts (2001) UN Doc A/56/10..31
Draft Code of Crimes against the Peace and Security of Mankind (1991)
  UN Doc A/46/10 (1991) 36, 38

TABLE OF INSTRUMENTS

Draft International Convention on the Condition and Protection of
 Civilians of Enemy Nationality Who Are on Territory Belonging to or
 Occupied by a Belligerent (Tokyo Draft) (1934) reprinted in Dietrich
 Schindler and Jiri Toman (eds), *The Laws of Armed Conflicts: A Collection
 of Conventions, Resolutions, and Other Documents* (Fourth rev edn Leiden:
 Martinus Nijhoff Publishers, 2004) 21

European Convention for the Protection of Human Rights and
 Fundamental Freedoms (1950) 213 UNTS 222 .... 56, 92, 184, 190, 195
 Protocol No 6 to the Convention for the Protection of Human Rights and
  Fundamental Freedoms concerning the abolition of the death penalty
  (1983) 1496 UNTS 281 60

Final Act of the Conference on Security and Co-operation in Europe
 (Helsinki Accords) (1975) 14 ILM 1292 62

General Framework Agreement for Peace in Bosnia and Herzegovina
 (Dayton Agreement) (1995) 35 ILM 75 .... 151, 157
Geneva Convention of 1864 – *See* Convention for the Amelioration of the
 Condition of the Wounded in Armies in the Field (1864)
Geneva Convention of 1906 – *See* Convention for the Amelioration of the
 Condition of the Wounded and Sick in Armies in the Field (1906)
Geneva Conventions of 1929 – *See* Convention for the Amelioration of the
 Condition of the Wounded and Sick in Armies in the Field (1929) *and*
 Convention relative to the Treatment of Prisoners of War
Geneva Conventions (1949) 19–27, 29–31, 36, 38, 44, 46,
  48, 50–57, 60, 63, 87, 92, 118, 140, 143, 144, 173, 182,
  191–193, 196, 197, 200, 201, 203, 212–215, 217, 218,
  220, 222, 224, 225, 227, 230, 241, 292, 293
 Geneva Convention for the Amelioration of the Condition of the Wounded
  and Sick in Armed Forces in the Field (I) 75 UNTS 31 .... 20, 23
 Geneva Convention for the Amelioration of the Condition of Wounded,
  Sick and Shipwrecked Members of Armed Forces at Sea (II) 75 UNTS 85 ... 20
 Geneva Convention Relative to the Treatment of Prisoners of War (III) 75
  UNTS 135 .... 20, 52, 206, 212–216
 Geneva Convention relative to the Protection of Civilian Persons
  in Time of War (IV) 75 UNTS 287 .... 6, 20, 21, 22, 27, 53, 205, 206, 230
 Protocol Additional to the Geneva Conventions of 12 August 1949, and
  relating to the Protection of Victims of International Armed Conflicts
  (Additional Protocol I) (1977) 1125 UNTS 3 .... 23, 24,
   33, 36, 38, 49, 50, 55, 88, 140, 154, 191,
   192, 200, 201, 203, 206–209, 220–224, 241, 292
 Protocol Additional to the Geneva Conventions of 12 August 1949, and
  relating to the Protection of Victims of Non-International Armed
  Conflicts (Additional Protocol II) (1977) 1125 UNTS 609 .... 33, 36,
   38, 49, 50, 88, 92, 93, 140, 154, 158, 191,
   192, 200, 201, 203, 206, 218, 220–224, 227, 241
Genocide Convention – *See* Convention on the Prevention and Punishment of the Crime of Genocide

Hague Convention II – *See* Convention with respect to the Laws and
    Customs of War on Land and its annex: Regulations concerning the
    Laws and Customs of War on Land
Hague Convention IV – *See* Convention respecting the Laws and
    Customs of War on Land and its annex: Regulations concerning the
    Laws and Customs of War on Land
Hague Regulations – *See* Convention respecting the Laws and Customs
    of War on Land and its annex: Regulations concerning the Laws and
    Customs of War on Land
Helsinki Accords – *See* Final Act of the Conference on Security and
    Co-operation in Europe

ICC Statute – *See* Rome Statute of the International Criminal Court
ICJ Statute – *See* Statute of the International Court of Justice
ICTR Statute – *See* Statute of the International Tribunal for Rwanda
ICTY Statute – *See* Statute of the International Tribunal for Prosecution
    of Persons Responsible for Serious Violations of International Humanitarian
    Law Committed in the Territory of the former Yugoslavia since 1991
Instructions for the Government of Armies of the United States in the
    Field (Lieber Code) (1863) reprinted in Dietrich Schindler and Jiri Toman (eds),
    *The Laws of Armed Conflicts: A Collection of Conventions, Resolutions, and Other
    Documents* (Fourth rev edn Leiden: Martinus Nijhoff Publishers, 2004) 19, 46
Inter-Allied Declaration (St. James Declaration) (1942) reprinted in *Punishment
    for War Crimes: The Inter-Allied Declaration Signed at St. James Palace,
    London on 13 January 1942, and Related Documents* (New York: United
    Nations Office, undated) 83
International Covenant on Civil and Political Rights (1966) 999 UNTS
    171 .... 44, 58, 59, 92, 118, 183, 184, 188,
                                                                    194–196, 197, 243, 244
    Second Optional Protocol to the International Covenant on Civil
        and Political Rights, aiming at the abolition of the death penalty (1989)
        UN Doc A/RES/44/128 60
International Covenant on Economic, Social and Cultural Rights (1966)
    993 UNTS 3 .... 44, 194

Lieber Code – *See* Instructions for the Government of Armies of the
    United States in the Field
Lomé Peace Agreement – *See* Peace Agreement between the Government
    of Sierra Leone and the Revolutionary United Front of Sierra Leone
London Charter – *See* Charter of the International Military Tribunal – Annex
    to the Agreement for the prosecution and punishment of major war criminals
    of the European Axis

Mine Ban Treaty – *See* Convention on the Prohibition of the Use,
    Stockpiling, Production and Transfer of Anti-Personnel Mines and on their
    Destruction
Moscow Declaration – *See* Declaration of German Atrocities

Paris Declaration – *See* Declaration Respecting Maritime Law

Peace Agreement between the Government of Sierra Leone and the
    Revolutionary United Front of Sierra Leone (Lomé Peace Agreement) (1999)
    UN Doc S/1999/777 158

Rome Statute of the International Criminal Court (1998) 2187 UNTS
    90 .... 40, 50, 68, 88–91, 95, 114,
                                            141, 143, 147, 149, 154, 156, 158–167, 169,
                                                      171–174, 177, 193, 209, 222, 234, 280

Slavery, Servitude, Forced Labour and Similar Institutions and Practices
    Convention of 1926 (Slavery Convention) (1926) 60 LNTS 253 193
St. James Declaration – *See* Inter-Allied Declaration
St. Petersburg Declaration - *See* Declaration Renouncing the Use, in Time
    of War, of Explosive Projectiles Under 400 Grammes Weight
Statute of the International Court of Justice (1945) 59 Stat 1055 .... 31, 241, 269
Statute of the International Tribunal for Prosecution of Persons
    Responsible for Serious Violations of International Humanitarian Law
    Committed in the Territory of the former Yugoslavia since 1991
    (ICTY Statute) (1993) UN Doc S/25704 at 36, annex and
    S/25704/Add.1 .... 32, 33, 35, 36, 58, 84, 88–92, 100, 101, 103, 104, 107,
                                  113, 117, 118, 124, 125, 130, 147, 184, 185, 187–189,
                                  194, 195, 201–205, 218–220, 222, 226, 229, 247, 280, 282, 292
Statute of the International Tribunal for Rwanda (ICTR Statute) (1994)
    UN Doc S/RES/955 .... 39, 58, 88–92, 100, 103, 104,
                                107, 147, 184, 186, 187, 201, 203, 224, 226, 260, 280, 282, 292

Tokyo Charter – *See* Charter of the International Military Tribunal
    for the Far East
Tokyo Draft – *See* Draft International Convention on the Condition and
    Protection of Civilians of Enemy Nationality Who Are on Territory Belonging
    to or Occupied by a Belligerent
Torture Convention – *See* Convention against Torture and Other Cruel,
    Inhuman or Degrading Treatment or Punishment
Treaty of Peace with Turkey (Treaty of Lausanne) (1923) 28 LNTS 11 82
Treaty of Peace between the Allied and Associated Powers and Germany
    (Treaty of Versailles) (1919) 225 Parry 188 .... 81, 82
Turku Declaration – *See* Declaration of Minimum Humanitarian Standards

United States Army Field Manual (1956) United States Department of
    the Army, *Field Manual No. 27–10: Law of Land Warfare* 292
Universal Declaration of Human Rights (1948) UN Doc A/810 .... 20, 44, 62–65

Vienna Convention on the Law of Treaties (1969) 1155 UNTS 331 .... 24, 26, 55, 172

INDEX

As per usual Oxford University Press practice, names of authors mentioned only in the footnotes have not been indexed.

Academia
  author's appointment as professor in Geneva 8–9
  author's education 3–4
  author's interest in Shakespeare developed at Oxford 11–15
  author's teaching post at NYU 7–8
  contributions by Judge Buergenthal 244–5
Accountability
  see also Responsibility for crimes
  criteria for success of international criminal justice 146
  independent judiciary 266
  peace vs justice controversy 156–7
  peace vs justice in Uganda 160–4
  shift from reciprocity to individual responsibility and rights 22–5
Address at Memorial Cemetery at Potočari, Srebrenica 297–9
Amnesties 29–30, 82, 153, 158–9
Appeals
  decision-making
    diversity of staff and judges 281–3
    procedure 283–4
  self-representation on appeal 189
Armed conflicts *see* Internal conflicts; International conflicts
Arrest and detention
  impact of human rights law 45, 185–6
  obligation of states to cooperate in apprehension 173–6
  treaty developments 49
  unlawful confinement of civilians 205

Bias *see* Impartiality of judiciary
Buergenthal, Judge T.
  advancement of human rights law
    extraterritorial applicability of ICCPR 243–4
    interpretation of American instruments 242–3
  impact on academia 244–5
  importance 239

Cambodia tribunal 141, 145, 157
Child soldiers 40
Civilians *see* Crimes against civilians
Command responsibility
  customary humanitarian law jurisprudence of ICTY 34–5, 37, 228–9
  lessons from Shakespeare 286, 291–4
  liability of heads of state 80–1
  trial of senior figures after WWII 84–7

Yamashita principle 292
Complementarity
  relationship between ICC and national jurisdictions 152, 167–9, 172–3
  scrutiny of admissibility challenges and complementarity 161–4
Crimes against civilians
  actions of non-state actors 66–7
  classic principles of law of war 43
  impact of Geneva Conventions 20–2
  impact of human rights law 46–7
  important contributions by ICTY 36
  jurisprudence of ad hoc Tribunals
    crimes against humanity 202–4
    history and development of protections for civilians 200–1
    protections in Tribunals' founding documents 201–2
    significance 209–10
    war crimes 204–9
  sentencing 246–54
  treaty developments 48
Crimes against humanity
  definition of 'civilian population' 202–4
  impact of human rights law on ad hoc Tribunals' jurisprudence 192–6
  impact of human rights law on interpretation 55–6
  jurisdiction 89–90
  rape 89
  persecution 193–6
Customary humanitarian law
  see also International humanitarian law
  application by human rights courts 29–30
  continuing revival 41
  creation of expert group by ICRC 8
  genocide 201
  ICRC study on customary humanitarian law 36, 38, 50, 222
  increase in importance 240–1
  jurisprudence
    ICC 40
    ICJ 23, 26, 29–32
    ICTR 39
    ICTY 32–8, 228–9
    Special Court for Sierra Leone 39–40
  legality principle 32–5, 93–5, 112–4
  prisoners of war 214
  revival at Nuremberg 28–9
  terror 206

Decision-making
  commitment to transparency 278–9

Decision-making (*Cont.*)
  diverse decision-makers 280–1
  diversity of staff and judges 281–3
  procedure 283–4
  uniqueness of ad hoc Tribunals 279–80
Deportation 36
Detention *see* Arrest and detention
Discrimination
  gender offences 89
  impact of human rights law 45
  relevance of UDHR fundamental values 64
  treaty developments 49
Due process
  challenges of ICTY
    right to self-representation 124–5
  criterion for success of international criminal justice 147–8
  customary humanitarian law jurisprudence of ICTY 37–8
  desire for speedy completion not to affect rights 107–9
  developments after Nuremberg 90–2
  fairness in sentencing
    exercise of discretion 247–54
  ICTY distinguished from earlier tribunals
    procedural and evidentiary rules 100–2, 104–5
  impact of human rights law generally 45
  impact of human rights law on ad hoc Tribunals 184–5
  legality principle 111–2
  treaty developments 49

Enslavement 36, 192–3
Evidence
  availability of various types of evidence 83–4
  challenges of ICTY
    blending common and civil law traditions 120–4
    gathering of evidence 83–4, 99–100, 119–20
  evidentiary standard in ICJ opinion on genocide 232
  ICTY distinguished from earlier tribunals
    blend of civil and common law traditions 105–7
    procedural and evidentiary rules 100–2

Fair trial *see* Due process
Forced labor 205–6
Forcible displacement 36

Genocide
  Address at Memorial Cemetery at Potočari, Srebrenica 297–9
  ICJ opinion
    cooperation with ICTY 234–5
    importance of case 231

reliance on principles of criminal responsibility 231–4
impact on establishment of international courts 75
Tribunals' role in civilian protection 201
Grave breaches 20, 25, 53, 92, 143, 173, 201, 218–19, 230
Guilty pleas 121, 133

Human rights law
  see also Customary humanitarian law; International humanitarian law
  achievements and potential of UDHR
    need for cross-cultural improvements 64–5
    relevance of fundamental values 62–4
    role of UN 64–5
  contributions by Judge Buergenthal
    extraterritorial applicability of ICCPR 243–4
    interpretation of American instruments 242–3
  impact on jurisprudence of ad hoc Tribunals
    arrests 185–6
    due process 184–5
    enhancement of humanitarian law 197–8
    enslavement 192–3
    jurisdiction 183–4
    legality principle 196–7
    persecution and 'other inhumane acts' 193–6
    rape 191–2
    right to self-representation 187–9
    torture 190–1
  impact on law of war
    interpretation 44–5, 55–60
    protected persons 53–4
    reciprocity 54–5
    repatriation of POWs 52–3
    reprisals 55
    treaty developments 48–51
  increase in number of human rights courts 239–40
  international humanitarian law distinguished 59
  interpretation by ad hoc Tribunals and ICJ 57–60
  relationship with international humanitarian law
    increasing symbiosis 182–3
    traditional separation 181–2
    revolution brought about by WWII 43–5
Humanitarian law *see* Customary humanitarian law

Impartiality of judiciary
  institutional design and management 265
  means of accountability 265–6
  recusal 261–5

Inalienability of individual rights
  impact of Geneva Conventions 25–7
  impact of human rights law 45
Independence of judiciary
  importance 255–7, 266
  judicial assignments 258–60
  selection procedures 257–8, 271–2
  underlying justifications 267–8
Individual responsibility
  criminalization of international legal norms 92–3
  impact of Geneva Conventions 22–5
  impact of human rights law 45
  lessons from Shakespeare 287–91
Internal conflicts
  applicability of customary law 49–50
  applicable rules of international humanitarian law 229–30
  blurring of distinction with international conflicts 220–3
  forces fighting on behalf of foreign powers 223–4
  impact of changes in relationship between human rights and humanitarian law 182
  importance of international customary law 241
  lingering distinctions from international conflicts 228–9
  nexus with armed conflict 226–7
  prisoners of war 212–4
  responsibility of public agents under humanitarian law 224–5
  Tadić decision 217–20
International Committee of the Red Cross (ICRC)
  author's work with 8
  commentaries on Geneva Conventions 23–6
  study on customary humanitarian law 36, 38, 50, 222
International conflicts
  applicability of customary law 49–50
  applicable rules of international humanitarian law 229–30
  blurring of distinction with internal conflicts 220–3
  internal forces fighting on behalf of foreign powers 223–4
  protected persons 53–4
International Court of Justice (ICJ)
  application of customary humanitarian law 23, 26, 29–32, 38
  application of human rights law 57–60
  author's cases before court 9–10
  genocide opinion
    importance of case 231
    reliance on principles of criminal responsibility 231–4
    reliance on rulings of ICTY 234–5
    questions regarding choice of ICJ as venue 235
  judicial selection 257–8
  Nicaragua finding on fundamental rights 25
International Criminal Court (ICC)
  deterrence of crime 148–50
  difficulties in apprehending perpetrators 145
  due process 91
  challenges 154–5
  greatest change to international law 75
  judicial assignments 258
  jurisdiction 90, 168–9
  obligation of states to cooperate
    ratification and arrests 173–6
    relationship between efficacy and cooperation 176–7
    treaty obligations 171–3
  peace vs justice controversy
    history and development 156–9
    political considerations 165–6
    Uganda situation 159–60
  promotion of peace and healing 152
  relationship with national jurisdictions
    duty to cooperate 172–3
    outreach 152
    role of complementarity 152, 167–8
    self-referrals 168–9
  sources of law 95
  Uganda situation
    peace vs justice controversy 159–60
    scrutiny of admissibility challenges 161–4
    suspension of investigation 164–6
International criminal justice
  see also Accountability; International humanitarian law; Responsibility for crimes
  challenges 154–5
  criteria for success
    deterring crime 148–50
    fair trials 147–8
    finding and trying perpetrators 142–7
    promotion of peace and healing 150–3
  establishment of well-developed standards 153–4
  importance of ICTY and ICTR 140–1
  increased commitment of international community 154
  origins at Nuremberg and Tokyo 139–40
  relevance to ICJ opinion on genocide 231–4
International Criminal Tribunal for Rwanda (ICTR)
  blend of civil and common law traditions 105–7
  customary humanitarian law jurisprudence 39

International Criminal Tribunal for Rwanda
  (ICTR) (Cont.)
  decision-making
    commitment to transparency 278–9
    diverse decision-makers 280–1
    diversity of staff and judges 281–3
    effectiveness 284–5
    procedure 283–4
    uniqueness of ad hoc Tribunals 279–80
  desire for speedy completion not to affect
      rights 107–9
  deterrence of crime 95–6, 148–50
  difficulties of finding and trying
      perpetrators 144–5
  due process 90–2, 107–9
  gender offences 89
  impact of human rights law
    arrests 186
    rape 191–2
    right to self-representation 187–9
  impact of human rights law on
      interpretation 58
  internal conflicts
    nexus with armed conflict 226–7
    responsibility of public agents 224–6
  judicial assignments 258–60
  jurisdiction 89–90
  legality principle
    due process 111–2
    reliance on customary law 112–4
  Nuremberg and Tokyo distinguished
    basis on which established 99–100
    criminalization of international legal
        norms 92–3
    due process 90–2
    gathering of evidence 83–4, 99–100
    gender offences 89
    judicial selection 102–3
    jurisdiction to prosecute 89–90
    legality principle 93–5, 103–4
    procedural and evidentiary rules 100–2,
        104–5
    prosecution of abuses against
        civilians 83
    sources of law 93–5
    trial of senior figures 85–7
  promotion of peace and healing 150–3
  role in developing law on civilian
      protection 200–9
  sources of law 93–5
  trial of senior figures 84–7
International Criminal Tribunal for the
    former Yugoslavia (ICTY)
  author's election as President of
      Tribunal 11
  avoiding appearance of judicial bias 263
  blend of civil and common law
      traditions 105–7, 120–4
  challenges

    blend of common and civil law
        traditions 120–4
    establishment of regional courts 126–7
    gathering of evidence 83–4, 99–100,
        119–20
    right to self-representation 124–5
    rules of procedure and evidence 116–7
    sentencing scheme 125–6
  command responsibility 292–3
  criminalization of international legal
      norms 92–3
  customary humanitarian law
      jurisprudence 32–8
  decision-making
    commitment to transparency 278–9
    diverse decision-makers 280–1
    diversity of staff and judges 281–3
    effectiveness 284–5
    procedure 283–4
    uniqueness of ad hoc Tribunals 279–80
  desire for speedy completion not to affect
      rights 107–9
  deterrence of crime 95–6, 148–50
  difficulties of finding and trying
      perpetrators 144–5
  due process 90–2, 107–9
  fairness in sentencing 247–54
  focus on due process 90–2
  gender offences 89
  impact of human rights law
    arrests 185–6
    due process 184–5
    enslavement 192–3
    jurisdiction 183–4
    legality principle 196–7
    persecution 193–6
    rape 191–2
    right to self-representation 187–9
    torture 190–1
  impact of human rights law on
      interpretation 58
  internal conflicts
    blurring of distinction with international
        conflicts 220–3
    forces fighting on behalf of foreign
        powers 223–4
    nexus with armed conflict 226
    relevance of customary rules
        traditionally applied 229–30
    Tadić decision 217–20
  judicial assignments 258–60
  jurisdiction 89–90
    Tadić decision 217–20
  legality principle
    due process 111–2
    reliance on customary law 32–5, 112–4
    length and complexity of trials 118–9
  Nuremberg and Tokyo distinguished
    basis on which established 99–100

criminalization of international legal
  norms 92–3
due process 90–2
gathering of evidence 83–4, 99–100
gender offences 89
judicial selection 102–3
jurisdiction to prosecute 89–90
legality principle 93–5, 103–4
procedural and evidentiary rules 100–2,
  104–5
prosecution of abuses against
  civilians 83
sources of law 93–5
trial of senior figures 85–7
obligation of states to cooperate 174
origins of international criminal
  justice 140–1
peace vs justice controversy 157–8
prisoners of war
  captor responsibility 216
  internal and international conflicts
    distinguished 212–4
  when duties cease to apply 214–16
promotion of peace and healing 150–3
role in developing law on civilian
  protection 200–9
social and political goals 115–6
sources of law 93–5
statement by author to Security Council
  completion strategy 129–35
  cooperation of regional states 131–2
  need for continued commitment to
    international criminal justice 135–6
superior orders 290–1
trial of senior figures 85–7
International humanitarian law
see also **Customary humanitarian law;
  Human rights law**
author's early interest 8–9
classic principles of law of war 43–5
historical development of war crimes law to
  present 79–97
human rights law distinguished 59
impact of atrocities 45–7
impact of Geneva Conventions
  growth of importance over time 27
  inalienability of individual rights 25–7
  protection of civilians 20–2
  review of historical context 19–20
  shift from reciprocity to individual
    responsibility and rights 22–5
impact of human rights law on
  interpretation 44–5, 51–5, 57–60
increase in number of courts
  applying 239–40
internal conflicts 222
interpretation by human rights bodies 55–7
non-state actors
  problems posed by 66–7, 96–7

need for more strategic and long-term
  policy 70–1
protection of civilians 200
relationship with human rights law
  increasing symbiosis 182–3
  traditional separation 181–2
International Military Tribunal (IMT)
due process 90–2
forerunner to international courts 75
gender offences 89
ICTY distinguished
  basis on which established 99–100
  blend of civil and common law
    traditions 105–7
  legality principle 93–5, 103–4
  procedural and evidentiary rules 100–2,
    104–5
lasting influence 95–96
new approach to war crimes 77–8
origins of international criminal
  justice 139–40
revival of customary humanitarian
  law 28–9
role in criminalization of international legal
  norms 92–3
si omnes clauses 22
sources of law 93–4
trial of senior figures 84–7
**International Military Tribunal for the Far
  East**
due process 90–2, 140
gender offences 89
ICTY distinguished 99–100
role in criminalization of international legal
  norms 92–3
trial of senior figures 84–7

Joint criminal enterprises 37, 293
Judges and justices
  Barak, Chief Justice A. 273
  Baxter, Judge R. 4
  Buergenthal, Judge T. *see* **Buergenthal,
    Judge T.**
  Cassese, Judge A. 217
  Hewart, Lord Chief Justice G. 261
  Higgins, Judge R. 255, 257
  Jackson, Justice R. 77–78, 97, 115, 139, 149
  Jennings, Judge R. 30
  Kennedy, Justice A. 255
  Meron, Judge T. *see* **Meron, Theodor**
  O'Connor, Justice S.D. 255
  Odio Benito, Judge E. 263
  Posner, Judge R. 273, 284
  Robertson, Justice G. 262–3
  Scalia, Justice A. 276
  Woolf, Lord Chief Justice H. 255
Judiciary
decision-making
  diverse decision-makers 280–1

Judiciary (Cont.)
    diversity of staff and judges 281–3
    procedure 283–4
    uniqueness of ad hoc Tribunals 279–80
  fairness in sentencing
    exercise of discretion 247–54
  impartiality
    means of accountability 265–6
    institutional design and
      management 265
    problems of perception 260–1
    recusal 261–5
  independence
    electoral pressures 108–9, 271–2
    importance 255–7, 266
    judicial assignments 258–60
    selection procedures 257–8, 271–2
    underlying justifications 267–8
  participation in public life
    affiliations and contacts 275–6
    arbitration 274–5
    codes of conduct 269–70
    for-profit organizations 274
    need for discretion 276–7
    non-judicial actions and
      engagements 272–3
    non-profit organizations 273–4
    political activities 273–4
    public speaking and publications 273
    role 265–6
Jurisdiction
  of ICC
    relationship between ICC and national
      jurisdictions 152, 167–9, 172–3
    scrutiny of admissibility challenges 161–4
    self-referrals 168–9
    state responsibility 168
    Uganda situation 161–5
  of ICTR 89–90, 201
  of ICTY 89–90, 201–2, 218–20
  impact of human rights law on ad hoc
    Tribunals' jurisprudence 183–4
  problem of states outside
    jurisdiction 142–3
Jus ad bellum 71
Jus cogens 26–7, 30, 49
Jus in bello 24, 43

Law of war *see* International humanitarian law
Lebanon tribunal 141, 157
Legality principle
  application by ICTY and ICTR
    due process 111–2
    reliance on customary law 32–5, 103–4,
      112–4
    sources of law 93–5
  customary humanitarian law jurisprudence
    of ICTR 39
    of ICTY 33–4

    of Special Court for Sierra Leone 39–40
  defined 110

Marten's Clause 48
Meron, Theodor
  Address at Memorial Cemetery at Potočari,
    Srebrenica 297–9
  appointment as professor in Geneva 8–9
  education 3–4
  election as President of ICTY 11
  election by UN as ICTY judge 11
  impact of WWII 3–4
  interest in Shakespeare 11–15
  statement to Security Council regarding
    ICTY
      completion strategy 129–35
      cooperation of regional states 131–2
      need for continued commitment to
        international criminal
        justice 135–6
  teaching post at NYU 6–8
  work with ICRC 8
'Methodological conservatism' 34
Murder 56

Non-state actors
  problems posed by 66–7, 96–7
  compliance with international
    humanitarian law 67–8
  history and emergence after WWII 66–7
  need for more strategic and long-term
    policy 70–1
  responsibility to prisoners of war 212
Nullem crimen sine lege see Legality principle
Nuremberg *see* International Military
  Tribunal
Nuremberg tribunals *see* International
  Military Tribunal

Opinio juris 30
'Outcome conservatism' 34

Peace
  peace vs justice controversy
    history and development 156–9
    Uganda situation 159–60
Persecution 193–6
Precedent 30
Prisoners of war
  captor responsibility 216
  classic principles of law of war 43
  forced labor 206
  inalienability of individual rights 25–6
  internal conflicts 212–4
  need for protection 211
  problems of custody transfer 211–2
  repatriation 52–3
  when duties cease to apply 214–6
Protected persons 53–4

Rape *see* Sexual violence
Reciprocity
    classic principle of law of war 43–4, 54
    impact of Geneva Conventions 22–5
    impact of human rights law 45, 54–5
    non-state actors 68
Recusal of judges 260–5
Repatriation of POWs 52–3
Reprisals
    impact of human rights law 55
    non-state actors 71
    shift from reciprocity to individual
        responsibility and rights 23–4
Responsibility for crimes
    command responsibility
        customary humanitarian law
            jurisprudence of ICTY 34–5, 37,
                228–9
        history before WWII 79–82
        lessons from Shakespeare 286, 291–4
        liability of heads of state 80–1
        trial of senior figures after WWII 84–7
        Yamashita principle 292
    individual responsibility
        criminalization of international legal
            norms 93
        history before WWII 79–82
        impact of human rights law 45
        impact of Geneva Conventions 22–5
        lessons from Shakespeare 288–91
    joint criminal enterprises 37, 293
    lessons from Shakespeare
        command responsibility 286, 291–4
        superior orders 288–91
    prisoners of war
        captor responsibility 216
        when duties cease to apply 214–6
    public agents 224–6
    superior orders 288–91

Self-representation
    impact of human rights law on Tribunals'
        jurisprudence 187–9
    matters for future clarification 124–5
Sentencing 246–54
Sexual violence
    customary humanitarian law jurisprudence
        of ICTY 36
    gender offences 89
    impact of human rights law on Tribunals'
        jurisprudence 191–2
    treatment as war crime 220
Shakespeare, W.
    author's interest at Oxford 11–5
    author's writings at NYU 7–8
    command responsibility 286, 291–4
    leaders' awareness of responsibility 288
    role of advisers 286–8
    role of leaders 286–8

superior orders 288–91
Si omnes clauses 22, 54
Special Court for Sierra Leone
    customary humanitarian law
        jurisprudence 39–40
    hybrid court 141
    peace vs justice controversy 157–8
    prevention of appearance of judicial
        bias 262

Terror
    actus reus 207
    elements of crime 206–8
    customary humanitarian law 206–7
    responsibility for 206–9, 246–7
Terrorism *see* Non-state actors
Tokyo tribunal *see* International Military
    Tribunal for the Far East
Torture
    impact of human rights law 45, 182
    impact of human rights law on Tribunals'
        jurisprudence 190–1
    important contributions by ICTY 36
    treaty developments 49
Treaties
    in history of war crimes law 80–3
    impact of Geneva Conventions
        growth of importance over time 27
        inalienability of individual rights 25–7
        protection of civilians 20–2
        review of historical context 19–20
        shift from reciprocity to individual
            responsibility and rights 22–5
    humanitarian treaties 48–51
    limitations on reprisals 24
    obligation of states to cooperate with ICC
        under Rome Statute 171–3
    protection of civilians 200

Uganda situation
    peace vs justice controversy 159–60
    scrutiny of admissibility challenges 161–4
    suspension of investigation 164–6
United Nations (UN)
    author's book about Secretariat 6
    selection of judges by UN 257–8
    statement to Security Council regarding
        ICTY
        completion strategy 129–35
        cooperation of regional states 131–2
        need for continued commitment to
            international criminal justice 135–6

War
    classic principles of law of war 43–5
    impact of atrocities 45–7
    impact of human rights law
        interpretation of law of war 55–60
        protected persons 53–4

War (*Cont.*)
  reciprocity 54–5
  repatriation of POWs 52–3
  reprisals 55
 influence upon author 4, 5–6
 lessons from Shakespeare
  leaders' awareness of responsibility 288
  responsibility of subordinates 288–91
  role of advisers 287–8
  role of atrocity and chivalry 12–5
War crimes
 see also Internal conflicts; International conflicts; International humanitarian law
 establishment of international courts 75
 Nuremberg and Tokyo distinguished from modern tribunals
  criminalization of international legal norms 92–3
  due process 90–2
  gathering of evidence 83–4, 99–100
  gender offences 89
  jurisdiction to prosecute 89–90
  prosecution of abuses against civilians 83
  sources of law 93–5
  trial of senior figures 84–7
 history and development of law
  after WWI 80–2
  before WWI 67–8
  need for multi-faceted approach to prevention 95–7
  new approach at Nuremberg 77–8
  protection of civilians 204–9
  responsibility of public agents 224–5
Weapons
 bans resulting from changes in relationship between human rights and humanitarian law 182
 civilian protection against war crimes 206
 impact of human rights law 47
 new means of warfare 47
 treaty developments 49–51

Yamashita principle 292